DICTIONARY OF
JEWISH
LORE AND LEGEND

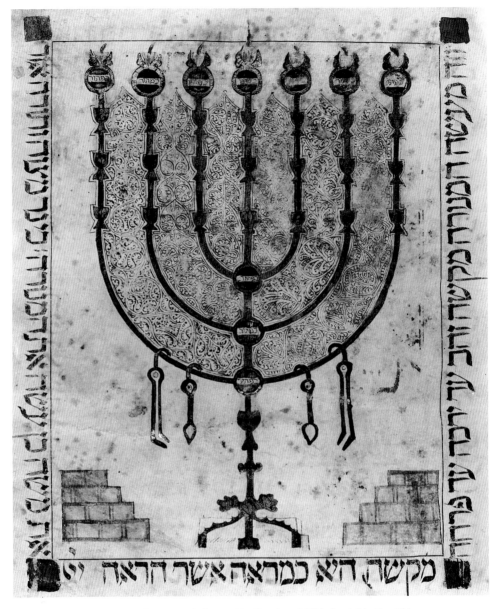

Illustration of a **menorah** from a 14c. illuminated Bible (probably Spanish).

ALAN UNTERMAN

DICTIONARY OF JEWISH LORE AND LEGEND

222 illustrations

THAMES AND HUDSON

Designed by Liz Rudderham

Printed and bound in Singapore

Contents

Introduction

7

Abbreviations

9

THE DICTIONARY

10

Further Reading

213

Sources of the Illustrations

215

For Doudi Wachsstock
to whom the legendary past
spoke in clear terms

Introduction

Since the period of the Enlightenment, when the ghetto walls began to crumble and Jews started to adopt Western culture, it has been customary to depict Jewish religion in terms of its more rational elements. The Judaism which emerged in the writings of 19c. and 20c. Jewish savants was a religion of ethical monotheism whose rituals inculcated the moral and theological values associated with the belief in a creator God, the master of human history and the divine author of the torah.

Such a portrait of Judaism was already prefigured in philosophical works of the Golden Age in medieval Spain, but it diverged markedly from the actual religion of the ordinary Jew. This rationalization of Jewish religion, though intellectually acceptable to modernists, was not recognizable as a description of the colourful beliefs and lifestyle of the majority of Jews. They subscribed to a corpus of legends, folklore and superstitions which we may call the aggadic corpus (from the Talmudic term aggadah, 'story'). References to the darker side of this aggadic corpus, if found at all in works about Judaism, were allegorized or explained away as quaint residues of a ghetto mentality rather than offered as an essential part of Jewish consciousness. These so-called residues, however, are just as important for understanding Jews and Judaism as the sophisticated faith of intellectuals.

The situation has not changed substantially today. Many ordinary Jews, as opposed to professional theologians, either accept large parts of this corpus literally or simply do not question these elements of Jewish teaching. This legendary tradition which contributes so much to the vitality of contemporary Jewish life, still recovering from its confrontation with the evil of the Nazi Holocaust, has remained an embarrassment to Jewish modernists. They practise prescriptive theology, writing about their faith in a polemical manner in order to present Judaism, long a pariah in Christian consciousness, in a form acceptable to the non-Jewish world.

This book seeks to help remedy the situation with a fuller picture of the irrational side of Judaism, expressed in the elements of Jewish lore and legend which are at the heart of the religion as it is lived by the traditional scholar and layman alike. Not that every traditional Jew believes all the material in this dictionary − far from it, for many may not even be aware of some of the more obscure themes and ideas. But they all take seriously elements which to outsiders, or even to Jewish modernists, will seem bizarre. The more traditional a Jew's faith or the more Orthodox his practice, the more likely it is that he lives in a world divided between yidden (Jews) and goyim (Gentiles) and populated with characters who spring alive from the pages of the Hebrew Bible to share that world with him. Many of the exploits of these biblical heroes and villains are not actually found in the text of the Hebrew Bible but are known from midrashic literature, from the classical Bible commentators or from the stories told by parents, and by teachers in cheder, to Jewish children.

The scientific picture of nature, from the subatomic world of mesons and quarks, through the biological world of viruses and bacteria, to the astronomical world of black holes and supernovae, in so far as it is known to traditional Jews, competes with the aggadic world of angels and demons, of souls that reincarnate in new bodies or haunt people and places, of wonder-working sages and Kabbalists, of strange creatures unknown to zoologists which are so large they blot out the sun or small but so powerful they can split rocks by the merest touch, of magical substances which protect man from fire or from the evil eye, of remedies for disease which depend on prayer, charms and amulets and of lucky and unlucky days and numbers which determine a Jew's life. This is a world of hope for a Messianic era when those who are dead will arise once again to bodily life, nations will put aside their military might, nature will become less hostile, wild animals and men will live in harmony and trees will provide an abundant harvest of fruit the whole year round.

This legendary material is not easily reconciled with scientific concepts. Apart from anything else, the scientific time-scales for the age of the world, for the evolution of man from earlier primates and for the extent of human history are measured in millions of years. The aggadic time-scale, by contrast, comprises only 5,750 years, counting from the moment that Adam and Eve were created by God on the sixth day of the creation. Scientific theories are not integral to the traditional Jewish outlook: they may be dismissed as temporary models which will change in the light of new discoveries; they may be compartmentalized and kept apart from their aggadic competitors; or they may be ignored altogether.

A major clash can be avoided because Judaism itself never sought to promote one coherent system of aggadic doctrine. Aggadah is continually being reinterpreted, and even contradictory elements are allowed to coexist side by side, as will be apparent from some of the conflicting elements presented in this book. Legends may, after all, be 'true' without actually being true.

The material for this work has been drawn mostly from written sources. Midrashic, Talmudic, Zoharic, Kabbalistic, Chasidic, halakhic and magical texts have been used, as have the stores of localized folklore which are the life-blood of the Ashkenazi and Sephardi cultures. Confronted with such a rich, multifaceted and ancient religious tradition, deciding what to exclude is as much a problem as deciding what to include.

The transliteration of Hebrew, Aramaic and Yiddish words has been undertaken in a simple manner so that the reader will be able to recognize the words as they are used among Jews. Some of the common spellings of words in English are also preserved. The modern Israeli pronunciation of Hebrew has been used in preference to the different varieties of Ashkenazi and Sephardi pronunciation. References have been kept to a minimum and used only when a biblical verse or passage is at issue.

Within the dictionary, cross-references to other entries are printed in SMALL CAPITALS. In the captions to the illustrations, the words in **bold type** refer to the relevant dictionary entry.

Abbreviations

The following abbreviations are to be found in the text:

BCE	before Christian Era	Josh.	Joshua
c.	century	Judg.	Judges
CE	Christian Era	Lam.	Lamentations
Chr.	Chronicles	Lev.	Leviticus
Dan.	Daniel	Mal.	Malachi
Deut.	Deuteronomy	Num.	Numbers
Exod.	Exodus	Prov.	Proverbs
Ezek.	Ezekiel	Ps.	Psalms
Gen.	Genesis	Sam.	Samuel
Isa.	Isaiah	Zech.	Zechariah
Jer.	Jeremiah		

Aaron First Israelite HIGH PRIEST, and brother of Moses and Miriam. Aaron is depicted as a lover of peace who would go in turn to each of the two parties to a quarrel and, by telling a white lie, would apologize in the name of the other party; when they next met, their quarrel was over because each believed the other had apologized. This characteristic made Aaron suitable as High Priest, whose sacrifices brought peace between Israel and their father in heaven. He possessed a miraculous rod, created at twilight on the sixth day of creation (*see* TETRAGRAMMATON), which burst into almond blossom overnight to vindicate him when his suitability as High Priest was challenged (Num. 17). When he died, it was through a kiss of the shekhinah, the easiest form of death, and God Himself prepared his funeral bier and a golden candelabrum to light the way. He was also very popular among the Israelites, and this explains why 'all the House of Israel' mourned him (Num. 20:29). Symbolic of the great loss his death represented was the cessation of the Pillar of Cloud and of Fire, which until then had guided the Israelites through the desert because of Aaron's merits. Although Aaron was responsible for making the GOLDEN CALF, he did so because he did not want the Israelites to be guilty of the greater sin of killing their High Priest if he refused. Aaron is one of the Seven Faithful Shepherds of Israel, a title given to outstanding biblical leaders, who are invited to the sukkah each evening as spiritual guests. *See also* TABERNACLE.

Aaron of Baghdad (9c.) Babylonian mystic, also known as Abu Aaron Ben Samuel Ha-Nasi, who brought the mystical traditions of the East to Italy. Aaron's pupils, particularly members of the Kalonymus family, carried his teachings into Germany where they became the basis of the German pietist movement known as Chasidei Ashkenaz. Many legends are recorded about Aaron's life, particularly in the medieval *Chronicle of Ahimaaz*. For instance, when a lion ate the ass that turned his father's mill, Aaron harnessed the lion to grind the corn. His father disapproved of this exploitation of the 'king of beasts' and sent Aaron into exile. On his wanderings he found the son of a Spanish Jew who had been turned into a donkey by witchcraft, so he turned him back into a human and sent him home to his family. On another occasion he came across a young man who was an excellent prayer leader, but who never mentioned the name of God in his prayers. Aaron realized that this youth was really a dead spirit, and he eventually discovered that he was being artificially kept alive by the ineffable name of God which had been inserted into the flesh of his right arm. Aaron cut out the name, and the youth's body immediately turned to dust, like someone long dead. In Italy Aaron acted as a judge, claiming the authority only possessed by a member of the Sanhedrin in a previous age. He sentenced sinners to death and carried out the trial by ordeal of a woman suspected of adultery (sotah). Aaron is referred to as 'the master of all secret mysteries'.

abba (Aramaic for 'father') A word used as a first name in the early Rabbinic period but also a title of respect and one of the names of God. Its use is illustrated in a Talmudic story about the miracle-working saint Chanan, grandson of the famous Choni Ha-Meaggel. At a time of drought children would come to him and say: 'Abba, abba, give us rain.' He would then pray for rain to be sent for the sake of these children who could not distinguish between God, the Abba who gives rain, and Chanan, the human abba who cannot give rain. Jewish mystics use 'abba' to denote the sefirah of wisdom (chokhmah) which is the 'father' of all the other SEFIROT. For Abba the Tall, *see* RAV.

Abed-Nego *see* HANANIAH, MISHAEL AND AZARIAH

Abel *see* CAIN AND ABEL

ablution (Hebrew 'tevilah') The use of water for purificatory purposes is a common theme of Penta-teuchal legislation on ritual purity and impurity. The most important means of ablution is the total immersion in a MIKVEH, or pool of 'living water' as opposed to drawn water. The mikveh is usually made from a rain-water source to which an adjoining bath of tap-water is connected. Women after menstruation (*see* NIDDAH), converts to Judaism (*see* PROSELYTES) and men before YOM KIPPUR immerse themselves in a mikveh. Under the influence of the Kabbalah the custom of immersion every morning before prayers has been adopted by Chasidic Jews. It is also necessary to immerse certain types of new food utensils bought from a Gentile. Second in importance to full immersion is ritual hand washing when water is poured from a vessel over each hand in turn. This is done on waking up in the morning to remove the unclean spirit residing on the fingertips, before prayers, before eating bread, before reciting the PRIESTLY BLESSING and after visiting a cemetery or coming into contact with the dead. The water which had been poured over the hands was formerly considered a potential source of danger; it was not to be thrown out in a public place, and if it fell into the hands of witches, they could use it to harm people, so it had to be disposed of with care.

Abrabanel, Don Isaac (1437–1508) Iberian statesman and scholar. Abrabanel had to flee from Portugal in 1483, after false accusations were made against him as court treasurer. He re-established himself in Spain only to flee once again, this time to Italy, with the expulsion of Spanish Jews in 1492. As an important Bible commentator, using Christian as well as Jewish sources, Abrabanel occasionally questioned the traditional authorship of some biblical books although he sub-scribed to their divine origin. His own experience of the precariousness of political power led him to a critical estimation of biblical kingship and urban culture. Abrabanel put forward scriptural sources for the doctrines of the Resurrection of the Dead and the transmigration of souls. Indeed he claimed that the latter doctrine was the only way of making sense of levirate marriage and was necessitated by a belief in divine justice. In his discussion of the scriptural doctrine of the Messiah, he argued strongly for a Jewish interpretation and took issue with Christian teachings. Abrabanel's method of Bible commentary was to ask a whole series of questions about a text before presenting his answers. Jewish folklore, in a jocular vein, holds him responsible for the 'unbelief' of some of his readers. It depicts a Jew sitting down after a heavy Sabbath lunch of cholent to study the Bible with Abrabanel's commentary; he only manages to read the questions before falling asleep in his chair and never actually comes to the author's answers which would resolve his doubts.

Abraham First PATRIARCH and founder of Hebrew MONOTHEISM, who migrated to the land of Canaan with his wife SARAH according to God's command. Abraham came to believe in one God by reflecting on the nature of the universe and rejecting idolatry. He broke the heads of all the idols in his father's idol shop except for the largest, before which he left an offering. His father was amazed at what looked like a fight among the idols, so Abraham asked him how he could worship statues if they were incapable of such activity. For his heretical views he was forced by King Nimrod into the fiery furnace, from which he emerged unscathed. As a sign of his COVENANT with God, Abraham was commanded to undergo CIRCUMCISION when he was already very old, and after he circumcised himself, Sarah miraculously gave birth to a son, ISAAC. One of the ten trials of faith that God put Abraham through was the demand to offer up his son as a sacrifice to God (*see* AKEDAH). Abraham kept the whole torah before it was revealed by God, including the many Rabbinic additions. He also instituted the practice of reciting the morning prayers (*see* SHACH-ARIT). His especially compassionate character manifested itself in his HOSPITALITY, in his attempt to persuade God not to destroy Sodom despite the wickedness of its citizens, and in the magical stone he wore round his neck with which he cured the sick. Abraham was buried in the Cave of MACHPELAH. He now sits at the gates of gehinnom and saves those who are circumcised from its fires. Abraham was instructed by an angel in the secrets of the Hebrew language and made a golem, and the early mystical work *Sefer Yetzirah* is ascribed to his authorship. All converts to Judaism have Abraham as their spiritual father because he was the first missionary on behalf of monotheism (Gen. 12:5), and they enter the divine covenant originally made with him. Male proselytes usually take 'Abraham' as their Hebrew name. In each generation there are thirty people who are as righteous as Abraham and who sustain the world. *See also* ZEKHUT AVOT.

Abraham Ben David of Posquières (*c.* 1125–98) Provençal rabbi and mystic, commonly known as the Rabad. He was the most important critic of Moses Maimonides and defended the unsophisticated beliefs of Jewish pietists against Maimonides' philosophical strictures. He argued that some of those who believed in the corporeality of God, although mistaken, were better men than Maimonides and not to be considered as heretics. The prophet Elijah revealed himself to the Rabad, and he claimed that the Holy Spirit (*see* RUACH HA-KODESH) had appeared over a number of years in his house of study. Maimonides said that no one had ever outwitted him except for Rabbi Abraham, whom he described as a 'craftsman with only one skill'.

Moses, accompanied by **Aaron**, spreads out his hands to heaven outside the city gates to end the plague of hail, the seventh of the Ten Plagues (14c. Spanish haggadah).

Wall painting from the 3c. CE Dura Europos synagogue of **Abraham** with his hands crossed in prayer.

Absalom A son of King DAVID who led a popular rebellion against his father (II Sam. 15). When David's army crushed the revolt, Absalom was killed after he was caught in a tree by his long hair while trying to escape. He attempted to cut his hair with a sword to release himself but saw the abyss of gehinnom open under him, so he remained hanging and became an easy prey to his pursuers. Absalom is one of those who have no share in the World to Come (olam haba) because of his utter disregard of the commandment to honour one's parents. He inherited the hair of Adam and kept it long because of his vanity and because he had taken a Nazirite vow.

Abulafia, Abraham (1240–91) Spanish mystic and Kabbalist. Abulafia wandered in search of the Ten Lost Tribes and the Sambatyon River. When he was unable to continue his search, he took up the study of the *Sefer Yetzirah* and had visions. He aimed to achieve prophecy through meditation on letter combinations of the Hebrew alphabet and on the mystical names of God. Believing himself to be the Messiah, he went to Rome in 1280 to convert Pope Nicholas III to Judaism. Abulafia was arrested and was due to be burnt at the stake. His life was saved, however, when the pope died, and after a short period of imprisonment he was released. Abulafia then went to Sicily where he proclaimed himself the Messiah and claimed that he possessed the Holy Spirit (ruach ha-kodesh). Rabbi Solomon Adret said of him: 'That fool ... that Abraham who claimed to be a prophet and the Messiah ... He seduced the Children of Israel with his lies.' Abulafia believed that the Messianic age would dawn in the year 1290.

Academy on High The heavenly YESHIVAH where God and the unborn Messiah study torah with the souls of departed sages. In this academy the subjects studied are the same as on earth, with the different views of the sages on issues of halakhah being quoted and debated. When there is a disagreement between God and the rest of the academy, the opinion of a living sage may be sought. He dies in being called to the Academy on High to adjudicate, though not necessarily always in God's favour. From this idea the expression 'called to the Academy on High' came to be used as a euphemism for the death of a scholar (*see* RABBAH BAR NACHMANI). Behind the whole concept of such an academy lies the belief in the supramundane value of torah study.

acharit ha-yamim *see* ESCHATOLOGY

Adam The first man, who was made on Mount MORIAH out of dust taken from the four corners of the earth into which God breathed the breath of life, so that he was formed in the image of God (Gen. 2). All the angels accepted Adam as the master of the earthly domain, except for SATAN, who refused to subordinate himself to man and was expelled from heaven. Ever since that time he has been man's enemy and accuser. Man was created after the animals so that, if he grows conceited, he can be told that the gnat preceded him. He was also created alone to convey the message that, if one destroys a single life, it is as if one destroyed the whole world. Since all men are descended from Adam, no one can claim more noble birth than anyone else. Adam was created as a hermaphrodite in the form of the divine male and female aspects (shekhinah), from which God split away the female half. Before EVE was thus separated, Adam's first wife had been LILITH, representing his evil inclination, but she left him. Originally Adam was like one of the angels and of enormous size, but he was reduced to ordinary human dimensions when his sin in the GARDEN OF EDEN awakened his lust and drew upon him and upon all his descendants the power of impurity (*see* ORIGINAL SIN). According to Kabbalistic teaching the souls of all men were once parts of the great soul of Adam, and those individuals who are able to help each other in life have souls which belonged to a similar area within Adam's original soul. Adam was shown what would happen in each future generation, and he gave seventy years of his own life so that King David could live. The mystical *Book of the Angel Raziel* is ascribed to Adam, and the angelic book he used in the Garden of Eden was passed on to be used by those of his descendants in each generation who were divinely inspired. Adam and Eve are buried in the Cave of Machpelah.

adam kadmon (Hebrew for 'primordial man') A being of light formed, according to Kabbalah, at the beginning of the process of emanation. Adam kadmon is a transcendent manifestation of God Himself, a personalized structure made out of the sefirot. The earthly Adam, who was created in God's image (Gen. 1:26–7), was actually made in the likeness of adam kadmon, and it was the latter whom Ezekiel saw in a vision as the appearance of a man on the heavenly throne. All worlds are reflected in the primordial man and, at a more hidden level, in his human counterpart, who may use adam kadmon as a focus of contemplation for his own spiritual nature (*see* MICROCOSM). In the teachings of the Lurianic Kabbalah (*see* LURIA, ISAAC), some of the lower sefirotic lights forming adam kadmon broke the vessels that were meant to contain them, shevirat ha-kelim, leaving sparks of light trapped in the broken pieces. Although the creative process was partially rectified by God, it is up to man to complete the rectification (*see* TIKKUN) by raising the remaining sparks back to their divine source.

Adar Twelfth lunar month of the Hebrew calendar, counting from Nisan, the month of the Exodus, or sixth month from the New Year festival (rosh ha-shanah). Adar usually begins sometime in February or March, and its zodiacal sign is the fish. When 'Adar begins, joy should be increased', because the carnival-like festival of PURIM falls in this month. A leap year has two months of Adar; the second Adar is regarded as the real Adar in which purim falls and in which the bar mitzvah of a boy born in the Adar of a non-leap year will take place. If two boys are born in the separate Adars of a leap year, then they will both be considered bar mitzvah and religiously adult on their birth date in the Adar of their thirteenth year, even if this is not a leap year. It can happen, therefore, that the younger boy (born say on 3 Adar II) reaches 'maturity' weeks before the older boy (born say on 25 Adar I). The seventh of Adar is the anniversary of both the birth and death of Moses; the thirteenth of

Adar, the day before purim, is the Fast of Esther; and the fifteenth of Adar is shushan purim.

ade-lo-yada (Aramaic for 'until he does not know') On the festival of purim a Jew is encouraged to drink alcohol to the point where he can no longer differentiate (ade-lo-yada) between blessing MORDE-CAI, the hero of the Book of Esther, and cursing HAMAN, the villain of the story. The origin of the custom reflects both the role played by wine in the purim story and the message of the festival that God works behind the scenes and not simply at the level of rational understanding. Some rabbis, who were averse to encouraging DRUNKENNESS, interpreted the practice to mean that one should drink a little more than usual and then sleep it off, for during sleep one loses the power of discrimination. In the modern state of Israel there are ade-lo-yada carnivals with floats parading through the streets.

a-do-nai *see* TETRAGRAMMATON

adon olam (Hebrew for 'Lord of the world') Popular hymn usually sung at the end of the shabbat morning service. Although adon olam is of unknown origin, it has been ascribed to the 11c. Spanish poet Solomon Ibn Gabirol. The theme of the hymn is that God is an eternal and unique king who has no second. He is man's redeemer and refuge. Adon olam concludes with the words: 'Into His hand I entrust my spirit at the time I sleep, and I will awaken. And with my spirit, also my body, the Lord is with me and I shall not fear'. It is therefore included among the prayers to be recited at night before going to bed.

Adret, Solomon (1235–1310) Leading Spanish rabbi and mystic, commonly known as the Rashba. In 1305 Adret issued a ban (cherem) against the study of 'Greek wisdom', i.e. secular studies, for anyone under the age of twenty-five. The spread of allegorical interpret-ations of scripture among those influenced by the philosophical writings of Maimonides was the major factor that led Adret to issue the ban. The allegorists understood Abraham and Sarah to represent matter and form and the Twelve Tribes to represent the twelve signs of the zodiac. Although Adret defended Maimonides against his more extreme critics, as a halakhist he insisted that the rituals are meant literally. Tefillin, for instance, are not merely a symbolic way of remembering God but involve the ritual of putting on the phylacteries. People are not to use their human intellect to judge what is possible and what is impossible for God or what the torah actually means. *See also* AVILA, PROPHET OF; SHABBOS GOI.

adultery Sexual relations between a married woman and a man other than her husband constitute adultery, while those between a married man and a single woman are not adulterous since polygamy (*see* MON-OGAMY) is allowed by the Bible. Adultery, which is prohibited in the Decalogue, is considered one of the three sins for which a Jew should be prepared to die rather than commit (the other two being idolatry and murder). In ancient times both the man and the woman caught committing adultery were executed (*see* CAPITAL PUNISHMENT) if there were two witnesses

Figure of **Adam** by Sir Jacob Epstein.

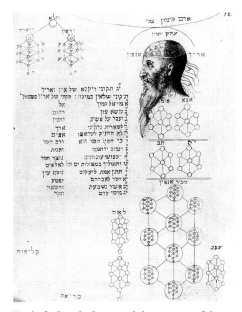

Head of **adam kadmon** and the structure of the sefirot (17c. Kabbalah Denudata).

to testify to the act, and a woman suspected of adultery had to undergo the ordeal of the SOTAH in order to prove her innocence. Today, if it is known that adultery has taken place, the husband has to divorce his unfaithful wife while she, in turn, is not allowed to marry her paramour. A child born from adulterous relations is considered to be a MAMZER. The prophets used the image of adultery to depict Israel's worship of strange gods. Indeed the prophet Hosea brought his own personal experience of love for his adulterous wife into his prophecies about the love which God still feels for unfaithful Israel. *See also* DIVORCE.

afikomen (from the Greek for 'dessert') A piece of unleavened bread (*see* MATZAH) which is the last thing eaten at the SEDER meal on pesach and after which no dessert is served, hence its name. The afikomen, a piece taken from the middle of the three portions of matzah on the seder plate, symbolizes the Pascal lamb which was eaten at the end of the meal in ancient times. It has become customary for the head of the household to hide it and for the children to try and 'steal' it from him. The afikomen is usually only returned if a gift has been promised in its place. Since the afikomen, like the Pascal lamb, has to be eaten before midnight, the negotiations between father and children have to be concluded by then. The purpose of this charade is to keep the children awake during the long ritual. What remains of the afikomen is sometimes kept as a good luck charm, or as an AMULET against evil. It may also be hung on the wall of a house to protect it against fire.

afterlife Although a belief in IMMORTALITY is expressed in the Bible, little is said there about the condition of man's soul after death. This subject is dealt with extensively, however, in Rabbinic literature, the Kabbalah, and Jewish folklore. The SOUL remains attached to the physical body after death for the first seven days, when it flits from its home to the cemetery and back. This explains why the initial mourning period is one week. For twelve months after death the soul ascends and descends, until the body disintegrates and the soul is freed. During this time the soul of a righteous person who has not been attached to physical existence can return to earth in a quasi-physical form. It is even reported of Judah Ha-Nasi that he would appear to his family on Fridays in his shabbat finery and make kiddush for them. Mourning thus continues for this period, and the KADDISH said by a son of the deceased for eleven months helps the soul to rise from this attachment and from the purgatorial period in GEHINNOM to its place in PARADISE. The purified soul there 'enjoys the radiance of the Divine Presence (shekhinah)'. The soul is thought to have its root in the divine world and after death to return to its spiritual home, its life on earth being merely a form of exile. Some Jewish thinkers have regarded both the life of piety and the stage of prophetic illumination on earth as of a similar level to that attainable after death. Moses, for example, attained to the highest form of union with God while on earth, and at death he entered directly into the most hidden recesses of the Godhead, avoiding the usual judgment of the soul. Belief in the TRANSMIGRATION OF SOULS involves a different image of the afterlife in which the soul, after death, returns to a new body until it has fulfilled its destiny. *See also* OLAM HABA; RESURRECTION OF THE DEAD.

age The usual age of man is given in the Bible as 70 years (Ps. 90:10). The ideal age to live to, however, is 120, which God set as the limit of man's life after an initial period of great old age. The first biblical character described as aged is Abraham, who requested that old people should actually look old. Until then people would speak to Isaac, Abraham's son, thinking they were talking to Abraham and vice versa. Respect must be shown to the aged and even to an aged heathen since there is a strong association between the elder (zaken, from zakan 'beard') and wisdom. According to one Rabbinic description of the ages of man, 'at thirty a man attains full strength, at forty understanding, at fifty advice, at sixty old age, at seventy grey hairs, at eighty new vigour, at ninety he is bent with years, and at one hundred he is like one who is already dead.' *See also* BIRTHDAY.

aggadah (Aramaic for 'story') Rabbinic lore dealing with ethics, theology, history, folklore and legends. Aggadah does not concern itself with legal and ritual matters and is thus to be distinguished from HALAKHAH. The importance of aggadah is expressed in the statement that those who truly wish to know God should study aggadah. There were rabbis in the Talmudic period, however, who spoke disparagingly of this branch of Jewish learning and knew little about it, as they concentrated mainly on halakhic topics. On one occasion Akiva, a leading halakhic expert, was reprimanded by ISHMAEL BEN ELISHA for his attempts at aggadic exposition and told to restrict his comments to matters of ritual purity. Aggadic literature grew out of sermons and MIDRASH, there being thirty-two rules of aggadic interpretation of the Bible. The homiletical basis of aggadah accounts for its vernacular expressions and for the inclusion of parables, folktales, polemics and speculations about redemption and the Messiah. The popular traditions of angels and demons emerged from the aggadah, and its images were particularly influential among the mystics of the Kabbalah. Aggadic texts are replete with strange and bizarre tales about God, biblical characters and the Talmudic rabbis. These stories were criticized by some Karaite thinkers as ridiculous and were played down by Jewish rationalists who feared they would encourage anthropomorphism. Some of the leading geonim (gaon) in post-Talmudic Babylonia stated that aggadah should not be relied upon where it conflicted with reason: it merely represented the opinions of individual rabbis and had no binding doctrinal character. Other authorities in the Middle Ages insisted, by contrast, that aggadah should be understood literally and must be believed in as part of the ORAL TORAH.

Agrat Bat Mahalat A queen of DEMONS who stalks the world with her destructive cohorts. Agrat is described as a concubine of SAMAEL, the king of demons, and as a granddaughter of the biblical Ishmael. Ishmael abandoned Agrat's grandmother in the wilderness where Agrat's mother was born. She then married a demon who became Agrat's father. Agrat's destructive activity was limited by the sage Chanina

Ben Dosa to Tuesday and Friday nights, after she pleaded with him not to banish her from the world altogether. The *Talmud* therefore recommends that people should not go out alone on these nights. *See also* MOON.

Agudat Israel *see* MITNAGGEDIM; NETUREI KARTA

agunah (Hebrew for 'a tied woman') A married woman whose husband has disappeared, leaving no evidence of his death, or whose husband has left her and refuses to give her a DIVORCE is known as an agunah because she cannot remarry. A man in a similar situation is in a more advantageous position. Among the Sephardim, who do not prohibit polygamy, he can usually marry again. Even among the Ashkenazim, who insist on MONOGAMY, he is able to remarry in such circumstances if one hundred rabbis are prepared to give their consent. A period of great upheaval, such as a pogrom or a war, is usually followed by problems of such 'tied women' who apply to the rabbinical courts to have their status resolved. Since it is a mitzvah to help an agunah, a bet din might allow her to remarry on flimsy evidence of her husband's death, such as her own testimony, that of an apostate or even on the basis of merely documentary proof. The rationale for this is that, if the husband were still alive, people would be afraid to give false testimony since he could turn up at any time. In cases where a mistake is made in allowing the woman to remarry, the reappearance of her first husband means any child born from her new marriage is a MAMZER, and she is forced to leave her second husband since they have committed ADULTERY. Many attempts have been made to build a special clause into the marriage document (ketubbah) that would annul the marriage retroactively if she becomes an agunah, but these have not won the acceptance of the Orthodox rabbinate.

Ahab *see* ELIJAH; JEZEBEL; NAAMAN

Ahasuerus *see* ESTHER; HAMAN; INTERMARRIAGE; MORDECAI; WANDERING JEW

Ahijah the Shilonite *see* BAAL SHEM TOV, ISRAEL; JEROBOAM

akedah (Hebrew for 'binding') The story of ABRAHAM's test of obedience to God's command to offer up his son ISAAC on Mount Moriah as a sacrifice (Gen. 22). At the last minute the archangel Michael stayed Abraham's hand. Isaac is depicted in some Rabbinic accounts as thirty-seven years old at the time; nevertheless, he voluntarily submitted to being bound on the altar. In the liturgy the story of the akedah is read as a reminder to God of the devotion of the Patriarchs and of God's compassion towards Isaac. On rosh hashanah, as well as the reading of the akedah, the shofar is blown as a reminder of the ram which was used by Abraham as a substitute sacrifice (*see also* PSALMS). Isaac became the symbol of Jewish martyrdom in the Middle Ages, and the legend arose that he had indeed been killed, only to be brought back to life again. The killing of children by their parents in the face of Christian persecution and forced baptism was thus modelled on a biblical precedent and accompanied by

A Chasid of advanced **age** wearing a shtreimel at a melavveh malkah feast. Notice the peot tucked behind the ear of the young Chasid on his left.

Synagogue mosaic of the **akedah** showing Abraham about to offer up his son Isaac as a sacrifice (6c. CE, Bet Alpha Synagogue, Israel).

the hope of the Resurrection of the Dead. *See also* ZEKHUT AVOT.

Akiva (2c. CE) Mishnaic sage who started out as an ignorant shepherd. He fell in love with Rachel, his employer's daughter, who agreed to marry him on condition he studied TORAH. Akiva was already forty years old and was only convinced that knowledge would penetrate his mind when he came upon a stone which had been worn away by a constant, but gradual, drip of water. His father-in-law disapproved of the match, refusing any financial support to the couple, so Rachel had to sell her hair to support Akiva in his studies. She would sit beside him holding burning wooden splits so he could study undisturbed. He became the leading scholar of his generation and a major contributor to the *Mishnah*. Akiva was one of the four rabbis who made the mystical journey into PARADISE, and only he emerged from his mystical experiences unscathed. From his teacher, Nachum of Gimzu, he took as his guiding maxim the idea that everything that God does is for the best. On one occasion when travelling on an ass, with a cockerel and a lamp, he arrived at a town but was unable to gain admittance. Undaunted, he slept in a nearby field. During the night his lamp was blown out, his cockerel was eaten by a wild animal, and his ass ran off. Next day he found that the town had been sacked by brigands during the night, and he was left unmolested because they saw no light and heard no cockerel crowing or ass braying. Everything that God did was thus for the best, even though at the time it seemed like one catastrophe after another. Akiva was a strong supporter of the BAR KOKHBA revolt against the Romans and believed that Simeon Bar Kokhba was the Messiah despite the misgivings of his colleagues. He was martyred at the age of 120 during the Hadrianic persecutions. While he was being tortured, he smiled as he recited the shema, since he was now able to fulfil the commandment to love God with all his soul, i.e. by giving up his life in martyrdom. *See also* AVINU MALKENU; HEIKHALOT; LEVI ISAAC OF BERDICHEV; MOSES; OMER, COUNTING OF; SIMEON BEN AZZAI; SONG OF SONGS.

akkum (Hebrew acrostic of oved kochavim umazalot, 'worshipper of stars and zodiacal signs') A common term in Jewish literature for heathens and for Gentiles in general, originally coined to refer to star worshippers. It was used widely in the Middle Ages in reference to non-Jews to avoid Christian censors, who objected to some of the harsh things that Jews said about Gentiles. Some medieval rabbinic authorities went out of their way to indicate that the discriminatory laws against the akkum did not apply to Christian and Moslem Gentiles.

alchemy The esoteric quest to turn base metal into gold and to find the elixir of youth. A number of Kabbalists were involved in alchemy. Judah Loew Ben Bezalel of Prague had a reputation as an alchemist, and it was thought that he used alchemy to make a GOLEM. Among Christians it was believed that Jews possessed alchemical secrets, and the Kabbalist Samuel FALK was much sought after in 18c. London as a wonder-working alchemist. Even rabbis who did not practice alchemy still believed in it, and they assumed that the great characters of the Bible were possessed of alchemical knowledge. It was through such knowledge that the antediluvians, like Methusaleh, reached such an old age. According to a midrash, Abraham wore a stone round his neck which could cure all those who looked upon it, and Solomon received the philosophers' stone as a present from the Queen of Sheba. The practical Kabbalah proffers a number of recipes for making gold out of base metal, and there were even stories of it being made from herbs. Indeed, the techniques of letter combination, which allowed mystics to control the divine creative power, were thought of as parallel to the combinations of chemical elements at the heart of alchemical experiments (*see* ALPHABET, HEBREW; GEMATRIA).

alcohol Intoxicating beverages play an important role in a number of Bible stories and prohibitions. Thus NOAH had too much wine to drink after the Flood and was abused by one of his sons. A drunken Lot was made to father the children of his two daughters, after the destruction of Sodom, without being aware of what was happening. The service of God should be undertaken free from alcohol, so a priest could be punished from heaven with the death penalty if he fulfilled his priestly function while intoxicated (Lev. 10). If a judge had taken intoxicating beverages, he was not allowed to sit in judgment on a case. The NAZIRITES, who lived a life of greater holiness than ordinary Israelites, were forbidden to touch alcohol. One should not pray while drunk, and if one does so, it is akin to worshipping idols. The biblical HANNAH was suspected of being drunk when she prayed with great emotion at the Shiloh Tabernacle, and she was reprimanded by Eli, the High Priest. Yet any business dealings undertaken by a drunk are considered valid, and a person is even responsible for sins committed while intoxicated, unless he is as drunk as the biblical Lot, when he is excused all his actions. WINE is the recommended beverage for a number of rituals. On the festival of purim Jews are encouraged to drink alcohol and become intoxicated to the point where they cannot distinguish between the hero and the villain of the Esther story (*see* ADE-LO-YADA). Members of the CHASIDIC MOVEMENT use alcohol as a way of enhancing their religious practices.

aleinu le-shabbeach (Hebrew for 'it is our duty to praise') A prayer, composed by Rav and originally part of the rosh ha-shanah liturgy, which is used to conclude each daily service. Aleinu offers thanks to God for not having made the Jewish People like the other nations of the world, who do not know the true God. On the festivals of rosh ha-shanah and yom kippur, aleinu is sung to a solemn tune, and the chazzan and congregation prostrate themselves when they come to the line: 'But we bend the knee, bow down and give thanks before the King, the King of kings.' At other times they simply bow their heads at these words. Martyrs would chant aleinu to this haunting tune on the way to their death. In 1171 the Jews of Blois, in France, were accused of the ritual murder of a child (blood libel). They refused to save their lives by converting to Christianity, and the whole community perished in the flames singing aleinu.

Those who witnessed their deaths are reported to have said that they never heard a song like it. In the late Middle Ages one line of aleinu referring to the idolatrous worship of Gentiles, 'For they bow down to vanity and emptiness', caused a bitter controversy. Christians maintained that 'and emptiness' was a cryptic reference to Jesus since its numerical value (gematria) is the same as that of the Hebrew name of Jesus. Jews replied that the prayer was pre-Christian in origin, but they were forced to censor the offending line from the prayer-book in Christian countries. Those communities which preserved this line had the custom of spitting on the floor as they recited it, a custom objected to by some rabbis but with only limited success. The second paragraph of aleinu looks forward to a time when idolatry will cease and all peoples will accept the yoke of the kingdom of heaven. This contributed to the popularity of the prayer in the liturgy because it raised the spirits of downtrodden Jews and inspired hope for the coming of the Messiah.

Alexander the Great *see* GARDEN OF EDEN; SIMON THE RIGHTEOUS

aliyah (Hebrew for 'going up') Someone who is called up to recite the blessings over the reading from the SEFER TORAH is said to be 'going up to the torah', aliyah la-torah. The term is used because the BIMAH on which the torah is read is usually a raised platform with steps leading up to it. Originally, people who were called up read the torah portion themselves, but today a trained reader does this so as not to embarrass those who cannot read the unpunctuated text. They are received with a special GREETING. The order of precedence for an aliyah is a Kohen, then a Levite and then other Jews. Members of the congregation are entitled to an aliyah on special occasions. These include a bridegroom on the shabbat before his wedding and a boy celebrating his bar mitzvah, both of whom would usually be given MAFTIR and HAFTARAH, someone on the anniversary of the death of a relative (yahrzeit), and the father of a newborn child. In an Orthodox synagogue only male adults are given an aliyah, but in Reform congregations women are also called up. There is a custom in some communities to auction off the various portions to be read on a sabbath or festival to the highest bidder, who can then decide whether he wishes an aliyah himself or wants to honour someone else with it. Since certain torah sections are considered especially important or auspicious, the bidding for them may become very competitive.

The term 'aliyah' also has the different meaning of visiting, or emigrating to, the Land of Israel which is referred to as aliyah la-aretz ('going up to the land'). It is only the journey to Israel from the flat terrain of Egypt or the desert which is obviously one of going up. Yet the image of ascending was preserved for any journey to Israel, because the Holy Land was considered spiritually higher than other lands. Modern waves of immigrants to Israel are referred to as the First Aliyah (1881–1903), the Second Aliyah (1904–14), etc. *See also* BRIDEGROOM OF THE TORAH, GABBAI; GELILAH.

aliya le-regel *see* PILGRIMAGE

A 16c. woodcut of Rabbi **Akiva** from an Italian haggadah.

Picture of a laboratory used for **alchemy** (17c. manuscript)

The clandestine **aliyah** of Jewish immigrants disembarking on the shores of Palestine in 1939.

Alkabetz, Solomon (1505–76) Poet and mystic who lived in Safed, northern Palestine. Alkabetz migrated to the Holy Land from Turkey after an unusual experience during the night of the shavuot festival. He was with Joseph CARO studying the torah, when Caro was possessed by the spirit of the *Mishnah*. This spirit (maggid) spoke to them from Caro's mouth and advised them to settle in the Land of Israel. Alkabetz later expressed the belief that only in the Holy Land could the secrets of the Kabbalah be truly revealed. He was one of the circle of mystics who used to go out into the fields on Friday evening, dressed in white, to welcome the shabbat. The hymn he composed for this occasion, LEKHAH DODI, spread throughout the Jewish world and quickly became a popular liturgical piece. Alkabetz was killed by an Arab who buried him under a fig tree which immediately began to bloom. This strange occurrence led to an investigation: the body was dug up, and the murderer was eventually hung from the very same tree.

Alliance Israelite Universelle *see* MORTARA CASE

almemar *see* BIMAH

alphabet, Hebrew The HEBREW alphabet, the alef-bet, is made up of twenty-two letters and five final letters. The square script now in use differs from the old Hebrew script, and there is one Talmudic view that Ezra adopted it after returning from Babylonian exile, leaving the old rounded script for use by the Samaritans. This view is not generally accepted, however, since the current form of the letters is regarded as holy and is therefore assumed to be the original one. The letters are seen as conveying messages based on the alliteration of their names. Each Hebrew letter also has a numerical value, words having the value of the sum of their letters. Thus words, phrases or sentences with the same value may be related together in an association of ideas known as GEMATRIA. The mystic traditions, including MAASEH BERESHIT, MAASEH MERKAVAH and KABBALAH, regarded the letters of the alphabet as having creative power, since God created the world through words (*see* YETZIRAH, SEFER). Knowing how to combine the letters correctly not only gives the mystic the ability to engage in contemplation, taking him closer to God, but also enables him to create animals and men (*see* GOLEM). The biblical craftsman BEZALEL built the Tabernacle in the wilderness through combining Hebrew letters. The sanctity of prayers relates to the spiritual forces in the letters which the utterance of the words liberates. Any small changes in the prayers, therefore, upset the balance of these forces, as do any mistakes in the writing of a torah scroll, tefillin or a mezuzah. The SCRIBES of old counted every letter in the Bible, and it was believed that there were 600,000 letters, one for each Israelite who participated in the Exodus. The Kabbalists tell how Isaac Luria came across a simple man whose prayers were particularly efficacious. The man told Luria that in fact he could not read, so what he did was to recite the alphabet and tell God to take the letters and make them into words Himself.

Alroy, David (12c.) False Messiah from Kurdistan. Alroy, who was a skilled magician, declared himself the Messiah and led a revolt against the Sultan, promising to take his followers to Jerusalem. He also sent out letters to his co-religionists urging them to go to war against the Moslems. The leaders of Babylonian Jewry tried to discourage him from acting on his Messianic pretensions but to no avail. Legend relates how Alroy was captured by the Sultan but escaped by magically crossing a river on his cloak. He met his end when he told those Jews who doubted him to cut off his head and see for themselves that he would continue to live. They cut off his head, and he died. According to another version, he was killed by his father-in-law, who had been bribed and who wanted to avert the massacre of the whole Jewish community which would have resulted had Alroy remained at large. Some of his followers among the Jews of Persia continued to believe in him even after his death. They were fraudulently tricked out of their wealth by two men claiming to act in Alroy's name, who told them they would fly that night from their rooftops to Jerusalem. The ruse was discovered at daybreak, but by then the two imposters, to whom they had given their precious belongings for safekeeping, had fled. *See also* TETRAGRAMMATON.

altar (Hebrew 'mizbeach') The altar symbolized the peace which existed between Israel and their Father in heaven; hence, no iron was allowed in its construction since iron is used in instruments of war. When sacrifice ceased with the destruction of the Second Temple, acts of loving kindness were regarded as effecting atonement like the sacrificial ritual itself. Thus a Jew's table, at which he makes blessings over his food and to which he invites poor guests, substitutes for the altar. The table, therefore, must be treated in a respectful manner, must not be sat on or used to put one's feet on. Death was also seen as a form of atonement, and the souls of martyrs were pictured as sacrifices being offered up to God on a heavenly altar by the angel Michael, who is the High Priest among the angels. After death the souls of the righteous are sheltered under the heavenly altar. *See also* URIEL.

al tikrei (Hebrew for 'do not read') An exegetical technique used by the Talmudic rabbis to give the unvocalized text of the Bible a different vocalization, or a different spelling, from the standard form. The use of al tikrei never actually negates the original reading of the text and therefore is best explained as 'do not read it only in the normal way but also in another way'. It thus allows a new interpretation, even when the laws of grammar and syntax necessitate the standard reading. The use of this technique is based on the verse: 'God has spoken once, I have heard this twice' (Ps. 62:12), namely, the words of the Bible lend themselves to senses other than the standard one.

Amalek A tribe, descended from Esau (Gen. 36:12), which attacked the Israelites from the rear on their way to the Holy Land during the Exodus (Deut. 25:18). The Amalekites at first befriended their kinsmen the Israelites, but when the opportunity arose, they ambushed the unprotected old people and children who made up the rearguard and killed them. They then made fun of their circumcised victims by cutting off their genitals and throwing them up to heaven, as if taunting God with the sign of the covenant between

Him and Israel. In the subsequent war between the two nations Moses positioned himself on a hill over-looking the battlefield. As long as Moses held his hands up, the Israelites prevailed, but when he grew tired and let his hands drop, the Amalekites prevailed (Exod. 17:8–12). The *Mishnah* asks how the hands of Moses could determine the fate of a battle and answers that, as long as Moses pointed to heaven, the Israelites looked up to God and trusted in Him. Their faith made them strong. When they ceased to focus on their father in heaven they became weak and started losing the fight. Amalek came to symbolize the archetypal enemy of Israel in each generation, particularly those Gentiles who preyed upon Jews who were easy victims because of their sins or lack of faith. The Rabbinic stories about Amalek reflect attitudes to circumcision in Roman times and later Christian attempts to convert Jews. HAMAN, the villain of the purim story, was a descendant of the Amalekite King Agag whose life was spared by SAUL (I Sam. 15:9). Thus, the passage about remembering the deeds of Amalek is read on the shabbat before purim, and Haman's name is accompanied in the synagogue by booing and hissing to fulfil the commandment to blot out the memory of Amalek (Deut. 25:19).

amen (Hebrew for 'true' or 'faithful') Liturgical response, indicating assent, uttered after hearing the BENEDICTIONS and prayers of the CHAZZAN and others. In ancient times few knew the prayers by heart, as there was no printed prayer-book and illiteracy was widespread, so responding to prayers was a substitute for reciting the prayers themselves. It is said that in the age of the Messiah punishment in gehinnom will cease, and the gates of the Garden of Eden will be opened for those who say 'amen' with all their might to the KADDISH prayer recited in heaven. This prayer will be heard from one end of the world to the other, so that even the wicked in hell will be able to respond 'amen'. God will then send angels down with the keys of hell to open its doors, pull out its denizens, wash and clothe them anew and present them to God.

am ha-aretz (Hebrew for 'people of the land') Term used in Rabbinic literature to refer to peasant farmers who were lax about agricultural tithes and did not eat their food in ritual purity. While Jerusalem was a centre of learning and sophistication, the main area of the am ha-aretz was in the Galilee. Galilean religious leaders were more charismatic than scholarly, and their followers adhered to a popular form of Judaism, expressing their religion through simple belief. The *Talmud* has some positive things to say about the religious commitment of the am ha-aretz and rec-ommends that great care should be taken with their children because they might grow up to be scholars of the torah. Nevertheless, there was considerable antagonism between the Rabbis and the peasants. The former believed that they were hated by the am ha-aretz and would be harmed physically by them if the opportunity arose. They discouraged intermarriage with peasant families and regarded the religiously primitive life of the am ha-aretz as no real life at all, since an am ha-aretz could not be truly pious. In the post-Talmudic period the expression 'am ha-aretz' came to mean an ignorant person not acquainted with

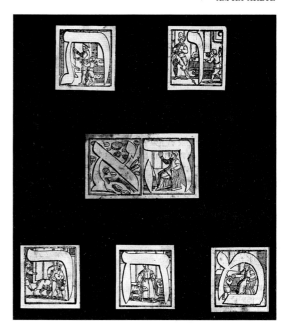

Letters of the Hebrew **alphabet** with pictures showing Passover rituals (15c.).

Illustration from a 13c. French Bible showing the **altar** table with the twelve loaves of the shewbread.

the rudiments of Talmudic lore and lacking moral sensitivity.

amidah (Hebrew for 'standing') Main PRAYER of the LITURGY, which forms the centre of every service. It is modelled on the daily SACRIFICE in the Temple. The weekday amidah, said at SHACHARIT, MINCHAH, and MAARIV, is known as the shemoneh esreh, 'eighteen', because it originally contained eighteen BENEDICTIONS. A nineteenth benediction against heretics, presumably Jewish Christians, was added in the 2c. On shabbat and festivals a shorter version of the prayer is recited (*see* MUSAF). The amidah prayer is said silently while standing with the feet together, facing towards the place of the Temple in Jerusalem (*see* MIZRACH). Before commencing, the worshipper takes three steps backwards and then three steps forwards to bring himself symbolically into God's presence. At the end he withdraws from God's presence by repeating this procedure. It is forbidden to interrupt the amidah even if, as the *Mishnah* puts it, a king greets one or a serpent wraps itself around one's leg. Other people should not walk within the four cubits (approximately six feet) in front of those reciting the amidah because it is like coming between them and God. The prayer should not be said if one is feeling sad or sluggish or light-headed, but only with a feeling of joy. *See also* RESURRECTION OF THE DEAD.

Amnon of Mayence (10c.) A rich and influential Jew who was pressured by the Archbishop of Mainz (Mayence) to convert to Christianity. Amnon asked for three days to think it over. At the end of this period he was ashamed of having even given the impression that he might consider conversion and asked the archbishop to cut out his tongue. Instead, Amnon was punished by having his hands and feet cut off. Thus mutilated, he asked to be carried to the synagogue, arriving in the middle of the rosh ha-shanah service. He recited a prayer, unetane tokef, expressing the awe and grandeur of the divine judg-ment which takes place at the Jewish New Year festival, and then died. He subsequently appeared in a dream to one of the rabbis and taught him his prayer. It has become a central part of the liturgy for rosh ha-shanah and yom kippur and is sung to a solemn and mournful tune.

amora (Aramaic for 'speaker', 'interpreter'; pl. amoraim) Title applied to sages of the TALMUD. The term originally indicated an assistant who stood beside a teacher during a lecture and repeated his words out loud to large gatherings of students, adding explanations as he went along. It came to refer to the Talmudic rabbis who explained the text of the MISHNAH. An amora could not explicitly contradict the teachings of a Mishnaic TANNA which were uncontested in tannaitic literature; he could only interpret them. On the completion of the Palestinian and Babylonian *Talmuds*, the interpretation of Judaism presented by the amoraim was accepted as authorit-ative.

Amos (8c. BCE) Israelite prophet of humble origins who described himself as 'neither a professional pro-phet nor the son of a prophet, but a herdsman and a dresser of sycamore trees' (Amos 7:14). Amos criticized the people for their sins and predicted their EXILE, but he was mocked because he stuttered. He met his death at the hands of King Uzziah who struck him with a hot metal object. The Book of Amos concludes with a message of comfort about the end of the captivity of Israel, when 'they shall rebuild the waste cities ... plant vineyards ... make gardens ... And I [God] will plant them upon their land and they will not be plucked up any more out of the land' (9:14–15). The *Talmud* views Amos' expression of God's teaching, 'seek Me and live' (Amos 5:4), as representing the basic idea behind all the commandments of the torah.

Amram of Mayence Medieval rabbi who left a request in his will that his body should be buried in his home town of Mainz (Mayence). Just before he died in Cologne he told his pupils that, if they found it difficult to take him to Mainz, they should put his body in a boat and it would find its way there. This they did, and the boat navigated the Rhine to Mainz on its own. When it arrived, however, the Christian community of Mainz claimed that the body must be that of a Christian saint, and they would not allow the Jews to take it for burial. The Christians themselves were unable to move the body from the river bank, so the bishop ordered that a church be built on the spot. Amram appeared to his pupils in a dream telling them to remove his body secretly from the vault of the church and to rebury it in the Jewish cemetery, leaving another body in its place.

amulets (Hebrew 'kemea') Texts and drawings used as protection against demons, the EVIL EYE, sickness, nosebleed, fire, burglars and enemies. Amulets are also used to gain someone's love, to cross the sea in safety, for a barren woman to have children, for easy childbirth, for the welfare of newborn babes, to catch fish, to find water and to obtain wisdom. They are usually inscribed on small pieces of parchment and include magical signs, letter permutations (*see* ALPHA-BET, HEBREW) and the names of God or of angels, such as Raphael. Three powerful angels, Sanvi, Sansanvi and Semangelaf, guarantee protection against LILITH, a demon queen who attacks women in childbirth and causes the death of infants. In order for an amulet to be effective, it has to be written by a holy person who is an expert in the practical KABBALAH. If it has cured someone on three different occasions, then it is regarded as a proven amulet. Amulets are worn round the neck or sometimes attached to the wall of the home. Some amulets include a magen david. Among Jews from Islamic lands a wall amulet in the shape of a hand (*see* YAD) is very popular for protecting the home and family against the evil eye. Amulets are also made from ritual objects like a piece of the afikomen, a mezuzah which girls often wear on a chain round the neck and tefillin. Red garments or some salt in a pocket are regarded as protection against the evil eye. Although amulets seem to have been widely used in the Talmudic period, Maimonides and other, more philosophically minded rabbis like Ezekiel LANDAU opposed them as empty superstitions. Nevertheless, their use was supported by mystics and by popular belief. Even Christians sought to obtain amulets from Jews in the Middle Ages. *See also* BAAL SHEM; MEZUZAH; RAZIEL; URIEL.

Anan Ben David (8c.) Founder of the KARAITE movement. Anan was disappointed at being passed over in favour of his brother for the position of EXILARCH, because he was considered to be insufficiently God-fearing. Under his leadership disaffected elements among Babylonian Jewry and remnants of various anti-Rabbinic sects came together. When he proclaimed himself Exilarch in 767 CE with their support, he was arrested by the Moslem authorities who backed the establishment candidate. While in prison Anan was advised by a Moslem sectarian, who was a fellow prisoner, to declare that he was the head of a new religion and thus to escape further punishment. Anan preached a form of religion which interpreted the biblical text more literally than the Rabbinic tradition, in a manner reminiscent of the SADDUCEES. He told his followers to search the torah thoroughly for themselves and not merely to rely on his view. His strict interpretation of the halakhah forbade any light or fire to burn on the Sabbath day, and he also prohibited sexual relations since 'ploughing and reaping' are prohibited on shabbat not only in agriculture but in the human world, as well. Anan favoured an ascetic approach to life and put forward his belief in the transmigration of souls, both of which were modified in later Karaism. He originally gave some support to Mohammed as a prophet of the Arabs and also regarded Jesus as a prophet. He maintained that followers of his movement had objected to the killing of Jesus in the 1c. CE.

androgyne Greek term used in Rabbinic literature to refer to hermaphrodites, i.e. those who possess both male and female sexual characteristics. According to one view ADAM was created androgyous since the biblical text (Gen. 1:27) says that God created man 'male and female'. The formation of EVE as a separate being was thus the splitting of the originally androgynous creature in two. Since an androgyne is of unknown sex, or represents a third sex, he/she has to be treated halakhically sometimes as a man, sometimes as a woman, sometimes as both and sometimes as neither. He has to be circumcised and keep all the commandments like a man and may marry a woman but not a man. If he did go through a marriage ceremony with a man then, according to some opinions, a divorce is necessary. The androgyne is distinguished from the person with no sexual characteristics, the tumtum, who is of indeterminate sex.

Angel of Death (Hebrew 'malakh ha-mavet') One of the ANGELS whose specific task is to end human life. The Angel of Death is covered with eyes, so that those who see him gape in amazement, and a drop of poison from his sword falls into their open mouthes. When someone dies, therefore, all water in the house should be poured away in case poison from the angel's sword fell into it. In Kabbalistic literature the Angel of Death is identified with SAMAEL, the prince of the dark forces of the SITRA ACHRA, and with his consort LILITH who kills infants and women in childbirth. Dogs are aware of the presence of death, and they either freeze in their tracks or growl as the angel approaches. Ashkenazim do not call their children by the same name as a living relative because this might lead the Angel of Death to make a mistake and kill the wrong person. This

Moroccan silver yad **amulet** in the shape of a hand with the divine name engraved on the palm.

Figure of an **androgyne** from a 15c. German manuscript with the male on the right and the female on the left.

Hebrews marking the lintels of their doors with the blood of the Pascal lamb so the **Angel of Death** will pass over their houses. This 'passing over' is the literal meaning of the name pesach or Passover.

propensity to make mistakes may also be used to save lives. When someone is seriously ill, it is customary to give him or her an extra name so that the angel is not able to identify his intended victim. Another tactic is to sell a child to a new set of parents so as to confuse the Angel of Death, who knows people by their name and their patronym. Apart from these attempts to outwit the Angel of Death, one can nullify his power by giving charity or by studying torah. King David knew that he would die on shabbat, so he spent each Sabbath day studying and only died because the angel distracted him (see also LUZ). The Talmudic sage JOSHUA BEN LEVI managed to jump into the Garden of Eden while still alive after having taken the sword of the Angel of Death. Though God made him return the sword, He allowed Joshua to remain in Paradise from where he sent descriptions of heaven and hell to his colleagues using the Angel of Death as his messenger. In the World to Come (olam haba) the Angel of Death will be slain by God.

angels (Hebrew 'malakhim', meaning 'messengers') Angels appear in the Bible in a variety of forms. There are the mysterious CHERUBIM who guard the entrance to the Garden of Eden (Gen. 3:24), winged creatures singing God's praises in heaven, angels in human form who visited Abraham (Gen. 18) and wrestled with Jacob (Gen. 32). Some angels (e.g. GABRIEL, META-TRON, MICHAEL, RAPHAEL, RAZIEL, SANDALFON, SATAN, URIEL and the three angels Sanvi, Sansanvi and Samangelaf) are named individually in biblical, midrashic or Kabbalistic literature, and references to them occur in prayers. Some, like the ANGEL OF DEATH, play a major role but are not fully personified, and others seem to exist only for a short time, having been created for a specific task. Every nation has its guardian angel, and each embryo is taught torah in the womb by an angel (see BIRTH). The father of the family is accompanied by two angels when he returns from the synagogue on shabbat eve, and they are welcomed into the Jewish home with a song of greeting, 'Shalom Aleikhem'. Angels officially have no evil INCLINATION, yet the whole tradition of DEMONS involves the belief in angels of destruction who frustrate man's attempts to keep the commandments (see also EVIL EYE). Angels carry people's prayers to God, but it is forbidden actually to pray to them. The liturgy contains songs ascribed to angels, some of which come from HEIKHALOT literature. The MAASEH MERKAVAH mystics had to learn the passwords that enabled them to ascend to heaven past angelic guardians, an experience which they claimed transformed them into angels. There are also a number of works of practical Kabbalah which contain magical formulae for controlling angels, but strong warnings were issued against indulging in these practices because a person should not conjure angels for his protection. Instead he should pray to God. On yom kippur all Jews are like angels, dressed in white (see KITEL), living without food and reciting the angelic response after the first line of the shema aloud. See also KEDUSHAH.

ani maamin (Hebrew for 'I believe') A highly stylized reformulation of Maimonides' thirteen ARTICLES OF FAITH, each beginning with the words: 'I believe with perfect faith ...'. Ani maamin became a popular

catechism and, although it misrepresents Maimonides' ideas, was included in many editions of the daily PRAYER-BOOK to be said privately at the end of the weekday shacharit. Those Jewish groups who objected to Maimonides' philosophical bias refused to recite the ani maamin or to incorporate it into their prayer-books. The modernist prayer-book of Reconstructionism, in the USA, has replaced the 'I believe' formula with one which sets out the conditions of Jewish loyalty. Reconstructionists believe that Jews do not need to express their religion in terms of dogma but in terms of what they want and expect from the Jewish heritage. The twelfth ani maamin is about the Messiah: 'I believe with a perfect faith in the coming of the Messiah, and even though he delay, I will wait for his coming every day'. This was sung by Jews before they were murdered in the Nazi concentration camps, a poignant expression of hope in God's salvation.

animals For the purposes of Jewish life the animal kingdom is divided up into KOSHER animals which may be eaten and those whose meat is forbidden (see DIETARY LAWS). Although animals can be exploited for food and clothing, cruelty to animals is prohibited, as is hunting them for sport. Originally, mankind was vegetarian, and meat-eating was only allowed by God after the Flood as a concession to human weakness. Jews have to feed their animals before they themselves eat, and they must slaughter them for food in a swift and painless manner (see SHECHITAH). They must also allow their animals to rest on shabbat. Consideration for animal welfare is expressed in a Talmudic story about Judah Ha-Nasi, the leading figure of 2c. Palestine. He was stricken with illness because he refused to help a calf on its way to slaughter, which sought refuge with him. He was only cured when he saved some mice from being killed by one of his servants at home. All animals worship God each day, and Jewish liturgy contains a collection of songs of praise uttered by them (see PEREK SHIRAH). Demons appear in animal form, and Jewish folklore knows of fantastic animal creatures such as the BEHEMOTH and the LEVIATHAN, whose flesh will be eaten at the great banquet in the days of the Messiah. See also MIXED SPECIES.

anointing The use of oil to anoint a person or a cult-object indicated that it had entered into a new status and was brought under special divine guidance, set aside from the profane world or returned to a normal condition. Thus a king, a High Priest, a priest appointed for war, or someone who had recovered from leprosy were all anointed. The oil for anointing kings was originally prepared by Moses and used to anoint kings until the period of King JOSIAH, who hid it away until the time of the Messiah. The term 'Messiah' itself is an anglicization of the Hebrew word 'mashiach' which means 'anointed', since the Messiah will be a king of the line of David appointed by God for his redemptive task.

anshei keneset ha-gedolah see SYNAGOGUE, THE GREAT

anthropomorphism The language of the Hebrew Bible, Rabbinic literature, the Kabbalah and the liturgy is replete with descriptions of God in human terms. Since the Bible forbids any attempt to depict God, the Talmudic rabbis, when using grossly anthropomorphic expressions, sometimes added the remark 'kiveyakhol' meaning 'if it were really possible (which of course it is not)'. Nevertheless, ordinary Jews continued to think of God in very mundane terms. For this reason Aramaic translations of the Bible (Targum) paraphrased certain expressions, and medieval philosophers like Maimonides wrote at length about the heresy entailed in taking anthropomorphic language literally. Maimonides argued that, in fact, such language simply refers to man's understanding of God's activity in the world and does not refer to God Himself. The mystics were more inclined to meditate on the 'physical' dimensions of God, particularly in the SHIUR KOMAH literature, and they avoided the problem of anthropomorphism by maintaining that the physical world was but a lower-order reflection of divine structures.

anti-Semitism Term coined in the late 19c. to refer to anti-Jewish attitudes and activities. It is used nowadays to include prejudice against Jews down the ages from pre-Christian times to modern political persecution. The nature of anti-Semitic prejudice has varied in different periods. Its pre-Christian form was partly nationalistic, since Jews could not be assimilated by other national cultures, partly religious mockery, since Jews worshipped an invisible God, and partly economic dislike for Jews, who competed in business with their GENTILE neighbours. Christianity introduced accusations of deicide, an identification of Jews with the devil, the need to show the superiority of the New Israel (Christianity) over the Old Israel, the negation of Judaizing trends in Christianity itself (*see* JUDAIZERS) and xenophobia of the Jew as cultural stranger. These themes are found in a variety of forms, from the writings of the New Testament to those of modern churchmen. Jews were perceived as embodiments of the Antichrist, were massacred during the CRUSADES, made to wear a distinguishing Jewish BADGE, accused of desecrating the Eucharistic host and of using the blood of Christians in their rituals (*see* BLOOD LIBEL), restricted to GHETTOS, expelled from Christian countries and forcibly baptized. Even after a more positive approach to Jews began with the liberal policies of the 18c. Enlightenment, renewed European nationalism alienated them once again and led to anti-Jewish works like the *Protocols of the* ELDERS OF ZION. Racists and fascists have used Christian anti-Semitism for political purposes (*see* POGROM), culminating in Nazi attempts to solve 'the Jewish problem' through genocide (*see* CONCENTRATION CAMPS; HOLOCAUST). Islamic antagonism to Jews usually took a more moderate form, and Jews had the status of a protected people (*see* DHIMMA). They were, however, sometimes forcibly converted to Islam. In modern times anti-Zionism has drawn upon classical anti-Semitic images for political purposes. *See also* MARTYRDOM; SHTADLAN; ZIONISM.

Antoninus *see* JUDAH HA-NASI

apikoros (Hebrew for 'heretic', from the Greek philosopher Epicurus) A Jew who does not believe in revelation, denies the validity of the Rabbinic tradition, or makes fun of the Rabbis. The apikoros is

*The Purple **Angel*** by Marc Chagall.

Evidence of **anti-Semitism**: a Dutch poster advertising an anti-Semitic film about 'the Eternal Jew'.

one of those said to have no portion in the World to Come (olam haba) and is condemned to eternal punishment. The term is used commonly in Yiddish to apply to anyone who expresses views at variance with Orthodox teaching, particularly where the person concerned is knowledgeable about Judaism. The halakhah recommends the ostracization of the apikoros, who is excluded from all religious functions, and where possible he should be killed, or if he is in danger, his life should not be saved. People should at least know what to reply to the questions of the apikoros.

Apocalypse Works containing visionary revelations about the secret teachings of God concerning angels, the Messiah and the End of Days (see DAY OF JUDGMENT). There are many motifs from the AGGADAH in apocalyptic literature, reflecting the mysticism of the Talmudic period, but there is also a strong heretical tendency in the mysteries revealed to the elect. During the heavenly journeys undertaken by the heroes of Apocalypse, they are instructed by angels about God's purpose in the Creation, about good and evil spirits (see DEMONS) and about the fate of mankind. They are also told the meaning of the signs of the times which point to the Messianic Age. The DEAD SEA SCROLLS contain apocalyptic writings.

Apocrypha Non-canonical, semi-sacred writings claiming the status of revelation. In order to prevent confusion between apocryphal works, which sometimes contained heretical teachings, and the inspired literature of the Hebrew biblical canon, the former were taken out of circulation by being consigned to a GENIZAH, and their public reading was prohibited. This rejection meant that the Hebrew or Aramaic originals of most works of Jewish Apocrypha were lost or were preserved only in translation. See also BEN SIRA; MACCABEES.

apostasy An apostate Jew who leaves the Jewish faith for another religion or becomes a heretic is known as a mumar, 'someone who has changed', or a meshumad, 'someone who was forced to abandon his faith'. A special benediction was added to the eighteen blessings of the AMIDAH against apostates who had become Gnostics or had adopted Christianity. An apostate is still regarded as a Jew for certain purposes, but he or she does not have any claim to the privileges associated with Jewish status. The sin of apostasy was regarded as so heinous that it was even claimed that an apostate could never genuinely repent, although this claim was not accepted by the halakhah. One of the best-known apostates of the early Rabbinic period, ELISHA BEN AVUYAH, refused to return to Judaism because he mistakenly believed that God would accept the repentance of all other sinners except himself. In the Middle Ages a sympathetic view was taken of those who were forcibly baptized during the CRUSADES and in Christian Spain during the INQUISITION (see MARRANO), or who chose Islam when fanatical Moslem rulers offered them the alternatives of conversion or death. Jews have been far less sympathetic to co-religionists who voluntarily converted to other faiths. Parents would go into full mourning for an apostate child, sitting shivah on low chairs and being comforted by relatives and friends. Thereafter the child was

treated as dead and his name never mentioned in the home again. This negative feeling was mutual, with the most zealous opposition to Judaism coming from those Jews who had become Christians through conviction. The latter were behind some of the worst anti-Jewish measures, claiming that the *Talmud* should be burnt because of its supposedly anti-Christian teachings and instigating persecution of their former co-religionists. See also DOENMEH; SHABBETAI TZEVI.

Aramaic A Semitic language related to HEBREW. In ancient times Aramaic was spoken throughout the Near East, and it became an integral part of Jewish linguistic culture. There is even a Talmudic view that Adam spoke Aramaic. Different dialects of Aramaic, representing Palestinian and Babylonian forms, are found in Jewish literature. Large sections of the Bible (the books of Daniel and Ezra) are in Aramaic, as are the TARGUM texts and most of the TALMUD. The *Zohar* is written in a literary Aramaic. Those parts of the liturgy which were intended for popular use are also in Aramaic, e.g. the mourner's KADDISH which was recited by Jews who were not learned enough in Hebrew actually to lead services. It was said, however, that, since the angels who carry prayers to God do not understand Aramaic, it is better not to pray in that language. In most communities the marriage document (ketubbah) is still written in Babylonian Aramaic.

arbaah minim *see* FOUR SPECIES

arba kosot *see* FOUR CUPS

Aristeas, Letter of Greek work telling of the translation of the torah in the 3c. BCE for the library of the Egyptian king, Ptolemy Philadelphus, in Alexandria. The High Priest in Jerusalem sent seventy-two elders, six representatives from each of the twelve tribes, whose translation of the Bible into Greek impressed the king. According to PHILO JUDAEUS each sage was filled with divine inspiration which guided him in his work. This belief about divine inspiration meant the Greek translation, identified with the Septuagint, was highly valued by Christians and was preferred to the Hebrew original. In the Talmudic version of the story, each elder was confined to a different house while the translation was made, so that they produced totally independent renditions. Their hearts were filled with divine wisdom, however, and they produced identical versions. They all made the same changes in their translations, so as not to raise any doubts in the king's mind, which might have accompanied a literal rendition of the Hebrew. See also TEVET.

ark, holy (Hebrew 'aron ha-kodesh', also 'heikhal', 'tevah') The cupboard containing the SEFER TORAH, which is situated in the Jerusalem-facing wall of the synagogue, is called the holy ark. Its name derives from the ARK OF THE CONVENANT, which contained the TABLETS OF THE DECALOGUE, and was situated in the HOLY OF HOLIES in the TABERNACLE and later on in the TEMPLE. Since the congregation turn towards Jerusalem in prayer, the ark is the focus of synagogue worship, and the eternal flame (see NER TAMID) hangs above it. The sermon is preached from a platform in front of the ark, and the PRIESTLY BLESSING is also recited from there. The curtain (see PAROKHET) of the ark is drawn and the doors are opened when a sefer torah is removed or when especially important prayers are said, and the congregation stand out of respect for the torah (see PETICHAH). On SIMCHAT TORAH when all the torah scrolls are taken out, a lighted candle is placed in the ark symbolizing the light of torah. The doors and surrounds of the ark often used to be elaborately carved and decorated, the lion motif being particularly popular.

Ark of the Covenant (Hebrew 'aron ha-berit') A box-like container of wood overlaid with gold, which was kept behind a veil in the HOLY OF HOLIES of the desert TABERNACLE and then of the TEMPLE in Jerusalem (Exod. 25). On top of the ark were two golden angels, known as cherubim (see CHERUB), and inside were the two TABLETS OF THE DECALOGUE. The ark miraculously occupied no space in the Holy of Holies, even though its physical measurements are given in the Bible. When it journeyed before the Israelites in the wilderness, it carried its LEVITE bearers along. It also levelled mountains, so that the people could travel without hindrance, and destroyed any snakes or scorpions in their path. The Philistines captured the ark, but found that it caused the idol they worshipped to collapse and brought them disease and misfortune (I Sam. 5). When they returned it, the cattle pulling the cart it was on sang as they made their own way home. At the end of the First Temple period, the ark was hidden away by JOSIAH so as not to be captured by the Babylonians, and it will only reappear when the Messiah comes.

ark of Noah (Hebrew 'tevah') The ship built by NOAH at God's command to save himself, his family and the animals from the FLOOD (Gen. 6). The ark had three stories: the top was for humans, the middle for the animals, and the bottom for refuse (though other views about its threefold structure are also found). The 'skylight' in the roof of the ark (6:16) was made from a luminous stone, since the world was darkened by rainclouds and an ordinary window would not have sufficed. Apart from Noah's wife, three sons and daughters-in-law, the ark also carried the giant Og, king of Bashan, who clung onto the outside during the whole of the flood period. This explains why Og's lifespan, as recorded in the Bible, extends beyond the traditional date of the flood. After the flood, the ark landed on Mount Ararat, where travellers still occasionally report sightings of it (see BENJAMIN OF TUDELA).

aron ha-berit see ARK OF THE COVENANT

aron ha-kodesh see ARK, HOLY

art, religious Jewish artistic expression is conditioned by reservations about making graven images. Thus not only is it forbidden to make idolatrous images of other gods (see IDOLATRY), it is also forbidden to fashion any likeness of God Himself. It was also forbidden to reproduce any of the Temple implements (see MENORAH). By extention it is considered sacrilegious to use any art forms as central features of religious worship. This was not a universal prohibition

A 6c. mosaic of the **Ark of the Covenant** from the Bet Alpha Synagogue, Israel.

Picture of the hand-washing ablution during the Passover seder ritual. The birds' heads replace human heads to satisfy objections to representing human figures in Jewish **art** (14c. German haggadah).

in the past, however, and there are fine examples of both mosaics and frescoes from synagogue remains of the first six centuries CE (*see* DURA EUROPOS). It is possible that Islamic opposition to representational art affected Jewish attitudes, and there is some evidence of synagogue figures having been defaced in the Islamic period. Throughout the Middle Ages rabbis objected to the use of images in synagogues and even to designs on prayer-books, since they might detract the worshipper from the idea' of 'a God without form'. In ILLUMINATED MANUSCRIPTS the opposition to representing human figures led to strange pictures of people with the heads of birds and to MICROGRAPHY. Most religious creativity went into purely decorative artefacts and ritual objects used both in the synagogue and in the home. Since these did not usually involve representational art, they did not raise any problems of graven images. The area of greatest artistic creativity was not in plastic art but in sound expression: music, song and particularly in story-telling, because the imagination was able to range freely without limitation. *See also* ARK, HOLY; ARK OF THE COVENANT; LION; PAROKHET; SHIVVITI.

articles of faith (Hebrew 'ikkarim') Until the Middle Ages Jewish religion had no systematized doctrine. Neither the Bible nor the *Talmud* discussed the central tenets of belief in any detail, though a number of items of faith, such as the belief in MONOTHEISM, played a central role. Biblical theology was concerned with specific issues like the challenge of idolatry or the question of whether God was concerned with worldly affairs, rather than with dogma. Talmudic passages which deal with matters of Jewish belief were similarly directed at particular problems. Thus, the *Mishnah* enumerated among those who have no portion in the World to Come (olam haba): 'He who says that there is no RESURRECTION, that the TORAH does not come from heaven, and the APIKOROS ... also those who read non-canonical books, who utter a charm over a wound ... or who pronounce the TETRAGRAMMATON with its letters.' In the Middle Ages contacts with Christianity, Islam and Greek philosophy made it necessary for Jewish thinkers to formulate the main beliefs of Judaism and thus to distinguish it from these other religions. The most important formulation was that undertaken in the 12c. by Maimonides, who argued for thirteen articles of faith which must be subscribed to by the believing Jew. These consist of the belief 1) in a creator God, who is 2) unique, 3) incorporeal, 4) eternal, and 5) is the sole object of worship; that 6) the biblical prophecies are true, 7) Moses was the greatest of the prophets, 8) the torah was given to Moses, and 9) will not be changed; that 10) God knows the deeds of men, and 11) rewards and punishes them; that 12) the Messiah will come, and 13) there will be an afterlife. Somewhat altered and shortened versions of these principles have been incorporated in the prayer-book in the hymns, adon olam and YIGDAL, and in the ANI MAAMIN formulae.

arvit *see* MAARIV

asceticism Judaism does not encourage institutionalized asceticism in the form of monasticism, celibacy or vows of poverty, although these were found in sectarian movements (*see* ESSENES). The world created by God is a good world, and people will have to give an account for all the pleasures they could have enjoyed in this world but did not. Nevertheless, there are many examples of individual and group ascetic practices. The biblical NAZIRITE gave up wine and the cutting of hair. Adults go without food and drink on official FAST DAYS or undertake optional fasts. Fasting is regarded as a kind of sacrifice in which the fat and blood of the individual are offered up to God on the altar. Some holy men even fasted for long periods to avert tragedies, and we are told of one Mishnaic sage, Rabbi Zadok, who fasted over a period of forty years in an unsuccessful attempt to prevent the Temple being destroyed. There was also a well-attested practice of fasting from one shabbat to the next which was popular in the late Middle Ages. Meat and wine are not consumed at the beginning of the month of Av as a sign of mourning for the destruction of the Temple, though the Rabbis disapproved of attempts to ban these items completely. Some scholars, like Simeon Ben Azzai, did not marry because they 'desired the torah itself' rather than women. Sexual abstinence was indeed encouraged by a number of medieval authors who regarded asceticism as necessary for ethical perfection. Other sages curtailed their sleep so that they could study torah. Elijah the Vilna Gaon, for example, only slept two hours a night for most of his life. Under Kabbalistic influence people engaged in penitential practices like rolling in the snow, which were meant to hasten the coming of the Messiah. In some of the sectarian Messianic movements, like that of the followers of Shabbetai Tzevi, these ascetic practices were taken very seriously.

aseret ha-dibberot *see* DECALOGUE

aseret yemai teshuvah *see* TEN DAYS OF PENITENCE

ashamnu (Hebrew for 'we have sinned') Confession of SINS listing a variety of different sins in alphabetical order. Ashamnu is chanted on fast days, on yom kippur and in some liturgies even every day. A bride and groom say ashamnu prior to their marriage, since at their wedding all their sins are forgiven and they begin life anew. A dying person should be encouraged to confess his sins but should be informed that such a confession does not mean he will certainly die. If, however, saying ashamnu distresses him, then those at his deathbed should not press him to do so. It is customary to bang one's chest above the heart as each sin is mentioned, and on special occasions ashamnu is sung to an evocative tune intended to instil a feeling of REPENTANCE.

Asher Ben Yechiel *see* BERLIN, SAUL

Ashkenazim Jews originally of German extraction. The biblical name Ashkenaz (Gen. 10:3; I Chr. 1:6; Jer. 51:27) was thought in the Middle Ages to refer to Germany. Since most of the Jews of Christian countries in Western, Central and Eastern Europe from medieval to modern times were both culturally and demographically the descendants of the Franco-German Jews, the term Ashkenazim came to be applied to them all. The Ashkenazi cultural complex involves the use of different dialects of YIDDISH as a Jewish lingua franca and distinctive rituals, customs, liturgy, synagogue architecture (*see* SHUL), methods of study and pronunciation of HEBREW which differentiated Ashkenazi Jews from their co-religionists among the SEPHARDIM and Oriental Jewries. Since most of the latter sub-groups lived in Islamic lands and the Ashkenazim lived in Christian lands, they maintained separate identities for about four hundred years until modern times and were influenced by different host cultures. In the State of Israel there are two Chief Rabbis, one Ashkenazi and one Sephardi. *See also* CHASIDIM, SEFER; GERSHOM, RABBENU; JUDAH HA-CHASID; KHAZARS; SHTETL.

Asmodeus Mischievous demon king. Asmodeus knew the whereabouts of the fabulous SHAMIR which King SOLOMON needed for building the Temple. Solomon managed to capture the intoxicated demon king after he arranged for the well that Asmodeus drank from to be filled with wine. While he was being brought to Solomon, Asmodeus cried as he passed a wedding, laughed at a man who was ordering shoes to last for seven years and scoffed at a magician who was showing off his magic tricks. The demon later explained to Solomon that he could see beyond appearances, and so he knew that the groom would soon die, the man buying shoes would not survive for seven days, let alone seven years, and the magician was standing over a buried treasure of which he was completely unaware. Solomon gained control of the shamir and came into possession of a book of magic given to him by the demon. He was, however, tricked by Asmodeus who sent him into exile and sat on the throne in his place. People suspected that Asmodeus was not the real king because he never appeared in public, and the reports which circulated about his sexual behaviour with Solomon's wives showed that his actions were not in accord with Jewish practice. After much wandering as a beggar, Solomon returned and banished Asmodeus. *See also* BENJAMIN OF TUDELA.

ass (Hebrew 'chamor') In biblical and Rabbinic literature the ass is the symbol of stupidity and insensitivity; even at the height of summer asses feel cold. An image of a foolish undertaking is an ass trying to climb a ladder. Gentiles were depicted as people who were like asses, and Jews themselves are regarded as asses compared to their forefathers who surpassed them in wisdom and insight. Yet it was BALAAM'S ass which perceived an angel blocking Balaam's path and by speaking saved his master from death (Num. 22). This same ass had carried Abraham to the akedah and will one day carry the Messiah into Jersualem on his triumphal journey (Zech. 9:9). Since the root of the Hebrew word for ass also has the meaning of 'gross matter', the idea of the Messiah riding on an ass is interpreted to mean that he will have overcome his own earthly desires. The *Talmud* remarks that, if someone sees an ass in a dream, he should expect salvation.

Assembly of Jewish Notables Council of Jewish leaders called together in 1806 by Napoleon, from France and Northern Italy, as part of the process of Jewish emancipation. The Assembly consisted of 111

English ceramic figure of an **Ashkenazi** Jewish peddlar.

Bronze medal commemorating the **Assembly of Jewish Notables** and the Grand Sanhedrin called together by Napoleon, showing Napoleon presenting submissive Jewry with a new Decalogue.

participants who had to respond to twelve questions, among which were ones about intermarriage of Jews and Gentiles, whether Frenchmen were regarded as brothers, whether France was seen as their homeland by Jews and Jewish attitudes to usury. The Jewish Notables, who were made up of Orthodox and non-Orthodox members, devised compromise answers so as not to alienate Napoleon. The Assembly was followed a year later by the convening of a modern SANHEDRIN to give religious authority to the Assembly answers. The Sanhedrin had seventy-one members, two-thirds rabbis and one-third laymen. They, too, came up with answers that would not be detrimental to Napoleon's positive attitude to the Jews, allowing marriage and divorce between Jews to follow state regulations, banning usury and claiming that Jews were citizens of their country of domicile.

assimilation The process whereby a Jewish minority adopts the values, culture and lifestyle of the Gentile majority. Since Jews throughout the DIASPORA had to struggle to retain a separate identity, outright assimilation was always perceived as a threat. Yet many cultural elements were assimilated by Jews from their hosts, and these in turn shaped the different local varieties of Judaism. The continuous battles of Jewish religious leaders against SUPERSTITION and Gentile mores were only partially effective. The extent of external influences on Jewish life can be seen in the use of YIDDISH (a German dialect) and LADINO (a Spanish dialect) by ASHKENAZIM and SEPHARDIM as their respective linguae francae. The customs and folklore of Judaism can, to a large extent, be traced back to parallel items in surrounding cultures, and there is no area of Jewish life and religion which has not been affected by this process of cultural assimilation. This does not mean that Judaism has been threatened with loss of identity because what has been absorbed has been 'Judaized' and integrated into the tradition. In the modern period the situation has changed radically through self-conscious attempts to adopt European culture and its life-style. In every community there are Jewish 'secularists', and they make up a large part of the population of the State of Israel. There is also a growing tendency for Jewish youngsters to marry Gentile partners (*see* INTERMARRIAGE) and to drift out of the Jewish community. This modern process of assimilation, with the accompanying disappearance of a distinctive Jewish life-style, has to some extent been arrested by the Holocaust. The death of six million co-religionists had a traumatic effect on those Jews who, until the Nazi era, believed they would simply be accepted by their Gentile hosts. ZIONISM and the rebirth of modern Israel have also awakened a new sense of Jewish ethnic solidarity. *See also* APOSTACY.

astrology Astrological influences determine a person's life, but Israel is under the direct guidance of God. Good deeds can thus annul astrological misfortune, and even predictions may not always turn out as imagined. Pharaoh was informed by his astrologers that the person who would redeem the Israelites from slavery would succumb to water, so he had all the Israelite children cast into the Nile. In fact, however, the downfall of MOSES came about when he struck the

rock to bring forth water in the desert, instead of speaking to it. People born on different days of the week will have specific personality traits: Sundays = distinction, Mondays = anger, Tuesdays = wealth and love of pleasure, Wednesdays = intelligence, Thursdays = benevolence, Fridays = piety, and those born on Saturdays will die on that day. Some days were regarded as lucky and others unlucky for specific undertakings. It was recommended not to drink water on Wednesday or Friday evenings and not to undergo blood-letting on Mondays, Tuesdays or Thursdays because of the negative planetary influences (mazal). An eclipse of the moon means bad luck for Jews, while an eclipse of the sun means bad luck for Gentiles. The remnants of this belief in astrological luck are preserved in the greetings of 'mazal tov' ('good luck') which Jews use for joyous occasions. Another view regards the dominance of heavenly bodies at the hour of birth as the decisive factor in a person's character. For example, someone born under the dominance of Mars will be a shedder of BLOOD, either a murderer, a ritual slaughterer (shochet) or a surgeon. While Kabbalists (*see* KABBALAH) and many medieval rabbis believed that the heavens were 'the book of life' and astrology the 'supreme science', Maimonides dismissed such ideas as forbidden superstitions. He explained away the Talmudic references to astrology as the isolated opinions of individuals which should be rejected since the Jew must rely on God alone. *See also* NOSTRADAMUS; SUPERSTITION; YETZIRAH, SEFER.

a-t-ba-sh Code in which the first letter of the Hebrew ALPHABET replaces the last letter and so on. The name of the code actually involves its key because a-t-ba-sh means aleph (first letter) tav (last letter) bet (second letter) shin (penultimate letter). Through the use of this code, words can be transposed into other words, leading to an association of ideas in biblical interpretation and in Kabbalistic literature. There are variations on a-t-ba-sh, such as those associating the first and the twelfth letters, the second and the thirteenth, etc.

atonement (Hebrew 'kapparah') The reconciliation of man and God which, in ancient times, was brought about through SACRIFICE, particularly the sacrificial ritual of YOM KIPPUR. After the destruction of the Second Temple, and the cessation of sacrifices, yom kippur continued to have an atoning power, but the main vehicles for atonement were considered to be repentance, prayer, HOSPITALITY, charity and good deeds. EXILE is also a form of atonement. It was also said that a man without a wife remained without atonement and that the People of Israel served as an atonement for the nations of the world. Between the Jew and God there need be no intermediaries to effect atonement. As the *Talmud* puts it: 'Happy are you, Israel. Before whom do you cleanse yourself and who is it who cleanses you? It is your Father in heaven.' Suffering (*see* JOB) and death both have an atoning aspect. When something bad happens to a Jew he may say: 'Let this be as an atonement', and the prayer of a dying person includes the words: 'May my death be an atonement for all my sins.' In the Middle Ages the atonement rite of KAPPAROT was introduced prior to yom kippur. This practice, however, was strongly opposed by some leading rabbis who regarded it as a pagan superstition. *See also* FORGIVENESS; JOCHANAN BEN ZAKKAI.

Auschwitz CONCENTRATION CAMP built by the Nazis in 1940 near the Polish town of Oswiecim. The Auschwitz complex became the largest of the Nazi extermination centres when the death camp of Birkenau was added nearby in 1941. Political dissidents, Russian prisoners, Jews and gypsies were all murdered at the death camp, some being selected for extermination on arrival by the notorious Dr Mengele, since they were considered unfit for work on labour units. Those who were selected for forced labour had a number tattooed on their arm. It is estimated that more than one million Jews, from all over Europe, were killed by gassing in rooms designed to look like showers so as not to alarm the victims. The bodies were then burnt in the crematoria ovens. Experiments were conducted on human beings, particularly on identical twins, by Mengele and other medical staff. Auschwitz has come to symbolize the whole Nazi policy of genocide and is the most infamous of the HOLOCAUST camps.

auto da fé (Portuguese for 'act of faith') Originally the proclamation of a verdict by the Catholic INQUISITION on backsliding Christians, many of whom were crypto-Jews (*see* MARRANO). Those found guilty of capital offenses were handed over immediately to the secular authorities for execution by being burnt at the stake, the Church itself not wishing to carry out the sentence. The local townspeople were summoned to an auto da fé, where a sermon was preached. The ceremony was accompanied by a public spectacle with processions and penitent sinners wearing special clothing indicating their sins. Before the auto da fé, the accused were tortured by the Inquisitors to make them confess and repent, and the property of those condemned to death was confiscated by the Church. In later usage the term 'auto da fé' was applied to the execution itself. The last recorded auto da fé took place in 1826 in Valencia, Spain.

autopsy The post-mortem dissection of a corpse is forbidden by the halakhah because it is regarded as showing disrespect for the dead. The only exception is where another life might be saved directly by the knowledge thus acquired. Most Orthodox rabbis maintain a narrow interpretation of this exception, which was first adumbrated by Ezekiel Landau in the 18c. They only allow a post-mortem when there is a patient, currently suffering from a life-threatening illness similar to that of the deceased, who might actually be cured by medical knowledge gained from the autopsy. This would rule out autopsies for the general purpose of advancing scientific research, since they involve no immediate situations of saving life. Although traditional Jews abide by those state laws which necessitate a post-mortem, they try to avoid them if possible. In the State of Israel autopsies are an emotive issue and have led to clashes between religious Jews and government authorities.

Av Fifth lunar month of the Hebrew calendar, counting from Nisan, the month of the Exodus, or the eleventh month from the New Year festival (rosh ha-

Jewish savant working on an **astrology** chart (16c. woodcut).

The main gate of **Auschwitz** concentration camp.

shanah). It begins in July or early August, and its zodiacal sign is the lion. Av is the saddest month of the year, during which both the First and Second Temples were destroyed, events commemorated in the fast of the Ninth of Av (see AV, NINTH OF). So 'when the month of Av begins, joy diminishes'. Nevertheless, the fifteenth of Av (see AV, FIFTEENTH OF) was once a minor festive day.

Av, Fifteenth of (Hebrew 'tu be-av') Minor festival celebrated in ancient times. It was on this day that marriage was allowed between the different TRIBES of Israel, and so the custom grew up for maidens to parade themselves before prospective suitors. According to the *Mishnah*: 'There were not such festive days for Israel as the Fifteen of Av and yom kippur on which the daughters of Jerusalem would go out in white garments, borrowed so as not to put those who did not have any to shame. They would dance in the vineyards and say "Young man, lift up your eyes and choose".' The attractive girls would encourage the bachelors to choose a beautiful wife. The less attractive ones from good families would encourage them to choose someone with a respectable family background (see YICHUS). Those who were neither attractive nor from a good family would encourage the boys to choose a wife for spiritual, rather than material, reasons.

Av, Ninth of (Hebrew 'tisha be-av') The saddest day of the Jewish year, marked by a fast commemorating the destruction of both the First and Second TEMPLES in JERUSALEM. Apart from the twenty-four hour fast, the day is one of semi-mourning (see EGG). Leather shoes are not worn, chairs are not sat on until midday, TEFILLIN are only put on at the afternoon service, the body is not washed and torah is not studied, as this brings joy. Since it is customary to sleep on a harder surface than normal, some people even put a stone under their head in place of a pillow. In the age of the Messiah the Ninth of Av will be turned into a festival, but he who does not mourn for the destruction of the Temple will not merit to see it rebuilt. Indeed, it is said that the Messiah was born on the day the Temple was destroyed, indicating that within destruction lie the seeds of redemption. Prayers in the synagogue are held in a dimmed light, the book of LAMENTATIONS is read and special KINOT hymns of lament are recited in a sad chant accompanied by sighing and crying. Some keep the custom of abandoning their kinot texts after use, to express the faith that before the next Ninth of Av the Messiah will come. The history of persecution, exile and martyrdom is related in the liturgical poems. In pre-modern times children used to add to the sombre atmosphere by throwing prickly plants into the beards of adults. The Fast of Av ends a period of THREE WEEKS OF MOURNING, which begins with the Fast of the Seventeenth of Tammuz, during which no weddings take place. It was on the night of the Ninth of Av that the Israelites cried in the wilderness, when the report of the spies about the Holy Land made them despair of ever being able to conquer it (Num. 14). This crying in vain and lack of faith was punished by God. Throughout Jewish history Jews have had something to cry about on this night. Among the

other tragic events which took place on the Ninth of Av was the expulsion of the Jews from Spain in 1492. *See also* LEVI ISAAC OF BERDICHEV; SIYYUM.

av bet din *see* BET DIN

avel, avelut *see* MOURNING

av ha-rachamim *see* CRUSADES; MEMORIAL PRAYERS

Avila, Prophet of (13c.) Illiterate Spanish wonder-worker named Abraham, who produced a large volume of mystical writing which he claimed was inspired by an angel. He also asserted that he had the gift of prophecy and was the Messiah. The leading Spanish rabbi of his generation, Solomon Adret, refused to support these claims of prophecy because an ignorant man could not be a prophet. Adret told Jews to bear the sufferings of exile patiently, and not to follow signs and wonders without thoroughly investigating the matter. Nevertheless, many members of the Avila community were impressed by the achievements of their 'prophet' and in the summer of 1295 dressed in white to await the dawning of the Messianic Age. According to a Christian version of what happened, crosses appeared on the white garments, and a number of Jews converted to Christianity. The Jewish leadership took this to be the work of Satan.

avinu malkenu (Hebrew for 'our Father, our King') A prayer, each verse of which begins with the words 'our Father, our King', recited on fast days and during the Ten Days of Penitence. Avinu malkenu is traced back to an incident during a drought when Rabbi Akiva recited five brief supplications, each of which began with the words 'our Father, our King'. Although the fasting and prayers of others had failed to end the drought, after Akiva's prayer it started to rain immediately. Seeing the effectiveness of the avinu malkenu formula, the rabbis expanded the prayer and incorporated it into the liturgy. The two forms of address, 'our Father' and 'our King', relate to the images of man as 'child' and 'servant' of God.

avodah zarah *see* IDOLATRY

ayin hara *see* EVIL EYE

Azazel The destination for the scapegoat which carried the sins of Israel into the wilderness on YOM KIPPUR (Lev. 16). Two identical goats were selected for the ritual. One was chosen by lot to be offered to God and the other sent to Azazel in the wilderness, to be pushed over a high cliff. The High Priest recited a confession of sins for the people over the head of the scapegoat, and a scarlet thread was wrapped partly around its horns and partly over a rock on the cliff top. As the goat fell, the thread turned white showing that the sins of the people were forgiven (see SIMON THE RIGHTEOUS). Although the word Azazel may be a description of the place, or of the goat, it was also explained as the name of a demon. The sins of Israel were thus being returned to their source of impurity. The Kabbalists thought of the goat as a bribe to the powers of evil, so that Satan would not accuse Israel but instead would speak up on their behalf. Azazel is also the name of a fallen angel (see SOLOMON).

baal ha-bayit (Hebrew for 'householder') A lay member of the Jewish COMMUNITY who is the head of a family is known as a baal ha-bayit, the Yiddish equivalent being 'baalebos'. These terms imply a level of responsible behaviour and a solid, virtuous life-style. Thus, someone might be commended for behaving in a baalebatisher manner, and it is a compliment to refer to a married woman as a baalebosta, meaning that she is a good housewife and runs a clean, well supplied home. The baal ha-bayit is contrasted with the RABBI and CHAZZAN, who have a higher status in the community. He, in turn, has a higher social standing than poor people or itinerant workers whom he is expected to support.

A painting by William Holman Hunt of the scapegoat sent into the wilderness to **Azazel** on yom kippur.

baal shem (Hebrew for 'master of the name') Title of a miracle-worker or folk-healer who had control over the name, or names, of God. The designation was first used in the early Middle Ages, and there is an 11c. reference to a baal shem who was seen in two places at once. Among the activities of a baal shem were writing AMULETS, EXORCISM, healing mental illness, protecting people against demons, controlling spirit possession (dibbuk) and dispensing herbal cures. While some of those to whom the title baal shem was applied were only semi-literate, others were saintly scholars. Many stories are told of how they flew through the air and worked wonders by means of practical KABBALAH. Elijah the Baal Shem of Chelm (16c.) made a golem which was animated by a piece of paper with the TETRAGRAMMATON placed under its tongue. When the paper was removed the golem returned to dust. Joel Baal Shem Heilprin (17c.) saved a ship from sinking by writing a divine name on the ship's bottom. Samuel FALK the Baal Shem of London (18c.) was sought after by the English aristocracy for his knowledge of ALCHEMY and could protect buildings from fire. The most famous of these miracle-workers was Israel BAAL SHEM TOV, who himself inherited Kabbalistic teachings from the legendary Adam BAAL SHEM.

Baal Shem, Adam Legendary wonder-worker whose exploits are recounted in Yiddish tales. Adam found Kabbalistic manuscripts which had been written by the Patriarch Abraham hidden in a cave. These enabled him to become a BAAL SHEM and to perform wonders. He once invited a king to a banquet at his humble home. One of the anti-Semitic ministers of state unsuccessfully tried to persuade the king not to attend, but when they arrived at the Jew's home, they saw a luxurious palace full of wonderful food instead of a small house. Adam had seen a neighbouring monarch constructing a palace in which he was to hold a reception on that day, so he simply whisked the palace away to his own street. Adam told his guests that they must not remove anything from the palace, and if they put their hand in their pockets, they would find what they really wished for there. When the minister withdrew his hand, he found that it was covered in excrement which he could not wash off. Adam informed him that it would only disappear if he swore

The **baal ha-bayit** at the head of the seder table, from Artur Szyk's illustrations for the Passover haggadah.

not to hate Jews and if a Jew urinated on his hand. The king, against his host's advice, removed two glasses from the banquet, thus preventing the return of the palace to its original owner. At the end of his life Adam asked God to whom his Kabbalistic texts should be given and was told in a dream that they should go to Israel Ben Eliezer (*see* BAAL SHEM TOV, ISRAEL). When Adam's son journeyed to Israel's home, he was disappointed when he realized that the only person he could find there by that name was a lowly synagogue attendant. Nevertheless, he left pages of the manuscript next to Israel while he slept and found him studying them during the day. He came to realize that Israel was indeed a skilled practitioner of KABBALAH, but the Baal Shem Tov prohibited him from revealing his true identity.

Baal Shem of London *see* FALK, SAMUEL

Baal Shem Tov, Israel (1700–60) Folk-healer, mystic and charismatic leader of the fledgling CHASIDIC MOVEMENT, originally named Israel Ben Eliezer and commonly known as the Besht. Young Israel grew up as an orphan in southern Poland and had little formal education. He was, however, initiated into the secrets of the KABBALAH by studying the texts left to him by Adam BAAL SHEM and learnt the practice of heavenly soul-ascension from heavenly teachers like the prophet Ahijah the Shilonite. During one such ascension the Besht met the Messiah and was told that the Messianic Age would begin when his teachings had spread far and wide. He is said to have known the identities of the LAMED VAVNIKS of his generation. He liked to spend time in fields and forests, experiencing the divine in the natural world, and eventually became a wandering folk-healer. As such he was known as a Baal Shem Tov, or Master of the Good Name, who used herbal cures, amulets and exorcism, made a GOLEM and taught a form of popular Kabbalah. His religious teaching had a wide influence since it was geared to the needs of simple and barely literate Jews. He showed them how to serve God through their everyday activities by fixing their minds in devotion on God (*see* DEVEKUT). Prayer was a more important form of devotional expression than torah study, and even the 'strange thoughts' which inevitably beset a man in prayer should be followed through to their root in God. In this way the sparks of the divine which are trapped in the world of matter can be raised back to their source. This task of rectifying the sparks (*see* TIKKUN) can be carried out in all the activities of the Jew, not just by keeping the commandments. The Besht emphasized the need for joy in the service of God, particularly to those whose lives were beset by suffering and hardship. He encouraged them to shun extreme asceticism and to drink alcohol, sing and dance in ecstatic self-transcendence.

Babel, Tower of (Hebrew 'migdal bavel') Tower built by the generation after the Flood to reach into the sky (Gen. 11). Their purpose was to take heaven by storm, defeat God and set up idols in His place. They knew that God had control over water, for He had brought the Flood, but they thought that they could shelter in a high tower from any future deluge. The builders were more concerned about the building material than about the workmen, who were expendable. The death of a worker was less disturbing than the loss of bricks falling off the tower, since it took such a long time to hoist them up. The builders were eventually punished by having their original language of communication, HEBREW, split up into many languages. They could thus not understand each other or cooperate and were scattered in all directions. Some of them were turned into animals and demons. They were not punished more severely because they had at least manifested social unity and worked together, whereas people in the generation before the Flood had practised violence against each other and so were destroyed by God.

Babylonian Captivity *see* EXILARCH; EXILE; EZEKIEL; EZRA; GEDALIAH, FAST OF; HOLY OF HOLIES; LEVITES

badchan (Aramaic for 'joker') A jester whose task it was to enliven wedding feasts among Eastern European Jews with songs, jokes and riddles, especially about the bride and groom. The badchan usually worked together with the band of musicians, klezmer, who played at weddings. Sometimes the badchan's words were very cutting, making fun of all those present and not even sparing the embarrassed newlyweds. This led to criticism of the whole institution of wedding jesters, because their coarse and unseemly remarks seemed to make a mockery out of a holy occasion. It was claimed that such merry-making should not really be allowed since Jews were supposed to be in mourning for the destruction of the Temple. This type of entertainment persisted, however, and even the officiating rabbi would sometimes make jokes and sing light-hearted songs in the absence of professional jesters. The *Talmud* tells how the prophet ELIJAH on one of his periodic visits to earth from heaven, pointed out two jesters who were guaranteed a place in the Messianic World to Come (olam haba) because they made those who were sad smile and laugh. *See also* OSTROPOLER, HERSHELE.

badge, Jewish Distinguishing mark worn by Jews on their clothing so they could not be mistaken for Christians. The badge was introduced all over Christian Europe by the Church after the Fourth Lateran Council in 1215, ostensibly to prevent sexual contact between Christians and Jews. It consisted of a piece of cloth sewn on an outer garment, a special hat or a scarf for women. Any Jew caught without one would be fined, though some managed, through bribery, to gain permission not to wear a badge. Since the badge made Jews conspicuous, it was dangerous to travel with one. Jews would sometimes travel in disguise to avoid becoming easy prey for robbers, occasionally travelling as monks and nuns. In the Islamic world distinctive dress for Jews and other non-Moslems was introduced in the 8c. and 9c. After 1939 when the Nazis occupied Poland, with its large Jewish population, Jews had to wear a yellow star (*see* MAGEN DAVID) sometimes with the word 'Jude' on it. This throwback to the Dark Ages of Christian prejudice was put into effect throughout the countries of Nazi-controlled Europe. It was resisted by Dutch Gentiles who themselves wore yellow stars, thus undermining the whole project, and it was also not implemented by the Danes.

Bahir, Sefer Ha- (Hebrew for '*Book of Brightness*')
Early medieval work of Jewish mysticism, and the
first book of the KABBALAH. The *Bahir*, which is
ascribed to a 1c. CE Mishnaic sage, seems to be of
Babylonian origin but was edited in late-12c. Provence
by disciples of the mystic Isaac the Blind. It teaches
how the lower world symbolizes the upper divine
world through the SEFIROT, which are the active
divine powers manifesting themselves through the
biblical COMMANDMENTS. A true understanding of
these commandments is thus to be found only in their
mystical interpretation. The evil of this world is a
result of the revolt of Satan and his demonic hordes
against God. Much is made of the doctrine of TRANS-
MIGRATION OF SOULS, which is used to explain that
just people suffer because they have sinned in a previous
life. Rebirth is compared to a vineyard which must
be replanted so that it can bring forth good grapes.
The *Bahir* is based on the letter mysticism of the *Sefer*
YETZIRAH and its magical use of sacred names.

Balaam Grandson of Laban and a Midianite prophet
who was as great among the Gentiles as Moses was
among the Israelites. Since he alone could tell exactly
when God was angry, he was brought by the Moabite
King Balak to curse the Israelites at such a moment
of divine wrath (Num. 22), when his curse would
thus be especially potent. This stratagem proved
unsuccessful, however, for Balaam was inspired by
God to bless the Israelites instead. En route to his
assignment, God sent an angel brandishing a sword to
discourage him from any thought of cursing the
Israelites. Balaam's ASS saw the angel and refused to
go on, although his master beat him. Eventually the
ass spoke to its master, asking him why he was beating
him. Balaam then saw the angel and realized that his
ass had saved him from danger. The miraculous mouth
of Balaam's ass was one of the things created at twilight
on the sixth day of Creation, though some medieval
rabbis regarded the speaking ass incident as a dream
or a vision. Balaam, who was lame and blind in one
eye, was essentially a prophet who became an evil
magician. When he found he could not curse Israel,
he sought to lead them astray by advising the Moabites
to send their women to prostitute themselves in the
Israelite camp (Num. 25). He never repented and is
continuously punished in gehinnom in boiling semen.
Even there he declares that one should not seek the
peace and welfare of Israel. *See also* JETHRO; PROPHECY.

Balak *see* BALAAM

Balfour Declaration Letter from the British Foreign
Secretary, Arthur J. Balfour, to Lord Rothschild
dated 2 November 1917 conveying His Majesty's
Government's agreement in principle to the setting up
of a Jewish National Home in Palestine. Zionist leaders
had been in negotiation with the British government
for some time prior to 1917, with a view to winning
British support for the rebirth of a Jewish state in the
Holy Land. For Zionists, the Declaration was a historic
document containing recognition of Jewish claims to
Palestine, although the letter did add the rider that
such a Jewish National Home should not prejudice
the rights of the non-Jewish population of Palestine.
Religious Zionists hailed it as a text of crucial religious

The building of the Tower of **Babel** (11c. English
manuscript).

Balaam *and the Ass* by Rembrandt, showing the
angel with a sword blocking their path.

import since there were objections in the *Talmud* to Jews attempting to re-establish political domination of the Holy Land without the agreement of the Gentile nations. From the British point of view the letter seems to have been intended to win the backing of North-American Jewry for the allied cause and to pressure Russian Jews to help keep Russia in the First World War on the side of Britain. The sentiments of the Balfour Declaration were supported at the San Remo Conference of 1920 and in the League of Nations mandate over Palestine in 1922. *See also* ZIONISM.

Barak *see* DEBORAH; JAEL

Bar Kokhba, Simeon (2c. CE) Rebel commander who led a revolt of Palestinian Jewry against the Romans from 132–5 CE. His name was originally Bar Koziba, and he used the appellation 'Bar Kokhba' as a Messianic title meaning 'Son of a Star'. AKIVA supported Bar Kokhba's claim to be the Messiah, although his rabbinic colleagues made fun of him and told him that grass would grow out of his cheeks before the Messianic 'Son of David' would come. The revolt failed with the fall of the last stronghold of Bethar. This was despite some notable military successes, including the capture of Jerusalem, and despite the commitment of Bar Kokhba's soldiers, who each cut off a finger to show their bravery. God rejected Bar Kokhba because he prayed that God need not help him as long as He did not help his enemies. *See also* NASI.

bar mitzvah (Hebrew for 'son of commandment') At the age of thirteen years and one day a boy is considered a responsible adult for most religious purposes. He is now duty bound to keep the COMMANDMENTS, he puts on TEFILLIN, and may be counted to the MINYAN quorum for public worship. He celebrates his bar mitzvah by being called up (*see* ALIYAH) to the reading of the torah, usually on the next available shabbat after his Hebrew birthday. The boy's father makes a blessing thanking God for having released him from responsibility for the actions of his child. The celebration of a bar mitzvah is an important milestone in the life of the whole family, and the parents host a party for relatives and friends. It is also a rite of passage for which the boy has to spend long hours preparing, especially practising the singing of the HAFTARAH. While the age of thirteen has been fixed as the time for the onset of puberty, the real criterion of adulthood is the growth of at least two pubic hairs. Since a thirteen-year-old boy may not yet be physically adult, he is unable to participate in certain rituals which need a genuine adult, such as the baking of the matzah for Passover. In some communities a bar mitzvah boy is also not allowed to read certain Pentateuchal sections which are prescribed by biblical law. *See also* BAT MITZVAH; REBELLIOUS SON.

Barnacle Goose A bird whose sudden migratory appearance during the summer led to the folk belief that it grew on trees like fruit. The *Zohar* mentions a rabbi who claimed to have seen geese growing on trees. Doubts about its status led to a halakhic debate about whether the Barnacle Goose actually needed ritual slaughter (shechitah) like other birds or was to be classed as a type of fruit. Opinions were even expressed that the Barnacle Goose was not kosher at all because it was a forbidden sea creature or a reptile. The main law code, the *Shulchan Arukh*, ruled that it should not be eaten, but Jacob Emden told of male birds which fertilize mussels to produce new birds and was inclined to allow such offspring to be eaten even though mussels themselves are not kosher.

Bathsheba Favourite wife of King David and mother of his successor Solomon. David fell in love with her when he glimpsed her bathing and had an affair with her. When she became pregnant, he arranged for her soldier husband, Uriah the Hittite, to be sent home so that he would regard the child as his own. This ruse failed, and Uriah was posted to the front line so he would be killed in battle. NATHAN the prophet upbraided the king for his evil doings in taking away another man's wife (II Sam. 11,12). Despite the Bible's negative portrait of David's relationship with Bathsheba, the *Talmud* maintains that he did not in fact commit adultery. All soldiers in the king's army had to give a conditional get, or bill of divorce, to their wives in case they never returned from the battlefield. Thus, Bathsheba was a divorcee, and David's affair with her was not an adulterous one. She was in fact a very young girl at the time of her first contact with David and still a virgin, for Uriah had not consummated the marriage. Even when she eventually gave birth to Solomon, her first child having died in infancy, she had still not reached her teens.

bat kol (Hebrew for 'daughter of a voice') Heavenly voice which continued to communicate God's messages to man after biblical PROPHECY came to an end. The High Priest would hear a bat kol while officiating in the Holy of Holies, and after the destruction of the Temple, visitors to its ruins could hear a heavenly voice expressing God's mourning. At times when there is no High Priest, no Sanhedrin and no respect for torah, a bat kol issues forth to reprimand mankind. Indeed, each day one emanating from Mt SINAI may be heard declaiming: 'Woe unto creatures for neglecting the torah.' A bat kol also brings comfort to people in distress, tells of events happening far away and announces the future marriage partner of an embryo forty days before it is fully formed. In a dispute between the rabbis in the 2c. CE, a bat kol supported the view of ELIEZER BEN HYRCANUS, but objections were raised to such interference from heaven about an issue that had to be decided by a MAJORITY OPINION of the sages. Nevertheless, the arguments between the followers of HILLEL and those of Shammai were finally resolved in favour of the Hillelites by a bat kol. The nature of a bat kol has been interpreted as someone overhearing God talking to Himself, the voice of angels, the name of a special being who speaks to man, or even a heavenly echo. In an urban setting it sounds like a man's voice, while in the desert it sounds like a woman. A bat kol is less authoritative than a prophetic message, and there was some discussion among rabbis as to whether a woman should be allowed to remarry if the only evidence for the death of her husband had come from a heavenly voice. A bat kol may publicize the merits of saintly persons in their lifetime, or pass judgment on men immediately after their death, particularly when they have suffered martyrdom, declaring that they have gone to the World to Come (olam haba).

batlan (Aramaic for 'idle man') Originally a title applied to scholars of the highest virtue who spent their time in torah study and did not work. They constituted the judges (*see* DAYYAN) of the law court (bet din) and helped to run the affairs of the congregation. A batlan was either of independent means or else was supported by the community, and the very definition of a town was a place that could support ten batlanim. Since the smallest number for a prayer quorum (minyan) was ten, these batlanim guaranteed the availability of public prayers. The minimum of ten verses of the Pentateuch read during services on Mondays, Thursdays and Saturday afternoons was said to symbolize the ten batlanim. In more recent times the term has taken on a pejorative connotation, and in Yiddish is used to refer to underemployed ne'er-do-wells with little prospects. This latter type of batlan might eke out a living as a paid member of a minyan or by receiving emoluments from the family of someone who died without leaving any sons for reciting kaddish for the deceased.

bat mitzvah (Hebrew for 'daughter of commandment') A girl at the age of twelve years and one day, according to her Hebrew birthday, is considered an adult woman who has to keep the COMMANDMENTS. Synagogue ceremonies are held for bat mitzvah girls in Reform and Conservative communities, where they are called up (*see* ALIYAH) to the torah in a similar way to BAR MITZVAH boys. In many modern Orthodox synagogues a bat mitzvah celebration also takes place. The major differences between the ceremonies for boys and girls in traditional synagogues are that the bat mitzvah usually takes place for a number of girls together, often on a Sunday rather than on a Saturday, and the girls read selections of other texts rather than being called to the torah. This bat mitzvah innovation has not won the universal approval of the Orthodox rabbis, however, since many regard it as too much of a concession to Reform and object to the use of a synagogue for an essentially social occasion. *See also* PROVERBS, BOOK OF.

Bavli *see* TALMUD

bedikat chametz (Hebrew for 'search for leaven') Since all leavened bread must be removed for Passover (*see* PESACH), a special search for any hidden crumbs takes place the night before. It is customary to search by the light of a candle so that nooks and crannies can be investigated, to use a feather to clean the CHAMETZ away, and to renounce ownership of whatever leaven has not been found. In order that the blessing pronounced before the search should not be entirely in vain, ten carefully wrapped breadcrumbs are hidden in different rooms to be found during the search. All the leaven is burnt next morning. Since leaven symbolizes haughtiness and arrogance, the 'risen dough' in man, the search for chametz was understood by Jewish moralists as entailing an inner cleansing. Man has to search out his own hidden egoism and remove it.

A bronze coin issued by Simeon **Bar Kokhba** showing a lyre (132–135 CE).

A painting by Rembrandt of **Bathsheba** at her toilet.

Ritual of **bedikat chametz** from a 15c. German haggadah, showing the relevant benedictions and an illustration of a Jew searching for leaven.

beggar *see* SCHNORER

Behemoth (Hebrew for 'beast', or more literally 'beasts') Animal of gigantic proportions mentioned in the Bible (Job 40), and the land equivalent of the LEVIATHAN sea monster. The Behemoth is the size of a thousand mountains and drinks so much water each day that a special river flows out of Paradise to quench its thirst. It roars once a year in the month of Tammuz to frighten the wild animals of the world and keep them in control. In the age of the Messiah the Behemoth and the Leviathan will slay each other, and their flesh will be eaten at the great Messianic banquet.

bein ha-metzarim *see* THREE WEEKS OF MOURNING

bekeshe *see* DRESS

bekhor *see* FIRSTBORN

beli ayin hara *see* EVIL EYE

Belz Chasidim *see* NETUREI KARTA

bemidbar *see* CHUMASH

benedictions (Hebrew 'berakhot') Liturgical blessings usually beginning with the formula: 'Blessed are You, O Lord our God, King of the universe.' The most important types of benedictions are those associated with food or drink, where God is recognized as the source of human sustenance (*see* GRACE AFTER MEALS), those recited prior to the performance of MITZVAH, which serve to point out the ritual nature of the act, and those forming part of the LITURGY of the synagogue services. The form of these benedictions was fixed in the period of the Second Temple and is regarded as sacrosanct. There are benedictions for almost every occasion and eventuality, from leaving the toilet to seeing a rainbow in the sky, from recovery from illness (*see* GOMEL BLESSING) to lighting the shabbat candles. A Jew should make one hundred blessings a day acknowledging God to be the source of all blessings. On hearing a benediction, it is customary to respond 'blessed be He and blessed be His name' after the name of God and AMEN at the end. Apart from liturgical blessings there is another form of benediction where a priest blesses the congregation (*see* PRIESTLY BLESSING) or where a father blesses his child at the beginning of shabbat. This does not involve the standard formula of blessings directed to God. *See also* PRAYER-BOOK.

Bene Israel Marathi-speaking Indian Hebrews from the Bombay area. Bene Israel do not use the designation 'Jew', because this is the Hebrew word for an inhabitant of the Kingdom of Judah, whereas the Bene Israel claim descent from the TEN LOST TRIBES of the Kingdom of Israel. According to another version the original Bene Israel left Palestine in the 2c. BCE. Seven couples were saved from a shipwreck off the western coast of India. In the course of time the Bene Israel forgot their religion but retained some knowledge of shabbat and festivals, dietary laws, circumcision and the SHEMA. They repeated the shema on every occasion, and a Jewish visitor who recognized this re-established con-

tact between them and the wider Jewish community. They were known by their Hindu neighbours as Saturday oilmen because they earned their living by pressing oil but did not work on Saturdays. The Bene Israel are divided into two groups. The 'whites' who are descended from the original settlers and the 'blacks' who are descended from Bene Israel who intermarried with natives. White and black Bene Israel did not marry one another or even dine with each other in the past, and though today they share the same synagogues, the 'blacks' play a secondary role. Nevertheless, dark skin-colour is found among both groups. A religious revival took place among the Bene Israel when David Rahabi, a Jew from Cochin, came to the community. He wanted to test whether the Bene Israel were really Jews so he gave the women of the community different kinds of fish to prepare for a meal. Their selection of only the kosher fish convinced him of their Jewish status. The first Bene Israel synagogue in Bombay was built in 1796. Though they have no priests, they use priests from among the Baghdadi Jews of Bombay for ritual purposes. Many of the Bene Israel community have emigrated to Israel where questions were raised about their Jewish status by the Chief Rabbinate.

Benjamin of Tudela (12c.) Traveller who kept a record of his journeys from Spain, through the Holy Land, to Baghdad, Persia and Egypt. Benjamin included in his writings the legends which he heard from various Jewish communities en route. He tells of the tomb of Ezekiel near the Euphrates River in which a light, first kindled by Ezekiel, still burns and where a torah scroll, written by Ezekiel, is to be found in a library many of whose books go back to the First Temple period. He mentions Noah's ark on Mount Ararat over which a mosque had been erected, SOLO-MON's palace in Lebanon which was built by the demon king ASMODEUS, the pillar of salt which was once Lot's wife and which could still be seen in Palestine, the coffin of DANIEL suspended from a bridge and an enormous bath made out of a giant's skull in which three people could bathe at once.

Ben Sira (Hebrew for 'Ecclesiasticus') Greek text of the APOCRYPHA, based on a Hebrew original, which is regarded as part of the scriptural canon by some Christian denominations. Ben Sira is a collection of proverbs and maxims, like those of biblical Wisdom Literature, teaching moderation, the virtues of family life and the fear of God. The author Simeon (or Joshua/Jesus) Ben Sira showed a marked tendency towards the religious ideas of the Pharisees, emphasizing the greatness of Israel and the enjoyment of this-worldly pleasure within prescribed limits. The work was highly thought of in Rabbinic literature, and indeed there was an unsuccessful attempt to have it included in the Hebrew canon. Its public reading was eventually outlawed, however, to prevent it being confused with scripture. According to a bizarre Jewish legend Ben Sira was the son and grandson of the prophet JEREMIAH. He was conceived when Jeremiah's daughter took a bath in some water into which Jeremiah had been forced to emit semen. The name Sira has the same numerical value (gematria) as Jeremiah; hence, he was called Ben Sira (i.e. the son of Sira) to mask his shameful origins. He was born with his teeth fully formed, and he could talk from birth. As an infant prodigy he learnt the alphabet and made each letter into the beginning of a proverb. With his father he studied the *Sefer Yetzirah* and at the end of three years created an artificial man (golem). His abilities so impressed King Nebuchadnezzar that the latter offered him the throne, but Ben Sira refused because he was not of the Davidic line. He also refused the king's daughter in marriage because she was not Jewish, thus upsetting the king. The hoard of manuscripts in a Cairo genizah was discovered after an English scholar, Solomon Shechter, was shown a page of the Hebrew original of Ben Sira which came from there. Among the manuscripts he later recovered were large parts of the original Ben Sira.

ben sorer umoreh *see* REBELLIOUS SON

Berab, Jacob *see* SANHEDRIN; SEMIKHAH

berakhot *see* BENEDICTIONS

bereshit *see* CHUMASH

berit *see* COVENANT

berit milah *see* CIRCUMCISION

Berlin, Saul (1740–94) Rabbinic author who favoured the enlightened ideas associated with Moses MENDELSSOHN and his circle. In a number of his writings he introduced thinly veiled criticism of the obscurantism of his colleagues. His modernist attitudes came out most strongly when he published a volume of responsa, *Besamim Rosh*, which he fraudulently ascribed to a leading medieval authority, Rabbi Asher Ben Yechiel. Berlin claimed that the work came from a manuscript purchased in Italy to which he had added his own commentary, but in fact a number of the rulings supposedly written in the 13c. reflected the liberal views of Berlin's age. Indeed, some of them contradicted Asher's known opposition to philosophy and secular knowledge and his conservatism with regard to halakhah. The book caused a storm of protest when the true significance of its contents became apparent to some scholars. Berlin was defended, however, by other Talmudists, and the book is still quoted in halakhic literature, although with reservations.

Beruryah (2c. CE) Wife of the Mishnaic sage Rabbi MEIR and the most outstanding female figure of the whole Talmudic period. Beruryah had a considerable scholarly reputation, and on occasion her view was preferred to that of the sages who opposed her. Her husband valued her advice, and she taught him not to pray for the destruction of sinners but only for the removal of sin so that the sinners would repent. When their two sons died on the shabbat, she kept their death a secret from her husband so as not to spoil his Sabbath joy. At the conclusion of the Sabbath she asked Meir whether she had to return some objects given to her in trust. He answered that she must, so she took him to see his two dead sons saying: 'God has given, now God has taken away.' A legend, found in post-Talmudic literature, relates how Meir

The fight between the **Behemoth** and the Leviathan in the age of the Messiah (14c. South German illuminated manuscript).

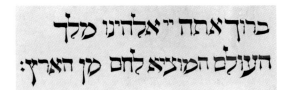

The **benediction** recited before eating bread.

Bene Israel baking matzah, from a Passover haggadah with Marathi translation (Poona, 1874).

instructed one of his students to try and seduce Beruryah because she was too confident about her own virtue and her ability to resist temptation. Meir only intended to teach her a lesson, but when Beruryah realized that she had indeed been on the verge of succumbing to the seduction, she committed suicide.

besamim *see* SPICES

Besht *see* BAAL SHEM TOV, ISRAEL

bet din (Hebrew for 'house of judgment') Religious court usually consisting of three judges (*see* DAYYAN) which deals with supervision of kosher facilities, DIVORCE, civil disputes and PROSELYTES. The senior judge is known as the av bet din, the 'father of the law court'. In ancient times larger courts of twenty-three, or seventy-one, judges dealt with major cases involving CAPITAL PUNISHMENT (*see* SANHEDRIN). Each Jewish community would have its own bet din which used to sit on market days, originally Mondays and Thursdays. Since Jews are not allowed to take disputes among themselves to Gentile courts, the Jewish law court has a wide role to play in Orthodox communities. It is believed that God Himself participates with the judges in their deliberations. He also presides over a heavenly bet din which assesses the deeds of men and metes out rewards and punishments. *See also* TAM, JACOB.

bet ha-keneset *see* SYNAGOGUE

bet ha-kevarot *see* CEMETERY

bet ha-midrash (Hebrew for 'house of study') Combined SYNAGOGUE and study hall, particularly the central study hall of a YESHIVAH. Services are held in a bet ha-midrash so that the students can pray where they study without interruption. The early biblical characters, Shem and Eber, founded a bet ha-midrash where the Patriarchs studied the torah. Many other biblical heroes are said to have established a bet ha-midrash or studied at one. When Balaam blessed Israel with the exclamation 'How goodly are your tents O Jacob' (Num. 24:5) he was referring to the 'tents of torah'. In Talmudic times entry to a bet ha-midrash was often difficult for poor students, as they had to tip the attendant. Rabbi Gamaliel, the 1c./2c. CE leader of Palestinian Jewry, insisted that only students whose 'inside was like their outside', i.e. who were of the highest integrity, could enter a bet ha-midrash. This meant that many were excluded, and it eventually led to popular opposition which helped bring about Rabbi Gamaliel's deposition. Thereafter, the doors of the bet ha-midrash were opened to all those who wanted to study, and hundreds of extra seats had to be made available. The Rabbis prescribed the following prayer on entering a bet ha-midrash: 'O Lord my God may it be your will that I do not stumble in understanding the HALAKHAH, and that my colleagues do not rejoice at my mistakes. That I do not declare what is permitted to be forbidden, or vice versa. That my colleagues do not stumble in understanding the halakhah, and that I do not rejoice at their mistakes.' On leaving the bet ha-midrash one should say: 'I give thanks to you, O Lord my God, that you have put my portion among those who sit in the bet ha-midrash, and have not placed my portion among those who sit on street corners. For we both get up early in the morning, yet while I arise to the words of the torah, they arise only to spend their time in vanities.' *See also* SHUL.

bet ha-mikdash *see* TEMPLE

Bet Hillel; Bet Shammai *see* HILLEL; SHAMMAI

Bethlehem (Hebrew 'bet lechem', meaning 'house of bread') Town in the tribal territory of Judah situated south of Jerusalem. The Matriarch RACHEL is buried nearby (Gen. 35:19), and the story of Naomi and RUTH is set in the town. King DAVID was born in Bethlehem (1 Sam. 16), and since the Messiah will be of the Davidic line, the town is regarded as the origin of the future Messianic king (Micah 5:1). Although Christians understood this literally, Jewish commentators take it to mean that Bethlehem will be his ancestral home and not that the Messiah will necessary be born or live there.

Bezalel Israelite craftsman who built the TABERNACLE in the wilderness and made its sacred furnishings (Exod. 31). Moses was unclear how to fulfil God's instructions about the Tabernacle, so he had to consult Bezalel and let him design and execute the work. Bezalel was filled with 'the Spirit of God', and in a homiletic play on his name ('in the shadow of God'), Moses said that he must have obtained his artistic knowledge because he dwelt in God's shadow. Bezalel used the magical power of the letters of the Hebrew ALPHABET to create the Tabernacle, just as God had used letter combinations in His creation of the world. Bezalel was only thirteen years old when he built the Tabernacle.

Bible (Hebrew 'tenakh' or 'kitvei ha-kodesh', meaning 'holy writings') The central scripture of Judaism consists of twenty-four books divided into three sections. The most important of these sections is the TORAH which comprises the Five Books of Moses or CHUMASH. This was revealed directly by God to Moses in the wilderness during the Exodus and was written down by him. God also taught Moses the ORAL TORAH which contains explanations of the written text. There is a difference of opinion in the *Talmud* as to whether Moses also wrote down the last six verses of Deuteronomy, which tell of his death and burial. One view is that he wrote them before he died with tears in his eyes, and the other is that Joshua wrote them after his death. The other two sections were written under the inspiration of the Holy Spirit (*see* RUACH HA-KODESH). The second section, the Prophets, comprises the historical books of Joshua, Judges, SAMUEL (I & II) and Kings (I & II) plus the collections of prophetic sayings in the books of ISAIAH, JEREMIAH, EZEKIEL and the twelve minor prophets (HOSEA, Joel, AMOS, Obadiah, JONAH, Micah, Nahum, Habakkuk, Zephaniah, Haggai, Zechariah and Malachi). The third section, the Hagiographa or the Writings, comprises the books of PSALMS, PROVERBS, JOB, SONG OF SONGS, RUTH, LAMENTATIONS, ECCLESIASTES, ESTHER (*see also* MEGILLAH), DANIEL, EZRA, Nehemiah, and Chronicles (I & II). Before the canon was fixed there were doubts about whether some of these books should be taken out of general circulation and kept in a genizah (*see* APOCRYPHA). Several teachings of the Book of Ezekiel, for instance, seemed to conflict with other biblical passages, and these needed to be reconciled before the book was allowed to circulate freely as canonized scripture. There were also problems about whether Proverbs, Ecclesiastes, the Song of Songs and Esther were divinely inspired. Ultimately these issues were resolved in favour of the scriptural nature of the books. There are four basic methods of biblical interpretation (*see* PARDES) including PESHAT and MIDRASH. *See also* TARGUM; TENAKH.

bimah (Hebrew for 'platform'; also called 'almemar') Raised structure in the synagogue from which the SEFER TORAH is read (*see* ALIYAH) and from which prayers are led. Although Reform practice is to have the bimah at the end of the synagogue in front of the ark, most Orthodox congregations insist on the bimah being in the centre to convey to the worshippers the idea that the torah belongs to everyone. The bimah is reached by steps from the floor of the synagogue and is surrounded by railings. On the festival of sukkot it is circumambulated with the Four Species and on simchat torah with the torah scrolls (*see* HAKKAFOT).

birds Chickens, turkeys, geese, ducks and doves are among the birds allowed to be eaten by the Jewish DIETARY LAWS while most other birds, particularly birds of prey, are prohibited. The Bible does not specify the characteristics that determine which birds are KOSHER but simply lists twenty-four varieties of birds which may not be eaten. Not all the birds on the list are unambiguously identifiable, and so Jewish communities only eat those birds which have been eaten in the past. Birds need to be slaughtered (*see* SHECHITAH) before they can be consumed, and the Rabbis decreed that their meat may not be eaten with milk, although they do not come from a milk-producing species. The EGG of a kosher bird is pointed at one end and can thus be distinguished from non-kosher varieties which are completely round. Birds were thought to have been created from mud on the fifth day of Creation. There are a number of fantastic birds in Jewish folklore such as the BARNACLE GOOSE which grows like fruit on trees, the Chol which lives for a thousand years before being burnt in fire only to rise once again from its ashes, the phoenix which never dies and the ZIZ whose gigantic wingspan blocks out the sun when it flies. King Solomon to whom PEREK SHIRAH is ascribed, understood the language of birds, and in the Talmudic period messages were brought from heaven by birds to various rabbis. It was believed by Kabbalists that God used birds to reveal what He intended to do in the world. Nevertheless, it is forbidden to interpret the messages of bird calls because of the prohibition on soothsaying. *See also* DOVE; SHAMIR; SOLOMON.

birkat ha-gomel *see* GOMEL BLESSING

birkat ha-mazon *see* GRACE AFTER MEALS

birkat kohanim *see* PRIESTLY BLESSING

Bethlehem, a view to the east.

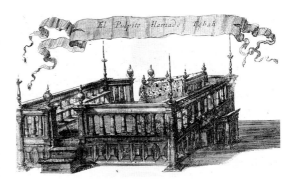

The elaborate **bimah** of the Portuguese synagogue in Amsterdam, from a 17c. drawing.

birth The process of birth was surrounded in the past with a number of magic practices which were intended to protect the mother and child from demonic forces. LILITH, the demon queen, is jealous of the happiness of motherhood since she became estranged from her husband early in their marriage. She therefore endangers the embryo, and AMULETS or charms used to be hung on the walls and on the bed to keep her away. Incantations were also whispered into the ears of women to ease their labour. If a woman died in childbirth, this was because she was negligent about the laws of menstrual separation (*see* NIDDAH) or about tithing the bread she baked (*see* CHALLAH) or about lighting the Sabbath LAMP. In the womb a candle burns, the light of which enables the embryo to see from one end of the world to the other. One of the angels teaches it the torah, but just before birth the angel touches it on the top lip so it forgets all it has learnt, hence the cleavage on a person's upper lip. *See also* MIKVEH, TZADDIK.

birth control The first command to Adam was to be 'fruitful and multiply' (Gen. 1:28), and this is the basis of the Jewish attitude toward birth control. Having a large family is seen as a blessing from God, and each couple should have at least one son and one daughter so as to reproduce themselves. Many Orthodox families do not practice any form of birth control, and nine or ten children are quite common. The *Talmud* elucidates various methods of contraception and allows their use by women under certain circumstances since it was Adam, and not Eve, who was commanded to be fruitful. Most later halakhists took a strict view of this permission and only allowed contraception where there was some health risk involved in pregnancy. The pill is the preferred method of contraception because it interferes least with the sex act, while methods like coitus interruptus, for which Onan was punished in the Bible (Gen. 38:9–10), or the use of a condom are prohibited.

birthdays Although birthdays as such do not play any significant role in biblical or Talmudic literature, traditions have arisen around different birthdays in the life of the individual. Some Jews begin the daily recitation of the Psalm whose number represents the age they enter on their Hebrew birthday. Among Lubavitch Chasidim verses from the appropriate Psalm are set to music and sung before their leader, the Lubavitcher Rebbe, on his birthday. The following are some of the images associated with different birthdays (*see* AGE). At three, sexual differentiation begins between boys and girls, and among those Jews who follow Kabbalistic tradition the boy's hair is cut for the first time, the head being shaved leaving only side curls (*see* PEOT). At five, Hebrew education begins at cheder. This is celebrated with the eating of sweet foods, usually honeycake. At twelve, a girl is BAT MITZVAH and enters adulthood, while a boy becomes BAR MITZVAH at thirteen. Eighteen is the age for marriage, since the two Hebrew letters numbering eighteen mean 'life' and thus the time to begin the procreation of new life has arrived. At thirty, a person comes into their full strength, since this was the age when the Levites used to do the main physical work in the Tabernacle. Forty is the age of understanding,

and one may begin the study of Kabbalah. At fifty, one is fit to offer counsel to others, since Levites retired from physical labour and became senior advisers at this age. At sixty, one attains to old age and acquires wisdom. At seventy, one has reached the normal lifespan of three score years and ten, while the eighty-year-old gains new strength. At ninety, one is bent over, and those who have achieved their century are as good as dead. Despite this it is customary to wish someone: 'Till one hundred and twenty' on their birthday, as Moses was still clear of mind and strong of body when he died at that age.

birth pangs of the Messiah *see* CARO, JOSEPH; ESCHATOLOGY; MESSIAH; MESSIANIC MOVEMENTS

bishul nochri *see* DIETARY LAWS; GENTILE

Black Jews Judaizing groups among blacks in the USA, most of whom have no historical links to the Jewish community and have not formally converted to Judaism. Such groups do, however, have a special affinity with the Hebrew Bible and claim that they originate with the FALASHAS, though their actual roots are among west-African slaves rather than the black Hebrews of Ethiopia. The Black Jews are a product of revivalist sects among black Americans. A few have followed the logic of their new identity and converted to Orthodox Judaism, studying at institutions like Yeshivah University. In the early 1970s a number of American blacks who had tried unsuccessfully to be resettled in Liberia emigrated to the State of Israel and settled in the city of Dimona. Though they were not recognized as Jews by the Israel Rabbinate, they were allowed to settle because turning them back might appear to be racism directed at blacks. The Black Jews of Dimona have Karaite leanings in their ritual, with a literalist attitude to scripture, very strict shabbat observance and a number of strange customs. They pronounce the tetragrammaton as it is written, a practice which is anathema to Jews of all persuasions.

blood It is forbidden to consume blood which has moved out of its natural place after an animal has been killed. It is removed by washing, salting and rinsing the meat or grilling it over an open flame. When birds or non-domesticated animals are slaughtered (*see* SHECHITAH), their blood must be covered over. The potency of blood is apparent from the story of how the Hebrews smeared the blood of the Pascal lamb on their doorposts so that the Angel of Death would not kill their firstborn during the last of the Ten Plagues. In the Middle Ages there was a custom for a MOHEL to hang his blood-stained towel at the synagogue door during the CIRCUMCISION operation to protect the child from harm. There are many folkloristic beliefs about the powers of blood. People who are born under the sign of Mars will have a blood-related occupation, such as a murderer or a surgeon, and it is dangerous to perform bloodletting when Mars is in the ascendent (*see* ASTROLOGY). During the solstices and equinoxes one should not drink water from wells since they have been polluted by the menstrual blood of LILITH, the demon queen. Indeed if a menstruating woman (*see* NIDDAH) looks into a mirror, spots of blood will appear on the glass. Human blood is supposed to help alleviate LEPROSY, and the Egyptian Pharaoh, who was a leper, used to kill Israelite children in order to bathe in their blood. Up to modern times Jews were accused of killing Christians in order to use their blood (*see* BLOOD LIBEL) to treat the haemorrhoids with which Jews were thought to be afflicted. The blood of horses cures warts, and the blood of the SALAMANDER makes someone fireproof if it is smeared on the skin. No one may claim that his blood is redder than that of another, as an excuse for saving his own life by killing someone else. Just as the blood of Abel called out for vengeance from the ground, after he was slain by his brother, so the blood of murdered righteous people continues to boil until their murderer is punished.

Blood Libel Accusation that Jews practice ritual murder of Christians to obtain blood for use in the making of matzah. These accusations were widespread from the Middle Ages until the 20c. As late as 1911 Mendel Beilis was accused in Czarist Russia of killing a Gentile boy to use his blood in Jewish ritual and was only acquitted after a long pre-trial imprisonment. Behind the Blood Libel were beliefs about Jews needing blood as medicine to remedy their ghastly appearance and to sustain their quasi-human existence, since they were in league with the Devil. They were also responsible for the death of Jesus, and the killing of a Christian child was thought of as a latter-day crucifixion. Although accusations about the use of blood were made in pre-Christian times against Jews, as well as against the early Christians themselves, the first fully fledged Christian Blood Libel accusation against Jews was in 1144 in the case of William of Norwich. A number of Jews were tortured until they admitted their guilt, and many were massacred in consequence. The case entered English literature, most notably in Chaucer's *Canterbury Tales*. Secular and Church leaders who investigated the Blood Libel in the 13c. found no basis for the charges against Jews. Even Jewish converts to Christianity, who were usually very antagonistic to their old faith, completely exonerated the Jews. Nevertheless, the Blood Libel remained ingrained in popular prejudice, and accusations would flare up around Easter time. Jewish authorities even encouraged Jews to drink white wine during the Passover seder since red wine might be mistaken for Christian blood by a hostile mob. Any Christian, particularly a child, who died in mysterious circumstances might lead to accusations against Jews, and some of these children were turned into martyrs. The Nazis spread stories of the Blood Libel as part of their anti-Jewish propaganda (*see* ANTI-SEMITISM). *See also* NIDDAH.

bobe mayse (Yiddish for 'grandmother's tale') An incredible story or old wives' tale which need not be taken seriously. In Yiddish it is common to dismiss something with the remark: 'That is just a bobe mayse.' The origin of the expression, however, had nothing to do with the kind of stories grandma used to tell. It meant a story from the *Bove Bukh*, a Yiddish translation of the *Buovo d'Antona* which was first published in Italy in 1540. The book was a romantic tale, and its Yiddish version was popular among Jewish women. In the course of time the expression bobe mayse came to mean any imaginary story, eventually

Amulet from the *Sefer Raziel* to protect a mother and child after **birth**. The two boxes contain the names and seals of the three angels who guard humans against Lilith (Amsterdam, 1701).

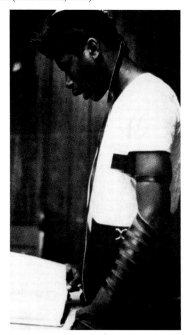

A **Black Jew** in New York wearing tefillin.

Woodcut of a **blood libel** showing Simon of Trent subject to supposed Jewish atrocities.

taking on a pejorative connotation as something beyond belief.

Book of Beliefs and Opinions *see* SAADIAH GAON

Book of Brightness *see* BAHIR, SEFER HA-

Book of Formation *see* YETZIRAH, SEFER

Book of the Pious *see* CHASIDIM, SEFER

Botarel, Moses (14c.–15c.) Spanish mystic and pseudo-Messiah. Botarel wrote a Hebrew commentary on the *Sefer Yetzirah* for a Christian patron which is full of bogus quotations from non-existent works of previous scholars. He justified teaching torah to a non-Jew with reference to the Talmudic saying that a Gentile who studies torah is like the High Priest. After Botarel had himself anointed Messiah, he survived an ordeal by fire, for a fiery furnace could not harm him. His followers claimed that he was surrounded by a cloud and that they saw an angel talking to him. He described himself as a great and holy rabbi to whom Elijah appeared. Botarel's teachings involved the use of charms and amulets and the practice of asceticism leading to prophetic dreams revealing the future. He believed that philosophy and Kabbalah were compatible with one another and that Aristotle should be regarded as a sage.

Brazen Serpent (Hebrew 'nachash nechoshet') Serpent of bronze which Moses set up on a pole in the wilderness during an epidemic of snake bite. The snakes came as punishment for the complaints of the people against God. The snake itself is a symbol of evil speech, as exemplified by the SERPENT in the Garden of Eden which spoke deceitfully to Eve, and thus, snakes bit those who had spoken evil about God's dealings with the Israelites. Those bitten by a snake had merely to look up to the Brazen Serpent to be cured (Num. 21). This serpent image eventually became an object of idolatrous worship and was destroyed by King HEZEKIAH (II Kings 18:4). The *Mishnah* asks how a bronze serpent could affect the life or death of a human being and answers that, when the Israelites looked up to heaven and subordinated their hearts to God, they were cured.

bread (Hebrew 'lechem') As the staple Jewish food, bread is consumed at all religious meals. The hands have to be ritually washed before eating it, and the main GRACE AFTER MEALS is recited at the end of the meal. Special loaves of CHALLAH bread, named after the tithe separated from the dough, are baked for shabbat and festivals. Two such loaves, representing the double portion of MANNA which the Israelites had on these occasions in the wilderness, are eaten at each meal. The manna is referred to as 'bread from heaven' (Exod. 16:4). On the Passover (*see* PESACH) only unleavened bread, MATZAH, may be eaten. This is the 'bread of affliction', eaten by slaves and the poor, and reminds Jews that their ancestors were slaves in Egypt. On rosh ha-shanah there is a folk custom to throw breadcrumbs into the water during the TASHLIKH ceremony to represent man's sins. The Hebrew term for bread, 'lechem', is also used for food in general,

so that Adam is told after his sin, 'By the sweat of your brow you will eat lechem ('food')' (Gen. 3:19). The Talmudic image of a foolish person is someone who eats bread with bread, i.e. starch with starch, the equivalent of a sandwich with a slice of bread in the middle.

bridegroom of the torah (Hebrew 'chatan torah') On SIMCHAT TORAH the person called up for an ALIYAH to recite the blessings over the concluding section of the torah is known as 'bridegroom of the torah'. Based on this nomenclature the person who recites the blessings over the first section of the Pentateuch is called 'chatan bereshit' ('bridegroom of Genesis'). It is customary for both these bridegrooms to host a party for the congregation after the service in honour of the siyyum of the torah. The term 'bridegroom' is extended to the person called up to recite the torah blessing with all the pre-bar-mitzvah boys, who is known as 'bridegroom of all the boys'. These titles are related to the idea of the marriage between Israel and the torah and to customs in olden times of crowning the bridegrooms with the head-dress worn by genuine bridegrooms and bringing them to the synagogue under a wedding canopy (chuppah). The term 'chatan' ('bridegroom') is also used metaphorically as an expression of honour for a child undergoing circumcision and for a bar mitzvah boy. In some Reform communities the women called up for the special torah readings on simchat torah are called 'brides of the torah'.

Bund Jewish socialist organization, founded in Vilna in 1897, with a strong emphasis on YIDDISH culture and an equally strong antagonism to both religion and Zionism. Bundists refused to practise circumcision or even allow the name of God to be mentioned on their premises. They believed that Jews could survive as a separate cultural entity, rather than as a religious group, in the diaspora. Their social ideals were based on Marxism, and Bundists were very active in organizing self-defence groups to fight outbreaks of anti-Semitism (*see* POGROM). The movement was suppressed in post-revolutionary Russia by the Bolsheviks, one-time allies, but continued to flourish in Poland and Lithuania where Bundists were prominent in Jewish partisan resistance to Nazism and particularly in the Warsaw Ghetto Uprising. Though the Bund still exists today with its youth movement, its Yiddish newspapers and Yiddish schools, it is only a shadow of its former self having been decimated by the Holocaust.

burial (Hebrew 'kevurah') The traditional method of disposal of the dead is by burial in consecrated ground as an affirmation of the belief in the RESURRECTION of the body in the age of the Messiah (*see* LUZ). CREMATION is regarded as a negation of the idea of resurrection and is not sanctioned in Orthodox practice, though not unusual among Reform Jews. Jewish literature traces the custom of burial back to Adam, the first man, who did not know what to do with his dead son Abel until he saw a raven burying a dead raven in the ground. Before burial, members of the CHEVRA KADDISHA burial society wash the body, anoint it and dress it in a shroud (*see* KITEL), a process known as taharah. Some earth from the Land of Israel is placed in the coffin or in the grave so that the dead Jew is, as it were, buried in the Holy Land. It is customary to place a small stone on the grave after visiting the CEMETERY. This relates to a time when it was necessary to mark a grave with a heap of stones. Some communities have the custom of circumambulating the corpse seven times and of throwing money in the four directions as a bribe to evil spirits to keep away. Burial has to take place as soon after death as possible, preferably on the same day, since the soul cannot be at rest until the body is buried. The Kabbalists saw a delay in burial as interfering with any proposed reincarnation (*see* TRANSMIGRATION OF SOULS) that God may have arranged for the deceased. In Jerusalem burial even takes place at night because of the reluctance to keep a dead body overnight in the holy city. Among the most important duties a Jew has is the burial of a corpse for which no one is willing to take responsibility, the met mitzvah. This takes precedence over any other positive commandment and must even be done by a priest, despite the ritual impurity involved through contact with the dead. The burial of Moses by God Himself on Mount Nebo is taken as an example (imitatio dei) for man to emulate. *See also* MOURNING; PILGRIMAGE; TALLIT.

Burning Bush The bush on Mount Sinai from which God first revealed Himelf to MOSES, commanding him to return to Egypt and bring the Israelites out of slavery (Exod. 3). Moses had wandered up the mountain to retrieve a lamb that had strayed from his flock, and this show of compassion convinced God that he was suitable to be the shepherd of Israel. Moses was curious about a bush that burned but was not consumed by fire. God addressed him from the midst of the bush and told him to remove his shoes because he was standing on holy ground. This method of revelation was chosen by God to teach Moses that, although Israel may be persecuted like the bush, it will not be consumed. The bush also showed that God was willing to lower Himself to man's level, for nothing is more lowly than a bush on a hillside, and by dwelling among the thorns of the bush, God expressed His participation in the suffering of Israel.

Cain and Abel The first two children of Adam and Eve, Cain was involved in agriculture while Abel was a shepherd (Gen. 4). They both made offerings to God, who accepted Abel's sacrifice but refused Cain's because it was of second-rate produce. In a fit of jealousy over the non-acceptance of his offering and over a twin sister whom Abel had married, Cain killed his brother. When asked by God where his brother was he said: 'Am I my brother's keeper?' (Gen. 4:9). Cain was not only responsible for the death of Abel but also for the death of Abel's descendants who would never be born. That is why the Bible states that the 'bloods' of Abel cried out to God from the earth. For this sin of fratricide Cain lost his portion in the World to Come (olam haba). He was cursed by God to wander the face of the earth, finding no rest, but he carried God's mark on him so that no one would kill

The **Brazen Serpent** by Albert du Hameel.

Anthropomorphic picture of God (symbolized by the pointing finger) addressing Moses from the **Burning Bush**. Notice that Moses has only taken off one of his shoes (14c. Spanish haggadah).

him, and he grew horns to scare off any animals that might attack him (see WANDERING JEW). Cain himself was really the child of Eve and the serpent, and his descendants show some of the wicked characteristics of their ancestor. It was eventually his own descendant, Lamech, who killed him with an arrow, having been misinformed that the horned Cain was himself a wild animal. See also SHAATNEZ.

Cairo Genizah see BEN SIRA; GENIZAH

calendar (Hebrew 'luach ha-shanah') The Hebrew calendar consists of twelve lunar months (see MOON) set in the framework of a solar year: Nisan, Iyyar, Sivan, Tammuz, Av, Elul, Tishri, Marcheshvan, Kislev, Tevet, Shevat and Adar. Since there is a discrepancy of just over eleven days between the 354 days of the lunar year and the 365 days of the solar year, a leap year containing an extra month (see ADAR II) is intercalated seven times every nineteen years. This enables the festival of Passover (pesach) to fall in springtime (Deut. 16:1), and the other festivals to match the agricultural seasons. Originally, months were fixed when witnesses testified to the sighting of the new moon before a bet din in Jerusalem, which would then declare the sanctification of the new month. If no witnesses arrived on the thirtieth day, then the thirty-first day of the old month became the first day of the new month and was celebrated as the NEW MOON festival day, rosh chodesh. Fires would be lit on mountain tops, starting with the Mount of Olives, and lookouts stationed on other mountain tops would light their own signal fires in turn, until the news of the declaration of the new month passed into the Jewish communities of the diaspora. When sectarians, who had their own calendar system, interfered with this process by lighting fires at the wrong time, the news of the new month was conveyed by messengers sent to outlying communities. Those Jews who lived too far away to find out about the new month would keep two days for each of the festivals instead of one, since they had doubts about the exact day. After the destruction of the Second Temple, JOCHANAN BEN ZAKKAI transferred calendar calculations from Jerusalem to Jabneh. In the 4c. CE, when Christian persecution made the activities of calendar determination very difficult, the new months were fixed by mathematical calculation rather than sighting of the moon. This calculation is currently in use throughout the Jewish world, but it is slightly inaccurate and means a day is gained every 216 years. Eventually Passover will cease to be a spring festival. See also JUBILEE; SAMARITANS; SAMUEL, MAR; SHEMITTAH.

Cantonists Jewish children forcibly conscripted into the Czarist army to serve for a period of twenty-five years once they had reached military age. The Cantonist conscription began in 1827 and was only abolished in 1856. The name 'Cantonist' came from the cantons, set up originally to look after the children of Russian soldiers, where these Jewish youngsters were indoctrinated. Special schools in the cantons educated Jewish child conscripts until the age of eighteen when their army service proper began. The

teachers there imposed a cruel regime of discipline in order to convert their pupils to Russian Orthodox Christianity, and once in active military service they were stationed far from Jewish communities so as to break any connections with their past faith. Each Jewish community was given a quota of conscripts to fulfil, and since many adults managed to evade conscription, poor children, even as young as eight years old, were seized by professional 'kidnappers' and handed in to the Jewish leadership to make up the numbers. Many of the Cantonists did not survive the harsh treatment meted out in the cantons and to Jewish soldiers in the Czarist army. Most of those that did survive had completely adopted a Christian identity by the time they emerged from their forced conscription. See also PALE OF SETTLEMENT.

cantor see CHAZZAN

capital punishment There are four methods of capital punishment in the Bible: stoning (being pushed off a cliff), burning (having molten lead poured down the throat), beheading (with a sword) and strangulation (by means of a scarf round the throat). The sins for which these different forms of DEATH penalty are prescribed are homicide, blasphemy, idolatry, adultery, incest, bestiality, striking one's parents or rebelling against them, shabbat breaking, witchcraft and kidnapping. Capital punishment could only be applied if there were two witnesses who had warned the perpetrator of the consequences of his actions and he had acknowledged the warning. In court the witnesses were cautioned about the seriousness of their testimony and told that Adam was created alone to show that a single life is like a whole universe. Capital punishment was an uncommon penal measure, and a Sanhedrin which executed someone once in seven years, or according to another version once in seventy years, was known as a murderous bet din. Various rabbis who lived after the destruction of the Second Temple, when the death penalty was abolished, said that they would never have passed a death sentence on anyone. Before capital punishment was carried out, the sinner confessed and said: 'May my death be an ATONEMENT for all my sins.' It was necessary to make the execution as easy as possible, since the commandment 'to love one's neighbour as oneself' applied to the sinner, yet the family did not hold any official mourning rites after the execution. In the Middle Ages there were a number of cases of Jewish informers who worked as spies for the government being killed by their co-religionists after a makeshift trial. They were usually drowned in the mikveh.

Caro, Joseph (1488–1575) Halakhist and mystic of Spanish origin. Caro left Spain during the great expulsion of the late 15c. and after a long stay in Turkey settled in Safed, northern Palestine. His code of ritual law, the SHULCHAN ARUKH, became the most authoritative halakhic text for Sephardim, but Caro was no dry legal scholar and was guided by a daemon (see MAGGID). This heavenly guide was the spirit of the *Mishnah* and sometimes it took possession of Caro, speaking out of his mouth with a strange voice much to the consternation of colleagues who were present at the time. The maggid also communicated with Caro privately, answering questions, commending him on halakhic decisions and revealing Kabbalistic secrets and knowledge of the future. He kept a diary of these contacts from heaven. Like many of the Kabbalists in Safed, Caro believed that the expulsion of the Jews from the Iberian peninsula represented the 'birth pangs of the Messiah', and he expected the Messianic Age to dawn in 1540. He was deeply involved in attempts to revive the ancient rabbinic ordination (semikhah) and was himself ordained in order to prepare for the coming of the Messiah. The example of Solomon MOLCHO, an ex-Marrano who returned to Judaism and was burnt at the stake by the Inquisition, had considerable influence on Caro. He, too, sought a martyr's death, and his maggid confirmed that his desires would be fulfilled. In fact, however, he died peacefully at a ripe old age. Although he was part of the circle of Kabbalists in Safed, Caro was unable to study with Isaac Luria, the leading mystical teacher there. Luria told him that he was not a suitable pupil, and every time Caro attended one of Luria's lectures he fell asleep.

cemetery (Hebrew 'bet ha-kevarot', meaning 'the house of graves') Consecrated ground which is assigned eternally to the dead who occupy it and also known euphemistically as 'the house of life'. The spirits of the dead are thought to hover over the cemetery, as is apparent from the Talmudic story of a man who slept in a cemetery overnight and overheard the dead conversing. From their conversation he was able to find out what had been decreed in heaven for mankind. Since the dead are unable to keep the commandments, one must be careful not to mock them by ostentatiously performing commandments in a cemetery. Thus it is forbidden to carry a torah scroll there, wear tefillin or have one's tzitzit showing. It is customary to visit the graves of relatives prior to the rosh ha-shanah festival to ask for their intercessory prayers. Objections were raised, however, to any prayers actually addressed to the dead since prayer can only be directed to God. Those of priestly descent (*see* PRIEST) are buried at the entrance to a cemetery so that their families can visit them without defiling themselves through the proximity of other graves. In some cemeteries men and women are buried in different rows, or if buried together they do not have a member of the opposite sex, except a spouse, next to them. These considerations of modesty look ahead to the RESURRECTION when the dead will rise out of their graves, even though they will be clothed. A similar reason underlies the prohibition on burying religiously observant people in the same section of the cemetery as those who were known as religiously lax or wicked. Indeed, those who committed SUICIDE and apostates were once buried at the edge of the cemetery proper, away from all the other graves, though this is uncommon today. The graves of saintly individuals are centres of PILGRIMAGE, and visitors place written requests for intercessory prayer on their TOMBSTONES. *See also* BURIAL; DEATH; HAKKAFOT; OLIVES, MOUNT OF.

Chabad *see* LUBAVITCH; SHNEUR ZALMAN OF LYADY

chad gadya (Aramaic for 'one kid') Popular ditty in the HAGGADAH sung at the SEDER service on Passover. The song tells of a father who buys a kid goat for two coins. The kid is eaten by a cat, which is bitten by a

Synagogue mosaic showing zodiacal signs for the months of the Hebrew **calendar** (Bet Alpha Synagogue, Israel).

Stonemason engraving a tombstone in a Russian Karaite **cemetery**.

dog, which is beaten by a stick, which is burnt by fire, which is doused by water, which is drunk by an ox, which is slaughtered by a butcher, who in turn is killed by the Angel of Death. The sequence ends with God destroying the Angel of Death. Chad gadya took on a symbolic meaning in Jewish consciousness. The kid was thought to represent the People of Israel mistreated by the great nations of the world, who in turn were punished by being subjugated to other nations. In the era of the Messiah justice will finally be done when the work of the Angel of Death is nullified at the Resurrection of the Dead. Though chad gadya may have originated as a children's song, it came to be taken very seriously. There are even reports of those who made fun of it being excommunicated (cherem) since they were thought to be belittling the rabbis who accepted the song as part of the Passover ritual.

Chafetz Chaim *see* ISRAEL MEIR HA-KOHEN

chag *see* FESTIVALS

chag sameach *see* GREETINGS

Chaim of Volozhin (1749–1821) Lithuanian rabbi and the main disciple of ELIJAH THE VILNA GAON. Chaim founded the Volozhin yeshivah in his home town, on the instruction of his master, in order to teach *Talmud* using the Gaon's methods. These involved the study of the whole of Talmudic literature, rather than the few treatises which other academies concentrated on, and the rejection of artificial dialectics (pilpul). In the Volozhin yeshivah there was always somebody studying torah, with a rota of students who would study at night or during festivals when the rest of the world was otherwise occupied. Chaim was the author of the main ideological work of the MITNAGGEDIM, *Nefesh Ha-Chaim*, in which the study of torah is portrayed as the prime religious duty of man and the central way of relating to God. The book is full of Kabbalistic imagery, but it uses this imagery very differently from texts of the Chasidic Movement. On a number of occasions in the work, Chaim criticized Chasidic religiosity, and his argument that the worship of the divine element in a saintly man was itself idolatry was directed against the worship of the Chasidic tzaddik. When he was a young man, serving his first community as a rabbi, Chaim was once asked by one of his congregants when the birth of the new moon (molad) was due to take place. Chaim had to admit that he simply did not know, and there was consternation among the unlettered members of his community who suspected their rabbi of being an ignoramus. Armed by this experience of the expectations of simple Jews, Chaim always used to present a Hebrew calendar (luach ha-shanah) to graduates of his yeshivah who had just received semikhah. In the introduction to their father's *Nefesh Ha-Chaim* Chaim's sons explain that his life's motto was, 'Man must participate in the sufferings of others and help them.'

chakham (Hebrew for 'sage') One of the most general terms for a scholar of Jewish lore, used particularly of the wise men of the Talmudic period who expounded the ORAL TORAH. The chakham is the ideal religious type for Rabbinic Judaism, taking precedence even over the prophet. To emphasize the fact that sages study continually, an alternative title is 'talmid chakham' or student-sage, and one of the definitions of a chakham is someone who is willing to learn from every man. Among the characteristics of a true sage are silence in the presence of wiser people, being aware of one's own faults, not interrupting colleagues, asking direct and relevant questions, acknowledging the truth when wrong and admitting when one does not know something. Breathing the air of the land of Israel, eating breakfast every day and travelling South were all supposed to help make the foolish wiser. It is pride which makes wisdom leave the wise, and in Yiddish the expression 'chokhom' is often used sarcastically of someone who is too clever and impractical, as in the stories of the CHELM 'sages'. Elijah the Vilna Gaon explained that he became a chakham in five minutes, i.e he used the few minutes between one activity and the next to study when most people would simply waste their time. Among Sephardim the title chakham is used to refer to the rabbi of the community.

chalitzah *see* LEVIRATE MARRIAGE

challah Tithe taken from dough before baking and given to a priest. Originally this TITHE only applied to produce of the Holy Land, but the Rabbis extended it to the diaspora. Today, since priests are ritually unclean, the challah cannot be eaten by them and so a small amount of dough is separated off and burnt in the oven in which the BREAD is baked. The name challah has come to be used of the plaited loaves of bread eaten on shabbat and festivals. Two of these loaves are present at each meal to remember the double portion of manna which fell on Fridays and the eve of festivals (*see* DEW). The taking of the challah tithe was seen as the special task of the women of the family, and its neglect was punished by women dying in childbirth. *See also* SEUDAH SHLISHIT.

chametz (Hebrew for 'leaven') During the festival of Passover (*see* PESACH) it is forbidden to eat or even possess any leaven. This is defined as anything with yeast in it, as well as dough which has been allowed to rise. Thus BREAD is not consumed for the duration of the festival, and unleavened bread (*see* MATZAH) is eaten instead. All leaven is removed from the home and any remaining chametz must be searched for (*see* BEDIKAT CHAMETZ) and burnt. Chametz may also be locked away and sold to a Gentile before the festival begins, to be bought back afterwards. While leavened bread is the food of the rich and powerful, unleavened bread is the 'bread of affliction' which was eaten by the Israelite slaves in Egypt. Chametz symbolizes the 'risen yeast' in man, the egoism, arrogance and self-centredness which separate him from God. The mystics compared chametz to a dark cloud of egoism which blots out the divine light, and they likened eating it on Passover to worshipping idols.

chamin *see* CHOLANT

chamishah chumshei torah *see* CHUMASH

chammah *see* SUN

chamor *see* ASS

Chananiah Ben Teradyon *see* SEFER TORAH; SUICIDE

Chanina Ben Dosa (1c. CE) Galilean charismatic and wonder-worker. Chanina lived an ascetic life, being sustained every week by a small quantity of carobs, yet God said of him that 'the merits of My son Chanina sustain the whole world'. His intercessory prayers on behalf of the sick were much sought after, and he knew they had been successful when prayer came easily to him. Even the rabbis of the Jerusalem establishment turned to Chanina when in need, and one rabbi whose son was cured by such a prayer described Chanina as a servant of God who always had access to his divine master. His life was surrounded by miracles, and he even had an effect on the animals he came into contact with. His donkey refused to eat untithed food. When it was stolen, the thieves were unable to feed it and had to let it go, so it made its way back home. He and his family were very poor, and when his daughter found that she had nothing for the shabbat lights except vinegar, he encouraged her to have faith and light the vinegar. Just as God could make oil burn, so he could make vinegar burn. The vinegar lamps continued to burn for the whole of the Sabbath day. His wife found the dire poverty very difficult and persuaded him to take some of the reward for his good deeds in this life, rather than leaving it all for the afterlife. He agreed, and a golden table leg appeared from heaven. That night his wife dreamt that her husband's table in Paradise had only two legs, while the tables of all the other righteous had three legs. She insisted that Chanina pray that the golden leg be taken back to heaven. *See also* SIN.

chanukkah (Hebrew for 'dedication') Eight-day post-biblical festival of lights beginning the twenty-fifth of Kislev, usually in mid-December. Chanukkah celebrates the victory of the MACCABEES in 165 BCE over the Seleucid rulers of Palestine, who had desecrated the Temple and imposed their Hellenistic religion on the Jews. The Maccabees re-dedicated the Temple altar to Jewish worship and wished to rekindle the candelabrum (*see* MENORAH) but could only find one small jar of ritually pure olive oil with the seal of the High Priest still intact. This oil continued to burn miraculously for eight days, enabling them to prepare new pure oil. In commemoration of this miracle the members of each household light an ascending series of lights in an eight-branched menorah, one on the first night, two on the second, etc., followed by the singing of the hymn MAOZ TZUR. The lights are placed in the doorway or windows of the home to 'publicize the miracle'. The message of the story about the miraculous oil is that God enables something pure, however small it may seem, to give light well beyond its natural potential. Thus, the small army of the Maccabees fighting for true religion defeated the power of the Greek empire, and the small Jewish people preserving God's teaching continues to exist when mighty cultures based on false teachings have long perished. It is customary to eat food fried in oil on chanukkah and for children to be given gifts of money, chanukkah gelt, in order to gamble with a four-sided spinning top known in Yiddish as a dreidl.

Shabbat table covered by a white tablecloth showing the Sabbath candles, wine and cups for kiddush and round **challah** breads beside an embroidered challah cloth.

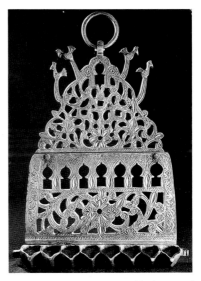

An 18c. Tunisian brass **chanukkah** menorah.

Adults often play cards during the festival despite the disapproval of many rabbinic authorities, some of whom pointed out that the Yiddish word for cards had the same numerical equivalent (gematria) as 'Satan'. For the mystics the chanukkah lights were seen as a manifestation of the hidden light of the Messiah.

charity (Hebrew 'tzedakah', meaning 'righteousness') There are many references to charitable laws in the Bible, ranging from the agricultural laws of LEKET, SHIKHCHAH, PEAH to consideration for widows, orphans, strangers and paupers. Prophets often spoke up for the poor and encouraged people to treat them compassionately. The poor themselves give the rich the opportunity to perform a MITZVAH which is said to be as important as all the other commandments. Charity atones for sin, saves one from death and brings the Messianic redemption near. The demand to give charity applies to everyone, rich or poor, and the Kabbalists introduced the custom of giving charity before morning prayers each day and saying: 'Behold I fulfil the requirement to love one's neighbour as oneself.' The poor of one's own community have a prior claim to support over other paupers, but ultimately charity has to be given even to the non-Jewish poor to preserve harmony. The best form of charity is when both the giver and receiver are anonymous and the poor are thus not put to shame. The specific needs of the poor have to be catered for, e.g. if a rich man became impoverished, he should receive sufficient charity to maintain his previous life-style. Normally, one should verify the bona fides of a poor man seeking assistance, but on the festival of PURIM anyone who asks for charity should be helped without question. *See also* SCHNORER.

charoset Food eaten during the Passover seder meal symbolizing the mortar used by the Israelite slaves in Egypt or the clay they had to form into bricks. It usually includes chopped fruit and nuts, mixed together to form a paste, and is sweetened with wine or dates. The bitter herbs, MAROR, are dipped into the charoset to make them more palatable.

Chasidei Ashkenaz *see* AARON OF BAGHDAD; CHASIDIM, SEFER; JUDAH HA-CHASID

chasidei umot ha-olam *see* RIGHTEOUS GENTILES

Chasidic Movement Revivalist movement, based on the teachings of Israel BAAL SHEM TOV, which began under the leadership of DOV BAER OF MEZHIRECH in mid-18c. Poland. Chasidism addressed itself to those Jews who were left spiritually and physically impoverished by the Chmielnicki Massacres. In place of scholarly elitism, the Baal Shem Tov's followers put forward an interpretation of KABBALAH which taught that God was to be found in all aspects of life, since the world existed within Him, and He could be served through everyday activities. This mystical panentheism attracted scholars to the movement and also appealed to the mass of uneducated Jews. People were encouraged to cleave to God (*see* DEVEKUT) and experience Him in ecstatic joy through song, dance and even the use of tobacco and alcohol. At the centre of each Chasidic community was a charismatic leader, the TZADDIK, who was believed to work miracles and act as a channel for divine energy (ruach ha-kodesh) to flow into the world. Chasidim sought the tzaddik's blessings for all their undertakings and told stories about his wonderful deeds. They set up their own autonomous synagogues (*see* SHTIBL), created a new LITURGY based on the Lurianic rite, introduced changes in ritual, neglected the set times for prayers because prayer had to be a matter of inner feeling, and adopted specific modes of DRESS. The opponents of the new movement (*see* LANDAU, EZEKIEL; MITNAGGEDIM) regarded them as latter-day followers of the Messianic heretics Shabbetai Tzevi and Jacob Frank. They were incensed by Chasidic neglect of torah studies and the wild behaviour of those Chasidim who turned somersaults during prayers in the synagogue. They burnt their books, pronounced a ban (*see* CHEREM) against them and had some of their leaders imprisoned. As Chasidism spread, however, it ceased to be a religion of protest and came closer to institutionalized Orthodoxy. Today it is a major conservative force in opposing the encroachments of modernity on traditional Jewish life. For the Satmar and Belz Chasidic sects, *see* NETUREI KARTA. *See also* KAVVANAH; LUBAVITCH; SHTREIMEL.

Chasidim, Sefer (Hebrew for 'Book of the Pious') The main literary product of the medieval German pietists, Chasidei Ashkenaz. Its author was JUDAH HA-CHASID (13c.) who came from a family of mystics of Babylonian origin. The awe in which its author was held gave the *Sefer Chasidim* a dominant position in the culture of the Ashkenazim. The book, first published in 1538, emphasized the importance of ethical behaviour, the consciousness of sin and the need for repentance, all of which characterized the pietistic movement. The importance of inner piety is illustrated by a story in it about an ignorant cowherd who did not know how to pray. He used to say to God that, if He had cattle, he would look after them for nothing. A sage came across him speaking in this way to God and told him he must use only formal prayers. That night the sage was told in a dream that God was angry with him for having deprived Him of the cowherd's spontaneous prayers and that he must return to the cowherd and persuade him to revert to his original way of praying. The *Sefer Chasidim* expressed and shaped the popular beliefs, customs and folklore of German Jewry throughout the Middle Ages, and its influence persisted until modern times.

chatan *see* BRIDEGROOM OF THE TORAH; MARRIAGE; SIMCHAT TORAH

chavruta *see* YESHIVAH

chazak u-varukh *see* GREETINGS

chazir *see* PIG

chazzan (Hebrew for 'cantor') The synagogue official who leads the prayers, particularly on shabbat and festivals, and who may also read from the sefer torah and teach the children of the congregation. He is also known as the sheliach tzibbur, or 'messenger of the community', since he recites the prayers which can only be said with a minyan quorum on behalf of the worshippers. In modern times the chazzan is appointed primarily for his singing ability, and a whole category of cantorial music has grown up for the virtuoso chazzan. In theory he must be worthy to represent the community: he should be married, bearded, of good reputation, of pleasing appearance, of good voice and acceptable to the congregation. If his voice failed, he could be retired, but the community was still responsible for his support. There was much criticism in the late Middle Ages of the liberties which the chazzan took with the text of the liturgy, singing some pieces at inordinate length, repeating words out of context and ignoring the basic rules of grammar and syntax. The 'prima donna' chazzan would pause in the middle of singing his prayers to see how he was affecting his hearers. A Yiddish folk saying takes the three letters of the word, ch-zz-n, as an acrostic for the three Yiddish words 'chazzonim zaynen naaronim', meaning 'cantors are fools'. This is somewhat qualified by the further saying: 'Maybe all cantors are fools, but not all fools are cantors.' *See also* HAGBAHAH; KADDISH; KEDUSHAH; KITEL; KOL NIDREI; MUSIC.

cheder (Hebrew for 'room') Religion classes often held in a room attached to a synagogue or in the private home of a teacher, melamed. It was traditional for boys to start cheder at three or five years old, learning to read Hebrew from a *Reshit Daat* primer and studying the Book of Leviticus, which was mechanically translated into Yiddish. Because of a shortage of texts, in poor communities several cheder children shared the same book. This led to the peculiar situation among Yemenite Jews where some children could only read Hebrew upside down, having always sat at the top of a book they were sharing with other boys. Children spent most of the day in cheder, and the teachers believed in corporal punishment, keeping control with a strap. Soon after bar mitzvah the student left cheder and went on to a yeshivah or to work. Girls did not attend cheder at all in the pre-modern world. Today cheder classes, for boys and girls, are usually held on Sunday mornings and after school on weekday evenings. In colloquial Yiddish, 'spending time in cheder' is a euphemism for going to prison.

cheese (Hebrew 'gevinah') Orthodox Jews only eat cheese from the milk of a KOSHER animal which was made by a Jew or by a Gentile under rabbinic supervision. The prohibition on unsupervised Gentile cheese extends even to cheese made with vegetarian rennet, although some medieval halakhists allowed it. In the *Talmud* the prohibition on eating meat and milk together is expressed in terms of meat and cheese, since milk was not commonly used in its natural state. After eating hard cheese, it is customary to wait for several hours before eating meat. Cheese was regarded by the rabbis as the food of the poor and was not recommended for sick people as it was thought to prolong their illness. It is customary to eat cheesecake on the festival of shavuot. One explanation for this custom is that the Israelites received the torah on shavuot and therefore had to make do with cheese until they could prepare their meat in accordance with the Jewish DIETARY LAWS.

Polish wooden figurine of a Jew with beard and peot, wearing the dress characteristic of a member of the **Chasidic Movement**.

A **chazzan** at the reading desk in synagogue, his face replaced by a bird's head to satisfy objections to representing human figures in Jewish art (14c. German haggadah).

Chelm Polish town whose inhabitants were the butt of many stories of foolish behaviour. A khelmer khokhem, a wise man of Chelm, was a typical foolish sage. These wise men of Chelm would propose simple solutions to complicated problems. Thus one rabbi stood up in his pulpit and declared he would solve the problem of poverty, for from now on the poor would have cream and the rich would have to make do with milk. 'How, how?' the congregation asked. 'From now on we shall call milk cream, and cream milk', he replied. Once the sages of Chelm were arguing whether the sun or the moon was more important. One rabbi answered: 'The moon of course, since who needs the sun during daylight? We all need the light of the moon at night because it is so dark.' The community leaders decided to turn Chelm into a pilgrimage centre by trapping the moon in a barrel of water so that Jews could look into the barrel and recite the special new moon prayers which require the moon to be visible. They closed up a barrel of water in which they had seen the moon and took it indoors for safekeeping. When they checked whether the moon was still there, however, they found it had been stolen. The community was known for its kindness and compassion. When the beadle (shammash) who had fulfilled the task of waking the Jews of Chelm for morning prayers over many years grew old and infirm, they decided not to sack him. Instead, they gathered the shutters from all the houses into his home so that every morning, instead of doing his rounds to knock on people's windows to wake them up, he could now do so without leaving his house.

cherem (Hebrew for 'excommunication') Exclusion from the community. The punishment of excommunication, also known as niddui, was laid down for twenty-four offences, including insulting rabbinic authority, testifying against a fellow Jew in a non-Jewish court, flouting Jewish customs, blaspheming and selling non-kosher meat as kosher. A cherem was enacted in the synagogue. The ark was opened, a sefer torah taken out, the shofar was blown, curses were pronounced and the candles were extinguished. The lighter forms of cherem involved social ostracization for a limited period, e.g. for seven days no one would associate with the person, no one would eat with them, they would not be counted as part of the quorum (minyan) for prayers, or called up to the torah reading. The person excommunicated was expected to go into mourning, thus showing contrition. Stronger forms of cherem would involve complete ostracization and treating the person concerned as if he were no more a Jew. This did not end even in death, since the coffin of someone in cherem would be symbolically stoned and the family would not keep any mourning rites. Although the use of cherem was discouraged, it was widely applied as a means of control of dissent. It was used against Talmudic sages who refused to abide by the majority view, against individuals like Spinoza, who was excommunicated by the Amsterdam Jewish community, against movements like the Chasidic Movement which was outlawed by the MITNAGGEDIM of eastern Europe, against the study of philosophy in the Middle Ages and against the study of Kabbalah before a mature age after the collapse of the mystical Messianism of Shabbetai Tzevi. The best known and most enduring cherem is that ascribed to Rabbenu GERSHOM which prohibited Ashkenazim from practicing polygamy and divorcing their wives without their consent.

cherub, cherubim Biblical winged ANGELS with the faces of young men or children, whose name is thought to derive from the word for 'youth'. The cherubim occupy a prominent place in the prophet Ezekiel's vision of heaven (Ezek. 10) and God is depicted on a number of occasions in the Bible as 'dwelling on the cherubim'. This was interpreted by mystics as meaning that the names of the Lord of Hosts dwell on the cherubim (cf. II Sam. 6:2), i.e. divine names, representing male and female sefirot, were engraved on their foreheads. A cherub with a fiery sword guards the entrance to the Garden of Eden to prevent man re-entering. In Solomon's Temple cherubim were woven onto the curtain before the Holy of Holies and carved on the Temple doors. There were also two golden cherubim, one male and one female, standing above the Ark of the Covenant though it was believed that they existed in a miraculous manner occupying no physical space. God revealed Himself to Moses in the Tabernacle from between these two cherubim (Num. 7:89). When Israel was faithful to God, the two cherubim embraced each other, signifying God's love for his people and the promise of fruitfulness for human sexual union. The curtain before the Holy of Holies was drawn back so that pilgrims who came to Jerusalem for the pilgrim festivals could see this symbol of divine love. When Israel was unfaithful, however, the cherubim turned away from each other signifying God's anger and foreshadowing calamity. The existence of these cherubic figures was something of an embarrassment to the philosophically minded supporters of Jewish monotheism, and Maimonides explained that there were two cherubim to ensure that people would not mistake them for an image of God Himself. Nevertheless, when the Temple was destroyed, Jews were mocked by Gentiles for worshipping the cherubim.

chet see SIN

chevra kaddisha (Aramaic for 'holy fellowship') The Jewish burial society whose male and female members undertake the process of purification of a corpse, taharah, before BURIAL. It is customary for all members of the chevra to fast one day a year, in case they have somehow infringed the dignity of those they have buried, and then to break their fast with a feast. A popular day for this is the seventh of Adar, the anniversary of the death of Moses who was buried by God Himself (Deut. 34:6). Members of the chevra also tend to the needs of the sick and try to be with the dying at the time of death. In many communities the chevra kaddisha is made up of volunteers, who must be available to leave their places of work at short notice to wash and dress corpses, since burial usually takes place on the day of death. Though their work is difficult, it is highly valued as the ultimate expression of kindness.

chilazon see TEKHELET

children The first commandment given to Adam and Eve was to have children, expressed in the words 'be fruitful and multiply' (Gen. 1:28). Children are the main purpose of marriage, and since they are seen as a blessing from God, many Orthodox Jews do not practice BIRTH CONTROL. A couple should have at least one son and one daughter (*see* PARENTS), so that they reproduce themselves, and if a marriage remains childless for ten years, this is grounds for divorce. A son is given his Hebrew name at the CIRCUMCISION ceremony and a daughter is named in the synagogue when her father is called up to the torah reading (aliyah) soon after birth. It is customary for the father to bless his children on Friday night at the shabbat table, and he is responsible for educating them, teaching them a trade, seeing that they get married, providing a dowry and teaching them to swim. In many Orthodox families there is little differentiation between the sexes until the age of three, since till that time a boy grows his hair long. Thereafter boys and girls are given distinctive roles. A child inherits its identity as a Jew from the mother, but its status as a priest or a Levite comes from the father. Children born from an adulterous or incestuous relationship have the status of a MAMZER and cannot freely marry with other members of the community. *See also* BIRTHDAY; FIRSTBORN; REBELLIOUS SON.

chillul ha-shem (Hebrew for 'profanation of the divine name') Jews are commanded not to profane God's name and to sanctify Him in the midst of the community of Israel (Lev. 22:32). This involves avoiding any behaviour that brings God's teaching into disrepute and acting so that people come to praise God and his torah. If necessary, a Jew should be ready to accept MARTYRDOM as the ultimate sanctification of the divine name. Since sinning in public is worse than sinning in private, a person who is overcome by temptation should dress in dark clothes and go to a place where he is not known before sinning. By doing so, there is at least no desecration of the divine name. It is also said that an offense against a Gentile is worse than a similar offense against a fellow Jew because God's name is desecrated thereby. While it is possible to repent (*see* REPENTANCE) and atone for ordinary SINS, it is very hard to atone for the sin of profaning God's name. On occasion the law of the torah may be set aside in order to avoid chillul ha-shem, and actions which are normally permitted become prohibited if they may be misconstrued by onlookers.

Chinese Jews There is no clear evidence of when Jews first arrived in China. Legends relate the origin of Chinese Jewry to the TEN LOST TRIBES or to refugees fleeing from the destruction of the Second Temple in the 1c. CE. By the 9c. Persian Jewish silk traders had established trading posts in China, and there are travellers' reports of meetings with them. They were known as 'those who remove the sinew of the thigh of animals before eating', reflecting an aspect of the Jewish dietary laws. Modern information about Jewish life in China came from Jesuit missionaries. One 17c. Jesuit was visited by a Jewish mandarin who mistook a picture of Mary and the infant Jesus for Rebecca and Jacob. The main Jewish settlement at that time was in Kai Fung, the capital of Honan Province in

The two **cherubim** above the Ark of the Covenant in the Temple (13c., France).

Chasidic **child** beside a chuppah at an Orthodox marriage ceremony. Note the headcoverings and peot.

central China, where the large synagogue bore a stone inscription dating back to 1163. Chinese Jews had already assimilated the culture of their surroundings and were indistinguishable from native Chinese. When they first came across Portuguese Jews, they could not believe that these white foreigners were Jews at all. The Kai Fung memorial book of the dead (15c.–17c.) shows how Hebrew names gave way to Chinese names. Chinese Jews only knew a rudimentary Hebrew, were ignorant of many rituals and practised ancestor worship in the Chinese style, which they thought was merely a way of honouring the dead. They kept their torah scrolls in a receptacle known as the Holy of Holies, above which the shema was engraved, and the torah reading took place from a chair with Hebrew inscriptions on it. They removed their shoes before entering synagogue, a custom also found among certain communities of Sephardim, and the person reading from the torah would cover his face with a veil, just as Moses did according to the biblical account (Exod. 34:33). The form of liturgy used by Chinese Jews was similar to that of Persian Jewry with some elements from the Yemenite prayer-book.

chinukh *see* EDUCATION

Chmielnicki Massacres Massacre of Jewish communities during the Cossack uprising against Polish rule in the Ukraine from 1648 to 1649. The Cossack leader, Bogdan Chmielnicki, and his men attempted to annihilate Ukrainian Jewry, who were hated middle men between the Polish aristocracy and the Ukrainian peasants. Not only were the Jews identified with the Poles, but they were also despised because of Christian anti-Jewish prejudice (*see* ANTI-SEMITISM). During the massacres, synagogues were destroyed, torah scrolls desecrated, and approximately 100,000 Jews killed. Many others fled as refugees, while some converted to Christianity in order to save their lives. The massacres were followed by a period of general mourning, and for many years afterwards the Jews of Eastern Europe fasted on the anniversary of the first massacre. The Chmielnicki uprisings led to economic depression among Jews and to the spiritual disintegration of organized Jewish community life. They played a major role in the spread of Messianic beliefs about Shabbetai Tzevi, since the great sufferings of Ukrainian Jewry were identified as the birth pangs of the Messiah and 1648 was itself regarded as a date with Messianic portent.

cholent (also choolant, shalent, schalet) Sabbath dish kept hot on a stove, or in an oven, overnight and served as the main course for Saturday lunch. Among Ashkenazim the main ingredients of the cholent are meat on the bone, beans, onions and potatoes. These are often eaten with stuffed chicken's neck, helzl, and stuffed intestines, kishke, which are cooked together with the cholent. Some Sephardim call their cholent chamin, 'hot dish', and use mutton or chicken, rice and hard-boiled eggs seasoned with oriental spices. In the shtetl of eastern Europe each family left their cholent overnight in the oven of the communal bakehouse, and the older children would bring it home at midday. The origin of the Yiddish word 'cholent' is obscure, and it may be derived from the

Old French word 'chald', meaning 'hot'. Jews are required to eat something hot on Saturday not merely to enhance the joy of shabbat, but also to differentiate themselves from Karaites who refuse to allow any fire to burn on the Sabbath.

chol ha-moed (Hebrew for 'profane time of the festival') The middle days of the two longer festivals PESACH and SUKKOT which are semi-holy days, and only necessary work is allowed to be undertaken on them. Marriages are not performed on chol ha-moed because they would detract from the joy of the festival itself, and although burials take place, mourning is muted until after the festival is over. While most Ashkenazim put on tefillin during chol ha-moed, Sephardim and members of the Chasidic Movement do not since the mystics regarded the wearing of tefillin as forbidden on these days. On chol ha-moed the world is under the influence of the divine tefillin, and putting on human tefillin represents a failure to submit to this heavenly influence.

Choni Ha-Meaggel (1c. BCE) Miracle-worker and saint. Choni earned his name Ha-Meaggel ('the circle maker') from an incident which occurred during a severe drought. He was asked to intercede with God and so drew a circle round himself, refusing to move until God sent exactly the right quantity of rain. One of the leading rabbis of the time, Simeon Ben Shetach, wanted to excommunicate (cherem) Choni for this brazen attitude towards God but was powerless to interfere, since God answered Choni's prayers. Choni once came across a man planting a carob tree and asked him why he was doing that since the fruit took seventy years to develop. The man answered that he was doing it for his grandchildren, just as his own ancestors had planted trees for him. Soon after this Choni fell into a deep sleep behind a rock and slept for seventy years. When he awoke, he saw the carob tree and the grandson of the man who planted it eating its fruit. He also returned to his village to find his house occupied by his grandson and all his contemporaries long dead. He prayed to God to be allowed to die, since without friends death was preferable to life. *See also* ABBA; RAIN.

Chosen People The idea that the Jewish people have been chosen from among the nations of the world to receive the divine revelation goes back to God's COVENANT with Abraham (Gen. 15), and subsequently with Moses and the Israelites (Exod. 19). ISRAEL is to be 'a kingdom of priests and a holy nation' and become a light to the Gentiles (Isa. 60:3). The Jewish People were chosen out of divine love, but it was also because they accepted God and His torah. Indeed the liturgy links the election of Israel to the torah, which the Jews have to keep. During the Middle Ages, when Jews were treated as pariahs by Christians and suffered almost continual persecution, their self-image as God's Chosen People was an important support. The ALEINU prayer, which gives expression to the distinctive nature of Israel, became one of the most frequently repeated parts of the service. The *Talmud* makes disparaging comparisons between the morality of Jews and the animalistic values of the heathen, while the Kabbalah emphasizes the difference in spiritual make-up between

Jew and Gentile and the superiority of the Jewish soul. In recent times the notion of the Jews as the Chosen People has been somewhat of an embarrassment to modernist Jewish thinkers. It has been given a more universalistic interpretation as signifying that each nation is chosen for a particular purpose.

Chuetas MARRANO inhabitants of the Balearic Islands, descended from Jewish forced converts to Catholicism who chose baptism rather than death in the 14c. and 15c. The word 'chueta' means 'pig', or 'pig eater', and was given to the new Christians as a pejorative nickname or because they ostentatiously ate pork to show that they were not Jews. In the 16c. and 17c. a number of Majorcan Marranos were executed for Judaizing and their property confiscated. They were originally banned from the army, public office, guilds and the priesthood and only after 1782 were these restrictions lifted. Although the Chuetas today are pious Catholics, having their own church in a former synagogue, they are still treated as pariahs, living apart from other Christians and even being buried separately. Various attempts have been made to resettle the Chueta community in the State of Israel, but these failed and the Chuetas returned to Majorca.

chukkat ha-goi (Hebrew for 'Gentile practices') Certain forms of GENTILE behaviour must not be imitated by Jews on the basis of the biblical prohibition of 'not walking in the ways of the Gentile' (Lev. 18:3 and 20:23). In its narrow interpretation this avoidance of chukkat ha-goi refers to aspects of Gentile religion and SUPERSTITION which should be rejected by Jews. For example, the practice of covering the head (*see* HEAD-COVERING) was made mandatory because Christians prayed bareheaded in churches, and kneeling during prayer was prohibited by Judaism since it was associated with Christianity. Chukkat ha-goi is used in a broader way by some Jews to outlaw any changes in the traditional style of DRESS and appearance. Thus they disapprove of wearing suits in place of the long black coats of the pre-modern ghetto, of shaving off the beard and of men having modern hair-styles. They also criticize the practice of rabbis wearing clerical gowns as 'goyish' and regard the decorum and style of Reform synagogues as church-like. The prohibitions on chukkat ha-goi have preserved the unique identity of the Jewish life-style over the centuries. Nevertheless, a number of superstitious practices have been adopted by Jews from the host cultures in which they have lived.

Chumash (Hebrew for 'Fifth') The Pentateuch with its division into five books, the Five Books of Moses, is called a Chumash, a shortened form of chamishah chumshei torah, 'the five fifths of the TORAH'. These 'fifths' are bereshit (Genesis), shemot (Exodus), vayikra (Leviticus), bemidbar (Numbers), and devarim (Deuteronomy). *See also* BIBLE; TENAKH; SAMARITANS.

chuppah (Hebrew for 'canopy') The wedding canopy symbolizes the groom's home, under which he stands, wearing a KITEL, and waits for the bride to join him for the wedding ceremony. The veiled bride comes with her parents and in some communities circumambulates the groom three or seven times (*see* HAKKAFOT).

Traditional portrait of Bogdan **Chmielnicki**, leader of the Cossack rebellion in the 17c.

Conclusion of the Book of Leviticus from an illuminated **Chumash** manuscript. The picture shows the education of a young boy by a cheder teacher who holds a whip (14c.).

Marriage ceremony with the bride and groom standing under a cloth **chuppah** (15c. French manuscript).

The Jewish mystical tradition lays stress on the need to decorate the chuppah in honour of the heavenly bride, the feminine aspect of God, who comes to rejoice with the earthly bride. The chuppah is thus often an elaborately embroidered velvet cloth held on four poles, but among some communities of Sephardim it may simply be a TALLIT held aloft by four men. Ultra-Orthodox Ashkenazim erect the chuppah outside under the open sky, as the stars are a symbol of fertility. The more general custom is to set up the chuppah inside a synagogue, despite objections from a number of Orthodox rabbis that this is an imitation of church weddings. The canopy which surrounds the bride and groom has been interpreted as representing the light of God which surrounds all creation. When the couple leave the chuppah they are, as it were, created anew and begin their MARRIAGE purified of all their past sins.

chutzpah (Hebrew for 'cheek', 'impudence') A popular term used in Yiddish to apply to that quality of lovable audacity thought to be characteristic of Jews and particularly characteristic of the SCHNORER. Traditional texts actually describe the people of Israel as the cheekiest of nations. The concept is sometimes defined in the story of the man who murdered both his parents and then asked for mercy from the court because he was an orphan. Chutzpah is often thought of in a positive way, as in the Talmudic expression that 'impudence, even when directed towards God, is beneficial'. It is also used negatively, however, and a law court (bet din) which sat with only two judges instead of the minimum of three was referred to as an 'impudent bet din'. Similarly in the period preceding the Days of the Messiah social values will crumble and 'impudence will increase'.

circumcision (Hebrew 'berit milah', meaning 'covenant of circumcision') The removal of the foreskin of a baby boy on the eighth day after birth, or of a male proselyte, goes back to God's COVENANT with ABRAHAM (Gen. 17:11–12). Those who are circumcised are saved from punishment after death by Abraham. Some of the great men of old were reputed to have been born already circumcised, a sign of special status, and circumcision for them merely consisted of the removal of a drop of blood from the penis. If a child is sick, the operation is delayed and may be postponed indefinitely on health grounds. In such cases the uncircumcised child is regarded as if circumcised, and indeed even wilful failure to circumcise does not affect the Jewish status of the child. Most Jews, whatever their religious affiliation, have their sons circumcised with the exception of some members of the anti-religious Yiddishist BUND. Jews in the past were willing to undergo MARTYRDOM in order to circumcise their children. During the ceremony of circumcision, the child is momentarily placed on a chair set aside for the prophet Elijah, who attends every circumcision (see ELIJAH, CHAIR OF). The child is then placed on the knees of the godfather (see SANDEK), who holds the child while the professional circumcisor (see MOHEL) operates. The child is given a Hebrew name at the end of the ceremony. Parents are careful not to tell anyone the name beforehand because, according to the Kabbalah, only after the berit milah

takes place is the child truly attached to God and fully human. The night before the operation, various rituals are performed to protect the child from the demon queen LILITH.

city of refuge (Hebrew 'ir miklat') In biblical times cities were set aside as places of refuge for those guilty of manslaughter (Num. 35). They could go into exile there to save themselves from the relatives of the deceased, who as 'blood avengers' might seek to kill them if they found them outside such protected zones. These refugees lived a normal life in a city of refuge, but they had to stay there till the death of the High Priest. The High Priest, as the spiritual leader of the generation, was held responsible for the actions of the people during his reign. He therefore had to suffer the indignity of exiles in cities of refuge praying for him to die. The High Priest's mother would send gifts to inhabitants of these cities to encourage them to pray for her son's welfare. See also HEBRON; LEVITES.

Cochin Jews There were trading contacts between Israel and South India in the time of King Solomon, and a number of Jewish trading posts were set up in the subcontinent in the Middle Ages. According to a legend current among Jews of the Malabar coast, refugees fled there after the destruction of the First Temple. The early settlers, who through intermarriage eventually took on the racial characteristics of Indian natives, were joined in the Middle Ages by lighter-skinned Jews from other countries, particularly refugees from the Spanish expulsion of 1492. An early medieval copper plate, kept in the Paradesi synagogue of the White Jews in Cochin, records the rights granted to a Jewish leader, Joseph Rabban, and to his descendants by the local raja. Rabban was allowed to carry a parasol, have a drum and a trumpet played for him and was freed from paying taxes. Cochin Jews claim that there was once an independent Jewish state in the area. The state came to an end after internal warfare between white and black Jews, and the majority of its inhabitants fled to Cochin. They were eventually joined by the rest of the community who fled the religiously intolerant Portuguese. The Jews took up residence in Jew Town near the raja's palace so that they could live under his protection. Black and white Jews maintained separate synagogues in Cochin and did not intermarry. The black Jews had no priest or Levites among them, and both communities had groups of manumitted slave proselytes attached to them. These freed slaves originally were not allowed into the synagogue for prayers and sat on a veranda outside. Indeed, they were not called up to the torah except on the festival of simchat torah. In the early 19c. Jews from Cochin went to Bombay to educate the BENE ISRAEL in Jewish rituals, to perform circumcision and to act as ritual slaughterers (shochet) and teachers for them.

Commandments, The 613 (Hebrew 'taryag mitzvot') There is a tradition that the number of commandments in the torah is 613. This is based on the numerical value (gematria) of 'torah', to which Moses bound the Israelites (Deut. 33:4), plus the first two commandments of the DECALOGUE which were spoken directly by God. They are divided into 248 positive

commandments ('thou shalt...'), equivalent to the
organs of the human body, and 365 negative commandments ('thou shalt not...'), equivalent to the
days of the year. Although there are many works
which seek to enumerate the individual commandments which make up this number, there is no general
agreement among halakhists because the source of the
tradition is purely homiletic. The purpose of the
commandments is the purification of man (see TIKKUN),
since it makes no difference to God whether, for
instance, an animal is to be slaughtered from the back
or front of the neck (see SHECHITAH). Before a positive
commandment is undertaken, a blessing is usually
recited, and someone engaged in the performance of
one commandment is excused from others. Although
one is not meant to derive benefit from the commandments, there being no reward for them in this world,
nevertheless someone who fulfils a commandment
will be given the opportunity to perform other
commandments. Obedience to the rules laid down by
the Rabbis comes under the biblical commandment
not to turn aside from the decisions of the judges of
each generation (Deut. 17:11). See also BAHIR, SEFER
HA-; GOLDEN RULE; KAVVANAH; MITZVAH; TZITZIT.

community (Hebrew 'kehillah' or 'kahal') One of
the basic units of Jewish life is the community, made
up of heads of households (see BAAL HA-BAYIT). A
community usually has its own synagogue and perhaps
its own cemetery and chevra kaddisha. Larger communities employ a full range of religious officials such
as a DAYYAN, a rabbi, a chazzan, cheder teachers, a
ritual slaughterer (shochet), a scribe, a shammash and
a mohel. Because Orthodox Jews have to live within
walking distance of a synagogue for shabbat and
festival attendance, a traditional Jewish community is
spread over a limited geographical area. In pre-modern
times communities had a measure of self-government
and were able to control, not just their own charitable
and welfare programmes, but all aspects of their
members' lives. They meted out fines, sentenced
people to periods in the stocks as punishment, and the
ultimate sanction was ostracization and expulsion from
the community (see CHEREM). Although Rabbinic
literature emphasizes conformity with community
norms and customs, Jews have often formed subcom-
munities as a result of disagreements between them
and their lay or religious leaders. The story is told of
the Jew who was shipwrecked alone on a desert island.
When he was rescued he was asked what the two
buildings on either side of the island were. He replied
that one was the synagogue he prayed in and the other
was the synagogue he would never set foot in.

concentration camps Camps established by the Nazis
after their rise to power in Germany in 1933. The
original purpose of concentration camps was to incar-
cerate political prisoners and opponents of the regime,
but they began to be used more widely with the
mass arrests of Jews after the destruction of German
synagogues on 'Kristalnacht' 1938. Eventually, a new
type of camp came into existence as an extermination
centre for Jews, gypsies, homosexuals, Soviet prisoners
of war, etc. Those Jews considered unfit for slave
labour were exterminated in such camps after 1941,
while previously they would have been shot or killed

A mohel performing **circumcision** while the
sandek holds the baby (19c.).

Bodies of victims at the Belsen **concentration
camp**.

in specially constructed lorries using exhaust fumes. Jews destined for extermination were taken by rail transport in cattle trucks from overcrowded GHETTOS. Of the approximately six million Jews killed by the Nazis and their Fascist sympathizers in occupied Europe during the HOLOCAUST, it is estimated that about four million died in the camps. The extermination camp near AUSCHWITZ was responsible for nearly twenty thousand deaths each day at its peak. The camps were run by SS men, and experiments were carried out on human subjects by medical staff, who also controlled the procedure of selection which determined who was fit for labour and who would be killed immediately.

concubine (Hebrew 'pilegesh') A 'wife' who, though dedicated to one man, has not been married to him in a formal ceremony and does not possess a MARRIAGE document (*see* KETUBBAH). There are many examples of concubines (usually handmaids) in the Bible. Six of the Twelve Tribes descended from concubines (*see* MATRIARCHS). King Solomon had several hundred, but concubinage was discouraged by the Rabbis in the post-biblical period in the belief that it led to sexual license. At least one pre-modern halakhist, Jacob Emden, advocated a reintroduction of concubine 'marriage' as a way of dealing with marriage break-up and its associated problems. The advantage of concubine 'marriage' is that the two parties do not need a formal GET, or bill of DIVORCE, when it is dissolved. If the man disappears, the woman does not become an AGUNAH and there are no restrictions on the marriage of an ex-concubine to the kinsmen of her previous 'husband'. *See also* MONOGAMY.

Conservative Judaism Movement of North American origin which advocates traditional Judaism adapted to the modern ethos. Conservative Judaism emerged out of the Historical School in Germany which believed in Westernization of Jewish mores but was more traditional than REFORM JUDAISM. The Jewish Theological Seminary, which is the main educational institution of Conservative Judaism, was founded in New York in 1887 to train traditional rabbis. The Rabbinical Assembly of America, bringing together rabbis who subscribed to the movement's outlook, was founded in 1901 although it only became formalized at a later date. The character of Conservative Judaism was shaped by Solomon Shechter who came to New York from Cambridge, England, to head the Seminary in 1902. Schechter was quite traditional in his approach, rejecting the Higher Criticism of the Bible as a form of what he called Higher anti-Semitism. He created the United Synagogue of America in 1913, modelled on the United Synagogue in London, to incorporate all Conservative synagogues. This today is the largest organized synagogue movement in the USA. In 1922 a radical Conservative branch movement, called RECONSTRUCTIONISM, was founded by some members of the Seminary faculty, and it eventually broke away to constitute a new, independent stream appealing mostly to intellectuals. Conservatism has had an uneasy relationship with ORTHODOX JUDAISM almost from its inception. Conservative rabbis are not recognized by the Orthodox rabbinate, and thus conversions and divorces performed by them are regarded as invalid. A number of Conservative innovations in halakhah have widened the gap with Orthodoxy, and recent moves towards the ordination of women as rabbis have reinforced the view of many Orthodox leaders that Conservatism is merely the more traditional wing of Reform.

conversion *see* PROSELYTE

Cordovero, Moses (1522–70) Kabbalist who lived in Safed, northern Palestine. Cordovero was a prolific writer and summarized most of the main mystical ideas of his predecessors in his great work *Pardes Rimmonim*, attempting to harmonize the differences between them. He also wrote a book recording his practice of 'exile', in which he would 'exile' himself to the graves of the righteous in different parts of Galilee and also undertake an 'exile' in honour of the shekhinah, the female aspect of the divine, which was exiled from the male aspect of God. He depicts all reality as a manifestation of the divine immanent in the mundane world. Although ELIJAH would come to his house to teach him mystical secrets, his Kabbalistic teachings were eclipsed by the rather different mystical system of Isaac LURIA, who was a pupil of his in Safed for a short time. Cordovero's work came to be seen as merely an introduction or 'entrance hall' to the Lurianic Kabbalah. He was a reincarnation of Eliezer, the servant of Abraham, and a pillar of fire accompanied Cordovero's body during his funeral.

corporal punishment Flogging is prescribed as a punishment for the transgression of negative COMMANDMENTS in the torah (Deut. 25:3). Although forty strokes are mentioned in the Bible, the Rabbis limited the punishment to a maximum of thirty-nine strokes to prevent any mistakes. A doctor had to examine the sinner and decide whether he could take the maximum or whether some lesser amount should be administered on medical grounds. The sinner was then flogged on his chest and back with a leather whip while one judge (dayyan) called out 'strike' for each stroke, another judge counted and a third read passages from scripture. After the punishment was over, people had to forgive him his sins and receive him back into the Jewish community since the Bible refers to him as 'your brother'. Flogging was used in the post-biblical period to uphold MINHAG, to maintain standards within the Jewish COMMUNITY and to persuade people to perform positive commandments they had neglected. In DIVORCE proceedings it was also used on a recalcitrant husband who was made to give a GET to his wife 'voluntarily' by being flogged. The idea behind this was that corporal punishment helps to overcome the husband's obstinacy and that he really wants to abide by the halakhah. Some Jews undergo a symbolic flogging on the afternoon prior to yom kippur as part of the process of atonement.

Court Jews In the late Middle Ages some Jews in Western European lands were used by Christian rulers to act as agents for collecting revenues, as tax farmers, as mint-masters, as suppliers of silver for the mints and provisions for the army, as organizers of loans for the princes and as diplomats who undertook delicate missions for their masters. These Jews, who came to be known as Court Jews, were granted privileges

not available to their co-religionists, and they saw
themselves as Jewish aristocrats. Some of them converted to Christianity, but those who remained within
the Jewish community, though they were somewhat
assimilated, represented Jewish interests at the court
(*see* SHTADLAN). They were caught up in the intrigues
of court life and were despised by their Christian
rivals, as well as by those fellow Jews who were eager
to replace them in positions of power. They also
earned the suspicion of ordinary Jews who were
resentful of the riches and honours of the Court Jews.
One of the most famous Court Jews was the German
Joseph Suess OPPENHEIMER, who ended his life on the
gallows in 1738. In Eastern Europe, although the
institution of Court Jews was not found in quite the
same way as in the West, individual Jews did attain
positions of pre-eminence. According to a widespread
legend, one of these, Saul Wahl of Brest-Litovsk, was
even appointed king of Poland for a day in the early
17c. while the Polish nobility was deciding exactly
who should succeed to the throne. *See also* JOSEPH OF
ROSHEIM.

covenant (Hebrew 'berit') The special relationship
between God and man is known as a covenant. The
covenant with Israel (*see* ISRAEL, PEOPLE OF) goes back
to the agreement between God and ABRAHAM (Gen.
15 and 17), which involved the CIRCUMCISION of his
male descendants. Jews who do not practise circumcision are considered to have 'broken the covenant of
our father Abraham' and have no portion in the World
to Come (olam haba). Keeping the covenant of
circumcision also entails avoiding forbidden sexual
activity, and thus helps to bring God's blessing into
the world. Included in the covenant with Abraham is
the gift of the Land of Israel, which is promised to his
seed. The covenant was renewed at Mount SINAI and
involved the commitment of the Israelites, known as
'sons of the covenant', to keep the ordinances of God's
torah. The torah is the foremost expression of God's
covenant with the world, and without it the heavens
and the earth would not continue to exist. *See also*
CHOSEN PEOPLE.

creatio ex nihilo *see* CREATION; EMANATION

Creation The doctrine of creatio ex nihilo is accepted
as the traditional interpretation of the Genesis story,
where the heavens and the earth were brought into
being by divine speech. There is, however, a Midrashic
view that the world was made from the remains of
previous worlds which God had destroyed because He
was not satisfied with them. The Kabbalah, by contrast,
preferred the idea of EMANATION, in which lower
levels of reality emanated from higher levels which in
turn emanated from the Godhead. There is general
agreement that implicit in these views is the depen-
dence of the world on God, who brought it into being
for His own honour and out of compassion for His
creatures. The torah is described as the blueprint
according to which the world was made. The earth
was begun from a foundation stone, the even shetiyyah.
This was the same stone on which the Patriarch Jacob
slept and dreamt of a ladder and was later incorporated
in the HOLY OF HOLIES in the Jerusalem Temple. A
number of the miraculous features of the Bible were

Solomon Shechter, one of the leading figures of
Conservative Judaism in the USA, at work on the
Cairo genizah manuscripts in Cambridge (England).

Diagram of the structure of the divine world
according to the Kabbalah, from the *Pardes
Rimmonim* of Moses **Cordovero**.

said to have been created towards twilight of the sixth day, just before the Creation process ceased. These include the manna, the mouth of Balaam's talking ass, and the grave of Moses which remains unknown to man. A branch of Jewish mysticism (*see* MAASEH BERESHIT) is devoted to understanding the divine creative process, the residue of which is contained in the world. This residue can be used to gain power over nature. *See also* YETZIRAH, SEFER HA-.

cremation Cremation of the dead is forbidden by the halakhah since it is seen as a denial of the belief in the RESURRECTION. The traditional method of disposal is BURIAL in consecrated ground so that at the Resurrection the body will be formed around the indestructible LUZ bone. Cremation is also seen as a desecration of the corpse and a practice introduced in imitation of Gentile customs (*see* CHUKKAT HA-GOI). The relatives of someone who has requested cremation would be advised by an Orthodox rabbi not to obey the wishes of the deceased but to bury them instead. Reform Judaism allows cremations, and Reform rabbis, unlike their Orthodox colleagues, will officiate at them.

Crusades During the Crusades Jewish communities which lay in the path of the Crusading armies were massacred. The Crusaders were influenced by Christian teachings that Jews were responsible for the crucifixion of Jesus. So they took revenge against the 'deicides', starting their battles against the Moslem unbelievers in the Holy Land by attacking the Jewish unbelievers on their doorstep. A number of bishops protested against these outrages, but they had little control over the mobs and some of them were themselves maltreated. They tried to persuade Jews to undergo baptism to save their lives. While some chose this way out, many refused to be converted to Christianity and some committed suicide. The worst massacres were during the First Crusade (1096–99) when the centres of Jewish life along the Rhine were destroyed. The OMER period between pesach and shavuot, which follows Easter, was henceforth commemorated as a time of Jewish MARTYRDOM for the Franco-German communities (Ashkenazim). During the Third Crusade (1189–92) the Jews of England were violently attacked after the coronation of Richard I, and this led to the mass suicide of the Jews of York who burnt themselves to death rather than face forced baptism and mob antagonism. The Crusades brought the period of medieval Jewish prosperity to an end and are remembered in Jewish liturgy as a period of Christian violence and Jewish submission to God. A special prayer, av ha-rachamim ('Merciful Father'), was introduced into the shabbat morning service asking God, the merciful father, to remember those communities who laid down their lives for the sanctification of His name.

crypto-Jew *see* MARRANO

daf ha-yomi *see* SIYYUM

Daniel Leading figure of the Babylonian EXILE whose exploits are recorded in the Book of Daniel. The book is written half in Hebrew and half in Aramaic, which was the vernacular of the DIASPORA Jews. Although not a prophet, Daniel, who was of Davidic descent, was inspired with divine wisdom, and a number of his apocalyptic visions are recorded. He achieved prominence in the Babylonian Empire because he was able to interpret dreams and could read the words 'mene mene tekel ufarsin' which appeared mysteriously on the palace wall. His faithfulness to the Jewish practice of praying three times a day led to him being thrown into a den of lions where he was protected by an angel (Dan. 6). Seeing the oppression of the Jews in exile, Daniel refused to praise God as 'mighty', for God did not show His might by punishing the Gentiles. Daniel was instrumental in arranging the return of the Jews to the Land of Israel. The medieval traveller Benjamin of Tudela reported in his book of travels that Daniel's coffin was suspended by a chain from the centre of a bridge over a river in Persia. It was placed there by the Persian Shah who wished to stop the Jews from both sides of the river quarrelling about where the coffin should rest. Until the Shah interfered, the coffin was taken every year to a different side of the river. Other travellers reported that the fishes which swam under Daniel's coffin had gold rings in their ears. *See also* PETAACHIAH OF REGENSBURG.

David King of Israel and descendant of Ruth, the Moabite convert to Judaism. David began as a shepherd in BETHLEHEM, showing God that he was suitable to be a future king of Israel by the concern he showed for the sheep under his care. In a famous incident he defeated the Philistine giant Goliath with a shepherd boy's sling and stone (I Sam. 17) after he had tricked him into looking up and exposing his forehead. David's ability as a musician helped to soothe King SAUL when he was depressed, but Saul's uncontrollable jealousy terminated their relationship. Saul's son Jonathan struck up a lasting friendship with David and helped him escape from his father. David was eventually anointed king by the prophet Samuel at the age of twenty-eight and ruled after Saul's death, making the newly conquered JERUSALEM his permanent capital. Not only was David a warrior king who extended the borders of his kingdom, but he was also a great religious figure. Above his bed hung a harp through the strings of which a wind blew at midnight, the music awakening David to sing God's praises and study torah. He composed psalms, edited the Book of PSALMS, and according to one view, also wrote the PEREK SHIRAH. David was told by God that he would die on shabbat, and so he would spend the whole Sabbath day studying torah to prevent the ANGEL OF DEATH from having power over him. Each Saturday night he would make a party to celebrate his survival, and this is the origin of the melavveh malkah ritual. David died on the festival of shavuot, which fell on a Saturday, after the Angel of Death had distracted him from his concentration on his studies. God chose his descendants as the true kings of Israel from among whom the MESSIAH will one day arise. Prayers are said for the restoration of the Davidic dynasty, and the declaration 'David, king of Israel, is alive and endures' is included in the liturgy. David's favourite wife was BATHSHEBA, and her son SOLOMON succeeded him. *See also* REPENTANCE.

day and night The 24-hour unit making one whole day, yom, always begins at sunset and ends the following night. This is based on the Creation story in Genesis where it says: 'And it was evening and it was morning' of each of the first six days (Gen. 1). Shabbat and festivals thus always begin the evening before. Day and night are each divided into twelve seasonal hours which vary in length between summer and winter. The times for prayers are calculated in terms of these seasonal hours, and some synagogues in Jerusalem have a clock with an adjustable pendulum which shows the time in seasonal hours. God is said to renew the work of creation every day with the emergence of the dawn light, just as His first act of creation was the formation of light from the darkness (Gen. 1:3). The international date-line, on one side of which it is one day and on the other the next day, has led to considerable halakhic discussion as to whether this convention should determine when shabbat is kept. An equally difficult problem affects Jews who live in areas of the extreme north where a day (i.e. the setting, rising and setting sun) may extend for many months, and the normal pattern of the 24-hour day does not exist. According to the *Talmud* and mystical literature, at night DEMONS stalk the world, but when day breaks Samael and his hosts return to their lair in the 'hole of the great abyss'. Therefore, people should not go out alone at night because of the danger from demonic forces.

Day of Judgment (Hebrew 'yom ha-din') At the End of Days in the time of the MESSIAH, when the RESURRECTION OF THE DEAD will take place, both Israel and the Gentile nations will be summoned to divine judgment by the blowing of the great shofar. The prophet ELIJAH will come back to earth to reconcile families, 'returning the hearts of fathers to their children and of children to their fathers, before the great and dreadful day of the Lord' (Mal. 4). The Day of Judgment will be a terrifying day of darkness (Amos 5:18), with tempest, thunder and consuming fire (Isa. 29:6). In the Jewish liturgy the New Year festival (*see* ROSH HA-SHANAH) is also called the Day of Judgment because the shofar is blown and God judges the world, deciding on the fate of individuals for the year ahead. *See also* ESCHATOLOGY.

dayyan (Hebrew for 'judge') A judge who serves on a religious court, whether a BET DIN or a SANHEDRIN, is known as a dayyan, and God is present with judges in their deliberations. A righteous judge is thus a partner with God and should feel awe at the responsibility of his office, as if a sword were pressed between his shoulder blades and gehinnom was open beneath his feet. Judges are constantly warned against corruption, showing favour to someone in court or judging unjustly. For a dayyan to take a bribe, even if he believes that it will not change his judgment, is forbidden since bribes cause psychological blindness, and the judge who takes them is eventually punished with physical loss of sight. Because of the need for a fair and unprejudiced trial, a dayyan should be joined by at least two other judges and not judge a case alone. Only God judges alone, and even He involves the ministering angels in his deliberations, as may be seen from the creation of Adam, when God said to the

Knights in battle during the **Crusades** (14c. Swiss).

Daniel in the den of lions (12c. Spanish).

Terracotta plaque of the young **David** playing the harp.

angels 'Let us make man' (Gen. 1:26). A blessing is recited by mourners before the burial of a relative which acknowledges that God is the true judge of men's lives. Appointing an unworthy judge is like planting an idolatrous tree in the midst of Israel, and if a community is beset by troubles then it is the judges who are most probably at fault. A judge who is a relation, a friend or an enemy of one of the litigants is not allowed to sit in judgment on their case. In biblical times priests and Levites were the judges of ritual and civil matters, but nowadays any suitably qualified Jew is able to act as a dayyan with the exception of proselytes and women (although *see* DEBORAH). Jews should not take their disputes before Gentile judges when a Jewish court is available, because this brings the divine laws of the torah into disrepute. *See also* CORPORAL PUNISHMENT; SEMIKHAH.

Dead Sea Scrolls Collection of ancient manuscripts which were discovered in 1947 by an Arab shepherd looking for a lost sheep. The bulk of the scrolls are thought to represent the library of the ESSENE community at Qumran which was situated close to the Dead Sea. They were hidden in nearby caves for safekeeping when the Qumran settlement was destroyed by the Romans in 70 CE, towards the end of the Jewish revolt against Roman rule in Palestine. The texts were preserved by the dry climate of the area, and some of them date back to the 2c. BCE. Many of the works found were previously unknown, being sectarian writings, although all the books of the Hebrew Bible (*see* TENAKH) except the Book of Esther are represented in whole or in part. There are manuals laying down a strict order of discipline for community members, who must adhere rigorously to the laws of ritual purity, and works of an apocalyptic nature about the End of Days. The scrolls depict the Qumran sect as a righteous community of people of light and those outside as wicked people of darkness who are to be hated and avoided.

deaf mutes (Hebrew 'cheresh') Deaf mutes were regarded in Jewish law as disadvantaged in a similar way to children and idiots. Babies are born as deaf mutes because their parents talked in a frivolous manner during the sexual relations which led to their conception. When the Israelites received the Decalogue at Mount Sinai, all deaf mutes among them were cured, and in the days of the Messiah the deaf will be able to hear once again (Isa. 29:18). Deaf mutes cannot be counted as part of the minyan quorum, be accepted as proselytes, deal in business or serve as witnesses in court. They are allowed to marry and divorce by Rabbinic, but not biblical, law on the basis of sign language, but a normal person who became a deaf mute after marriage would not be allowed to divorce his wife because his marriage has biblical validity. Those who are only mute but can hear, or only deaf but can speak, do not suffer from the same legal disabilities as the deaf mute. Today there have been moves among certain Orthodox rabbis to grant deaf mutes full status in Jewish life, regarding them as intelligent but handicapped. Many halakhic authorities, however, deny that the new techniques developed to educate deaf mutes can improve their status. It is

forbidden to curse the deaf (Lev. 19:14), and this is understood as prohibiting taking advantage of anyone who suffers from a disability.

death Death came into the world as a consequence of Adam's sin. The first human couple were expelled from the GARDEN OF EDEN to prevent them eating from the TREE OF LIFE and gaining immortality. Yet each individual dies only because of his own sins. Those who are especially holy, being free from the power of the ANGEL OF DEATH, die from the effect of the serpent's poison which contaminated Eve and her progeny. Death itself is viewed as part of the Creation, and God was referring to death when he declared that the world was 'very good' (Gen. 1:31). The righteous are still called 'alive' even after death, while the wicked are 'dead' even while still living. The easiest form of death is by a divine kiss, only as painful as removing a hair from milk, and this was the way a number of biblical characters died. At death all men have a vision of the divine presence (shekhinah). While the anniversary of someone's death is a sad occasion, the YAHRZEIT of a saintly person is celebrated by the Kabbalists as the day of their soul's wedding with God. The best known necrotic wedding day is that of the mystic SIMEON BAR YOCHAI on LAG BA-OMER. Since the dead are free from performing commandments, it is forbidden to perform any in their presence because this appears like a mockery of their condition (*see* CEMETERY). It is a meritorious act to wash a dead body (*see* CHEVRA KADDISHA), accompany it on its last journey and participate in the BURIAL. Indeed, the mitzvah of burying the dead when there are no relatives takes precedence over other duties. After touching a corpse, being in the same house with it, or visiting a cemetery the hands must be washed before returning to the world of the living. Though necromancy is forbidden, it is customary to visit the graves of parents and leave written requests beside the tombs of holy men, asking them to intercede with God. Stories are told of people who overheard the dead talking among themselves when they spent the night sleeping in cemeteries. *See also* CAPITAL PUNISHMENT; MARTYRDOM; MOURNING; ORIGINAL SIN; SUICIDE.

Deborah Prophetess who inspired a successful battle against the armies of the Canaanites circa 12c. BCE. Deborah sent for her husband, the Israelite leader Barak, and encouraged him to attack, but he would only agree to do so if she herself accompanied the troops. The Canaanites were defeated and their general, Sisera, was eventually slain by another woman, JAEL. After the victory Deborah sang a song of triumph (Judg. 4). Several Talmudic rabbis criticized Deborah's arrogance, expressed in her song and in the way she treated Barak. Although Deborah is described as a judge, there is some dispute as to whether a woman is allowed to serve in such a capacity. Those who maintain she actually was a judge explain that 'she sat under the palm-tree ... in the hill country ... and the Children of Israel came up to her for judgment' (Judg. 4:5) because, for reasons of modesty, she did not want to be alone in a house with the men who came to see her. The Kabbalists said of her 'Woe to the generation among whom there could not be found anyone to act as judge except a woman'.

Decalogue (Hebrew 'aseret ha-dibberot') There are two versions of the Decalogue, or Ten Commandments, given by God to the Israelites at Mount SINAI (Exod. 34 and Deut. 10). They differ in wording and in the explanations proffered, particularly with regard to the Sabbath. Both versions were communicated to MOSES at the same time, but the first version was written by the finger of God on the two TABLETS OF THE DECALOGUE which Moses broke when he found the people worshipping the Golden Calf, and the other version was on the second set of tablets written by Moses himself. In fact only the first two commandments, which are in the first person, were actually uttered by God to Israel; the rest were reported by Moses. The Jewish reckoning of the 'Ten Sayings', as the Decalogue is called, counts the opening statement 'I am the Lord your God' as the first of the ten and thus differs from the Christian reckoning of the Ten Commandments. The Decalogue was given in the desert to show it was meant for everyone and was proclaimed in the seventy languages of the world. Indeed, it was first offered to other nations, who refused to accept it when they heard it prohibited murder, adultery and robbery. The People of Israel, however, agreed to abide by its rules before knowing its contents, realizing they would come to appreciate it through use. The 620 letters of the Decalogue symbolize the 613 COMMANDMENTS plus the 7 NOACH-IDE LAWS. It is read in synagogue as the torah reading for the festival of SHAVUOT, which commemorates the revelation at Sinai. A special cantillation is used, and out of respect the congregation stand. The Decalogue does not appear in the liturgy to avoid the heretical belief that only the Ten Commandments were of divine origin and that the other parts of the torah did not come from God.

A scroll of the Book of Isaiah from the **Dead Sea Scrolls** found at Qumran.

demons were made on the Friday evening of creation, and God did not have time to give them bodies, as shabbat was approaching, so they remained disembodied spirits. They have no shadows or thumbs, fly through the air, know the future, and are mortal. Demons surround humans on all sides, rubbing against them to wear out their clothes and causing disease. If men could see them, they would be terrified. Their cock-like footprints may be traced by sprinkling special ash on the ground. Demons can be controlled by MAGIC power, by MEZUZOT and by AMULETS, and a number of rabbis claimed they could understand their speech. They haunt trees, ruins and toilets, and there was even a protective prayer to say before going into a lavatory. They attack those who sleep alone (see SHEMA), go out at night on their own (see DAY AND NIGHT), or do things in pairs (see also EVIL EYE). It was once considered dangerous to drink water at certain times because the menstrual blood of demonesses fell into it (see MINHAG). Modern halakhists maintain that human nature is now different and many of the dangers from demons do not apply any more. Some demons are fallen ANGELS. Others are personified like AGRAT BAT MAHALAT, a demon queen, ASMODEUS, a mischievous demon king, SAMAEL, the arch-demon who is identified with SATAN, and LILITH, who causes men to have nocturnal emissions in order to bear demon children. There is a custom, still found in Jerusalem, of driving away such children from the dead body of

Anthropomorphic image of Moses receiving the Tablets of the **Decalogue** from God at Mount Sinai (Moutier-Grandval Bible).

their father by circumambulating his corpse prior to burial and throwing coins in different directions to distract his demon children. One demon, Ketev Meriri, has a scaline body, a calf's head with a unicorn and is covered in hair with an eye on his breast. The mere sight of him is enough to kill someone (*see* THREE WEEKS OF MOURNING). On the Sabbath day demons have no power and return to their home in the 'hole of the great abyss' which is the area under the control of the SITRA ACHRA. The existence of demons was denied by Maimonides and other rationalist thinkers. *See also* DIBBUK; MOURNING; SHEVAT.

derush *see* PARDES

devarim *see* CHUMASH

devekut (Hebrew for 'cleaving') The biblical command to attach oneself to God was not interpreted literally by the Talmudic rabbis. For them it entailed following God's ways (*see* IMITATIO DEI) or associating oneself with the sages who are the living embodiment of God's teachings, since it is not possible actually to cleave to the divine consuming fire. The Kabbalists, however, understood devekut as an ecstatic state. The human soul is hewn out of the divine, and it finds its true home in God. Devekut therefore represents the highest spiritual state through which the mystic attains to eternal life while still alive by keeping God continually in his consciousness. This can be done at a more mundane level by visualizing the TETRAGRAMMATON, even while engaged in secular occupations or while having a conversation with other people. In the more ecstatic experiences of devekut, the body is in a trance-like state while the soul, by cleaving to God in thought, is able to bring the divine power down into this world and, afterwards, to work MIRACLES. In the CHASIDIC MOVEMENT devekut became a central concept, more important even than torah study, and involved the annihilation of the individual ego of the tzaddik. For the ordinary Chasidic Jew, faith itself involved devekut and a continuing sense of the presence of God, the 'sweet father' (*see also* LUBAVITCH). He was forbidden to turn God into a stranger, since a Jew may not worship strange gods. *See also* SHEKHINAH.

dew (Hebrew 'tal') Dew is considered so important for plant life that its absence constitutes a drought. The prayer for dew is introduced into the liturgy on the first day of pesach, at the onset of spring. The chazzan dresses himself in the white, shroud-like KITEL worn on yom kippur to indicate that the presence of dew for farmers is as much a matter of life and death as the forgiveness of sins. In the Middle Ages Jewish savants believed that dew rose up in the air towards the sun. Thus Rashi, in his Bible commentary (Exod. 16:14), writes that if someone were to fill an eggshell with dew, stop up the aperture and place it in the sun, the eggshell would rise upwards. The manna which appeared in the wilderness was covered with layers of white dew both above and below. This is the source of the custom of placing the shabbat loaves (challah), which symbolize the manna, on a white tablecloth and covering them with a white cover. When the torah was given on Mount Sinai, the Israelites died from fright when they heard God speak to them and

were revived with the dew of life. This same dew will be used in the age of the Messiah to bring about the RESURRECTION OF THE DEAD. *See also* ZION.

dhimma Protected status which Jews had in Islamic society, being classified as 'People of the Book'. This status entailed the payment of a special tax and the prohibition on missionarizing among Moslems. Jews had to wear distinctive DRESS and were granted limited rights as second-class citizens, which entailed some discrimination against employing them in government service. The killing of a Jew involved a smaller payment of blood money than the killing of a Moslem. Although their protected status enabled Jews to flourish in the Moslem world, their position was not always secure and they were sometimes forcibly converted to Islam, particularly under Shiite rule. According to a Moslem tradition, Mohammed himself will appear on Judgment Day to accuse those who harm Jews or Christians.

diaspora (Greek for 'dispersion') Term used to refer to Jewish communities outside the land of Israel. The diaspora originated towards the end of the Second Temple period when major Jewish centres sprang up in Babylonia, Alexandria, Rome and throughout the Graeco-Roman world. Life outside the Palestinian homeland was accompanied by a consciousness of EXILE and an institutionalized hope for the coming of the Messiah who would return them to their land (*see* INGATHERING OF THE EXILES). Yet Jews settled voluntarily in many areas of the dispersion and identified with their host cultures. The main forms of post-biblical Judaism after the end of the 2c. CE were shaped in the diaspora. Jewish religion adopted features from different countries and by the late Middle Ages had grown into a series of distinctive Judaisms, the major components of which were subgroups of the ASHKENAZIM and SEPHARDIM. Common to all forms of diaspora Judaism was a portable religion able to adjust to different environments and to survive the expulsions and persecutions of an often hostile Christian and Moslem majority. Jews took on the racial characteristics of the many peoples among whom they dwelt, through ASSIMILATION and the accumulation of proselytes, and adopted languages like LADINO (Judaeo-Spanish) and YIDDISH (Judaeo-German) as Jewish vernaculars. *See also* EXILARCH; SYNAGOGUE.

dibbuk (Hebrew for 'one that cleaves') A malignant spirit which attaches itself to the living and takes over their personality. A dibbuk is a 'naked soul' which is not at rest or subject to TRANSMIGRATION and must find an already occupied body left vulnerable by sin. The dibbuk speaks through a person's mouth with a new voice, and a change of personality takes place. It can be driven out through EXORCISM and leaves via the little toe, but it must first identify itself and rectification (*see* TIKKUN) must be made so that it finds rest, or else it will attach itself again. Sometimes the dibbuk is not a human soul but a demon which attaches itself to a woman who may turn into a witch. One of the first references to a dibbuk is a 17c. story about a man who had committed adultery and drowned at sea. He left behind a wife who could not remarry and eventually became a whore. The man

was first swallowed by a fish and then inhabited the
body of a cow. A Jew who bought the cow found its
behaviour erratic, so he slaughtered it in the presence
of a young man. The dibbuk took possession of this
young man until it was exorcised by local rabbis.
Before it departed, it informed two of the men
present that, from their foreheads, it knew they
were homosexuals. Chaim Vital told of a man who
committed adultery, giving birth to illegitimate children (mamzer). When he died, his soul wandered
around for twenty-five years. Eventually, it took
possession of a woman when she was angry, entering
her house through a door which had no mezuzah.
Another dibbuk was the soul of a pauper who died
after being refused food by a charity official. It attached
itself to the official, and Isaac Luria only managed to
expel the dibbuk on the condition that the official did
not look at a woman for three days. When his mother
arrived, however, he looked at her, and the dibbuk
returned to strangle him.

dietary laws (Hebrew 'kashrut') ANIMALS are KOSHER
if they have cloven hoofs and chew the cud, a limited
number of BIRDS are kosher (though not birds of
prey), and kosher FISH must have fins and scales. Some
species of LOCUSTS are kosher, but they are only eaten
where there is an established tradition of locust eating.
Blemished kosher animals are TEREFAH and cannot be
eaten. Animals and birds must be specially slaughtered
(*see* SHECHITAH) and the BLOOD removed using salt.
Certain animal fats and the sciatic nerve are not eaten,
the latter reminding Jews of the injury inflicted on
JACOB when he wrestled with an angel (Gen. 32). Meat
and milk must neither be cooked nor eaten together
(*see* PARVE), and after eating meat there is an interval
of several hours before CHEESE or milk are eaten. Milk
is kosher if it comes from a kosher animal, and many
Orthodox Jews only use milk which is produced under
supervision, so that there is no doubt about its origin.
A kosher EGG must come from a kosher bird and not
contain any bloodspots. HONEY is kosher, even though
the bee cannot be eaten, because it is not considered
an actual part of the bee's body. Vegetables which
might contain flies or worms have to be washed before
being eaten. Certain types of food, even though
kosher, must not be eaten if cooked by a Gentile,
under the rules of bishul nochri, and WINE produced
or handled by a Gentile must not be drunk. God
allows Gentiles to eat non-kosher foods, just as a
doctor prescribes a strict diet to a patient who has
some chance of recovery, while allowing another
patient who has no hope of regaining his health to eat
what he likes. Eating non-kosher food stops up a man's
heart and affects his attitudes, so that he becomes
attached to the evil of the SITRA ACHRA. The dietary
laws themselves have been explained as veiled health
measures, as means of testing Israel's obedience to God,
or as generating holiness and moral perfection. In the
age of the Messiah all animals will be kosher, and the
Behemoth and the Leviathan will be eaten at the
Messianic banquet. For reptiles, *see* PILPUL.

Dinah *see* JACOB; LEAH

disputations Compulsory religious debates conducted
in the Middle Ages between Jews and Christians with

The **diaspora** resulted in Jewish communities the
world over, like the Jewish ghetto in New York,
seen here in 1903.

Christians engaged in a **disputation** with Jews
(13c. Spanish).

the purpose of convincing the former that the religion of the latter was superior to their own. Jews were forced to attend these disputations, and Jewish scholars had to defend their religion in the presence of kings, lords and bishops. During the disputations Christians tried to show that Talmudic texts 'proved' that Jesus was the awaited Messiah and that Jewish teaching should be banned as anti-Christian. The Jewish participants were invariably considered to have lost the argument, and this often led to anti-Jewish measures such as the burning of the *Talmud* as blasphemous. The disputations were inspired by Dominican monks who used apostate Jews to debate on the Christian side, since they usually had a working knowledge of the *Talmud*. The first disputation took place in Paris in 1240, and the leading rabbis who participated were offered protection so that they could say what they liked. Subsequently, a large number of *Talmud* manuscripts were burnt. The second Disputation was at Barcelona in 1263. After it ended, Moses NACHMAN- IDES, the main Jewish participant, was forced to leave Spain because he had put up too successful a defence of Judaism. Jews were still being forced to engage in disputations as late as the 18c. when the Church pitted them against the followers of Jacob FRANK, a Jewish heretic who had sought the protection of the Polish Catholic authorities.

divorce (Hebrew 'gerushin') There was disagreement in the early Rabbinic period about the exact grounds on which divorce is allowed in the Bible (Deut. 24). The conservative School of Shammai forbade it except in cases of sexual misbehaviour by the wife (*see* ADULTERY), when the husband must divorce her. The School of Hillel allowed it if she behaved in an unseemly way, e.g. by spoiling her husband's food, and the later halakhah followed Akiva's view that a man can even divorce his wife if he finds another woman he prefers. Childlessness is also grounds for divorce (*see* CHILDREN). The initiative is taken by the husband who gives his wife a divorce document known as a GET. Such a document can be given even if the wife disagrees, though Ashkenazim have been prevented from divorcing women against their will since the cherem ascribed to Rabbenu Gershom in the 11c. After divorce, the maintenance laid down in the marriage contract (*see* KETUBBAH) is paid by the husband. The bet din which arranges the divorce must try to reconcile the couple before proceedings take place and should encourage the husband and wife to remarry after they are divorced. Such remarriage is not possible if the husband is a priest, who cannot marry a divorcee, so the get issued for him is a more complicated document. This allows time for a priest-husband to reflect on his decision. A woman can petition a court to order her husband to divorce her if he suffers from some physical defect which makes conjugal life impossible or his conduct has been atrocious. Although the husband must divorce his wife of his own free will, the bet din was able in the past to flog him (*see* CORPORAL PUNISHMENT) till he agreed. Since divorce is a tragedy for all concerned, the Temple altar sheds tears for each divorced couple. A divorced man is discouraged from marrying a divorcee while their spouses are still alive, because there are then four minds in the same marriage bed. The divorce

procedures of Reform Judaism are not recognized by Orthodox Judaism (*see* MAMZER). *See also* AGUNAH.

Doenmeh (Turkish for 'convert') Sect of Jewish converts to Islam, living until 1924 mainly in Salonika, who maintained Jewish practices and did not intermarry with Moslems. The Doenmeh originated when SHABBETAI TZEVI converted to Islam in 1666 and some of his supporters followed his example. They adopted Turkish names but kept secret Jewish names for their private use. Eventually they forgot Hebrew, and even the LADINO they spoke among themselves was replaced by Turkish. Many Doenmeh were integrated into Turkish society, and at one time all the barbers in Salonika were Doenmeh. Though these converts were suspected by Turkish Moslems, it is said that a number of the 'Young Turk' modernists, including Kemal Ataturk, were of Doenmeh descent. The sect retained the mystical Messianic beliefs associated with Shabbetai Tzevi and valued the *Zohar* above all other Jewish works. The three subgroups of the Doenmeh had little contact with each other, since they believed that Shabbetai Tzevi was a divine incarnation who after his death had been reincarnated in the human form of their own leader. The women of one subgroup used to go down to the sea-shore every shabbat to await the return of their leader, Jacob Querido, though he is known to have died on the way back from a pilgrimage to Mecca. These crypto-Jews were suspected by their Jewish co-religionists of incest and engaging in antinomian practices since they believed that they lived under a new Messianic torah. During the ceremony of 'extinguishing the lights' on 22 Adar, it would seem that adulterous sexual relations took place in a wife-swapping ritual. Since any child born from an incestuous marriage or from such orgiastic encounters would be a mamzer, the Turkish rabbis refused to accept Doenmeh back into Judaism.

Dov Baer of Mezhirech (1710–72) Leader of the CHASIDIC MOVEMENT from 1760 after the death of its founder, the Besht (*see* BAAL SHEM TOV). Dov Baer, known as the Maggid ('Preacher') of Mezhirech, first came to the Besht seeking a cure for his poor health, and the Besht tried to convince him of the futility of the extreme asceticism he practised by telling him stories and parables. These made little impression on Dov Baer, who was used to more scholastic instruction, so the Besht asked him to study a Kabbalistic text with him. Listening to Dov Baer's explanation of the passage they were studying, the Besht told him that he really knew nothing at all. He then explained the same passage in exactly the same way to Dov Baer, but while the Besht was doing so, the room was filled with the light of the angels who were conjured up by the holy words. 'Your learning has no soul', he said to Dov Baer. Once Dov Baer became a devoted follower, the Besht taught him Kabbalistic secrets and the language of birds and trees. After his master's death, Dov Baer gave the nascent movement a new direction since he was less a man of the people and more of a recluse than the Besht. He gathered a group of talented disciples around him who were sent out to spread the Chasidic teaching far and wide in Poland and the Ukraine. Many new members of the movement flocked to Dov Baer, and it is reported that he would ask each of his visitors to mention a scriptural verse, which he would then blend together into a sermon. Each participant thought the main thrust of the sermon related to his own verse and that his own situation had been addressed. The early opposition to the Chasidic Movement was directed primarily against Dov Baer. He was accused of teaching pantheism and antinomianism, of neglecting torah study and of introducing new rituals. A ban was pronounced against him and his followers. When Dov Baer died, the Chasidic Movement split up into many subgroups, most of which were led by his pupils, such as Levi Isaac of Berdichev and Shneur Zalman of Lyady.

dove (Hebrew 'yonah') The dove has become a general symbol of peace and innocence, based on the story of Noah who sent a dove out of the ark to see if the world after the FLOOD had reverted to its previous tranquillity. When the dove returned with an olive branch from the Mount of Olives in its beak, Noah knew that the world was once again inhabitable. For Jews the dove symbolizes the People of Israel since it is the most persecuted of birds, as Israel is persecuted by the nations of the world. It is renowned for its faithfulness to its mate, just as Israel retains its faithfulness to God. Indeed, it is said that if the torah had not been given, people could have learned sexual morality from the dove. A dove can also only defend itself with its wings, either through flight or by flapping them in a fight, as Israel can only defend itself through the commandments. The story is told in the *Talmud* of one pious man, Elisha Baal Kenafayim ('Elisha of the Wings'), who used to wear tefillin even at times of antireligious persecution. On one occasion while holding his tefillin in his hand, he was challenged by some Roman soldiers and told them that all he was holding were the wings of a dove. When they forced him to open his hand, that was all they found. He later explained that he mentioned dove's wings because Israel was often depicted as a dove. The dove is also used as an image of the Divine Presence or shekhinah, and young doves and turtle-doves were the only birds offered up as sacrifices in the Temple ritual. *See also* SAMARITANS.

dreams In the Bible dreams foretell the future and bring warnings or messages from God to man. Certain biblical individuals had the gift of interpreting dreams, as is apparent from the stories of JOSEPH and DANIEL. Maimonides even regarded some of the strange incidents in the Bible, such as the talking ass of Balaam (Num. 22), as having taken place in a dream. In the Rabbinic period dreams were considered as a minor form of PROPHECY, but fatalism was discouraged since impending calamities could be averted through prayer and repentance. After an evil dream, for instance, the dreamer is allowed to fast, even on the Sabbath, so that the dream may be nullified. A person's dreams show his inner state, and their significance always follows the interpretation given to them. Therefore, if someone has had a bad dream, it can be invalidated by saying 'I have had a good dream' in front of three people or by fasting (*see* FAST DAYS). It was considered a bad sign for someone to go for seven days without dreaming or to see certain things in a dream, e.g.

Turtle **Dove** by Ben Shahn.

The **Dream** *of Jacob* by Marc Chagall (stained glass, Metz Cathedral).

being given a present by a dead person in a dream or seeing TEKHELET was an omen of bad luck. Evil from the sitra achra can affect even the dreams of the righteous (see DEMONS), and all dreams have extraneous features which are not true or part of the dream message. Kabbalists would make heavenly ascents in dreams, and some mystics addressed inquiries to God to which replies were given in dreams, the subject matter ranging from technicalities of the halakhah to questions about when the Messiah would come. The best-known example of dream responsa were those of JACOB OF MARGEVE, some of which were collected and published.

dreidl see CHANUKKAH; GAMBLING

dress A person's clothes represent his status and honour. Thus a sage (chakham) should not go out with any stain on his clothing, and scholars should wear dark clothes, becoming to their position in the community. The *Talmud* comments that demons are also known to dress up in rabbinic garments. Distinctive Jewish dress goes back to biblical times. The Israelites maintained their identity in slavery by not changing their own dress for that of the Egyptians, and Pharaoh's daughter recognized the baby Moses as a Hebrew by his clothes. A priest wore a special uniform while performing the sacrificial ritual, and the High Priest wore a mitre, a breastplate (see URIM AND THUMMIM) and an apron. Prophets and Nazirites wore simple cloaks of animal hair. In the Middle Ages Jews were made to wear a distinctive BADGE on their outer garments, or a somewhat comical hat, in Christian and Moslem countries. Today, traditional Jewish dress prohibits the wearing of clothes made from a mixture of wool and linen, SHAATNEZ. Men wear a fringed outer shawl, TALLIT, with phylacteries, TEFILLIN, for morning prayers, a white shroud-like KITEL on certain festivals, a fringed undervest, TZITZIT, and a HEAD-COVERING. Orthodox married women cover their heads with hats, scarves or wigs (see SHEITEL). Members of the Chasidic Movement have preserved the dress of the shtetl, originally worn by both Jews and Gentiles, to distinguish themselves from the modern world. Their shabbat attire consists of a fur SHTREIMEL hat, a long black caftan, known as a bekeshe or a kapote, and white socks. They do not wear a tie, which represents an unnecessary division between the brain and the heart, but they do wear a gartel belt for prayers to separate the heart from the genitals. In some synagogues lay leaders wear top hats on Sabbaths and festivals, while the rabbi and chazzan wear caps and gowns which have been criticized by the Ultra-Orthodox as an imitation of the practices of the Church (see CHUKKAT HA-GOI).

Dreyfus Affair Anti-Semitic campaign against Captain Alfred Dreyfus (1859–1935), a French army officer, who was accused of spying for Germany and found guilty in 1894 on the basis of forged evidence. Dreyfus was publicly disgraced and sentenced to imprisonment on Devil's Island. The French government and reactionary army leaders, who had considerable mass support among anti-Semitic elements in the French populace, refused to consider new evidence clearing Dreyfus. Even some of those who suspected there had been a miscarriage of justice believed the honour of the army had to be maintained and that this was more important than the innocence of a single soldier, who was not really a Frenchman at all but a Jew. There was, however, considerable support for Dreyfus, and the novelist Emile Zola wrote an open letter, entitled 'J'accuse', to the President of the French Republic, in which he strongly defended the former's innocence. This led to a second trial in 1899, at which Dreyfus was found guilty only of the lesser charge of treason, and he was eventually exonerated in 1906. The whole Dreyfus Affair had a marked effect on Jews who realized the extent of anti-Semitic feeling (see ANTI-SEMITISM) even against as assimilated a Jew as Dreyfus. Theodor HERZL, who covered the trial as a journalist, was convinced by the Dreyfus Affair of the need for a national home for Jews and this led to his involvement in political ZIONISM.

drunkenness Noah was the first to discover the intoxicating effects of strong drink (Gen. 9), with disastrous consequences. There are a number of biblical warnings against ALCOHOL, despite the fact that it 'rejoices the heart of man' (Ps. 104:15). NAZIRITES must refrain from WINE, and a drunken priest is punished if he participates in the ritual (Lev. 10). This happened to the two sons of Aaron who were killed for officiating while intoxicated. From the example of HANNAH, who was wrongly suspected of being drunk in the Tabernacle (I Sam. 1), the lesson is learnt that one should be sober when praying. This requirement was ignored by members of the CHASIDIC MOVEMENT who used alcohol as a means of stimulating the service of God in joy. Drink is said to turn a person into an animal. First he becomes as mild as a sheep, then as aggressive as a lion, then like a pig, and in the final stage of drunkenness he is like a monkey. Despite this, a drunk is still considered responsible for his actions unless he is as intoxicated as Lot, who was seduced by his daughters (Gen. 19). The only time a Jew is encouraged to drink to excess is on the festival of purim when he is supposed to lose his ability to distinguish between heroes and villains, since God turns human power and arrogance to His own advantage (see ADE-LO-YADA). Although Jewish ritual involves the frequent use of alcoholic beverages, Jews regard themselves as a sober people and regard Gentiles as given to inebriation: there are a number of Yiddish songs which deal with the goi who is shikor ('drunk') because that is how he is. The Rabbis said that, of the ten portions of drunkenness which came into the world, nine portions were taken by the people of Africa and one portion by the rest of the world.

Dubno Maggid see KRANZ, JACOB

Dura Europos Archaeological site in Syria with a well preserved synagogue from the 3c. CE which was discovered in 1932. The synagogue building had been filled with sand as part of the defences of the city, and it was thus preserved with many of its extensive frescoes intact. They show that synagogue ART in an outlying Jewish settlement freely used human forms in depicting biblical and other scenes, and even included pagan motifs for decorative purposes. The artistic freedom extended to representing the hand of God reviving the dead in scenes from the story of Ezekiel, something that would have been unthinkable to later and more centrally located Jewish artists.

Eber *see* JACOB; MORIAH, MOUNT

Ecclesiastes (Hebrew 'kohelet', meaning 'a congregational leader') Biblical book containing the wisdom of Solomon, which he wrote down in his old age disillusioned with the indulgent style of royal life. There was some disagreement in the 2c. CE as to whether Ecclesiastes was an inspired work or merely the expression of worldly wisdom. There was also some disquiet at the internal contradictions of the book and the fact that it did not always advocate a position which accorded with normative Jewish religion. Despite these doubts, the book came to be accepted as part of the biblical canon, and every verse of the book was regarded by the mystics as containing secrets of heavenly wisdom. Ecclesiastes contains reflections and aphorisms on the vanity of life, and it expresses considerable criticism of conventional values. It is one of the five scrolls (*see* MEGILLAH) and is read in the synagogue on shemini atzeret or sukkot, at the happiest time of the Jewish year, to remind the congregation that ordinary life is a 'vanity of vanities'.

Ecclesiasticus *see* BEN SIRA

education (Hebrew 'chinukh') Parents are commanded in the shema (Deut. 6:7, 11:19) to teach God's words to their children. This command was understood to refer only to male children. To teach a girl torah was like teaching her to behave immorally, because she might use her knowledge for lewd purposes. In biblical times the priest and the Levite were the educators of the adult population, Moses himself being a Levite, and there were also schools of prophets where the traditions of prophecy were passed on. The rabbi in post-biblical Judaism was essentially a teacher of the ORAL TORAH, and from the 1c. CE a formal education system was introduced for children, transferring the responsibility from parents to a professional teaching class. Many ordinary Jews maintained a high standard of Hebrew literacy. Jewish boys would start CHEDER sometime after their third birthday and graduate to a YESHIVAH after their bar mitzvah. Adults would hear the torah reading on Mondays and Thursdays, and on shabbat and festivals. These readings would be accompanied by public translation-commentaries (targum) in ancient times, and there were special study months for Babylonian Jewish farmers, during those periods when they were not engaged in agricultural work. The synagogue itself was used as a house of study (*see* BET HA-MIDRASH) in the evenings and at weekends. To be known as an AM HA-ARETZ, or ignoramus, was the supreme insult. In modern times Jewish communities have devoted much of their resources to education, and even the restrictions on educating women have been removed, although there is still opposition to them studying *Talmud*. In the womb an angel teaches the embryo the whole torah

A 19c. Polish shtetl scene of two Jews in Chasidic **dress**.

The **Drunkenness** *of Lot* by Lucas Cranach the Elder.

Education of a group of pupils by a rabbi. Notice that the teacher is seated and the pupils are standing (14c. Spanish manuscript).

and then touches the child's lip before BIRTH so it forgets. Religious instruction is thus a form of spiritual recall. In the age of the Messiah, the whole world will be full of the knowledge of God (Isa. 11:9).

egel ha-zahav *see* GOLDEN CALF

egg (Hebrew 'betzah') Eggs are kosher if they come from permitted BIRDS and they can be distinguished from non-kosher eggs because they are pointed at one end and the yolk is surrounded by the albumen. If blood is found inside an egg it cannot be eaten, but there are no restrictions in the Jewish DIETARY LAWS on eating fully formed eggs with either meat or milk. The egg plays a prominent role in Jewish ritual where 'the size of an egg' is one of the standard measures of Jewish law. Eggs are a symbol of mourning, being round like a wheel and thus representing the cycle of birth and death. Mourners include hard-boiled eggs in the meal they eat on returning home from a funeral, and an egg dipped in ashes is the last thing eaten just before the fast on the Ninth of Av. On pesach an egg dipped in salt-water is eaten at the start of the seder, reminding the participants of the tears and suffering of the Israelites in Egypt, and a burnt egg on the seder plate represents the festive offering. Anyone who eats this egg the next day will have their wishes fulfilled. Finding a double yolk in an egg is an omen of good luck and guarantees fertility to a barren woman. Before taking eggs from a nest the mother bird must be shooed away (Deut. 22:6), and the reward for doing so is 'length of days'. Since there were cases of young people who went to the trouble of sending away the mother bird but died soon after, this was understood as referring to life in olam haba rather than to mortal existence. Indeed, stories are told of how people were led into heresy by taking 'length of days' literally.

eikhah *see* LAMENTATIONS, BOOK OF

Eldad Ha-Dani (9c.) Mysterious figure who claimed to come from an independent Jewish state in Africa where some of the TEN LOST TRIBES were situated. Eldad had many adventures en route to Jewish communites in Babylonia, North Africa and Spain, escaping from a tribe of African cannibals who ate his companions but did not bother about him because he was too weak and thin. He was taken to China as a prisoner where he was eventually ransomed, passing through areas where other members of the Lost Tribes lived and governed themselves. His own tribe of Dan lived in Ethiopia, and their neighbours were the tribe of LEVI, who lived on the other side of the river SAMBATYON. The Levites lived in peace in a land with no thieves where they did not need to lock their doors. The river, which surrounded their land, flowed with a wild mass of rocks and sand for six days each week, only resting on shabbat when it was surrounded by fire and cloud. Since Jews could not cross it without desecrating the Sabbath, communication between the tribes took place by people standing on opposing river banks and shouting or sending letters by pigeon-post across the Sambatyon. The African Jewish tribes had their own *Talmud*, written in Hebrew, in which each teaching began with the words: 'Thus we have learnt from Joshua, who in turn learnt it from Moses.' Eldad

quotes some halakhic rules from this *Talmud* which differ from the normative Jewish teaching of the communities he visited.

Elders of Zion, Protocols of the Anti-Semitic document purporting to show the details of the international Jewish conspiracy to take over the world, based on the medieval Christian image of the Jew as follower of the Devil. The forgery first appeared towards the end of the 19c., having been produced by the Czarist secret police on the basis of a French work about Napoleon III's desire for world domination, to foment anti-Jewish feeling. In the 20c. there were still people who believed the *Protocols* were genuine, and the document has been used by anti-Semitic propagandists (*see* ANTI-SEMITISM) in Nazi Germany and in the Arab world.

Eli High Priest of the Shiloh sanctuary who adopted the young SAMUEL after his mother, HANNAH, dedicated his life to God (I Sam. 1). Eli's own sons were corrupt priests who were able to ignore their father's censure because his eyesight was failing. They died when the Ark of the Covenant, which they had carried into battle, was captured by the Philistines. When Eli heard the news of the capture of the Ark and the death of his sons, he fell off his chair and broke his neck (I Sam. 4:18). He was ninety-eight years old when he died, and with his death the Shiloh sanctuary also came to an end. All of Eli's descendants were cursed with a short lifespan (I Sam. 2:31), but they could overcome this curse by the study of torah and acts of compassion.

Eliezer Ben Hyrcanus (1c.–2c. CE) Mishnaic sage and pupil of JOCHANAN BEN ZAKKAI, who said of him that he was equal to all the sages of Israel put together. Eliezer was often in disagreement with the more liberal opinions of his colleagues and favoured the stricter views of the school of Shammai, with its literal interpretation of scripture. For instance he is said to have understood the biblical 'eye for an eye' passage literally rather than in terms of monetary compensation. He had some association with the early Jewish Christians and indeed was once arrested by the Romans on suspicion of being a Christian. He realized this was a punishment for having accepted a halakhic ruling of JESUS from one of the latter's disciples. On one occasion Eliezer was in dispute with the other sages and was unable to convince them of his point of view. He asked for a nearby tree to aid him, and the tree uprooted itself to a new place, but the rabbis said that trees prove nothing. He asked for a local stream to aid him, and the stream flowed uphill, but the rabbis said streams prove nothing. He then called on the walls of the academy to prove his words correct, and the walls started falling inwards. Whereupon a colleague rebuked the walls for interfering, and they stopped falling. Then Eliezer asked for heaven to give his views support, and a heavenly voice (*see* BAT KOL) was heard which declared: 'The halakhah is in agreement with Rabbi Eliezer's views in all places.' Nevertheless, Eliezer was outvoted by MAJORITY OPINION and excommunicated (cherem) because he would not accept his colleagues' decision. After his death his views gained greater acceptance, and some came to be cited as the standard halakhah. It is said that in heaven God Himself quotes the teachings of Rabbi Eliezer.

Elijah Prophet of the Northern Kingdom of Israel in the 9c. BCE who protested about the idolatry of king Ahab and his foreign wife JEZEBEL (I Kings 17–22). Elijah is often identified with the High Priest PHINEHAS, a zealot like himself, who lived centuries before during the Exodus. Elijah did not die, but after appointing his successor, ELISHA, he ascended alive into heaven in a whirlwind with a chariot and horses of fire (II Kings 2:11). In heaven his task is to record the deeds of men and to guide the souls of the dead to Paradise. He often returns to earth, in many different guises (*see* SANDALFON), as God's messenger, sometimes as an agent of RAZIEL, helping people in time of need. A number of Talmudic rabbis and medieval mystics claimed to have met him and to have received mystical secrets from him. Once he was asked by a rabbi who among the crowd on a street had a portion in the AFTERLIFE, and he indicated a jailor and two professional jesters. Elijah explained that the jailor maintained morality among the criminals in his charge, while the jesters helped people by the laughter they aroused. Elijah attends every CIRCUMCISION ceremony, a special chair being set aside for him (*see* ELIJAH, CHAIR OF), and comes to each Jewish household to drink a cup of wine (*see* ELIJAH, CUP OF) at the seder. Elijah will return once more before the great and terrible DAY OF JUDGMENT (Mal. 3:23) to announce the coming of the MESSIAH. His task is to bring peace among men, lead them in repentance back to God and solve those problems in Rabbinic literature which have been left without a conclusion. He will blow the great SHOFAR and inaugurate the INGATHERING OF THE EXILES and the RESURRECTION. Since Elijah will not come on shabbat, at the end of the Sabbath songs are sung expressing the hope that Elijah will come quickly in the week ahead, heralding the Messianic age. Some rabbis believed that Elijah was an angel who temporarily took on human form to come down to earth. He thus has two bodies, one for his existence in heaven and one in which he appears to people on earth. *See also* MINCHAH; ZOHAR.

Elijah, the Baal Shem of Chelm *see* BAAL SHEM; GOLEM

Elijah, chair of (Hebrew 'kissei shel eliyyahu') Empty chair used in the rite of CIRCUMCISION which is thought to be occupied by the prophet ELIJAH. Elijah complained to God that the Israelites neglected the COVENANT of circumcision, and God therefore sends him from heaven to attend each circumcision ceremony, both as a reward for his zealousness and also to show him that he was wrong to condemn everyone. In the circumcision liturgy Elijah is referred to as the 'Angel of the Covenant' who is asked to stand at the right hand of the circumcisor (mohel) and support him. The baby is placed momentarily on the chair, and thus placed on the lap of Elijah, before circumcision takes place. Elaborately carved chairs of Elijah were often kept in synagogues to be used at circumcisions.

Elijah, cup of (Hebrew 'kos eliyyahu') At the Passover SEDER a special cup of wine is poured out for the

Elijah's Vision by Marc Chagall.

The chair of **Elijah**, used in the circumcision ceremony, from the Bevis Marks Synagogue, London.

prophet ELIJAH, the door of the house is opened and he is invited in. While the door remains open, the family ask God to punish those nations who do not recognize Him and who persecute the Jewish People. It is believed that Elijah visits every Jewish home on this night and offers his protection to the household. As the children look towards the door one of the adults spills a little wine from the cup to convince them Elijah has indeed called and drunk his wine, although he cannot be seen. The origin of Elijah's cup goes back to a dispute of the Rabbis as to whether, after the FOUR CUPS of wine, a fifth cup, representing God's future redemption, should be drunk at the seder. It is believed that Elijah will resolve all undecided disputes in future times, and therefore his name was given to this fifth cup. Since it is left standing on the table and nobody drinks it, it was assumed that Elijah would come to drink it. As Elijah is the forerunner of the Messiah, and the cup represents the Messianic redemption, it was also appropriate to regard the cup as one Elijah will drink at the onset of the Messianic age, which will begin at pesach time.

Elijah the Vilna Gaon (1720–97) Leader of the MITNAGGEDIM who were opposed to the CHASIDIC MOVEMENT. Elijah was a child prodigy who soon outgrew his teachers, knowing whole sections of the *Talmud* by heart. While still young, he mastered all branches of Rabbinic literature, including works largely ignored in the yeshivah curriculum and also became proficient in Kabbalah. He regarded some secular studies as necessary for a correct understanding of Jewish sources, but he bitterly opposed the study of philosophy which led people to deny the power of spells and charms. He studied by candlelight with the blinds of his room drawn, even by day, so as not to be distracted and slept only two hours a night in four half-hour shifts, keeping his feet in a bowl of cold water so that he would not drop off to sleep during the rest of the night. Even before his bar mitzvah he attempted to create a GOLEM but desisted when he received a sign from heaven. On another occasion he was offered an angelic guide (*see* MAGGID) to help him with his studies but refused as he did not want to know anything which he had not learnt by his own efforts. Although he never accepted any appointment as an official rabbi, claiming that he could not fulfil such office since he did not agree with so many of his predecessors, Elijah was the acknowledged spiritual leader of Lithuanian Jewry. Jacob Kranz served as his chaplain. He encouraged his main disciple CHAIM OF VOLOZHIN to start a new type of yeshivah where the whole of the Babylonian *Talmud* would be studied without any of the obscure dialectics (pilpul) of which he disapproved. He signed an order of excommunication (cherem) against the Chasidim in 1772, and again in 1781, declaring them heretics and forbidding marriage with them. He also supported the public burning of Chasidic books. When Shneur Zalman of Lyady came to see him to persuade him of the movement's respectability, he refused to see him. He knew the identity of a LAMED VAVNIK called Leib, whom he asked to accompany him to the Holy Land.

Elisha Israelite prophet of the 8c. BCE and disciple of ELIJAH, he was active for more than sixty years. He gained a double portion of his master's spirit as a reward for his loyalty and for staying with Elijah until he ascended into heaven in a whirlwind (II Kings 2). He was thus able to perform twice as many miracles as his master (*see* RUACH HA-KODESH). Elisha lived an especially holy life, and no flies were ever found at his table because of the fragrance which surrounded him. In some texts he is ranked second only to Moses as a prophet. Yet he was not without his weaknesses and was punished by ill health because on one occasion he caused some bears to attack a group of children who were mocking him (II Kings 2). He was also punished in a similar fashion because he was very severe with his servant Gehazi, who took money from the Syrian general NAAMAN after Elisha cured him (II Kings 5). When Elisha died, his miraculous power continued, and a dead man was revived when his corpse came into contact with Elisha's body. The prophet JONAH was one of Elisha's disciples.

Elisha Ben Avuyah (2c. CE) Mishnaic sage who became a heretic, thus earning himself the nickname 'acher' ('another') because of his change of belief. Elisha was one of the four rabbis who went on a mystical trip to PARADISE and emerged from this experience with dualistic beliefs of a Gnostic character. He is described as having 'destroyed the plants' of Paradise because he saw the angel Metatron in heaven and regarded him as a second deity. After his apostasy he denied that there was any reward for keeping the commandments, indulged in prohibited sexual acts and publicly desecrated the shabbat. His former colleagues shunned him, and only his pupil MEIR continued to study with him, justifying this by saying that he threw away the heretical skin of the pomegranate of Elisha's teaching and only swallowed the fruit. Meir claimed that his teacher repented before his death, and when he found Elisha's grave smouldering with fire from heaven, he threw his cloak over it to smother the flames saying: 'I will save you, even if God will not.' Through Meir's influence many of Elisha's sayings are recorded in Rabbinic literature.

Elul Sixth lunar month of the Hebrew calendar, counting from Nisan, the month of the Exodus, or the last month before the beginning of the New Year festival (rosh ha-shanah). Elul usually begins in late August, and its zodiacal sign is the virgin. Since Elul precedes the period of REPENTANCE associated with the new year, it is a time for soul-searching and spiritual preparation. Pietists of the Musar Movement in Eastern Europe used to isolate themselves from human company during the whole month of Elul, sometimes taking a vow of silence, and would engage in self-scrutiny. Some communities have the custom of blowing the SHOFAR every morning during Elul after prayers to awaken the worshippers to repentance.

emanation (Hebrew 'atzilut') The coming into being of the universe through the unfolding of God's essence in a series of stages. The idea of emanation was preferred by the KABBALAH to the more philosophical belief in creatio ex nihilo, but it was not understood as a temporal process, more as a structural analysis of reality. This involved the ten SEFIROT and the Four Worlds of Emanation, CREATION, Formation and

Action through which the outflow of the divine takes place. The belief in emanation lent itself to pantheism, which the mystics avoided by depicting the world as the flame from the divine coal or the garment of God within which divinity itself was contained. *See also* ADAM KADMON; SITRA ACHRA; TIKKUN; TZIMTZUM; ZOHAR

Emden, Jacob (1697–1776) German rabbinic author and controversialist. Emden's father Rabbi Tzevi Ashkenazi, known as the Chakham Tzevi, had been deeply involved in rooting out followers of Shabbetai Tzevi, the false Messiah, from the Jewish community, and his son devoted his life to continuing this task. He also defended his father's honour to the point of picking quarrels with those who succeeded Ashkenazi in the rabbinate of Altona. The main butt of Emden's critical zeal was Rabbi Jonathan EYBESHUETZ, the rabbi of Altona, in whose AMULETS Emden claimed to find hidden references to Shabbetai Tzevi. Using his private printing press Emden published a series of bitter and outspoken attacks on Eybeshuetz and was forced to leave Altona by the latter's supporters. Emden also turned his critical mind to an examination of the *Zohar*, maintaining that parts of this work were late forgeries and thus undermining Shabbetean claims that it supported their heretical views. His anti-philosophical bias led him to argue that Maimonides could not have written the *Guide for the Perplexed* because it was anti-traditionalist in character. Christianity fared better under Emden's scrutiny, and he wrote that Jesus had conferred a double blessing on the world in strengthening the values of the torah and in teaching the heathen to forsake idolatry and submit to morality. Faith in the Trinity was not a sin for Christians, and they would be rewarded by God for spreading belief in Him. Emden also advocated a reintroduction of CONCUBINE marriage. *See also* TZIMTZUM.

Endor, Witch of Biblical necromancer who raised the prophet SAMUEL from the dead so that King Saul could ask his advice (I Sam. 28). When Samuel returned to this world, the witch could see him because she had conjured him up, but she could not hear him speak. Saul could hear him but could not see him, and others there could neither see nor hear him. She was able to raise Samuel because he had been dead less than twelve months and the soul stays close to the body for this period. Other spirits, including Moses, accompanied Samuel up from the nether world because they thought that the Resurrection of the Dead had begun when they saw Samuel arise. Some commentators were of the view that the whole episode with the witch took place while Saul was in a trance, or it was brought about through deceit since necromancy has no real power to call up the dead.

Enoch Early biblical character who, because of his righteousness, did not die but was taken up alive into heaven. This is indicated by the verse: 'Enoch walked with God, and he was not, for God took him' (Gen. 5:24). While alive Enoch was a shoemaker who was completely devoted to God, and he bound the lower and higher worlds together as he stitched shoes. In heaven he was given a new body of fire and transfor-

The month of **Elul**, represented by the zodiacal sign of the virgin, from a synagogue mosaic at Hammath, Tiberias.

Enoch taken up to heaven and transformed into the angel Metatron (11c. English manuscript).

med into the angel METATRON, who is the chief of the angels and acts as a heavenly scribe. Enoch is associated with Elijah in Jewish mysticism, and is the subject of several works of the *Heikhalot* and Apocalyptic literature where his experiences are described. These works are thought to be taken from the original book which Enoch was given by the angels, containing the knowledge of the Tree of Life. By studying this original book Enoch was able to 'walk with God'.

en sof *see* SEFIROT; ZOHAR

Ephraim *see* TRIBES, THE TWELVE

eretz yisrael *see* ISRAEL

eruv (Hebrew for 'mixture') Eruv is a means of allowing various shabbat or festival activities which are normally prohibited. In order to extend the Sabbath boundaries, eruv techumim ('mixture of boundaries') is performed by leaving two meals at the boundary limits; the place therefore becomes a symbolic home, and one can travel a further two thousand cubits. In order to cook for the Sabbath on a festival falling on a Friday, some food is set aside before the festival begins and is eaten on Saturday. This eruv tavshillin ('mixture of foodstuffs') indicates that the cooking has already begun beforehand and thus may be continued. Eruv chatzerot ('mixture of courtyards') involves joining together the inhabitants of an area, ranging from a few houses to whole streets or even a whole town, to form one private domain on the Sabbath. This enables people to carry things throughout the area of the eruv, since it is normally forbidden to carry anything in a public domain. The area concerned must be surrounded by a real, or symbolic, wall for the eruv to be effective, and a loaf of bread is set aside to symbolize the meal in which all members of the new private domain participate together. The Karaites criticized this eruv as a deception, but the Rabbis defended it as having been introduced by King Solomon because it increased Sabbath joy.

Esau Son of ISAAC and Rebecca and older twin brother of JACOB. The two brothers were totally different in character and Esau's aggression towards Jacob showed itself even while they were together in the womb. Esau was an idolator and as an embryo struggled to get out of his mother's womb every time she passed a place of idol worship. He became a successful huntsman (Gen. 25:27) because he had stolen a magic cloak which had once belonged to Adam. On the day that he sold his birthright to his brother Jacob, he had just returned home after committing murder, rape and adultery. He mocked at belief in God and the Resurrection and said he had no use for the priestly role which the eldest son played in the family. He had managed to win his father's affection by pretending to be interested in religion when at home, asking questions even about minute details of ritual. His animosity towards his brother increased after the latter tricked him out of his father's blessing (Gen. 27), and he wished to kill Jacob. Esau met his death during a quarrel at Jacob's funeral. A grandson of Jacob cut off

his head when Esau would not let Jacob be buried in the Cave of Machpelah. Esau came to symbolize first the cruel Roman Empire and then the Christian world of the Middle Ages with its antagonistic attitudes to the descendents of Jacob. Among the mystics Esau is thought to represent the sitra achra, or side of evil in human affairs, which will only be finally destroyed in the era of the Messiah.

eschatology (Hebrew 'acharit ha-yamim', meaning 'the end of days') The doctrine of 'the last things' plays an important role in Jewish belief, bound up as it is with the coming of the MESSIAH and the RESURRECTION OF THE DEAD. In the pre-Messianic era there will be great upheavals and wars, known as 'the birth pangs of the Messiah' or 'the footprints of the Messiah', and Jewish experience of suffering and EXILE at various times was thought to presage the final redemption when mundane history would cease. The *Talmud* describes the footprints of the Messiah as a time when arrogance will increase. The government will turn to heresy, and there will be no one to rebuke their wrongdoing. The academies of torah will become brothels. The wisdom of scribes will putrefy. Young people will put the old to shame. A person's own family will become his enemies. The face of the generation will be like the face of a dog. 'On whom can we then rely? On our Father who is in heaven.' Eventually the armies of GOG AND MAGOG will be defeated, and there will be an INGATHERING OF THE EXILES to the Holy Land. The world will be at peace; Gentiles will recognize the one true God and accept the yoke of His kingdom, the earth being 'full of the knowledge of the Lord' (Isa. 11:9). In the Messianic era there will be the great DAY OF JUDGMENT for mankind, with the dead rising to new life from their graves. Afterwards in the period known as OLAM HABA the righteous will join in the great banquet of the Messiah; impure foods will be declared kosher; the world will speak one language; night will become like day; the warmth of the sun will heal the sick; trees will produce a fresh harvest of fruit every month; wild beasts will become tame; and the Angel of Death will be slain by God. Yet, lest one take this imagery too literally, it is said that there will be 'no eating or drinking but the righteous will simply enjoy the radiance of God's Presence (shekhinah)'.

eshet chayil *see* PROVERBS

Essenes Jewish sect which flourished from the 2c. BCE to the destruction of the Second Temple in 70 CE. It is generally assumed that the Jews of Qumran, the remains of whose library constitute the DEAD SEA SCROLLS, belonged to an Essene community. There was a strong monastic tradition of celibacy among the Essenes, with some communities excluding women altogether, although female skeletons were found in the Qumran cemetery. The different Essene subgroups do not seem to have had a completely uniform lifestyle, and divergent pictures of the sect emerge from the writings of Philo, Josephus, Pliny and the Qumran texts. There are no overt references to them in Rabbinic literature or in the New Testament, which may indicate that they were not directly involved in the religious life of Jerusalem in the 1c. CE. The Essenes believed that the Temple in Jerusalem was being run by a corrupt clique of priests, and so they kept away from the sanctuary. They were also much stricter about matters of ritual impurity than other Jews, wearing white linen garments as a symbol of purity. This restricted any socializing with non-Essene groups.

Esther Heroine of the Book of Esther whose Hebrew name was Hadassah but who is better known by her adopted Persian name. Esther was the orphaned cousin of MORDECAI, who brought her up and subsequently married her. At the age of forty she still looked like a young and beautiful girl, and Mordecai encouraged her to put herself forward as wife of the Persian king Ahasuerus. Although this would normally be forbidden for a Jewish woman, and particularly a married woman, Esther did not, in fact, have sexual relations with the king. A spirit which looked like her was sent by God to take her place in the king's bed. She managed to live as a secret Jewess in the royal palace, refusing to reveal her origins to her husband and his court but claiming truthfully that she was of royal descent since King Saul was one of her ancestors. Her position as queen allowed her to save the Jews of the Persian empire from annihilation at the hands of HAMAN and his followers. Before going to the king to plead for her people, she fasted, and God Himself dressed her and accompanied her. It is customary for Jews to fast on the day before PURIM in memory of Esther's fast, this being called the Fast of Esther (*see* ESTHER, FAST OF). It was Esther who persuaded the sages to institute the reading of the Book of Esther each year. The MEGILLAH was read on purim, and Esther's name was understood to symbolize the nature of the purim story, being read as the Hebrew word meaning 'I will hide', for God does not reveal Himself in the story and is not mentioned directly in the Book of Esther. *See also* TARGUM.

Esther, Fast of (Hebrew 'taanit ester') Daytime fast on the thirteenth of Adar, the day before PURIM. It is modelled either on the fast which ESTHER undertook before her visit to the Persian king to plead for her people (Esther 4:16) or on the fast of the Jews before defending themselves against their attackers (based on Esther 9:2). The custom of fasting only became widespread in the Middle Ages, and since it is of late origin, leniency is extended to those who have difficulty in fasting. It is strictly kept by many Persian Jewish communities, however, who insist that even the sick should fast. Karaite Jews keep the Fast of Esther for three days preceding Passover, that being the time she actually fasted according to the biblical account.

etrog Citrus fruit which is one of the FOUR SPECIES held together and shaken on the festival of SUKKOT (Lev. 23:40). There are rules for what constitutes a kosher etrog, and people try to buy a beautiful fruit to use for the mitzvah. Although the etrog cannot be eaten like other citrus fruits, it is customary to make etrog jam after the festival is over. There is also a view that the etrog was the fruit of the Tree of Knowledge that Adam and Eve ate in the Garden of Eden. The *Talmud* identifies the etrog tree as having the same taste as its fruit. When the etrog is shaken together

Illustration from a 13c.–14c. German haggadah showing **Esau** dwelling on Mount Seir. A bird's head replaces that of Esau in deference to objections to depicting human figures in Jewish art.

The excavated remains of the **Essene** monastery at Qumran.

Silver **etrog** containers.

with the lulav, or palm branch, it must be held the right way up, the way it grows from the tree. In the 19c. a leading German rabbi wrote at length about which way an etrog, grown in Australia, should be held in Europe, since up and down have a reverse meaning in the antipodes. *See also* TU BI-SHEVAT.

etz ha-chaim *see* TREE OF LIFE

etz ha-daat *see* TREE OF KNOWLEDGE

eulogy *see* HESPED

eunuch (Hebrew 'saris') The castration of humans and animals is forbidden, and a eunuch is not allowed to marry freely within the community of Israel. He can, however, take a proselyte or a freed slave woman as his wife. The definition of a eunuch is someone who has had both testicles removed, and there is a dispute as to whether someone with only one testicle is to be classified as a eunuch, since he may be able to have children. The prophet Isaiah encouraged eunuchs not to feel alienated from the family structure of the community, since God promised those eunuchs who keep shabbat that He would give them a reward which would be better than sons and daughters (Isa. 56:3–4).

Eve Wife of ADAM and mother of the human race. Eve was originally joined to Adam back to back as an ANDROGYNE and was then separated, since Adam needed a companion he could meet face to face. God Himself arranged the wedding of Adam and Eve and performed the marriage ceremony in the presence of the angels who celebrated with music and dancing. SATAN, who through the SERPENT tempted Eve to eat the forbidden fruit from the TREE OF KNOWLEDGE in the Garden of Eden, had sexual relations with her, and CAIN was born of this union, though his brother Abel was Adam's child. Through this act the serpent affected all her descendants with the taint of impurity (*see* ORIGINAL SIN). Eve's children in each generation are threatened by LILITH, Adam's first wife, who causes illness or death to babies. According to one view Lilith was a demoness who ran away from Adam because she refused to be subservient to him, or alternately she was thought to be the first Eve who had sinned and was replaced by a new Eve. Eve is buried beside Adam in the Cave of Machpelah in Hebron. *See also* NIDDAH.

even shetiyyah *see* CREATION; HOLY OF HOLIES; MORIAH, MOUNT

evil eye (Hebrew 'ayin hara') Originally the glance of an evilly disposed person, who has the power of harming someone through a spiteful look, but in Jewish folklore often thought of as an independent malicious force which stalks the world and is associated with the demonic. This force emanates from a bad angel which is called into being by an evil glance. Some people are thought to be especially prone to cast the evil eye on others, and they should be avoided, since out of one hundred deaths ninety-nine are caused by the evil eye. Certain kinds of behaviour draw the envy of others and expose one to the evil eye. Thus when Jacob sent his ten sons to Egypt to buy food, he advised them not to enter together through one gate, so as not to attract the evil eye. Indeed, any behaviour which draws attention, any ostentation or extravagance which arouses jealousy, is likely to bring the evil eye. People who are celebrating are particularly liable to harm from the evil eye, and for protection should wear a tallit, tzitzit, or be clothed with something red, carry SALT in a pocket or wear an AMULET round their neck. Among Oriental Jews the sign of a hand is attached to the wall of the home as a prophylaxis. Children used to be given ugly names to keep the evil eye away. A bridegroom should not be left alone on the day of his wedding, but if he walks backwards, he will be able to avoid the evil eye. Close male relatives are not called up to the torah reading (aliyah) one after the other nor the MINYAN counted, as this encourages the evil eye. A favourite way of removing the spell of the evil eye is to recite various formulae over the person affected and spit three times, so that the evil eye and whoever used it is exiled into wild, uninhabited places. In order to avoid giving the evil eye to someone who is being praised, it is customary to add the words 'without the evil eye' to one's remarks. In Hebrew this is 'beli ayin hara', and in Yiddish it is often expressed in the more garbled form of 'keneyna hore'.

excommunication *see* CHEREM

Exilarch (Hebrew 'resh galuta', meaning 'Head of the Diaspora') The leader of Babylonian Jewry, chosen on a hereditary basis from the line of the House of David. The position of Exilarch, parallel to that of the NASI in the Holy Land, is of unknown origin and was first mentioned in the 2c. CE. When Babylonia became the most important Jewish centre after the redaction of the Babylonian *Talmud*, the Exilarch was for several centuries recognized by Jews everywhere as the leader of the DIASPORA. His name was mentioned in the kaddish prayer and even today, long after the end of the institution, a prayer, yekum porkan, is still recited for the Exilarch's welfare in synagogues. Until the 11c. the Exilarch lived in great splendour, being supported by approximately one-fifth of the community's income. He maintained a court of semi-royal proportions with banquets, fine clothing, servants and professional musicians. He was in charge of the limited self-government granted to Jews in Babylonia and was able to apply criminal law as laid down by the halakhah. The Exilarch collected taxes for the Gentile authorities and appointed judges and market inspectors. In the synagogue, while ordinary Jews were called to go up to the sefer torah, the scroll was brought down to the Exilarch to recite the benediction. A number of major disputes took place between the Exilarchs and those who disagreed with their rulings or resented their abuse of power. The Karaites broke away from Rabbinic Judaism in the 8c. after a dispute over the succession to the position of Exilarch when ANAN BEN DAVID, the unsuccessful candidate, founded a new movement. In the early 10c. SAADIAH GAON began a long and bitter dispute with the Exilarch David Ben Zakkai.

exile (Hebrew 'galut') Jews in the DIASPORA felt themselves in exile after the destruction of the Second Temple though the experience can be traced back to the dispersion of the TEN LOST TRIBES and to the Babylonian Captivity in the 8c. and 6c. BCE. The sense of alienation was sharpened in the Middle Ages by the expulsion of Jews from host countries. When conditions worsened, the hope grew stronger for the coming of a Messiah who would lead the Jewish people back to the Holy Land (see INGATHERING OF THE EXILES). Their fast days encapsulated the exiles' mourning and their longing to return, yet exile guaranteed Jewish survival by dispersing an essentially vulnerable minority. It was seen both as an opportunity for Jews to win converts and as a punishment for sin. The Babylonian Captivity (see GEDALIAH, FAST OF) came about because of the sins of idolatry, sexual immorality and bloodshed, while the exile which followed the destruction of the Second Temple was brought about by the sin of causeless hatred. Christians interpreted Jewish exile as a sign that God had rejected Jews because they had crucified Jesus. In reply Jewish theologians maintained that Israel was the suffering servant of God (Isa. 53) who, through exile, atoned for the sins of the world. God Himself participated in Israel's suffering and the shekhinah accompanied Israel into exile. In the Lurianic Kabbalah, which was formulated after the great expulsion of the Jews from Spain in 1492 (see LURIA, ISAAC), the exile of the Jewish people reflects both the exile of God, who withdrew (tzimtzum) in order to make room for the world, and also the exile of the sparks of divine light trapped in the broken vessels (see TIKKUN). Galut is thus a condition of a universe in need of redemption. Kabbalists undertook self-imposed exile both as an atonement for sin and to participate through their own personal lives in the divine exile. The rise of modern ZIONISM and the State of Israel was intended to end the condition of alienation in the diaspora.

Exodus (Hebrew 'yetziat mitzraim', meaning 'going out from Egypt') The miraculous story of the redemption of the Israelites from slavery in Egypt and of their wanderings in the desert, led by MOSES, until Joshua led them into the Promised Land. This story is the main subject of the second book of the Pentateuch, the Book of Exodus. All future redemption is based on the prototype of the Exodus. The Messianic redemption will take place in the same month, Nisan, that the Israelites left Egypt, and the Messiah himself will be a latter-day Moses. The Exodus is also the focus of the liturgy and practices of the Jewish calendar, particularly of the three pilgrim festivals. Each Jew is meant to see himself as if he had actually gone out from Egypt, and the Passover ritual (see PESACH) recreates the experience. The main themes of the Exodus revolve around the protection and care provided by God to the Israelites. The Egyptians were punished by the Ten PLAGUES for enslaving the People of Israel, the RED SEA turned to dry land to let the Israelites through, the DECALOGUE was given to them at Mount SINAI, a well of water known as MIRIAM'S WELL followed them in the desert, they were led by a PILLAR OF CLOUD AND OF FIRE, the clothes they wore survived throughout their forty years in the wilderness, the ARK OF THE COVENANT lowered hills and raised valleys so that they could travel in comfort, and MANNA from heaven provided food for them. See also HAGGADAH; KORAH.

Adam and **Eve** hiding their nakedness behind fig leaves after eating the fruit of the Tree of Knowledge in the Garden of Eden (15c., Norfolk).

Bronze amulet against the **evil eye** (4c., Israel).

exorcism Procedure for expelling DEMONS or mal-evolent spirits (*see* DIBBUK) which take control of people or places. The ritual of exorcism involved the sounding of the shofar, the recital of prayers and anointing the person possessed with oil and water over which Psalms have been said. The demon or spirit concerned had to be identified, and in the case of a 'naked soul' which becomes a dibbuk, the sin which led it to attach itself to a human body had to be discovered. This sin needs rectification (tikkun) so that after expulsion the soul is at rest. The exorcism of haunted places involved various techniques such as chanting Psalm 91 and the PRIESTLY BLESSING, circum-ambulation of the building with a sefer torah, pouring water over the doorstep, making loud noises to scare off demons, reciting formulae prohibiting demons from dwelling there and putting up a kosher mezuzah on the doorpost.

Eybeshuetz, Jonathan (1690–1764) Kabbalist and rabbinic authority in Prague and Northern Germany. Eybeshuetz, despite his orthodoxy, was suspected of being a follower of Shabbetai Tzevi, a false Messiah many of whose disciples were outwardly Jews but secretly adhered to heretical beliefs. He was appointed as the rabbi of Altona because of his reputation as a writer of amulets which protected pregnant women against demons, since many women in Altona were dying in childbirth. Jacob EMDEN, the son of a previous rabbi of Altona and a fierce opponent of Shabbetean-ism, accused Eybeshuetz of being a crypto-Shabbetean and began a bitter campaign against him in a series of polemical books and pamphlets. Eybeshuetz consist-ently denied any involvement with the heretical movement and pointed out that he had signed an order of excommunication (cherem) against Shab-betean heretics. He managed to gain the support of rabbinic colleagues, who had no patience with Emden's zealotry, in closing down Emden's private press and in forcing him to leave Altona. Despite this support, Eybeshuetz's reputation was badly damaged by Em-den's accusations. These were strengthened by the fact that his own son and a number of his pupils became Shabbeteans, some of them even converting to Christ-ianity, and that letters from Eybeshuetz were found in the possession of known members of the heretical movement.

Ezekiel Prophet of priestly descent who was among the Babylonian exiles in the 6c. BCE. Ezekiel had already begun his career as a prophet while in the Land of Israel and continued in exile. He was granted a vision of the heavens opening (Ezek. 1–3), in which he saw four creatures and four wheels within wheels and on a THRONE OF GLORY a form like unto a man (*see* ADAM KADMON). This vision was the subject of mystical speculation by the Merkavah mystics (*see* MAASEH MERKAVAH), which for a time led to the vision being banned from public reading. The *Talmud* compares Ezekiel's vision with that of the prophet ISAIAH who also had a vision of heaven. Ezekiel was asked by Hananiah, Mishael and Azariah whether they should undergo martyrdom rather than bow down to idols, and he advised them to run away. They, in fact, did not heed him, and when they opted for a martyr's death, they were saved by God. Ezekiel encouraged

the people not to despair after the destruction of the Temple, and his prophecy to the dry bones to come to life again contains a great message of hope (Ezek. 37). One of the Talmudic rabbis even claimed descent from those whom Ezekiel resurrected. Ezekiel is buried in central Iraq, with a synagogue built over his tomb (*see* PETAACHIAH OF REGENSBURG; BENJAMIN OF TUDELA). This was a major centre of pilgrimage for Jews, and there are reports of a pillar of fire which once hovered over the grave. The torah scroll once read there on yom kippur was reputed to have been written by the prophet himself, and the shrine's library is said to have contained a number of books dating back to Temple times. The lamp above the grave was kept burning, having been originally lit by Ezekiel himself. There was once some discussion about whether the Book of Ezekiel should be taken out of circulation because some of its teachings seemed heretical. These problems were eventually overcome, however, and it was accepted into the biblical canon.

Ezra Priest and scribe of the 5c. BCE who led the return of the exiles from Babylonia to rebuild the TEMPLE, in which work he was aided by Nehemiah. Ezra was regarded as a second Moses, who himself was worthy of receiving the torah. He made the Jews abandon their Gentile wives (Ezra 10) and took with him all the families with genealogical problems, since he knew Babylonian Jewry would henceforth lack leadership. When the Jews of the Yemen refused to join Ezra, he cursed them that they should remain poor. He introduced the square Hebrew script for use in writing the torah (*see* ALPHABET, HEBREW). Among the practices which he, and the Assembly of Sages which he led (*see* SYNAGOGUE, THE GREAT), introduced was the thrice-weekly reading of the torah on Mon-days, Thursdays and Saturday afternoons. The great sage Hillel is sometimes described as a disciple of Ezra. *See also* TITHES.

ezrat nashim *see* MECHITZAH

Falashas (Amharic for 'strangers') The black 'Jews' of Ethiopia who call themselves Beta Israel, 'The House of Israel'. Their origin is obscure. Falashas trace themselves back to the Israelite entourage of Melenik, the son of the Queen of SHEBA and King Solomon, or to the Ten Lost Tribes, or to refugees from the destruction of the Second Temple. It is also claimed that Falashas originated with Yemenite or Egyptian Jews who intermarried with natives, or that they are JUDAIZERS with no actual Jewish ancestry. Traditional Falashas know no Hebrew and speak Amharic. Their religion is biblical, still involving the slaughter of the Pascal lamb, with no Rabbinic traditions and no prohibitions on mixing meat and milk dishes. Like other Ethiopians, some Falashas practise female cir-cumcision. They also still maintain a hierarchy of Nazirites and priests, who do not inherit their titles but are selected for office. The Shabbat, an angelic Queen of Heaven, plays a very important role in their ritual and mythology. On the Sabbath they hold a communal celebratory meal in the synagogue and do not allow any fire, sexual relations, crossing of rivers or fighting except in self-defence on that day. Indeed a Falasha legend tells how Melenik crossed a river on the Sabbath, and some of his followers, who later founded the Falasha community, refused to continue with him, while those who crossed eventually became Christians. Falashas are also strict in their application of purity laws. A menstruating woman (*see* NIDDAH), a woman in childbirth and mourners are kept in isolation. Contact with a non-Falasha generates impurity, and so Falashas live apart from their neighbours. Christian missionaries have tried to convert them, with only limited success, though many were forcibly converted in the past after their independent kingdom was crushed. In Israel some rabbis accept them as members of the tribe of Dan, while others insist they are Gentiles.

Falk, Samuel (1708–82) Kabbalist who was active in England where he came to be known as the BAAL SHEM of London. Falk fled from Germany to England in 1742 after being accused by Jacob Emden of being a Shabbetean heretic and practising black MAGIC. In London he ran an alchemical laboratory, dressed impressively in a gold turban and chain and was much sought after by royalty and the aristocracy for help in ALCHEMY, Kabbalah and providing talismans. He earned the reputation of a wonder-worker who could perform miracles. He made candles burn for weeks on end and could go without food or drink for long periods without any difficulty. When he pawned articles, they found their way back to his house on their own, and when the time for redeeming them arrived he would go to the pawnshop to pay but would explain that the goods had already been returned. On one occasion he saved London's Great Synagogue from a fire that was raging nearby by writing a Kabbalistic formula of four Hebrew letters on the synagogue door. When the fire reached the synagogue, the wind changed and the synagogue was saved. His portrait is often mistakenly reproduced in textbooks as depicting his contemporary, Israel Baal Shem Tov.

family (Hebrew 'mishpachah') The basic unit of ritual and ceremonial life is the extended family. In the past Jews and Jewesses were known by their Hebrew names and by their patronyms. Hence, the common endings of Jewish surnames: 'son' (e.g. Jacobson, Abrahamson), or 'ovitz' (Slavic for 'child of', e.g. Jacobovitz, Abrahamovitz), and the surname prefix 'ben' (Hebrew for 'son of', e.g. Bendavid, Bensusan). For most religious purposes the Hebrew name of a person and their father's name are used, but when prayers are recited for recovery from sickness, a person is referred to by his own name plus his mother's name. Membership of the Jewish people is passed down via the mother, but status as a priest or a Levite, or tribal affiliation, is patrilineal. A person's communal identity and social standing is dependent on their family YICHUS. The ideal family is monogamous (*see* MONOGAMY), although polygamy is allowed by biblical law and still practised by some Sephardim. The single individual is able to serve God, but lacks the joy, blessing and wholeness associated with MARRIAGE and procreation. CHILDREN are seen as a blessing from God. Many rituals can only

Ezekiel by Michelangelo from the ceiling of the Sistine Chapel in Rome.

Haggadah illumination showing the **family** assembled for the seder meal.

be performed in the home and involve both older and younger family members. *See also* PARENTS.

fast days (Hebrew 'taanit', 'tzom') Public fast days are either of the purely penitential kind like YOM KIPPUR, the most sacred day of the Jewish year, or are the penitential remembrance of sad events (*see* GEDALIAH, FAST OF). There are also many localized fast days, special occasions for fasting such as a parent's yahrzeit, and penitential fasts undertaken on a voluntary basis. It is forbidden to fast on shabbat, since this would indicate a rejection of the world which God created. The only exceptions are when yom kippur falls on a Saturday or when one has had a troubling dream on Friday night. In the latter case there might be no Sabbath joy if one ate, because of anxiety in response to the dream message. It is believed that an immediate fast after a nightmare annuls any evil implied in the dream. One needs to fast again on a subsequent weekday, however, to repent for having fasted on the Sabbath. Differing attitudes towards fasting are found in Jewish literature. Some Jewish thinkers see fasting as a sacrificial offering to God of the flesh of one's own body, while for others fasting is an essentially moral activity and involves giving the value of the food not eaten to charity. There are also those who believe that fasting should be discouraged except on official fast days, since it is a sin to overindulge in asceticism. Jewish mystics maintained that those angels who have sinned can only ascend once again to their place in heaven through the power of human fasting. Prayers recited on fast days include ASHAMNU and AVINU MALKENU. *See also* SIYYUM.

festivals (Hebrew 'moed', 'chag', 'yom tov') The Jewish year contains five major festivals of biblical origin: the three PILGRIM FESTIVALS or HARVEST FESTIVALS associated with the Exodus from Egypt (*see* PESACH, SHAVUOT and SUKKOT) and the penitential festivals of ROSH HA-SHANAH and YOM KIPPUR. There are also a number of minor festivals, the most important being the carnival-like festival of PURIM, the post-biblical festival of lights, CHANUKKAH, and NEW MOON days. They are determined by the Hebrew CALENDAR. On the major festivals profane work is forbidden, but work related to the preparation of food and to the use of fire is permitted, with the exception of yom kippur (but *see* ERUV). The purpose of a yom tov (literally 'good day') is to rejoice in the pleasures of God's world and serve Him in prayer and study. Half the festival time should be devoted to human needs and half to God, and people greet each other with special GREETINGS appropriate to the occasion. The fires of gehinnom do not burn on festivals, and the souls of those condemned to punishment are at rest. Although each person's wealth and the amount they will be able to spend is determined by God from the beginning of the year, these limits do not apply to expenditure for shabbat and festivals. *See also* KIDDUSH; MUSAF.

Firkovich, Abraham (1786–1874) Russian Karaite scholar who collected a mass of evidence intended to prove that KARAITES had a totally separate identity from Jews. Firkovich travelled widely in Palestine, the Ottoman Empire and the Crimea collecting manu-scripts and copying tombstone inscriptions supporting the antiquity of Karaism. Some of his Egyptian manuscripts came from what was later known as the Cairo GENIZAH. He claimed to have found Karaite tombstones which dated back to the first few centuries CE which would obviously undermine the accepted view that Karaism only began in the 8th century. It is now generally agreed among scholars, however, that his zeal to prove his case and his animosity to Rabbinic Judaism led Firkovich to forge much of his evidence.

firstborn (Hebrew 'bekhor') The male firstborn child has certain privileges denied to his siblings. He inherits a double portion of his father's estate (Deut. 21:15) and he has a holy status from birth necessitating a ceremony of redemption (*see* PIDYON HA-BEN) (Exod. 13:2). The firstborn also has the duty to fast on the day before Passover (*see* PESACH), in memory of the Israelite firstborn who were saved during the last of the plagues when the Egyptian firstborn were slain. In fact the firstborn usually break their fast at a party given on the completion of a *Talmud* tractate (siyyum) which is held on that day. In the Bible it is often CHILDREN who are not firstborn but younger sons who are the religious heroes, e.g. Isaac, Jacob, Joseph, Moses and David.

fish (Hebrew 'dag') Fish having fins and scales are kosher and may be eaten without being killed in any special way, according to the Jewish DIETARY LAWS. Fish and meat, however, have to be eaten separately because eating them together is considered a health risk (*see* PARVE). Fish are symbols of fertility, a popular part of the ritual diet, and herrings in particular are eaten at the third Sabbath meal (seudah shlishit). Fish is good for the eyes of normal people, though not for those who already have eye problems, but a fish diet in early spring can lead to leprosy. The TASHLIKH ritual on the New Year festival involves symbolically casting away sins into a stream which contains fish so they can carry the sins away to the sea. Fish are especially suitable for this task because their eyes are always open and being covered by water they are not subject to the evil eye. At the banquet in the age of the Messiah the LEVIATHAN, a monster fish, will be eaten. The involvement of the Jew with the torah is likened to the position of fish in water. If fish try to escape from the nets of fishermen by leaving the river, they die. So it is with Jews. If they are persecuted when they live fully as Jews, subject to the demands of the halakhah, how much more insecure will they be if they abandon their traditions. *See also* RABBAH BAR BAR CHANAH.

Flood, The (Hebrew 'mabul') The great deluge which took place in the time of NOAH destroying human and animal life (Gen. 6–8) lasted for forty days and forty nights. Noah started building his ARK 120 years before the Flood to give the people an opportunity to repent, but they only made fun of him. The sins of the wicked generation of the Flood consisted of robbery, sexual immorality and violence. Their disrespect for the property of others was the outcome of their own prosperity and lack of appreciation of God's bounty. Their sexual licentiousness was caused by the fact that

79

both men and women went around naked, and this led them to engage in acts of adultery. The extent of their violence is apparent from the way they even threw their children into the holes in the ground, through which the water was flowing, to try to stem the Flood. The animals were punished not only because they had illicit sexual relations with humans but because they also behaved corruptly by pairing off with members of other species (*see* MIXED SPECIES). The ark would only accept those animals that had not sinned, and all the occupants remained celibate while inside. The wild animals became tame for the duration of the Flood, but after it was over the lion injured Noah, causing him to limp, because he was late in feeding it. Some rabbis believed that the Flood affected the whole world except for the Land of Israel.

fool *see* SHLEMIEL

forgiveness (Hebrew 'selichah' or 'mechilah') The message of REPENTANCE for sin and of divine forgiveness runs through biblical and Rabbinic literature. 'Let the wicked forsake his way … let him return to the Lord for He will abundantly pardon' (Isa. 55:7). There are paradigmatic stories of divine forgiveness, for example that of the Golden Calf where the intercession of Moses led God to forgive the Israelites and to reveal Himself as merciful, gracious and long-suffering (Exod. 34). Moses was told that the quality of divine forgiveness was five hundred times more potent than the anger of God. Repentance, even on one's deathbed, always leads to divine forgiveness, no matter how serious the sins involved. Prayers, like KADDISH, can also win forgiveness. For major sins, the rituals of YOM KIPPUR, and ultimately the death of the sinner, may be necessary to complete the ATONEMENT. God wants to forgive and even prays to Himself that He should be forgiving. Man, too, must imitate God (imitatio dei) in being prepared to forgive his fellow man. It is a mark of the children of Abraham that they are forgiving, and indeed, a cruel and unforgiving person shows thereby that he is not a Jew. It is customary to seek forgiveness before the yom kippur fast from those one has wronged, and it is their duty to forgive.

four cups (Hebrew 'arba kosot') During the Passover SEDER four cups of sweet red wine are drunk to symbolize four characteristics of God's redemption from Egypt mentioned in the Bible (Exod. 6:6–7). A fifth cup, known as the cup of Elijah (*see* ELIJAH, CUP OF), is poured out but not drunk. It symbolizes God's promise to take the Israelites into the Holy Land, a promise which will be fulfilled once more only when the Messiah comes. The cups are also thought to represent the four cups of punishment which God will pour out on the nations of the world in future times. Red wine is used to remember the blood of the Pascal lamb which the Israelites smeared on their doorposts in Egypt (Exod. 12:7). When Jews suffered from BLOOD LIBEL accusations that they used Christian blood at PESACH time, white wine was drunk instead of red.

four questions (Hebrew 'mah nishtanah', meaning 'what is different') At the Passover SEDER the youngest child asks the head of the household four questions about why the seder meal differs from other meals.

*The Death of the **Firstborn*** by Sir Lawrence Alma-Tadema.

Mosaic of **fish**, the zodiacal symbol for the month of Adar (Tiberias).

14c. Venetian mosaic of the **Flood** showing Noah releasing a raven and a dove.

The questions refer to the eating of MATZAH and MAROR, to the custom of dipping food and of eating while leaning on the left side. These questions, contained in the HAGGADAH, are the formalized expression of an underlying theme of the seder that the rituals should lead the children to ask questions. The answer to the four questions is the story of the slavery of the Israelites in Egypt and how they were redeemed from there by God. It is this story which is behind all the various PESACH practices.

four species (Hebrew 'arbaah minim') The palm branch (*see* LULAV), citrus fruit (*see* ETROG), willow ('aravah') and myrtle ('hadas') are the four agricultural species held together and shaken on the festival of SUKKOT (Lev. 23:40). They are also paraded (*see* HAKKAFOT) round the synagogue each day of the festival and seven times on the seventh day, HOSHANA RABBA. The four species are shaken in celebration of God's bounty at the end of the harvest season and are associated with the prayers for rain on the last days of the festival. They are thought to symbolize the different types of Jew who go to make up the Jewish community. The palm produces fruit but has no pleasant odour and represents the Jew who studies torah but does not fulfil the commandments. The myrtle has a pleasant odour but no fruit; the willow has neither fruit nor odour; and the etrog has both. Just as all four must be held together, so the community must unite, for then the spiritually strong can help the spiritually weak. The four species have also been described as Israel's weapons of war. When they raise them, Jews indicate their victory, as the army of God, over His foes among the heathen.

Frank, Jacob (1726–91) Pseudo-Messiah and leader of a heretical sect. Frank was influenced by the more extreme antinomian followers of the Shabbetean movement (*see* SHABBETAI TZEVI) during his travels in the Ottoman Empire. Like a number of other Shabbeteans there, he seems to have converted to Islam while maintaining Jewish practices in secret, and when he returned to Poland, he preached an anti-Talmudic form of Judaism which involved indulging in orgiastic rites. To avoid persecution and excommunication (cherem) from the Polish rabbis, his disciples turned to the Catholic bishop of Kamenetz-Podolsk for protection, claiming that their movement had much in common with Christianity. The Frankists rejected the *Talmud* and wanted to maintain a form of Judaism based on the *Zohar*. The bishop arranged a DISPUTATION between them and their opponents in 1757 and declared that the Frankists had won. Unfortunately for Frank, the bishop died shortly afterwards, and the persecution of his followers was renewed. Another debate with the rabbis took place in 1759, and Frank led his adherents into the Catholic Church, putting himself and them out of reach of Jewish antagonism. He claimed that this conversion was another stage in the process of Messianic redemption, and his movement owed allegiance to the dictates of the hidden, mystical torah which transcended the limitations of the normative teachings of Judaism. The Catholic authorities soon became suspicious of the Frankists and investigated their beliefs and practices. Frank was arrested and imprisoned for thirteen years for heresy.

On his release he continued to lead the movement until his death, when he was succeeded by his daughter Eva.

free will The Bible presupposes that man can choose to obey or disobey God: 'I have set before you life and death, the blessing and the curse; therefore choose life' (Deut. 30:19). In the *Talmud* this notion of free will is expressed in the teaching that within man there are two inclinations, the good INCLINATION and the evil inclination. Man has the power to choose between them and should choose the former. God does not make this choice for man since 'everything is in the hands of heaven except the fear of heaven'. The Jewish philosophers of the Middle Ages sought to reconcile the conflict between the idea that God knows how man will act and man's freedom to act as he chooses. Most argued that God's foreknowledge does not determine man's actions since it is limited in scope, leaving an indeterminate area where real choice is possible and where God does not actually know what an individual will choose. Hasdai Crescas (14c.) argued, however, that despite his feeling of freedom, man is in fact not free since he cannot negate God's foreknowledge. A later Jewish thinker, the Chasidic leader Rabbi Mordechai Joseph Leiner (19c.), even went so far as to argue that every human action, including SIN itself, is caused by God. In the Messianic age we shall understand that sin, too, has a place and a meaningfulness within divine providence and that it is an expression of the divine will. Without the sin of Adam and Eve, for instance, human development would not have been possible. *See also* ORIGINAL SIN; TZADDIK.

fruit *see* ETROG; TREE OF KNOWLEDGE; TU BI-SHEVAT; VINE

gabbai (Hebrew for 'warden') Respected community official. In the wider community the gabbai plays the role of charity treasurer, collecting taxes and contributions and deciding how they are to be allocated. In the synagogue the gabbai is the warden, elected from among the laymen to administrate the religious life of the community. He allocates the honours associated with the opening of the ark and the calling up (aliyah) of congregants to the reading of the sefer torah. In the Chasidic Movement each Chasidic tzaddik is looked after by his personal gabbai who controls access to the rabbi and organizes his court.

Gabriel Archangel and Prince of Fire often mentioned together with MICHAEL, RAPHAEL and URIEL. Gabriel is in attendance at the left hand of God and guards the left side of man while he sleeps. He saved Abraham from the fiery furnace into which Nimrod cast him, and he later saved HANANIAH, MISHAEL AND AZARIAH from their ordeal in a furnace of fire. He was one of the three angels who visited Abraham, and he rescued Lot from Sodom before destroying the city with fire and brimstone. When Moses, as a child, was tested by

Pharaoh to see whether he would reach out for a fiery coal or a lump of gold, it was Gabriel who pushed the infant's hand into the fire. Pharaoh was thus convinced that this child was of little intelligence and would never be a threat to his rule. Although he is of lesser importance than Michael, taking two movements in flying to his target while Michael takes only one, Gabriel rules over Paradise, is in charge of the cherubim in heaven and the first fruits on earth. He speaks up for Israel in heaven, but when in the past they did not repent for their sins, he was forced to burn down the Temple. In the age of the Messiah Gabriel will fight a great battle with the LEVIATHAN.

galut *see* EXILE

Gamaliel A name current among the descendants of the great Mishnaic sage Hillel. The most important bearer of this name was Rabban Gamaliel of Jabneh, known as Gamaliel II, who lived during the 1c. and early 2c. CE. He is sometimes confused with his grandfather Gamaliel I who, according to the New Testament, was a teacher of Saul of Tarsus and was consulted about Jesus and his teachings. Gamaliel II became Nasi of Palestinian Jewry soon after the destruction of the Second Temple when the Sanhedrin moved to Jabneh from Jerusalem. He exercised strong leadership, standardizing halakhic practice, in order to preserve unity during the great religious ferment of that period, and pressuring his colleagues to conform. He ordered JOSHUA BEN CHANANIAH, who had calculated a different date for yom kippur than Gamaliel, to appear on that day dressed in his ordinary working clothes to show it was not a holy day. He also excommunicated (cherem) his brother-in-law ELIEZER BEN HYRCANUS for not bowing to the majority opinion of the sages. Although Gamaliel's tough policy helped to preserve the fabric of Jewish life, he was not popular among his colleagues (*see* BET HA-MIDRASH). They deposed him from his position for a time, only reinstating him when they had liberalized some of his more uncompromising regulations. Yet he played a crucial role in determining the character of post-Temple Judaism, adapting the Temple liturgy and ritual to the synagogue and home, outlawing Jewish Christians from the synagogue by introducing a prayer against heretics, establishing the views of the School of Hillel as normative rather than those of the School of SHAMMAI, showing concern for the welfare of his Gentile slaves to the point of keeping family mourning when his favourite slave died, and setting an example of concern for the poor. He requested that he be buried in simple garments so that no one should be put to shame for lacking rich burial shrouds. *See also* TARGUM.

gambling Professional gamblers are disqualified from giving evidence in a Jewish court since their activity is considered a form of robbery. In the Middle Ages compulsive gambling was regarded as an evil which was at the root of the breakup of marriages and could bring disasters on communities where it was uncontrolled. Impoverished gamblers were denied charity, the bet din would not collect their gambling debts, and they were not called up (aliyah) to the

A young Chasidic Jew holding the **four species** in a painting by Isidor Kaufmann.

The archangel **Gabriel** blowing his trumpet (woodcut by Geoffrey Whitney).

reading of the torah. Gamblers were even put under the ban (cherem) and flogged in some communities. Many Jews played cards for money during the CHANUKKAH festival, sometimes playing through the night. They also gambled with a chanukkah dreidl, which is a small spinning top with Hebrew letters on its four sides signifying a win or a loss. Christmas Eve was another favourite time for community gambling. This night was known as nittel ('natal') night, when Jews used to keep away from public expression of their religion so as to avoid Christian antagonism. There was no torah study, all classes were cancelled, and students would take the opportunity to relax by playing games and gambling. The religious authorities distinguished between occasional gamblers and professionals. While they disapproved of both, they only took strong measures against the latter. One 16c. rabbi, Leone MODENA, wrote a tract against gambling as a young man, but in later life he found himself addicted and unable to control his urge to gamble. A well-known 20c. Jerusalem sage, Rabbi Arye Levine, was asked by the wife of a gambler to persuade her husband not to spend all his money on lottery tickets. Levine managed to do so by telling the gambler that if God wanted him to win, one lottery ticket would be enough. The gambler then asked the rabbi why he did not buy a lottery ticket, seeing that he was such a saintly character and was bound to win. 'Yes, that is precisely why I don't gamble', the rabbi replied.

gan eden see GARDEN OF EDEN

gaon (Hebrew for 'eminence'; pl. 'geonim') Title used for the heads of the Babylonian academies from the 6c. to the 11c. CE. The Babylonian sages claimed spiritual leadership as guardians of the authoritative traditions of the Babylonian TALMUD. They used the title 'gaon' to emphasize their status and answered questions about the meaning of Talmudic texts from throughout the Jewish world, thus initiating the literature of RESPONSA. In later times the title was applied to outstanding sages whose pre-eminence was recognized, e.g. ELIJAH THE VILNA GAON, until eventually it came to be used simply as an honorific title of rabbis in general. See also SAADIAH GAON.

Garden of Eden (Hebrew 'gan eden') The idyllic garden from which ADAM and EVE were expelled after they ate the forbidden fruit from the TREE OF KNOWLEDGE, the path back being guarded by a CHERUB with a flaming sword (Gen. 3). The prophet Ezekiel describes the Garden of Eden as full of precious stones and stones of fire (Ezek. 28:13–14). It is situated at the very centre of the world, is of enormous dimensions, and everything on this earth has its form engraved in it. It is divided into a lower, earthly garden and an upper, heavenly one. Adam and Eve lived in the lower garden which contains beautiful fruit trees. The upper one is full of spiritual delights, where the souls of the righteous go after death to hear God expound the torah. When souls depart this life they pass into the Garden of Eden through the Cave of Machpelah where they are greeted by the Patriarchs. Alexander the Great is reputed to have found an entrance to Eden in an area of Africa near the equator, governed only by women, but was unable to enter.

The garden represents only a small part of Eden, the main part of which no human eye has ever seen. The odour of PARADISE wafts from the Garden of Eden, and helps neutralize the pungent breath issuing from the mouth of the LEVIATHAN. When the Messiah comes, the way to Eden will be revealed, and people will discover wonderful plants and trees. The Messiah himself will be the only one able to read the sefer torah in the Garden of Eden, which is written in a fire of many colours. See also TREE OF LIFE.

gartel see DRESS

Gedaliah, Fast of (Hebrew 'tzom gedaliah') Fast day falling on the third of Tishri, immediately after the rosh ha-shanah festival, which recalls the assassination of the last Jewish governor of Judah prior to the Babylonian EXILE circa 586 BCE. Gedaliah believed in cooperation with the Babylonian conquerors, and with his death all semblance of semi-independence for the Judaeans ended (Jer. 40, 41). The lesson of this fast is that the death of a righteous man can be as severe as the destruction of God's Temple, for which fast days were also instituted.

gehinnom (Hebrew for 'valley of Hinnom', also called gehenna) Hell or purgatory. Originally gehinnom was a valley near Jerusalem where idolatrous child sacrifices took place in biblical times. The name was later used to refer to the endless expanse of the netherworld, since it was believed that one of the gates of hell was situated there. Indeed, smoke is said to rise continually from the valley floor. Most people spend a period up to a maximum of twelve months in gehinnom, being purged of their sins by its river of fire (but see PEREK SHIRAH). Sons recite the KADDISH prayer during the first eleven months after the death of a parent to help them in this process of purification and MEMORIAL PRAYERS are said. The very wicked are incarcerated there indefinitely, though even they have some respite on SHABBAT and on FESTIVALS when the fires do not burn (see SEUDAH SHLISHIT). The punishments undergone in gehinnom are related to a person's sins. Thus, malicious gossip is punished by hanging from one's tongue, and BALAAM, who enticed the Israelites into sexual immorality, spends his time immersed in boiling semen. The *Talmud* remarks that even the best of doctors is destined for gehinnom. In the Messianic era those who remain in gehinnom will be able to answer 'AMEN' to the kaddish prayer recited in heaven. They will then be released and brought into God's presence.

gelilah (Hebrew for 'rolling up') The ceremonial rolling up of the sefer torah after it has been read in synagogue. The closed scroll is bound up, covered with a mantle, a breastplate, ornamental bells and a pointer (yad). In Talmudic times the last person to be called up for an ALIYAH to recite the blessings over the torah also rolled up the scroll. Since he completed the mitzvah, it was said that gelilah brought with it the spiritual benefit accumulated by all those who preceded him during the torah reading. When gelilah became a separate act, it lost some of its ritual importance though there are records of considerable sums of money being offered for the privilege of rolling up the torah. Today gelilah is often given to pre-bar-mitzvah boys.

gelt *see* CHANUKKAH

Gemara *see* TALMUD

gematria Homiletical rule which associates words or phrases with other words or phrases whose letters add up to the same numerical value. Gematria is possible because Hebrew has no separate number system. Each letter of the ALPHABET stands for a unique number, and larger numbers are made up of combinations of letters. Thus, the biblical text may be interpreted by means of gematria to reveal information about people, places and dates by its choice of words. For instance, Abraham is said to have taken with him 318 servants to a battle (Gen. 14). Since this number is the numerical equivalent of the name of his servant Eliezer, it is assumed that Abraham actually only took this one servant with him. The mystics attached special importance to gematria since God created the world with the letters of the alphabet. They used gematria for uncovering the secret meanings of texts, for devising powerful names of God or of angels and even for determining the exact number of words each prayer should contain. Speculation on the date of the coming of the Messiah sometimes relied on hints found by means of gematria. Apart from simple addition there are more complex methods of gematria in which each letter is spelt out in full before being added up, or the value of a word may be multiplied by itself or the letters rewritten according to the A-T-BA-SH code whereby the first letter is equivalent to the last, the second to the next to last and so on.

genizah (Hebrew for 'hiding place') A room or container in which worn-out holy texts and pages containing the name of God are stored. When the Mishnaic sages fixed the canon of the Hebrew Bible, they consigned non-canonical texts (*see* APOCRYPHA; TARGUM) to a genizah so that they would not be mistaken for scripture. The *Talmud* even mentions a book of medication which King Hezekiah placed in a genizah because people were inclined to rely more on its healing remedies than on God. The main function of a genizah today is as a repository for Bibles, prayer-books and other religious manuals which cannot be used any more. Since their holiness must be respected and the divine names they contain cannot be destroyed, they are left to disintegrate naturally. Such works are referred to as 'shemot' (Yiddish 'shaimos') or '(divine) names'. A genizah is usually a cellar or attic of a synagogue, and when it is full, the books are taken to a cemetery for burial. Some communities of Sephardim carry their old books to the cemetery in a public procession. They chant psalms, play music, dance and blow the shofar in order to prevent drought and to safeguard the community from trouble. Occasionally, the attic of an old synagogue used as a genizah was sealed up or abandoned. In the 19c. Abraham Firkovich removed the contents of Crimean synagogue store-rooms, in his attempts to prove the antiquity of the Karaites, and the English scholar Solomon Shechter

The serpent enticing Adam and Eve to eat the forbidden fruit from the Tree of Knowledge in the **Garden of Eden** (13c. French Bible).

The suffering of the dead in the purgatory of **gehinnom** is captured in this picture of hell by Jan van Eyck (15c.).

discovered a vast collection of manuscripts in the attic genizah of a Cairo synagogue (*see* BEN SIRA).

Gentile (Hebrew 'goi') A non-Jew, who is not 'a son of the COVENANT' and is only subject to the seven NOACHIDE LAWS, is referred to as a Gentile. In ancient times idolatrous Gentiles were suspected of immoral sexual practices and of having no regard for human life. They were distrusted so much that even their acts of kindness were thought to be for their own glorification. With the rise of Christianity and Islam, a number of rabbis sought to distinguish between the dissolute heathens of the past and those Gentiles who were subject to religious values and morality. This distinction did not win universal approval, however, due to idolatrous elements within Christianity, the savage persecutions suffered by Jews at the hands of both Christians and Moslems, and the Kabbalistic belief that non-Jews did not have a divine soul. Gentiles cannot testify in a bet din, they must not be taught the torah or allowed to keep shabbat. INTERMARRIAGE with a Gentile leads to ASSIMILATION and is considered tantamount to forsaking the religion of Israel. The family of a person who intermarries used to keep a week of mourning for them as if they were dead. Many food laws were introduced to maintain the separation of Jews from Gentiles, so that even certain kosher foods cooked by a Gentile are prohibited under the rules of bishul nochri (*see* DIETARY LAWS). Imitation of Gentile customs is expressly prohibited as CHUKKAT HA-GOI. Nevertheless, charity should be extended to Gentiles and their sick should be visited, because the ways of peace must be maintained. Negative attitudes towards Gentiles are expressed in the names used for them, e.g. 'nochri' ('stranger'), 'orel' and 'orelte' ('uncircumcised man or woman' [sic]), 'shaigetz' and 'shikse' ('abominable man or woman'), 'yok' and 'yaikelte' (onomatopoeic inversion of 'goi'). RIGHTEOUS GENTILES, however, have a portion in the World to Come (olam haba), and in the age of the Messiah all Gentiles will come to recognize the one true God. *See also* SUN.

ger *see* PROSELYTE

Gershom, Rabbenu (960–1028) Leading Franco-German rabbi who was known as meor ha-golah, 'The Light of the Diaspora'. According to the traditional view Gershom led a reforming synod of European rabbis which outlawed polygamy, divorce of a wife against her will, and other sundry matters such as opening correspondence without the permission of the recipient. These rules were adopted by all communities of Ashkenazim, and anyone who transgressed them was subject to excommunication (*see* CHEREM). Though the ban on polygamy was only initially for a period of just over two hundred years, MONOGAMY came to be established as a permanent part of Ashkenazi halakhah. Gershom lived at a time when Jews were persecuted and forced to undergo baptism, his own wife and son among them. He took a very lenient view of their predicament forbidding others from reminding them of their past once they had returned to Judaism. The yeshivah at Mainz where he taught attracted students from all over Europe, and Gershom was regarded as the spiritual father of

Ashkenazi Jewry. He composed a number of religious poems, some of which have been included in the liturgy.

ger toshav *see* NOACHIDE LAWS

ger tzedek *see* PROSELYTE

gerushin *see* DIVORCE

geshem *see* RAIN

get (Aramaic for 'document') The DIVORCE document which is needed to dissolve a MARRIAGE, though a get is not necessary where a man and his CONCUBINE wish to annul their relationship. The Bible describes this divorce document as a 'book of separation' which the husband must write for his wife and give into her hand before sending her out of his house (Deut. 24:3). The get today is actually written by a professional SCRIBE appointed by a bet din. Its Aramaic text contains an unambiguous statement of the names of the husband and wife, of the location, including the names of any rivers in the vicinity, and the date on which it is written. It is signed by two witnesses. The stringent requirements for a correctly written get were meant to avoid the disastrous consequences of an improperly divorced woman committing adultery by remarrying. In modern times intractable problems have arisen between Orthodox and REFORM communities, since the former do not recognize the validity of the divorce documents of the latter. The husband must give the get of his own free will and if pressure is exerted on him this may invalidate the whole divorce. Where the halakhah prescribes a divorce, however, the husband may be beaten (*see* CORPORAL PUNISHMENT) till he says: 'I am willing.' The force used is meant only to overcome his evil inclination which keeps him from agreeing to hand over a get as prescribed by the torah. The get is believed to originate in antiquity, and Abraham is said to have given a get to his handmaid Hagar when he sent her away at Sarah's insistence. Although the torah allows divorce, it is said that, when a husband gives his wife a get, the altar sheds tears and a great noise, inaudible to man, reverberates throughout the universe. A get was not only used for divorce but was also given by masters to their slaves in order to grant them their freedom.

gevinah *see* CHEESE

ghetto Restricted urban area set aside for Jews where they were separated from their Gentile neighbours. The term is derived from the Italian for an iron foundry and was first used to refer to the Venetian quarter, near a foundry, to which Jews were restricted in 1516. Throughout the Middle Ages Jews lived together both for protection from a hostile host majority and in order to live in proximity to their religious institutions. These ghettos were not hermetically sealed but were more like community areas, characteristic of the SHTETL in the PALE OF SETTLEMENT, of a type still found today among diaspora Jews. Occasionally, however, the restriction to ghettos was imposed upon Jews, and they were forbidden to live elsewhere. This happened in Rome in 1556 under Pope Pius IV, and it was only in the late 19c. that Roman Jews were able to live throughout the city. The separation of Jews from Christians was intended by the Church to protect the latter from contact with Jewish heresy and from the supposed evils of the BLOOD LIBEL. The ghetto walls and gates, which were closed at night, not only provided safety by shutting out rampaging Christian mobs (*see* POGROM), they also shut Jews in. Ghetto Jews were forced to live in overcrowded and dirty conditions, with their houses close together and subject to fire risk. In the old Jewish area of Prague the ghetto cemetery became so overcrowded that the dead were buried close to the surface in already occupied graves. Living in ghettos did, however, have the advantage of encouraging self-government among Jews and helped to prevent assimilation. During the Nazi HOLOCAUST Jews were herded together in ghettos en route to extermination in CONCENTRATION CAMPS. One of the largest was the Warsaw Ghetto where Jews staged a last ditch revolt against the German army on 19 April 1943. This uprising was only crushed by the physical destruction of the whole ghetto area.

gilgul neshamot *see* TRANSMIGRATION OF SOULS

glatt kosher *see* KOSHER

Gluekel of Hameln (1645–1724) German Jewess who wrote her memoirs in Yiddish intermittently for the last thirty-three years of her life. Gluekel began writing as a form of self-therapy to help herself cope with depression following the death of her husband, and she continued in order to leave a record for her descendants. Her diary provides information about her family and about the way historical events affected the Jewish community. It is also of interest because of the light it throws on the development of the Yiddish language and of Jewish social history. Gluekel, who was well educated by the standards of her age, married at fourteen, had twelve children and managed her husband's business after his death. She was a profoundly religious person and always found a moral message or some spiritual comfort in the stories she told. In her diary there is an account of Jewish life in Hamburg, where she grew up, with its scholars and thieves. On one occasion a Jewish diamond thief could have saved himself from the gallows by converting to Christianity but preferred to die a Jew. The community was caught up in the Messianic fervour which followed the news of Shabbetai Tzevi's appearance, and Gluekel said it was 'impossible to describe the rejoicing'. Her father-in-law was a believer in the Shabbetean claims and sent his furniture and provisions to the port so they could be taken to Palestine when the sign came from the Messiah. Some barrels of provisions were kept there for three years in readiness, and only then were they unpacked. She said of Judaism that the kernel of the torah was 'love your neighbour as yourself', but in her days 'we seldom find it so'.

Gog and Magog In the period immediately preceding the coming of the MESSIAH there will be a great war of Gog and Magog against Israel, bringing destruction in its wake (*see* ESCHATOLOGY). These

2c. Greek inscription on the gate of the Court of the **Gentiles** from the Temple in Jerusalem forbidding non-Jews to enter the Temple proper.

A **ghetto** sweatshop (E.M. Lilien).

legendary nations are based on the prophecy of Ezekiel about Gog from the land of Magog (Ezek. 38:2). Armilus, their king, was born from sexual intercourse between Satan and the stone statue of a girl in Rome. He will finally be defeated by the Messiah and his army in a war to end all wars. Some Gentiles who converted to Judaism (see PROSELYTES) in the Messianic era will forsake Judaism and flee when they see the impending war of Gog and Magog, but all those Jews who are careful to eat the three shabbat meals (see SEUDAH SHLISHIT) will be saved from the tribulations of this war. At times of persecution of the Jews, when the expectation of redemption was at its height, various cruel and warlike powers were identified as exemplars of Gog and Magog.

goi see DRUNKENNESS; GENTILE

Golden Calf (Hebrew 'egel ha-zahav') Golden idol worshipped by the Israelites while Moses was on Mount Sinai receiving the DECALOGUE. When Moses returned and discovered what they had done in his absence, he was angry and broke the two TABLETS OF THE DECALOGUE (Exod. 32). Of all the sins of Israel the worship of the Golden Calf is regarded as the worst, and the suffering and exile of later times can be traced back to it. This sin of idolatry was instigated by the 'mixed multitude' of non-Israelite slaves who left Egypt during the Exodus (Exod. 12:38). They led the Israelites astray when the latter were depressed by the delay in the reappearance of Moses. Satan had shown the people an image of Moses' coffin to convince them that Moses was dead. In order to prevent the making of an idol, AARON asked people to donate their wives' personal golden ornaments to its construction, in the belief that few women would be willing to part with their jewellery. This ruse did not work, however, and when their wives refused to comply with the request, the men brought their own ornaments to him without hesitation. Casting this gold into the fire for smelting, he was amazed when the Golden Calf emerged through the activity of magicians among the 'mixed multitude'. The LEVITES refused to participate in the idolatrous worship. They rallied round Moses when he returned and helped punish the sinners. Through Moses' intercession, the Israelites received God's FORGIVENESS.

golden rule Ethical rule of reciprocal action, 'doing as you would be done by', found in its positive form in the biblical commandment to 'Love your neighbour as yourself' (Lev. 19:18). Most rabbis interpret 'neighbour' here to refer to 'your neighbour in mitzvot' (see MITZVAH), i.e. only to someone who is subject to God's covenant, and thus not to Gentiles who are excluded from reciprocity because they do not recognize the basic ethical values of the torah. A minority of rabbinic commentators, however, take the positive golden rule to apply to all men and women. The great sage HILLEL, in the late 1c. BCE, formulated the golden rule in its negative mode: 'What is hateful to you do not do to your fellow.' The golden rule is at the essential core of the TORAH.

golem (Hebrew for 'unformed') Artificial man made through Kabbalistic magic. In Yiddish usage the term is one of abuse and means a 'zombie'. Earth from virgin soil was shaped into the form of a man, dances were performed around it, while names of God or letter combinations of the *Sefer* YETZIRAH were chanted. Once the golem arose, it was animated by writing the TETRAGRAMMATON on a piece of paper which was placed under its tongue or by engraving a Hebrew word on its forehead. Making a golem was one of the stages of development for the adept of practical KABBALAH and a goal of practitioners of ALCHEMY. Two Talmudic rabbis used to create an artificial calf every Friday to eat on the Sabbath. Another sage created a man whom he sent to a colleague. When the latter found it could not speak, he realized that it was a golem and told it to return to its dust. Many stories are told of people who created a golem. They include Jeremiah and his son Ben Sira, Abraham Ibn Ezra and Solomon IBN GABIROL, who made himself an artificial maid servant. Elijah Baal Shem of Chelm had to remove the divine name from his golem when it turned into a monster and threatened to destroy the world. His grandson raised the question in one of his responsa as to whether a golem could be counted to a minyan for prayer. Elijah the Vilna Gaon intended to make a golem while he was still a teenager but desisted when he received a sign from heaven. Israel Baal Shem Tov had a golem who acted as his personal servant. On one occasion Israel told him to grease his wagon, and when he found that the golem had smeared grease all over the wagon, he realized that he would prefer a human servant. Rabbi David Jaffe of Grodno made a golem to act as a SHABBOS GOI to light the fire on shabbat. Unfortunately, being a golem, it was not very careful and ended up burning down the town. Many stories are told about the golem created by JUDAH LOEW BEN BEZALEL of Prague.

Goliath see DAVID

gomel blessing (Hebrew 'birkat ha-gomel') Thanksgiving BENEDICTION recited after surviving a dangerous experience. The *Talmud* mentions crossing a sea or a desert, release from prison and recovery from serious illness as all requiring a gomel blessing. In Temple times a thanksgiving offering would have been brought, and today the gomel takes its place. The blessing offers thanks to God for doing good to the undeserving, and the congregation respond with the hope that God will continue to do good in the future. It is customary to make the blessing within three days of the event, after having been called up for an aliyah to the torah. Women after childbirth also recite the gomel in the presence of ten adult males, either in the synagogue or at home.

good and evil (Hebrew 'tov ve-ra') Judaism does not see evil as an independent power but as produced by God Himself. Thus, God says to the prophet Isaiah: 'I am the Lord, and there is no other. I form light and create darkness, I make peace and create evil' (Isa. 45:6–7). The Rabbis prescribe a blessing to be said both when good happens and when evil occurs, since 'all that the Merciful One does He does (ultimately) for the best'. One Talmudic sage said that even death itself, the prime image of evil, must be referred to in the words of the creation story, when God saw everything that He had created 'and behold it was very good' (Gen. 1:31). Many medieval Jewish philosophers played down the reality of evil, seeing it as the absence of good. The Kabbalists, however, gave it an important role in their outlook. Evil does indeed come from a divine source, but in its structure as the SITRA ACHRA, or 'other side', it is in continuous conflict with the powers of good. Since it has no life of its own, it must attach itself parasitically onto holiness, and it is enabled to do so by man's SINS. *See also* INCLINATION.

Grace After Meals (Hebrew 'birkat ha-mazon') The recital of special BENEDICTIONS after eating is based on the biblical verse: 'And you shall eat and be satisfied, and bless the Lord your God' (Deut. 8:10). Although this verse implies that a blessing need only be said after a satisfying meal, the Rabbis prescribed the full Grace After Meals after eating an olive-sized piece of bread, some bread and salt being left on the table as a sign of abundance. During weekdays any knives remaining on the table are covered before Grace is said. This is because the table is like an ALTAR for which no iron could be used. The main parts of the Grace After Meals were composed by Moses when the manna appeared in the wilderness, by Joshua when the Israelites entered the Holy Land, by David at the conquest of Jerusalem and by Solomon when the Temple was built there. Shorter forms of Grace are said after foods other than bread. Blessings are also recited before food, since deriving benefit from God's world without first thanking Him is considered tantamount to stealing. *See also* PRAYER-BOOK.

greetings The most common form of greeting between Jews involves a reference to peace. Either simply 'SHALOM', 'peace', 'shalom aleikhem', 'peace be to you', or 'shabbat shalom', 'a peaceful shabbat'. To the dead one says 'lekh beshalom', 'go in peace', but one does not say this to the living. The latter are not yet at rest and instead may be told to 'go towards peace', 'lekh leshalom'. On festivals people greet each other with 'chag sameach', 'a happy festival', or with the Yiddish 'gut yontov', literally 'a good good-day'. On rosh ha-shanah and yom kippur the traditional greeting is that someone should be written down, and subsequently sealed, for good in the heavenly books which are opened before God who sits in judgment on the world. Mourners are not usually greeted, but God is asked to comfort them, together with the other mourners of Zion and Jerusalem, or they are wished 'long life'. On happy occasions Ashkenazim usually exclaim 'mazal tov', 'good luck', while Sephardim say 'mabruk', 'be blessed', or 'siman tov', 'a good sign'. Some rabbis insisted that greeting should be accompanied by shaking hands. Indeed, in the diamond industry, where Jewish dealers have been influential, traders do not exchange written contracts. They reach verbal agreement on a deal and then shake hands, saying 'lechaim uleshalom', 'to life and peace'. This is considered an absolutely binding arrangement which both vendor and buyer will honour without reservation, and it is used by Jews and non-Jews alike. In the synagogue after someone is called up for an aliyah to the torah he is greeted with the words 'yeyashar kochekha', 'may your strength be made straight', among Ashkenazim (often in the abbreviated Yiddish

The Israelites worshipping the **Golden Calf** (Lucas van Leyden).

A **golem** banging in a frenzy on the doors of a synagogue.

form 'shekoach'), and 'chazak u-varukh', 'may you be strong and blessed', among Sephardim. 'Lechaim', 'to life', usually precedes the drinking of alcohol. One should always be the first to greet other people, and one may even interrupt certain prayers to do so.

Guide for the Perplexed *see* MAIMONIDES, MOSES

gut yontov *see* GREETINGS

hadran (Aramaic for 'return') Formula recited at the completion of the study of a Talmudic tractate (*see* SIYYUM) involving the last section of the tractate followed by an Aramaic piece beginning: 'We shall return [hadran] to you tractate So and So, and you shall return to us. Our thought is about you ... and your thought is about us. We shall not forsake you ... and do not forsake us, neither in this world nor in the World to Come.' The type of Talmudic discourse delivered on these occasions, often in the dialectic style of PILPUL, is also known as a hadran.

haftarah (Hebrew for 'conclusion') The reading from the Prophets which follows the SEFER TORAH reading on shabbat, festivals and fast days (*see* LITURGY). The haftarah is now fixed by community custom and usually reflects one of the topics found in the torah reading or is associated with the special nature of the day. In the Middle Ages, however, the situation was more flexible, and communities exercised considerable freedom in choosing the haftarah. Thus, at the death of Sherira Gaon, in the 11c., the Babylonian community read the passage beginning: 'Now the days of David drew near that he should die' (II Kings 2). They even replaced the name of Solomon, David's son and heir, with the name of Hai who was Sherira's son and heir. When Moses Maimonides died, the community in Egypt read the passage beginning: 'Moses My servant is dead.' (Josh. 1:2). It is thought that the haftarah was first introduced at a time when Pentateuchal readings were banned. It continued to be read, even after the ban was lifted, to counter the views of those sects who denied that the Prophetic writings were part of scripture. In order not to elevate a Prophetic reading to the same level as a Pentateuchal one, however, the person who recites the haftarah is first called up for an ALIYAH and says the blessings over a torah section (*see* MAFTIR).

hagbahah (Hebrew for 'lifting up') The lifting up of the opened SEFER TORAH so that the congregation can see at least three columns of the text. Sephardim perform hagbahah before the torah is read, while most Ashkenazim wait until the end of the reading and call up one person to do the hagbahah and one to roll up the torah (*see* GELILAH). As the scroll is lifted up the congregation stand, often point with their little fingers and sing: 'This is the torah which Moses set before the Children of Israel. By the mouth of the Lord through the hand of Moses' (Deut. 4:44 and Num. 9:23). The origin of the custom of hagbahah goes back to an

interpretation of the verse: 'Cursed be the man who does not raise up the words of this torah' (Deut. 27:26). This curse is taken to refer to a chazzan who does not raise up the torah scroll to show it to the congregation.

haggadah (Hebrew for 'Passover story') The haggadah text used during the SEDER contains the liturgy recited in the course of the Passover family meal and is often profusely illustrated (*see* ILLUMINATED MANUSCRIPTS). Its purpose is to enable each family to tell the story of the redemption from Egypt as commanded in the Pentateuch (Exod. 13:8). The haggadah is made up in the main of biblical selections about the EXODUS, Psalms of praise, Rabbinic homilies, hymns and children's songs which are sung at the end of the meal. It has instructions about the ritual eating of matzah and maror, and about the drinking of the Four Cups of wine. Among its contents are some of the best-known and best-loved images and themes of Jewish literature: the FOUR QUESTIONS asked by the youngest member of the family; the typology of the four sons (wise, wicked, simple and unquestioning), the first three of whom ask a different version of the child's questions about Passover; the list of the ten PLAGUES during the chanting of which a drop of wine is spilled for each plague; the request to God to punish the Gentile nations who have oppressed the Jews, which is recited after the cup of Elijah has been poured out and the door opened; the wish to meet 'next year in Jerusalem'; and the song about the young goat (*see* CHAD GADYA) bought by the father for two coins, whose death is avenged by God. Written in a popular style, the haggadah has a distinctive folk quality and avoids doctrinal matters. It does, however, convey the idea that it is not human agency but God who redeems man, and the name of Moses does not appear in the text, despite his central role in the Bible story of the Exodus.

Hagiographa *see* BIBLE; TENAKH

hair and beard It is forbidden to shave the beard with a razor or to remove the hair at the corners of the head (Lev. 19:27, 21:5). This has led to the custom of Jews wearing beards, even though it is permissible to remove facial hair with scissors or an electric shaver. Kabbalists believed that the beard should not be trimmed at all since there is mystical speculation on the beard of God and man should practise imitatio dei. Another objection to men removing their beards is that this makes them look like women and thus infringes the prohibition on men wearing women's clothes. The 19c. halakhist Rabbi Moses Sofer argued that the first man who removed his beard did indeed transgress this prohibition, but once it became common to have a smooth, hairless face, this ceased to be a distinguishing mark of women. It is said, however, that a man without a beard is like a eunuch. Although having a beard is an Orthodox characteristic, there is a Yiddish proverb which says there can be a Jew without a beard and a beard without a Jew (i.e. outward appearance does not determine the quality of one's religion). There is also a traditional comment that, if a beard were a sign of wisdom, then goats would be the wisest of creatures. The prohibition on rounding the corners of the head has led to the custom of growing long side curls called PEOT, found particularly among groups influenced by the Kabbalah. In biblical times a Nazirite would not cut his hair (*see* ABSALOM). When the Nazirite SAMSON was filled with the divine spirit, his hair rang out like a bell, and his strength left him after his locks were cropped. Some Jewish families do not cut the hair of a boy until he is three years old, and the ceremony of the first hair-cutting takes place on LAG BA-OMER with relatives participating in the tonsure. The child's hair is weighed against money before it is burnt, and the money given to charity. Male Jews wear a HEAD-COVERING, and Orthodox women cover their hair after marriage (*see* SHEITEL).

hakkafot (Hebrew for 'circumambulations') The processions round the BIMAH at the centre of the synagogue. These take place on the festival of SUKKOT when men, carrying the FOUR SPECIES, circumambulate the synagogue once chanting the hoshana prayers and on HOSHANA RABBA when seven hakkafot are performed. On SIMCHAT TORAH all the scrolls from the ark are carried round in seven hakkafot with much dancing and singing to celebrate the completion of the torah reading. At the end of each hakkafah the scrolls are handed to others, so that as many people as possible have the opportunity to rejoice with the torah. There is also a custom in some communities to circumambulate a corpse prior to burial, chanting verses to protect the deceased from the power of demons and scattering coins in different directions to encourage them to depart. The mystics recommended seven circumambulations of the graves of the righteous in times of drought, when seeking to avoid impending trouble, or when an individual wishes for children, health, etc. The purpose of this is to arouse the righteous to intercessory pray to help those in need. It is also customary for at least ten men (minyan) to walk around the perimeter of a cemetery seven times when consecrating the ground for Jewish burials and for a bride to circumambulate her groom under the CHUPPAH seven times in traditional marriage ceremonies.

hakhnasat orchim *see* HOSPITALITY

halakhah (Hebrew for 'way' or 'path') The legal tradition of Judaism which is usually contrasted with the theology, ethics and folklore of AGGADAH. Halakhic decisions determine normative practice, and where there is a dispute, these decisions, in theory at least, follow the MAJORITY OPINION of the rabbis, as illustrated in a dispute between ELIEZER BEN HYRCANUS and his colleagues. The situation of halakhic decision-making is complicated because the usually stricter legal views expressed in the literature of Kabbalah are preferred by some groups in place of Talmudic and post-Talmudic precedents. Local custom (*see* MINHAG) also often overrides the majority opinion found in law codes, like the SHULCHAN ARUKH, and in RESPONSA. *See also* JUDAH LOEW BEN BEZALEL; SHALOM; TALMUD; ZOHAR.

hallel (Hebrew for 'praise') A group of PSALMS (113–18) praising God, remembering the Exodus and expressing the hope in divine salvation, which are

The **hallel** Psalms from an illuminated **haggadah** manuscript.

Jewish Cantors in the Synagogue by Jack Levine. Notice the **hair and beard** and the tallit which are characteristic of an Orthodox rabbi or chazzan.

sung on festivals and new moon days. At the new moon a shorter form of the hallel is recited because, just as the moon waxes, so Israel will wax once again in the age of the Messiah. The shorter form is also said on the last six days of PESACH. One reason given for this is that the Egyptian army was drowned after the crossing of the Red Sea, at the end of Passover. The longer hallel was, therefore, considered inappropriate since God even rebuked the angels who sang to Him on that occasion saying: 'My creatures are drowning in the sea and you wish to sing?' During the festival of SUKKOT palm branches are waved to the four directions of the compass and towards heaven and earth as certain hallel verses are chanted. The tunes used for hallel on different festivals reflect the musical traditions of the festival LITURGY.

Haman Villain of the Book of Esther who gained permission from the Persian king Ahasuerus to exterminate the Jews of his empire. Haman's plans were frustrated by the Jewish Queen ESTHER, by MORDECAI and by the cries of the schoolchildren whom he had oppressed and who awakened God's compassion. Haman's anti-Jewish feelings were aroused by Mordecai who refused to bow down to him and worship him as a deity. Anti-Semitism was characteristic of his family, however, for he was a descendant of Agag, the king of AMALEK. Haman was eventually hanged, together with ten of his sons, on the very same tree he had prepared as a gallows for Mordecai (Esther 7:10). This tree was a thorn bush, all the other trees having refused to serve as the executor of the righteous Mordecai. Haman's grandchildren became converts to Judaism, and some of the Talmudic rabbis claimed descent from him. On the festival of PURIM when the story is read in synagogue Haman's name is greeted with boos and jeers, because the name of evil-doers must be blotted out. *See also* ADE-LO-YADA.

hamantaschen *see* PURIM

Hananiah, Mishael, and Azariah (also known by their Babylonian names Shadrach, Meshach and Abednego) Three Judaean exiles who, like Daniel, maintained their Jewish life-style even though they occupied important positions in the Babylonian court (Dan. 1). The particular merit that enabled them to resist temptation was their strict adherence to the dietary laws. They were perfectly righteous and would not worship idols. Instead they preferred martyrdom, despite being discouraged from such a course by the prophet EZEKIEL. They were made to pass through a fiery furnace and miraculously came out alive. The Angel of Hail came to God volunteering to save them by drenching the fire, but GABRIEL, the Angel of Fire, was chosen for the task since he offered to cool the fire at the centre of the furnace and heat up its extremities, thus increasing the quality of the miracle. During their time in the furnace, the three would-be martyrs sang songs of praise to God.

Hannah Mother of the prophet SAMUEL and a biblical prophetess. Hannah was originally barren and prayed for a child at the Shiloh sanctuary. The High Priest ELI thought she was drunk because she was not making any sound, but in fact she was simply praying silently with great emotion (I Sam. 1). Her prayers were answered, and at a very advanced age she gave birth to a son. Since God listened to her entreaties, the Rabbis held up Hannah's prayer as an example of how to pray. They therefore made the silent AMIDAH the centre of the liturgy.

Hannah and Her Seven Sons According to the Apocrypha Hannah was a pious woman who lived in 2c. BCE Palestine during the anti-Jewish persecutions of Antiochus Epiphanes. Jews were forced to eat pork to show they rejected their religion, and Hannah encouraged six of her seven sons to prefer a martyr's death rather than publicly break the rules of their faith. They refused to eat and were boiled alive in cauldrons. When the turn of her seventh son came, she was pressured to persuade him to eat pig's meat and live. Instead, she told him to follow the example of his brothers, and he too died a martyr. Hannah then committed SUICIDE by jumping into the fire so that no man would touch her. Rabbinic literature contains a somewhat similar story about a woman named Miriam who lived during the Hadrianic persecutions in 2c. CE Palestine. She, too, had seven sons who were martyred, and she supported them in their faith. She told them that, when they got to heaven, they should tell their father Abraham not to be proud, for he was called upon to offer up only one son (*see* AKEDAH), while she had to offer up seven. His experience was only a trial, while hers was for real.

Hannah Rachel of Ludomir (1805–92) Female Chasidic leader, born Hannah Rachel Werbemacher and later known as the Maid of Ludomir. As a girl Hannah Rachel studied Rabbinic literature with her father and had several ecstatic experiences. She used to visit the grave of her dead mother to pray there, and on one occasion she fell asleep by the graveside. When she awoke, she was afraid and ran away, only to fall into an open grave in the cemetery. This was a great shock to her, and she became ill. When she recovered, she claimed she had seen visions and received a new soul. She started putting on a tallit and tefillin, usually only worn by men, and when her father died, she recited the kaddish prayer which was the prerogative of a son. A group of Chasidic followers gathered round her, and she used to teach torah to them through the open door of her home, which led onto a synagogue specially built for this purpose. Eventually, other leaders of the Chasidic Movement pressured her into marrying at the age of forty, and thereafter she withdrew from any leadership role. Towards the end of her life she emigrated to the Holy Land where she was involved in a Kabbalistic attempt to hasten the coming of the Messiah.

har ha-zeitim *see* OLIVES, MOUNT OF

harvest festivals The three harvest or PILGRIM FESTIVALS have a historical dimension in commemoration of the Exodus, but they also celebrate the three harvest seasons of the agricultural year in the land of Israel. Thus PESACH is the beginning of the barley harvest, seven weeks later SHAVUOT is the time of wheat harvest and the beginning of the season of first fruits, and SUKKOT the time of ingathering of grapes and the remaining produce of the field. Sukkot is also the happiest of the festivals since the farmer rejoices at the completion of the year's harvest and is thankful for God's bounty. Various agricultural rituals are associated with the harvests, for instance the decoration of the synagogue with trees and flowers on shavuot and the use of the FOUR SPECIES on sukkot.

ha-shem *see* TETRAGRAMMATON

hashkavah *see* MEMORIAL PRAYERS

Hasmoneans Dynastic name of the MACCABEES who established a royal line after their successful revolt against the Seleucid rulers of Palestine in the 2c. CE. Since kings were ideally from the House of David, the Hasmoneans, who were a priestly family, had no real claim to kingship. Their reign was beset by opposition from the Pharisees, and the *Talmud* barely mentions them at all. Nevertheless, the Hasmonean kings ruled an independent Hebrew kingdom until 37 BCE when internecine disputes about succession to the throne led to Roman intervention.

hatikvah (Hebrew for 'The Hope') National anthem of the State of Israel sung to a folk tune of Moldavian origin. The words were composed by the Hebrew poet Naphtali Herz Imber, who led an unhappy life and died of alcoholism in the USA. The hatikvah was adopted by the Zionist Congress as an anthem and eventually by the new Jewish state, although it was never officially legalized as the Israeli anthem. The words of the hatikvah tell of the hope which lives within the heart of all Jews to be members of a free people in their own land, the land of Zion and Jerusalem. Some Orthodox Jews objected to the secular tone of the hatikvah and changed one or two words to give it a more religious flavour. Thus, for instance, in the modified version, instead of the hope of becoming 'a free people', which has libertine associations in Hebrew, there is the hope of becoming 'a holy people'. Anti-Zionist Jews regard the hatikvah as anathema.

havdalah (Hebrew for 'separation') Ceremony performed on Saturday night at the end of shabbat to mark the beginning of profane time and in a shortened form at the end of festivals. An initial havdalah prayer is part of the maariv service prior to the ceremony at home. In that ceremony a blessing is recited over wine or, if that is not available, over any drink which is considered a national drink and therefore of some importance. A blessing is then made before smelling SPICES, which are thought to revive the body after the departure of the special shabbat soul (*see* NESHAMAH YETERAH). A third blessing involves a candle of twisted wicks, since Adam first discovered the use of fire after the end of the Sabbath of Creation. The havdalah prayer is then recited, blessing God who distinguishes between the holy and the profane, between light and darkness, between Israel and the Gentiles, and between the seventh day and the working week. It is customary to extinguish the flame in some wine, which is spilled into a plate as a sign of plenty, and to rub some of this wine onto the eyelids and onto the corners of the pockets of one's clothing. At the termination of yom kippur only the wine and the candle are used, and at

Haman and his ten sons hanged on the gallows that they had prepared for Mordecai (14c. German).

the end of festivals the havdalah ceremony is performed without either the spices or the candle flame. One is not allowed to eat anything before havdalah, and if one forgets to perform the rite, it may still be performed until Tuesday evening or for the whole of the next day after a festival. The mystics understood havdalah as protection against the forces of impurity which begin to be active in the world after the Sabbath is over.

hazkarat neshamot *see* MEMORIAL PRAYERS

head-covering Men cover their heads during prayer, and many Orthodox men wear a small skull-cap, known as a yarmulke, kipah or kappel, at all times to remind them of God's presence. The custom itself seems to have developed from the Temple ritual, where a priest wore a head-covering, and the *Talmud* recommends covering the heads of young boys to ensure they will be pious when they grow up. There is some evidence, however, that during the Middle Ages covering the head even in the synagogue was not a universal practice. The special hats (*see* BADGE, JEWISH) that Jews were forced to wear in Christian and Moslem countries presumably fostered the custom. Today the wearing of a head-covering serves to differentiate Jews from Gentiles, particularly from Christians who bare their heads in church. In radical Reform congregations, however, the practice has been abolished, and some Orthodox Jews of German origin ('yekkes') only cover their heads in synagogue or while out of doors but not at home, except when reciting a benediction. The type of head-covering worn by Jews indicates their group affiliation. Thus, members of the Chasidic Movement usually wear a velvet skull-cap under a black hat or a SHTREIMEL, while many Israelis wear knitted skull-caps, indicating a positive attitude toward modernity. Orthodox women cover their heads after marriage out of modesty, since their exposed HAIR is regarded as a form of nakedness. In theory no benediction should be said or ritual performed in the presence of a married woman whose hair is uncovered. In practice, however, only a minority of Orthodox women keep their hair completely covered at all times with a SHEITEL, or a scarf, after marriage. The majority wear a hat only while attending a synagogue service. One modern halakhist, Y.M. Epstein (1829–1908), reluctantly admitted that, because it is now so prevalent for married women not to cover their hair, this can no longer be regarded as immodest.

heaven *see* PARADISE

Hebrew A Semitic language. The Jewish Bible is mostly written in consonantal Hebrew (*see* MASORAH), with no vowel signs, although some of the biblical books are in ARAMAIC. For Jews Hebrew is the holy tongue through which God created the world, and its ALPHABET still contains a creative power for those who know how to combine its letters. According to the Rabbinic tradition, everyone spoke Hebrew until the one language of the world was divided up into seventy languages after the building of the Tower of BABEL (Gen. 11). In Egypt the Israelites continued to speak Hebrew among themselves, and by retaining their identity, they merited redemption from slavery. For several centuries BCE, most people in Palestine and in the DIASPORA spoke in the vernacular, which was usually one of the Aramaic dialects, and Hebrew became a learned language used for literary and liturgical purposes. The Bible itself had to be translated into an Aramaic TARGUM so that ordinary people could understand it, and the *Mishnah* was written in a simpler Hebrew style than the Bible. Several different pronunciations of liturgical Hebrew grew up among Ashkenazim and Sephardim in the Middle Ages. With the rise of modern Zionism Hebrew began to be revived as a spoken language by Eliezer Ben Yehudah (1858–1922), who refused to speak any other language, coined new words and began a major Hebrew dictionary with no Aramaic or foreign words. Today in the modern State of Israel Hebrew is spoken with a modified Sephardi pronunciation. In the days of the Messiah, all nations will once again speak Hebrew.

Hebron (also known as Kiryat-Arba) City in the Judaean hills near Jerusalem and one of the holy cities of the Land of Israel. The cave of MACHPELAH in Hebron is the burial place of the Patriarchs. Originally Hebron was a CITY OF REFUGE (Josh. 20:7), and for a time it was King David's capital (II Sam. 2:11). During the Crusades the Jewish community of Hebron dwindled away but flourished once again under Moslem rule. From the 17c. it became a centre of the Kabbalah.

heikhal *see* ARK, HOLY

Heikhalot (Hebrew for 'halls') Works expressing the MAASEH MERKAVAH mysticism of the Talmudic and early medieval periods. Heikhalot literature is based on the vision of the prophet Ezekiel (Ezek. 1) who saw the heavens open and a divine chariot surrounding the THRONE OF GLORY. The heroes of the Heikhalot are the Mishnaic sages AKIVA and ISHMAEL BEN ELISHA whose mystical adventures and ascents through the seven halls are recorded. Before undertaking such an ascent, called a 'descent of the chariot', the mystical adept purified himself through fasting and prayers. He also mastered the special passwords made up of divine or angelic names which enabled him to pass the angels who guard the entrance to each hall and to return to earth once more. On this journey he traversed rivers of fire until he arrived in the highest hall of the highest heaven. There he met METATRON, an angel known as the little God, and he achieved his vision of the throne and contemplated the wondrous size of God expressed in the SHIUR KOMAH. The *Talmud* indicates the dangerous nature of the ascent in its story of the four sages who entered PARADISE. One died, another was driven mad by the vision, and a third became a heretic. Only Akiva returned in peace. The ecstatic hymns of the Heikhalot literature had a considerable influence on the poetry of the synagogue liturgy.

hekhsher *see* KOSHER

helzl *see* CHOLENT

heretic *see* APIKOROS

Herzl, Theodor (1860–1904) Austrian writer and founder of the Zionist Movement (*see* ZIONISM). As a young man Herzl was aware of the problems faced by Jews in Gentile society and advocated assimilation through the mass baptism of Jewish children. It was the anti-Semitism he found in France, while covering the DREYFUS AFFAIR as a journalist in the late 1890s, which convinced him that Jews needed their own homeland. He published a work, *The Jewish State*, in 1896 setting out the details of his somewhat idealized solution, and a novel, *Old-New Land*, in 1902 which opens with the words: 'If you will it, it is no dream.' The First Zionist Congress was organized by Herzl in Basle in 1897. He spent the rest of his short life trying to persuade wealthy Jews to give financial support to his project and meeting with a number of world leaders such as the German Kaiser, the Turkish Sultan, the King of Italy, the Pope and British and Russian government ministers. *See also* SHTADLAN.

hesped (Hebrew for 'eulogy') A speech usually delivered immediately prior to a BURIAL to honour the deceased and to stir the emotions of family and friends. There are a number of references to eulogies in the Bible, the most famous being David's lament for Saul and his son Jonathan which begins with the words: 'Your beauty, O Israel, is slain upon the high places. How are the mighty fallen!' (II Sam. 1:19). On joyous days of the Jewish year, eulogies are not delivered at funerals except in the case of important people. Although the orator who delivers the hesped is meant to praise the deceased, he should not exaggerate too much. The *Talmud* says that, just as the dead are judged and punished, so are those who deliver untruthful eulogies about them.

Hezekiah King of the Southern Kingdom of Judah in the 8c. BCE. Hezekiah was regarded as an outstanding religious monarch who purged Israelite religion of heathen accretions and destroyed the BRAZEN SERPENT which had been turned into an object of idolatry (II Kings 18:4–5). His mother saved him from death when he was a child by covering him with the fire-proof blood of the SALAMANDER. He was thus able to survive an idolatrous fire ritual. When in later life Hezekiah fell mortally ill, he was visited by the prophet ISAIAH who reprimanded him for not marrying and having children. Hezekiah repented, recovered from his illness and married Isaiah's daughter, by whom he fathered the wicked Manasseh. He lived a frugal life, subsisting on a daily meal of plain vegetables, and his reputation for piety led him to be considered as the Messiah by some rabbis.

High Priest (Hebrew 'kohen gadol') Chief functionary of the Tabernacle and in the Temple cultus and descendant of AARON the first High Priest. The holiness of the office meant that the High Priest could only marry an Israelite virgin, and not a widow, divorce or convert (Lev. 21:13–15). He alone entered the HOLY OF HOLIES as part of the ritual atonement on YOM KIPPUR. In order to do so he had to be married, and a second wife was always on standby in case his wife died. A rope was attached to his waist so that, if necessary, he could be brought out from the Holy of Holies should he die. Even Satan did not dare to accuse

A selection of skull caps used as **head-coverings** by religious Jews.

A page of **Hebrew** script from an illuminated haggadah manuscript.

Theodor **Herzl**, founder of political Zionism.

Israel when the High Priest entered the Holy of Holies, for the High Priest is said to be greater even than the angel MICHAEL, since the latter can only plead for Israel with words, while the former can also intercede on their behalf with ritual deeds. A High Priest should excel his fellow priests (*see* PRIEST) in strength, riches, wisdom and appearance. *See also* CITY OF REFUGE; KOHEN; METATRON; URIM AND THUMMIM.

Hillel (1c. BCE–1c. CE) Sage of the early Rabbinic period, commonly known as Hillel the Elder. Hillel was a descendant of the House of David and left his home in Babylonia to study under the Palestinian teachers Shemaiah and Avtalyon, both of whom were from families of converts to Judaism. As an impoverished Babylonian student, Hillel had to climb up onto the roof of their academy to hear the lectures since he could not afford to pay the doorkeeper for admittance. On one occasion during a severe snowstorm, he had to be rescued from the roof on the Sabbath, where he lay under a covering of snow. His passion for study was commended by his teachers, and he came to be the outstanding member of the academy, rising to the position of head of Palestinian Jewry (*see* NASI). As a religious leader he was less conservative, and more innovative, than his main colleague SHAMMAI, with whom he had a number of important disputes. His attitude to converts was generally accommodating. Thus he responded to a would-be convert, who wanted to know the whole TORAH while standing on one leg, by saying: 'What is hateful to you do not do to your fellow. The rest is commentary on this. Go and study.' In order to alleviate the plight of the poor, who needed to borrow money in the year before SHEMITTAH when debts were annulled, Hillel introduced a prosbul document which enabled debts to be assigned to a bet din so they could still be collected. Stories about Hillel came to occupy a special place in people's consciousness, as did his sayings, like: 'If I am not for myself, who will be for me, and if I am for myself alone, what am I? And if not now, when?' The followers of Hillel, Bet Hillel (*see* GAMALIEL), became the dominant party after his death, and in most of their disputes with the followers of Shammai, Bet Shammai, they were the winners since a BAT KOL gave them support.

Hirsch, Samson Raphael (1808–88) Leader of the Neo-Orthodox Movement in Germany. Hirsch was educated both at a yeshivah and at university and was thus steeped in modern German culture, as well as in Jewish tradition. After the publication of his first work in 1836, *The Nineteen Letters About Judaism*, he began the movement which later came to be known as Neo-Orthodoxy. The ideology of this movement was the combination of torah with general culture under the slogan of 'torah im derekh eretz'. Hirsch believed that Jews had to embrace the best of their Gentile cultural environment in order to express the values of Judaism, and he succeeded in reversing the assimilationist trend of German Jewry. Hirsch left an important position as District Rabbi of Moravia to lead a small Orthodox community in Frankfurt-am-Main in 1851. There he built up a separatist congregation, educational institutions and a journal to express his ideas. Hirsch was opposed by Reform Jews, who objected to his

traditionalism, by ORTHODOX Jews, who objected to his involvement with secular studies, and also by traditional German rabbis who did not want their congregations to separate themselves from the general Jewish community. He modified Jewish ritual just sufficiently to make it acceptable to moderns, introducing a German sermon and a choir into the liturgy, but otherwise insisted on a strict conformity with halakhic norms.

Holocaust Originally meaning a burnt offering that was totally consumed by fire, the term is also used of the Nazi extermination of Jews during the Second World War. The mass killing of Jews was the culmination of a process of Nazi anti-Semitism which began with anti-Jewish legislation and agitation. The idea originally was to encourage Jews to emigrate from Germany and Austria. The next development was the burning down of synagogues throughout Germany on 9 November 1938, known as 'Kristalnacht' ('Night of Glass') because the streets were covered with broken glass. Jewish businesses were looted, and mass deportations to CONCENTRATION CAMPS began. When millions of Jews came under Nazi rule after the occupation of Poland, the Nazis herded Jews into crowded ghettos (*see* GHETTO) or executed whole communities. This eventually led to an organized policy of genocide in the death camps, which was carried out in the main by gassing. It is estimated that around six million Jews were killed in the Holocaust under the Nazi extermination programme, which was also directed against other groups such as gypsies and homosexuals. Hitler even diverted valuable resources from the war effort to make Europe 'Judenrein' ('free of Jews'). Although there were many sporadic incidents of resistance and revolt, the most famous being the Warsaw Ghetto Uprising in 1943, the policy of extermination succeeded in gaining the passive participation of most of the victims through deception, dehumanization and their inability to believe that man's inhumanity to man could sink to such depths. The Holocaust has been described by survivors as a kingdom of hell on earth. The day on which the Warsaw Ghetto Uprising began, 19 April, is commemorated by Jews as Holocaust Remembrance Day. *See also* KRIMCHAKS; LADINO.

Holy of Holies (Hebrew 'kodesh ha-kodashim') The most sacred area in the TABERNACLE and in the TEMPLE where the ARK OF THE COVENANT was kept. It could only be entered by the HIGH PRIEST once a year, on YOM KIPPUR, to offer incense during the ritual of ATONEMENT. Workers had to be lowered into the Holy of Holies from above to make any repairs as they were neither allowed to enter it nor to stand on the holy ground. The Holy of Holies was curtained off from the rest of the sanctuary (*see* PAROKHET), and inside was the foundation rock, even shetiyyah. This rock is at the very centre of the world, and it was the base on which the world was created (*see* CREATION). Until the end of the first Temple period a flask of MANNA and the rod of AARON were also kept in the Holy of Holies, but in the second Temple the area was completely bare, since even the ark had been hidden away before the Babylonian Captivity. In the era of the Messiah a stream will flow from under the

Holy of Holies and will reveal all the buried Temple treasures. *See also* MORIAH, MOUNT.

honey (Hebrew 'devash') From biblical times honey has symbolized the sweetness and goodness of life, the manna in the wilderness being described as having a honey-like taste (Exod. 16:31) and the Holy Land depicted as a land 'flowing with milk and honey' (Exod. 3:8). Originally honey was made out of dates, but in post-biblical times bees' honey became the popular symbol of sweetness. It is specifically eaten on the ROSH HA-SHANAH festival, when bread is dipped into honey instead of into salt, and a piece of apple is dipped in honey to guarantee a sweet new year. Although the bee is non-kosher, its honey is allowed by the Jewish DIETARY LAWS because it is not considered as an actual part of the bee's body. According to the midrash a river of honey flows through Paradise.

horeb *see* SINAI, MOUNT.

Horwitz, Joseph Josel (1848–1919) Leader of one of the more extreme branches of the MUSAR MOVEMENT. Horwitz, who came to be known as the Grandfather of Novaredok, decided to devote his life to religion after meeting Israel Lipkin Salanter, the founder of Musar. When his wife died, Horwitz locked himself away from the world for several years, his only contact being the two holes in the wall of his room for food to be passed through, one for meat and the other for milk. He founded a Musar yeshivah in Novaredok, where he taught that life should be based on complete trust in God, and he always signed his own letters 'The one who has faith'. He prayed that his students should fail in their worldly undertakings, so that they would fall back on trust in God. Horwitz prescribed spiritual exercises to strengthen them against being swayed by the opinions of others, and when mixing with people outside the yeshivah, they dressed in shabby clothes. They were encouraged to go into chemist shops and, when their turn came to be served, to ask for nails or some other unlikely item, so that they became hardened to the mockery of others. The Novaredok students thus learnt to accept the truth according to their own inner conviction and not to follow the opinions of the crowd. Horwitz himself set up yeshivot all over Russia but would not hestitate to close them down if he felt they were not living up to his ideals. In the post-Holocaust period extreme Novaredok-style academies have become less common. There are still some that follow Horwitz's methods, but though they may have a full complement of staff, they have few students, so demanding are their standards.

Hosea Prophet of the 8c. BCE whose warnings of punishment and exile are collected in the Book of Hosea. Israel, like a faithless wife, had abandoned the covenant with God and worshipped idols, so God had temporarily forsaken her. Hosea's own wife was an adulteress, yet his love and forgiveness for her were to act as symbols of God's love and forgiveness for Israel. Hosea's call for repentance: 'Return, O Israel, to the Lord your God for you have stumbled in your iniquity' (14:2) is read in synagogues on the Saturday prior to yom kippur. God's words of hope and

Loading a transport of old people from the Theresienstadt ghetto to Auschwitz during the **Holocaust** (ink drawing by Leo Haas, 1943).

The **Holy of Holies** of a Canaanite temple at Hazor, Israel.

redemption to Israel: 'And I will betroth you unto Me for ever, . . . in righteousness, . . . in loving kindness, . . . in faithfulness, and you shall know the Lord' (2:21-2) are recited each weekday morning when the tefillin are wound round the hand. Some biblical commentators found Hosea's act of marrying and maintaining a 'loose woman' so repulsive that they treated it as an allegory or merely a dream.

hoshana rabba The seventh day of the SUKKOT festival is known as hoshana rabba because the hoshanna ('please save') prayers are recited in full on this day during seven circumambulations (*see* HAKKAFOT) of the synagogue carrying the four species. Seven torah scrolls are carried onto the bimah before the prayers begin, and as each circumambulation is completed, one scroll is returned to the ark. At the end of these prayers, a bundle of willow twigs is beaten on the ground by each worshipper five times, or in some communities until all the leaves drop off. These bundles are called hoshanot. On hoshana rabba the divine judgment of man which began on ROSH HA-SHANAH is concluded, and man's fate for the next year is decided. It is thus a minor yom kippur, and the white, shroud-like kitel is worn by the chazzan. There is a folk belief that if one cannot see one's shadow the night before hoshana rabba, or if one only sees a headless shadow, one will not survive until the next New Year festival. The mystics introduced the custom of staying awake all night and studying torah as an act of rectification (tikkun) to nullify any outstanding sins on the eve of hoshana rabba. Among the MOUNTAIN JEWS, the girls go out to dance on hoshana rabba.

hospitality (Hebrew 'hakhnasat orchim') Jewish tradition traces the practice of welcoming strangers into one's home back to Abraham, whose hospitality serves as a model for his descendants (*see* ZEKHUT AVOT). Abraham's tent had four doors so that he could see anyone who passed by and could extend an invitation to them. Even when suffering from the after-effects of circumcision, he left a conversation with God to invite three passing angels in, mistaking them for weary travellers (Gen. 18). This incident shows that hospitality is more important than being in God's presence. There are many other examples of hospitality in the Bible. Lot invited the same angels in and protected them at considerable risk to himself and his family (Gen. 29); the prostitute Rahab hid JOSHUA's spies in her home prior to the Israelite conquest of Canaan (Josh. 2); and the prophet Elisha was given a room by the Shunamite woman in her home (II Kings 4). After the destruction of the Temple, a man's table is an altar of atonement, and the hospitality he shows to poor guests is his sacrificial offering. One's house should, therefore, be open to all, and a host must go out of his way to make guests feel comfortable. It is even told of one Talmudic rabbi that, before sitting down to a meal, he would go to the door and say: 'All who are hungry come and eat.' This phrase is now part of the Passover seder ritual, at the beginning of which all who are hungry or needy are invited in. In the Middle Ages the SYNAGOGUE was used as a rest house for travellers, and today it is customary to invite strangers who attend synagogue services back home for a Sabbath or festival meal.

Huldah Prophetess of the 7c. BCE who was active in the Southern Kingdom of Judah. King JOSIAH turned to her for advice since, as a woman, she was likely to be more compassionate about the weaknesses of the Israelites than the male prophets. His emissaries found her teaching the oral torah to the elders in a yeshivah in Jerusalem. Her name means 'weasel', and she was known by it because of the disrespectful manner in which she replied to the king (II Kings 22:15). She is the only person not of royal descent buried within the walls of Jerusalem, and after her death, she was put in charge of one of the women's sections of Paradise.

Ibn Ezra, Abraham (1090–1164) Spanish Bible commentator and poet. He married the daughter of JUDAH HALEVI, but for much of his adult life Ibn Ezra lived as a poor wanderer, travelling from country to country. He visited London in 1158 and even reached India, writing his poetry, grammar books and biblical commentaries en route. His travels were undertaken to find his only son, who had been converted to Islam, and to bring him back to Judaism. Ibn Ezra ascribed his lack of success at business and his poverty to an astrological fate. 'If my trade were in candles, the sun would never set till I died. If I were a merchant who dealt in shrouds, no one would pass away all my days.' He believed in alchemy and astrology and that people could receive answers to their questions in dreams. He is also reputed to have created a golem, which he subsequently destroyed. Ibn Ezra was an unconventional writer, of an independent and critical mind, whose biblical exegesis sometimes differed markedly from Rabbinic orthodoxy. Later generations of pietists were wary of his commentaries, since they suspected him of heresy, and were disturbed by the sarcastic remarks he made against those whose opinions he could not accept.

Ibn Gabirol, Solomon (1021–58) Spanish poet and philosopher. Ibn Gabirol was orphaned when young and was forced to wander from place to place in Spain, because he made many enemies through his outspokenness. On his travels he composed poetry and also brought Neoplatonic ideas from Arabic sources to Christian Europe. His own mysticism, with its rejection of the illusions of this world and a deep yearning for God, had considerable influence on the Kabbalah. The liturgy still preserves Ibn Gabirol's philosophical poem 'Keter Malkhut', with its lofty spirituality, which is recited in some communities on yom kippur, and he is said to have written the ADON OLAM hymn. Ibn Gabirol created a female golem to be a woman servant in his house. He was denounced to the government for suspected immoral practices, and he had to show the investigators that she was really made of wood and hinges. Legend tells how he was killed by a Moslem who was jealous of his poetical gifts and was buried under a fig tree. The figs thereafter appeared early and were very sweet. In order to find out why this was so, an investigator dug under the tree, found Ibn Gabirol's body and eventually caught the murderer.

Ibn Latif, Isaac (1220–90) Spanish mystic. Ibn Latif was said to have had one foot in the Kabbalah and one foot in philosophy. He in fact believed that the two were reconcilable because Kabbalah was superior to philosophy and dealt with a higher level of reality: while the intellect only reached the back of God, mystical ecstasy could come before His face. His own system of Kabbalistic mysticism used a new terminology to express the way God was in everything and everything in God. He based this system on the philosophical writings of Maimonides, which he interpreted in a mystical way. Considerable criticism was directed against Ibn Latif, even from those who respected his saintly character. They suspected his Kabbalistic ideas, since he had not received them from a teacher but had made them up out of his own mind, and refused to rely on Ibn Latif's views.

Ibn Pakuda, Bachya (11c.) Spanish moralist and author of the first, and one of the most important, works of Jewish ethics. Ibn Pakuda called his work *Duties of the Heart* to contrast its contents with the laws of Judaism, which were duties of the body. He felt that the inner purity of man was somewhat neglected in Jewish literature and that the halakhah was followed in a mechanical and selfish manner by ordinary people. Religious morality should be based on the love of God and the contemplation of His greatness, the purpose of the laws being to subdue the animal side of man's nature, so that he should perfect himself. Although Ibn Pakuda includes philosophy in his work and argues for God's existence, he states that 'true philosophy is to know oneself'. He was not averse to quoting from non-Jewish, particularly Sufi, sources, and he divided his book into ten sections representing the stages of the spiritual life. Rabbi Joseph Caro was told by his maggid to study Ibn Pakuda's writings so as to subdue his evil inclination, and the *Duties of the Heart* was very influential on the Musar Movement in the 19c.

idolatry (Hebrew 'avodah zarah', meaning 'alien worship') Worshipping idols is prohibited in the Decalogue and the sin of the GOLDEN CALF was regarded as the lowest point of Israelite religion. Idolatry is viewed as a Cardinal SIN (*see* CAPITAL PUNISHMENT) and is forbidden even to save life. Legends of Jewish MARTYRDOM deal mainly with resistance to idolatry, whether pagan or Christian. Maimonides stated explicitly that the deification of Jesus was idolatrous, though this remark was deleted by Christian censors from the published editions of his code. Even those rabbis who did not regard the combined worship, shituf, of Jesus and God the Father as prohibited to Gentiles had no doubts that for Jews conversion to Christianity meant submitting to idolatry. Idolatry began when people began to show respect to God by worshipping His representatives, like the sun and the moon. In the course of time they focused their devotion not on the transcendent Creator God but on these intermediaries. God could not destroy such idols, because many of the objects worshipped were necessary for the running of the world. ABRAHAM rediscovered monotheism when he realized that the idols his father made were merely sticks and stones. Judaism today regards the evil inclination

Wood engraving showing a man with a headless shadow on the night of **hoshana rabba**. According to Jewish folklore, this was a sign that the person concerned would die within the year.

The **idolatry** of the heathen, from a 15c. Spanish Bible.

driving men to idolatry as having lost its force, with people simply continuing the idolatrous traditions of their fathers. Yet whoever denies idolatry is worthy of being called a Jew. The biblical condemnation of graven images has had a profound effect on Jewish attitudes to visual ART. Synagogue decorations are usually only two-dimensional, lacking both heavenly and human figures, and the medium of sound predominates in religious expression.

illuminated manuscripts A medieval ART form allowing artistic expression which was generally restricted because of the association between art and IDOLATRY. Illuminated manuscripts were widely used, despite opposition to pictures which might distract people from their devotions. Some of the illustrators employed were non-Jews, but the majority were Jews who adopted models used in Christian or Moslem texts. Thus, for instance, carpet pages were popular among Jews in Islamic lands, since Moslems did not approve of the depiction of human figures and preferred decorative motifs which gave the impression of a patterned carpet. God is not depicted except symbolically, e.g. as a hand at the edge of a scene. Human figures are quite common in texts from non-Moslem countries, which even show a naked Adam and Eve (perhaps from a Christian artist) and in one scroll of Esther (see MEGILLAH) used by Jews in China the figures are obviously Chinese. Sometimes, however, human figures appear without heads or with their faces masked by helmets. The Passover HAGGADAH was a favourite text for illustrators since, being read at home, it was not taken into the synagogue, and this allowed the artist to give free reign to his imagination. One illuminated haggadah has birds' heads instead of human ones on its figures to avoid objections about depicting people. A common form of illustration was MICROGRAPHY which meant writing a text using minute letters to form a picture. The invention of printing marked the end of manuscript illumination, although the tradition has continued with the decoration of hand-written marriage documents (see KETUBBAH) and even early printed versions of the MACHZOR.

imitatio dei The biblical command 'After the Lord your God you shall go ... and to Him you shall cleave' (Deut. 13:5) is understood by the *Talmud* to mean that one should imitate God's acts of compassion. Just as He clothed the naked Adam and Eve, so one should clothe the naked (see CHARITY); just as He visited the sick Abraham, so one should visit the sick; just as He comforted and blessed Isaac after the death of his father Abraham, so one should comfort mourners; just as He buried Moses on Mount Nebo, so one should bury the dead (see CHEVRA KADDISHA); just as God forgave the Israelites, so one should offer FORGIVENESS to one's fellow man.

immortality Different beliefs in the continued life of the soul after death exist side by side in Judaism. There is the belief that in the AFTERLIFE the soul continues in some disembodied state of consciousness in the heavenly GARDEN OF EDEN, or for a time in the purgatory of GEHINNOM. There is the belief in the RESURRECTION of the combined body and soul in the

age of the MESSIAH. There is also the belief of the Kabbalah in the TRANSMIGRATION OF SOULS which added a further dimension to Jewish ideas about immortality. Many of the Talmudic passages which talk about life after death are ambiguous because one of the terms used, OLAM HABA, means the 'World to Come', and this can refer both to the world to come after death as well as to the world to come in Messianic times. In both senses of the term, there is a strong folk aspect to the descriptions of the soul in olam haba. Thus, scholars after death continue their study of the torah in the next world, in parallel with the opinions and disputes of the academies on earth, the only difference being that God Himself is involved with the discussions of the ACADEMY ON HIGH.

inclination, good and evil (Hebrew 'yetzer tov' and 'yetzer ha-ra') Within man there are two inclinations, a good one and an evil one. FREE WILL gives man the power to choose between them. The good inclination urges man to the selfless service of God and his fellow men. The evil inclination, by contrast, represents man's drive for sexual pleasure, possessions, power and the worship of idols. Yet it is a necessary part of human life, for without it no one would marry and have children, or build a house, or engage in business (see GOOD AND EVIL). It is only evil because it easily leads man astray and dominates him, like yeast in dough or like a guest who eventually takes over as host (see SIN). In such circumstances it is identified with SATAN within man. Everyone is subject to its temptation; indeed, the greater a person is, the greater their yetzer ha-ra becomes. It can be subdued, primarily through the study of torah and deeds of loving kindness, and then directed to the service of God, so that man may serve Him with both inclinations. In the age of the Messiah, God will destroy the evil inclination (see also SHEMIT-TOT). The righteous who resisted its blandishments will then see it as a great mountain, and they will be amazed that they managed to overcome it. To the wicked who could not subdue it, it will seem as thin as a hair, and they will be amazed that they were unable to control something so puny. See also ORIGINAL SIN, PEREK SHIRAH.

ingathering of the exiles (Hebrew 'kibbutz galuyyot') In the Messianic age the Jewish people, including the Ten Lost Tribes, will be gathered from their exile all over the world to the Holy Land (see ESCHATOLOGY). This will be brought about by the prophet ELIJAH after a great blast on the shofar. At the Resurrection of the Dead which will follow, corpses will roll through underground channels from their graves to be resurrected in the Land of Israel. Many Jews see the suffering of the Jewish People during the Nazi Holocaust and the ingathering of exiles to the modern State of Israel as signifying that the time of the 'footprints of the MESSIAH' has arrived. See also OLIVES, MOUNT OF.

Inquisition The Holy Office of the Roman Catholic Church which investigated and tried heretics. From the late 13c. the Inquisition took a special interest in Jews, particularly in those who had been forcibly converted to Christianity and were maintaining Judaic practices in secret. Those investigated by the Inquisition were usually tortured to elicit penitential confession of their sins and, if found guilty, were handed over to the secular arm of the Church for punishment. In extreme cases the 'heretics' were burnt at the stake and their property was confiscated (*see* AUTO DA FÉ). Under Dominican influence the Inquisition became a major force during the reign of Ferdinand and Isabella, leading to the expulsion of the Jews from Spain in 1492 to prevent JUDAIZERS and crypto-Jews (*see* MARRANO) from having contact with their co-religionists. The Inquisition was also very active in Portugal, Italy and South America and was only abolished in Spain and Portugal in the early 19c. In Jewish folklore the Inquisition was seen as representing the true face of Christianity: cruel, intolerant and fanatical. *See also* APOSTACY.

intermarriage Marriage between Israelites and the heathen people of Canaan was forbidden in the torah, lest the latter lead their Hebrew spouses into idolatry and the service of strange gods (Deut. 7). During the return from exile in Babylonia EZRA made those Jewish men who had intermarried leave their Gentile wives (Ezra 9–10). The explicit cases of intermarriage mentioned in the Bible are not understood by the Jewish tradition as exceptions to the general prohibition of marrying a non-Jewish spouse. Thus, it is maintained that the Moabite women RUTH and Orpah either converted to Judaism before they married the sons of Naomi, or their husbands, indeed, died because they had transgressed. King Solomon, who married many foreign women, only did so after his wives underwent a ceremony of conversion. This conversion was not undertaken from sincere motives, however, and his wives continued to worship their own gods. ESTHER, who married the Persian king Ahasuerus, was forced to do so. She did not need to risk her life by resisting, since she was only the passive partner in their marital sexual relations. Intermarriage is one of the main factors in ASSIMILATION, but the desire to marry a Jewish partner also leads many would-be PROSELYTES to seek conversion to Judaism. Orthodoxy is strongly opposed to intermarriage, and there are even families who observe the MOURNING rituals for those marrying a Gentile. Some American Reform rabbis, however, are willing to officiate at mixed marriages, and extreme reformers have argued that marrying a Christian or Moslem monotheist should be allowed.

Isaac Biblical PATRIARCH and son of ABRAHAM and SARAH. Isaac was the child of his parents' old age and was circumcised when only eight days old (Gen. 21:4), setting the pattern for the subsequent circumcision ritual. He resembled his father in appearance, to the point of sometimes being mistaken for him, and this stopped the malicious gossip that Abraham was too old to be his real father. Isaac's name, from a root meaning 'to laugh', was given to him by God, as his parents had laughed at the idea of having a child so late in life. Because of its divine origin it was never changed, while both his father Abraham and his son JACOB had their names changed. Having undergone the traumatic experience of the AKEDAH, he withdrew from ordinary life, even though he was thirty-seven years old at the time it happened. His weak eyesight was due to having stared up into heaven and seen God

A decorative tribute from a scribe to his patron, from an 11c. **illuminated manuscript** of the Pentateuch found in the Cairo genizah.

The Spanish **Inquisition** burning heretics.

An angel restraining the Patriarch Abraham to prevent him from sacrificing his son **Isaac** during the akedah (Rembrandt).

while bound upon the altar. His eyes were also affected by the tears of the angels, which dropped upon him as they cried while he awaited slaughter. Isaac married his relative REBECCA when she was only three years old. While going out one afternoon to meet his future bride, he prayed to God and was thus the instigator of the MINCHAH prayer. After a long period of barrenness, Rebecca gave birth to twin sons ESAU and Jacob. Isaac's unworldliness accounts for his favouritism towards Esau, who was really a wicked child. Esau found it easy to create a good impression with the semi-blind Isaac. Jacob, too, managed to trick his father into giving him the blessing he had reserved for the elder son, since Isaac could not see clearly who was standing before him. Isaac was buried with his wife in the Cave of MACHPELAH. In Kabbalistic symbolism Isaac represents the aspect of stern judgment on the left side of God.

Isaiah Jerusalem-based prophet of the 8c. BCE and brother of King Amaziah of Judah, whose prophecies are recorded in the Book of Isaiah. Isaiah was born already circumcised. He had a vision of the heavens opening and saw the angels calling to each other 'Holy, holy, holy is the Lord of Hosts; the whole world is full of his glory' (6:3). His description of the heavens is less elaborate than that of the prophet EZEKIEL: Ezekiel was like a peasant who comes to the city and sees a king, while Isaiah was like a townsman who is more used to such sights. He reprimanded King HEZEKIAH for not marrying and having children, and the king replied that he had refrained because he feared he would father an evil son. Isaiah insisted that he nevertheless had a duty to marry and he should leave the rest to God. Hezekiah then proposed that he should marry Isaiah's own daughter, in the belief that their combined merits might ensure good offspring. A child of that union, however, was the evil king MANASSEH, who accused Isaiah of being a false prophet. When his grandfather ran away and hid in a tree, Manasseh killed him by having the tree sawn down. Isaiah's prophecies of rebuke and of comfort are widely used in the synagogue liturgy. Jewish theology has been shaped by his powerful images of the Messiah and of the Messianic age: 'The wolf shall dwell with the lamb, ... and a little child shall lead them ... And the lion shall eat straw like the ox ... They shall not hurt nor destroy in all My holy mountain, for the earth shall be full of the knowledge of the Lord, as the waters cover the sea' (11:6–9).

Ishmael *see* AGRAT BAT MAHALAT

Ishmael Ben Elisha (1c.–2c. CE) Mishnaic sage of priestly descent, sometimes called Ishmael the High Priest. As a child Ishmael was taken captive to Rome where he was rescued by Joshua Ben Chananiah, who recognized in him the potential for future greatness. Ishmael played an important role in the rebuilding of Judaism after the destruction of the Temple. He enumerated thirteen principles of biblical exegesis, expressed the view that the torah speaks in the language of men, and that therefore no significance should be attached to stylistic variations in the text, and his school edited some of the early midrash works. Ishmael's main colleague was Akiva, with whom he

had many disputes. On one occasion after Akiva had presented a homiletical interpretation of a verse, Ishmael told him not to involve himself with aggadah but to restrict himself to the legal aspects of Judaism (halakhah). Ishmael's realistic approach to life led him to encourage people to work and not to devote themselves totally to the study of torah, for the torah was not given to angels. He condemned the early Jewish Christians, and when his nephew was dying from snake bite, he refused to allow him to be treated by a Christian faith healer, saying: 'It is better for him to die than be healed by such a person.' He was associated with the mystical maaseh merkavah tradition and a number of mystical HEIKHALOT tracts refer to his exploits. During the Roman persecutions which led to his death as a martyr, he was sent up to heaven by his colleagues to see whether the decree of martyrdom came from God.

Israel Name given to JACOB after he wrestled with an angel (Gen. 32) and understood to mean 'he who has struggled with God'. Jacob's descendants were known as the Children of Israel or Israelites, and the land promised to them by God became known as the Land of Israel, eretz yisrael (*see* TRIBES, THE TWELVE). When the ten tribes (*see* TEN LOST TRIBES) broke away under JEROBOAM, to form an independent Northern Kingdom after the death of King Solomon, they took the name Israel, leaving the Southern Kingdom with the name JUDAH from which the term Jew originates. The designation 'Children of Israel' eventually became 'the House of Israel', 'the People of Israel' and then just 'Israel' as the collective name of all Jews, whether born of matrilineal descent from Jacob or converted to the faith of Judaism. 'Israel' thus became both an ethnic and religious concept incorporating all those subjects to the biblical COVENANT between God and the Jewish People. The modern Jewish state founded in Palestine in 1948 adopted the name Israel after some discussion of the alternatives (*see* ZIONISM). The People of Israel are thought to be characterized by three qualities: they are merciful, shy and generous in good deeds. They have the status of princes in God's eyes and are to be regarded as the sons of prophets who have insight into the correct way Jewish religion should be carried out. Even if an Israelite sins, he does not lose his status as a child of the covenant and must still try to be a member of 'a kingdom of priests and a holy nation'. God Himself guides Israel's destiny, and His CHOSEN PEOPLE are not under the control of any astrological force or mazal. The land of Israel is specially favoured by God, who keeps it constantly under his surveillance, and its very air makes people wise.

Israel Independence Day *see* IYYAR

Israel Meir Ha-Kohen (1838–1933) Polish halakhist whose real surname was Poupko but who was commonly known, after the name of one of his more popular books, as 'the Chafetz Chaim'. Israel Meir never served as the rabbi of a community and, indeed, was reluctant to accept ordination until late in life. He organized a yeshivah in Radun and supported himself through a grocery shop which his wife ran. In order not to be unfair to other grocers, he insisted that his wife close the shop each day after she had earned sufficient for their needs, since customers were attracted to his shop because of his saintly reputation. Apart from publishing a standard work on halakhah, he also wrote books offering guidance to Jewish soldiers serving in the Russian army and to Jewish migrants to America. His best known book, *Chafetz Chaim*, was about the sins of gossip and slander (*see* LASHON HA-RA). He was inspired to write this work when, as a young man coming under the influence of the Musar Movement, he heard Israel Lipkin Salanter talk about the need for such a book. It occurred to Israel Meir that many people who were very careful about ritual prohibitions hardly regarded evil talk as a sin at all. He was very careful about honesty in his dealings with others, and whenever he sent a letter by hand, he used to buy a stamp and then destroy it, for fear he might be defrauding the postal service of their due. On one occasion a rich man came to visit him and found him living in a very simple manner in a barely furnished home. 'Where is your furniture?', he asked. 'Where is *your* furniture?', Israel Meir asked him in turn. 'But I am a guest here', the rich man replied. 'So am I a guest here in this world', Israel Meir said.

Israel of Ruzhin (1797–1850) Chasidic leader and descendant of Dov Baer of Mezhirech. Israel became a tzaddik at the age of sixteen. He attracted many followers to the Ukrainian town of Ruzhin and lived in royal style on their donations, employing architects and decorators whom he brought from Paris and Italy. He rode among his followers in a golden coach and surrounded himself with servants. Other Chasidic leaders opposed this opulence and criticized the activities of Israel and his sons. Indeed, one of his sons grew disillusioned with Chasidism and wrote a bitter attack on the movement. When he repented, however, he was taken back by his family who defended him against his antagonists. Israel was accused by the Russian Czarist authorities of complicity in the death of a Jewish government informer, and after some time in prison, he went into self-imposed exile in Sadgora, in the Austro-Hungarian Empire. There he continued to live in the same royal style as before.

Isserles, Moses (1525–72) Polish halakhist and author of important Ashkenazi glosses to the SHULCHAN ARUKH, the main Jewish law code. Isserles was sympathetic to Maimonides' philosophic approach to Judaism and defended the latter against his detractors. In his writings he explained away demons as negative forces of nature and quoted the saying: 'Love Plato, love Aristotle, but above all love truth.' His own interpretation of the mystical 'journey to PARADISE' was that it signified the highest experience of philosophical contemplation of the divine. He was bitterly criticized by Elijah the Vilna Gaon, who said that neither Isserles nor Maimonides had ever seen Paradise. Although he was a student of Kabbalah, he made scathing remarks about unlettered people who engaged in mystical speculation when they did not know their 'right hand from their left hand and walked in darkness'. According to one popular, but unreliable, tradition Isserles lived for thirty-three years, wrote thirty-three books and died on the thirty-third day of the omer (lag ba-omer). His grave in Cracow became a place

The prophet **Isaiah** being sawn in two.

Dancers celebrating **Israel** Independence Day in Haifa, 1956.

of pilgrimage, and on his tombstone were engraved the words: 'From Moses [i.e. Maimonides] until Moses [i.e. Isserles] there was none like Moses.'

Iyyar Second lunar month of the Hebrew calendar, counting from Nisan the month of the Exodus, or eighth month from the New Year festival (rosh hashanah). Iyyar begins in April or May, and its zodiacal sign is the ox. The second Passover, pesach sheni, which was kept by those who were ritually impure or absent from Jerusalem on pesach, falls on the fourteenth of Iyyar. The fifth of Iyyar is Israel Independence Day, which is kept as a minor festival of thanksgiving by religious Zionists, and the eighteenth of Iyyar is LAG BA-OMER. The manna was provided for the Israelites in the wilderness for the first time on the sixteenth of Iyyar.

Jacob Last of the PATRIARCHS and younger twin son of ISAAC and REBECCA. Jacob's lifelong conflict with his brother ESAU was already apparent in their mother's womb. When she passed an idol Esau kicked and struggled to get out, and when she passed a yeshivah Jacob struggled to get out. Jacob indeed went on in later life to study torah in the academies of Shem and Eber. His name comes from a root meaning 'heel', primarily because he was born grasping his brother's heel. He also lived up to his name. He tricked his brother out of his birthright, although his intention was honourable, since he wished to serve God and knew Esau was unsuitable for the task. He also tricked his semi-blind father Isaac into giving him the main blessing which should have gone to his older brother. While escaping from his brother's anger, Jacob stopped at the future sight of the Temple to pray, thus initiating MAARIV. There he dreamt of a ladder reaching from earth to heaven, and God spoke to him from the top of the ladder, promising him His protection. Jacob himself was tricked by his uncle LABAN into marrying LEAH before her younger sister RACHEL, as a punishment for his own trickery. He eventually had twelve sons, the founders of the TRIBES of Israel, and one daughter, Dinah, from his wives and concubines. His favouritism towards his son JOSEPH led to fratricidal jealousy. On returning to be reconciled with Esau, Jacob was involved in a night battle with the guardian spirit of Esau, who was forced to bless him because Jacob would not let him go. Jacob was injured by the angel, and developed a limp, and Jews do not eat the thigh sinew of animals in memory of this encounter (Gen. 32). The angel told Jacob that he would have a new name, ISRAEL, implying that he had stood up in battle with both divine and human beings. According to MIDRASH, Jacob never really died, although the Bible describes his burial in the Cave of MACHPELAH, because God promised to redeem his servant Jacob in a future time.

Jacob Isaac of Lublin (1745–1815) Chasidic leader who was known as the Seer of Lublin because he was gifted with psychic powers of second sight which enabled him to see events at a distance and to foretell the future. Jacob Isaac could also see into men's souls and tell them what their previous incarnations were and whether or not they would be successful in their undertakings. His blessings were sought by his followers to enable them to have children or to help them in financial ventures. He only had to look at food to be able to tell whether it was kosher, and from a person's signature he would know all about their character. Jacob Isaac gained his extraordinary powers after he spent three years with a cloth wrapped around his eyes, so as not to be affected by the evils of the world, and his teacher, Rabbi Elimelech of Lyzhansk, bequeathed the light of his own eyes to him on his deathbed. The Napoleonic invasion of Russia was believed by Jacob Isaac to be the fulfilment of the biblical prophecy about pre-Messianic wars. He tried, unsuccessfully, to persuade other Chasidic leaders to concentrate their spiritual efforts in bringing the Messiah and to enlist their support on the side of Napoleon. Jacob Isaac died after a fall from an upstairs window, claiming that he had been pursued by the forces of darkness. He was one of the founders of Chasidism in Poland, and his pupils led important subbranches of the Chasidic Movement.

Jacob of Margève (12c.–13c.) French rabbi and mystic who was known as a saintly and holy man. Jacob would pose questions to God after meditating, praying and reciting various divine names. He would then receive an answer at night in a dream, usually hinted at in the form of a biblical verse. When he awoke in the morning, he would find the answers written down beside his bed. Jacob was able to obtain answers to his questions in this way because he had asked God to command His angels to respond to him. When, however, he asked whether it was permissible to control angelic powers in order to gain wisdom and wealth, he received the reply 'Holy, holy, holy is the Lord of Hosts', i.e. he should rely on God alone. Several of the dream answers contain an implicit Messianic message, namely that if more people followed the answer given in the dream, the Messiah would come. Jacob's dream answers were collected together in a work called *Responsa From Heaven*. Despite a well-established rule that halakhic decisions cannot be determined by prophecy – indeed a prophet who used prophecy for this purpose would be a false prophet – his dream RESPONSA did gain a measure of acceptance in halakhic literature.

Jael Kenite woman who slew the Canaanite general Sisera while he was fleeing from the army of Barak. She was able to overcome him by first seducing him so that he had sexual relations with her several times. She then gave him milk to drink, making him sleepy, and when he was asleep, she knocked a tent peg through his forehead. Jael did not kill Sisera with a sword because it would be inappropriate for a woman to use a man's weapon. The prophetess DEBORAH praised her with the words 'Blessed above women shall Jael be' (Judg. 5:24).

Jehovah *see* TETRAGRAMMATON

Jeremiah Prophet of Judah in the 7c. BCE of priestly origin. Jeremiah was descended from the proselyte

Rahab, and this led people to belittle his message. He devoted his life entirely to his prophetic mission, and little is known of his family. A daughter of his became pregnant after bathing in a bath into which some ruffians had forced Jeremiah to emit semen. The child of this strange conception was BEN SIRA, who was thus Jeremiah's son and grandson. Jeremiah went out to preach to the Ten Lost Tribes, who had been exiled from the Northern Kingdom of Israel, and to bring them back to Judah. He continuously warned people of the impending destruction of the Jerusalem Temple. His words of doom, and his criticism of the kings of Judah and the priestly establishment, made him very unpopular, and on several occasions he was imprisoned by the authorities. While Jeremiah was in Jerusalem, his merit protected the city and the Temple. During his absence, however, they were destroyed by the Babylonians, but not before he had arranged to have the Temple vessels hidden to protect them. After the destruction he wrote the Book of LAMENTATIONS, lamenting the fulfilment of his prophecies and the subsequent exile, yet he never lost faith in the ultimate return to ZION. He advised the Jewish exiles to become good citizens of their new land and to pray for the welfare of the Gentile government (Jer. 29:5). Jeremiah spent the end of his life in Egypt, where the philosopher Plato became his disciple. He was eventually killed by fellow Jews because he continued to upbraid them for their misbehaviour. The Egyptians, who held him in high regard because his prayers had rid the Nile of dangerous crocodiles, buried him in Egypt. *See also* RACHEL.

The prophet **Jeremiah** (12c. French stained glass).

Jeroboam Rebel king who broke away from Solomon's son Rehoboam to found the Northern Kingdom of Israel. He was supported by the prophet Ahijah the Shilonite and, nominally at least, by ten of the TRIBES. He was not entirely to blame for rejecting the divinely appointed House of David, since corruption had been prevalent under the rule of Solomon, who had married foreign wives. Jeroboam's wickedness lay, however, in introducing the worship of the two golden calfs he erected in order to prevent the people from going on pilgrimage to Jerusalem. He was held responsible for leading the people into sin for which no repentance is effective and is particularly blameworthy for his behaviour because he was well versed in the mystical lore of the maaseh merkavah, which he had learnt from his saintly teacher Ahijah. He is one of those who have no portion in the World to Come (olam haba), for though God wished to forgive him and offered him a place in the Garden of Eden, he arrogantly refused to enter since he was denied a higher status there than David.

Jerusalem (Hebrew 'yerushalaim') Holiest city of Judaism (*see* MIZRACH) and location of the first and second Temple. Jerusalem became the capital of the Hebrew kingdom after its capture by King DAVID and is the capital of the modern state of Israel. Adam, the first man, was formed out of its dust, and it was there that the akedah took place. While Jacob was asleep on the TEMPLE Mount in Jerusalem, he dreamt of a ladder which was planted on the earth and which reached up into heaven. Jerusalem was formed at the beginning of the Creation (*see* HOLY OF HOLIES); it is the heart of

A 15c. view of **Jerusalem**.

the world and contains nine-tenths of all mundane beauty. The city used to possess miraculous qualities, so that none of its inhabitants became sick, no building ever caught fire, and its area seemed to expand to accommodate all those who came within its twelve gates. Though full of visitors during the PILGRIM FESTIVALS, one of the miracles associated with the Temple was that no one ever complained that there was not enough space to stay in Jerusalem. Prayers are recited facing towards the holy city, and indeed, they rise up to God through Jerusalem which is the gateway to heaven. The journey to Jerusalem is always described as 'going up' (aliyah), not simply because it is a city of twelve hills but because it is spiritually the highest place. In the time of the Messiah Jerusalem will be rebuilt with divine fire, when the heavenly Jerusalem will descend complete in every detail. Then all nations will gather within its walls which will be formed out of a ring of angels. The memory of the destruction of Jerusalem is preserved in the liturgy, particularly in the dirges recited on the Fast of Av. The hope for the rebuilding of Jerusalem and the return to ZION is also a common theme of many prayers. At weddings a glass is broken so that an element of sadness is introduced at the moment of greatest happiness for the bride and groom, in fulfilment of the words of the Psalm: 'If I forget thee, O Jerusalem, ... if I do not set Jerusalem above my chief joy' (Ps. 137). *See also* OLIVES, MOUNT OF; TAMMUZ, SEVENTEENTH OF.

jester *see* BADCHAN

Jesus of Nazareth There are few direct references to Jesus in early Rabbinic literature, and some of these references are highly ambiguous. The image of Jesus which does emerge in the later Jewish tradition is very different from Christian stories and teachings about him. He appears as a mamzer, a child born from an adulterous union between his Jewish mother and a Gentile Roman soldier. He was excommunicated by one of the rabbis after a misunderstanding and thereafter left Jewish religion, worshipped idols and led Israel astray. He studied magic in Egypt and was able to smuggle out MAGIC formulae from there stuck in a fold of his skin. As a magician he used to make birds out of clay and then put life into them, but he was defeated in a magical contest with the rabbis. He was sentenced to death as a sorcerer but could only be hung from a cabbage stalk since he had conjured all other trees not to accept his body. Jesus was punished in hell for his sins, and there he recognized the error of his ways. The Roman aristocrat ONKELOS, a would-be convert to Judaism, summoned Jesus up from the dead to ask his advice and was told of the great value in which Israel was held. These legends, together with Jewish polemical writings against Jesus and Christianity, gave the medieval Jew the ability to cope with Christian persecution and to withstand missionary propaganda. The deification of Jesus was considered by Jews as IDOLATRY. *See also* SALAMANDER; WANDERING JEW.

Jethro The father-in-law of Moses. Jethro was a Midianite priest who came to reject the idolatry of his own culture. He eventually converted to the Hebrew

religion, thus setting an example for all later proselytes. He helped guide the Israelites through the wilderness (Num. 10) and advised Moses about the organization of the judicial system (Exod. 18). Jethro was one of the three original advisers of PHARAOH who were consulted about how to get rid of the Israelites. While the wicked Balaam suggested that the Israelite babies should be cast into the Nile and Job remained silent, Jethro opposed the plan and fled from Egypt. As a reward some of his descendants, the Rechabites, were members of the Sanhedrin.

Jew (Hebrew 'yehudi', Yiddish 'yid') A Jew is traditionally defined as someone born of a Jewish mother or converted to Judaism (*see* PROSELYTE), although there have been moves within Reform Judaism to consider a child born to a Jewish father and a GENTILE mother as a Jew (*see* INTERMARRIAGE). A convert becomes the spiritual child of Abraham and Sarah, and a Jew from birth takes his status as a priest or a Levite from his biological father. A Jew who sins, or rejects his role as a member of the CHOSEN PEOPLE, still remains a Jew, and to some extent a Jew retains his or her identity as a child of the COVENANT, even having completely abandoned the Jewish faith for another religion. The name 'Jew' originally referred to the Judaeans, i.e. inhabitants of the Southern Kingdom of JUDAH taken into captivity in 586 BCE, and was eventually applied to followers of the Jewish religion and to ethnic Hebrews in general. In English the term Jew is still used in a derogatory way to mean 'a usurer' and as a verb to mean 'to cheat', although dictionaries tend to regard these usages as archaic.

Jezebel Foreign wife of the 9c. BCE Israelite King Ahab. Jezebel introduced idolatrous Baal worship into Hebrew religion and persecuted the prophets who opposed her. It was the prophet ELIJAH who eventually persuaded the people to repent and return to the worship of God (I Kings 18), though even he was afraid of her. Ahab was a weak character, completely dominated by his wife, who led him into sin. In fact, Jezebel reigned with him as a queen in her own right. Despite her wickedness she showed compassion by never allowing a funeral procession to pass by without walking behind the bier, clapping her hands and wailing with the mourners. She also accompanied bridegrooms to their wedding feasts, participating in their joy. When she died and her body was eaten by dogs, her hands, head and feet were spared and given proper burial as a reward for the good deeds they had engaged in.

Job Hero of the Book of Job whose date and nationality are unknown. It is claimed that he was either a Jew or a pious Gentile, who lived at the time of Moses, and that the latter actually wrote the book about him. A host of other views are found in Jewish literature, including one which sees him as a purely legendary character. As an adviser to PHARAOH he kept silent when the plan to drown the Israelite children in the Nile was mooted. For this silence he was singled out to suffer in a test of his patience and his faith. This was brought upon him at the instigation of Satan, who was envious of Job's righteousness and feared that Job would eclipse Abraham in God's estimation. Indeed, it is asserted that Job's service of God was greater than that of Abraham. Like Abraham, Job was also very hospitable to visitors, and the doors of his house faced in different directions so that travellers could easily gain access. He bore his suffering with great patience. When his body was crawling with vermin he would not try to avoid them and would even replace any that fell from his open sores in the belief that they too had to submit themselves to God's will. His suffering saved his own generation from extinction and helped to atone for the world. In the end he was driven to blaspheme and to deny God's justice, because he could not fathom the workings of the world. God appeared to him in a storm, or according to another version in the hair of his head, to reveal His mysteries (a play upon the similarity of sound between the Hebrew words for 'storm' and for 'hair'). This indicated to Job that, although God's glory fills the whole universe, He is also present in the lowliest aspect of His creation.

Jochanan Ben Zakkai (1c. CE) Main rabbinic figure of the period following the destruction of the Second Temple. Jochanan, a disciple of Hillel, was in favour of surrendering the beseiged city of Jerusalem to the Romans, but the Zealots would not agree. So he was carried out of the capital by his followers in a coffin, pretending to be dead, and taken to the Roman commander Vespasian. He prophesied that Vespasian would become emperor, and when the news of Vespasian's appointment to this position arrived shortly afterwards, he offered to reward Jochanan for his prophetic insight. Jochanan asked for the rabbinic academy at Jabneh to be spared by the Romans when they crushed the Jewish revolt. It was there that he and his colleagues rebuilt Judaism when the sanctuary lay in ruins, teaching that good deeds now replaced sacrifices in their power of atonement. He gave Jabneh a status equivalent to that of Jerusalem, so that the calendar could be determined by the Sanhedrin there. Jochanan was involved in the mysticism of the maaseh merkavah and could understand the language of birds and of nature. He was the teacher of ELIEZER BEN HYRCANUS and Joshua Ben Chananiah.

Jonah Biblical prophet who ran away from God's call and refused to preach REPENTANCE to the Gentile people of Nineveh. Jonah was afraid that they might indeed repent and thus show up the failings of Israel. During his flight, he was thrown into the sea and swallowed by a large fish (Jonah 2), whose eyes were as big as windows and whose stomach was lit up by the glow from a precious stone. The fish was in danger of being eaten by the Leviathan, but Jonah scared this sea monster off by announcing that in the age of the Messiah he, Jonah, would capture the Leviathan, and it would be eaten at the Messianic banquet. Jonah eventually carried out God's original instructions and was thus taught that true compassion extends also to Gentiles and to the animal world. Jonah, as a child, had been revived from death by the prophet Elijah, and at the end of his life he entered Paradise alive. The Book of Jonah is read on the afternoon of yom kippur to show that true repentance can avert punishment if people change their behaviour.

An 18c. woodcut of a Jewish peddlar being stoned. **Jews** were often subject to anti-Semitism in Eastern Europe.

Job feasting with his family before his sufferings began (14c. Byzantine).

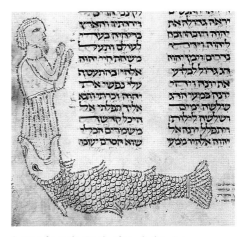

A page from the Book of Jonah showing a micrographic picture, made up of the masoretic notes, of **Jonah** being swallowed by the great fish (13c.–14c. Bible).

Joseph Son of the Patriarch JACOB and his favourite wife RACHEL. Joseph is the model of the biblical tzaddik, or righteous man, who is protected from harm by the Divine Spirit and whose descendants are not affected by the evil eye. His reports to Jacob about the immodest behaviour of his brothers (*see* LASHON HA-RA), and the preferential treatment his father showed him, led to fratricidal jealousy. Ten of his brothers plotted to kill him, casting him into a pit of snakes and scorpions, but in the end he was sold as a slave to Potiphar in Egypt. There he was able to resist the advances of Zuleika, his master's wife, because the image of his father appeared before his eyes and saved him from temptation. Eventually he was appointed Viceroy, in charge of the Egyptian economy, after interpreting Pharaoh's dreams to mean that seven years of plenty, followed by seven years of famine, were about to come upon the land (Gen. 41). When his family joined him, they found that he was not corrupted by power and had no thoughts of vengeance. Yet he died before his brothers because he adopted a leadership role which shortens a person's life. As a reward for personally accompanying the funeral cortege of his father back to the Holy Land, his own bones were taken back there for burial. They had been deposited in an iron coffin in the Nile so that the Egyptians should not treat them as idolatrous relics. Serach, the sole survivor of the early period of Israelite life in Egypt, told Moses the whereabouts of the coffin. Moses magically raised it and thereafter it travelled side by side with the Ark of the Covenant as the Israelites wandered in the desert. Joseph was honoured in this way because he had kept all the divine teachings contained in the Tablets of the Decalogue which were kept in the Ark. In the 2c. CE ten rabbis were martyred by the Romans on the pretext that the brothers of Joseph had gone unpunished for kidnapping him and selling him into slavery. *See also* TRIBES, THE TWELVE.

Joseph Della Reina (15c.) Kabbalist who tried to conjure up the devil in order to strip him of his powers. Joseph, together with five of his disciples, wanted to hasten the coming of the Messiah through practical Kabbalah. Their fasts, prayers and use of various combinations of the holy names of God succeeded in bringing Samael, the prince of demons, to meet them, but Joseph was unable to overpower him with Kabbalistic magic. Instead, Joseph himself fell under the dominion of the powers of darkness, and he was forced to worship Samael. He thus became a heretic and, after he died, was reborn as a black dog during the time of the great Kabbalist Isaac Luria. It was among Luria's followers that the story of Joseph Della Reina was told as a warning of the dangers of practical Kabbalah.

Joseph of Rosheim (1478–1544) Influential 'Court Jew' who represented Jewish interests to the German Emperor and channelled bribes from the Jewish community to avert anti-Jewish measures or expulsions. Joseph engaged in disputations with Jewish apostates and defended Jews against blood libel accusations, even gaining a letter from the Emperor stating that they were free from any guilt. At one point he needed to persuade Catholics that Jews were not the driving force behind Martin Luther, and at the same time he tried unsuccessfully to obtain a private audience with Luther to persuade him to modify his anti-Jewish views. He did manage to have the Strasbourg elders ban some of Luther's writings against the Jews. When Solomon Molcho, a pseudo-Messiah, was developing his plans for Messianic and political power, Joseph tried to dissuade him from putting them into operation.

Josephus Flavius (1c. CE) Palestinian historian from an upper-class priestly family. During the uprising against Rome, which began in 66 CE, Josephus was the rebel military governor of Galilee. When the Galilean rebels realized that they were unable to overcome the superior Roman forces, they decided on mass suicide. Josephus contrived to be the last one alive among his band of fighters and, instead of killing himself, gave himself up to the Romans. On meeting the Roman military commander Vespasian, Josephus predicted that he would become emperor, and Vespasian spared his life. Josephus was used by the Romans for propaganda purposes to persuade the rebels to surrender. He spent the rest of his life in Rome, writing works which were pro-Roman in character but which also explained Jewish history and beliefs to the Gentile reader. He claimed in his *Jewish War*, which is the main historical source for the events of the war against Rome, that the revolt was the work of a small band of Zealots and not the popular uprising it was generally assumed to be. He described the last days of the Jewish fort at MASADA, where most of the defenders committed suicide, and he depicted the Jewish sects as if they were Greek philosophical schools. There are some passing references to Jesus in Josephus' *Antiquities of the Jews*. Though these are now regarded as complete or partial Christian interpolations, nevertheless, they guaranteed the preservation of the Greek text of Josephus by the Christian Church. Josephus also wrote an autobiography defending his reputation and a reply to anti-Semitic attacks on Jews. During his lifetime, his fellow Jews regarded him as a traitor, but a pseudo-Josephus was produced in Hebrew in the Middle Ages, called JOSIPPON. This contained much material not found in Josephus' writings, but it did use the latter as a source.

Joshua Successor to Moses who led the Israelites into the Promised Land after their wanderings in the wilderness. Joshua received the oral torah from Moses, but in comparison with Moses, Joshua was like the moon compared with the sun. Hoshea, as he was then called, was one of the twelve spies sent in advance to investigate the Holy Land (*see also* PHINEHAS), and Moses added an extra letter from the name of God to his name, so that 'God would save him from the influence of the other spies'. Only he and Caleb brought back a positive report about the land to Moses and the Israelites. Joshua married the harlot Rahab who had converted to Judaism after she helped the Israelites conquer Jericho. He wrote the Book of Joshua, and according to one view, he also wrote the last eight verses of the Pentateuch which tell of the death of Moses. *See also* PEREK SHIRAH.

Joshua Ben Chananiah (1c.–2c. CE) Mishnaic sage and pupil of Jochanan Ben Zakkai. Joshua had a dispute with GAMALIEL, the NASI, about the correct date for YOM KIPPUR and was eventually persuaded to give in and publicly desecrate the day he had calculated to be the Day of Atonement for the sake of religious unity. In a dispute between the sages and ELIEZER BEN HYRCANUS, it was Joshua who rejected the intervention of a heavenly voice on the side of Eliezer by claiming that the torah was not in heaven and the law had to be decided by MAJORITY OPINION. In general he supported the underprivileged members of society, maintaining that righteous proselytes had a portion in the World to Come (olam haba) and claiming that the poor played an important role in accepting charity from the rich. His attitudes towards women were more negative, however, and he depicted them as essentially immodest shrews. He was known to be ugly in appearance, and on one occasion when the Emperor's daughter remarked how strange it was to find wisdom in such an ugly container, he replied that good wine is never kept in gold or silver vessels, otherwise it might spoil. He indicated thereby that a beautiful exterior was likely to generate feelings of pride and arrogance which would interfere with the acquisition of knowledge.

Joshua Ben Levi (3c. CE) Palestinian Talmudic sage who was renowned for his piety. As a mark of his saintly character, he was regularly visited by the prophet Elijah, but quite suddenly these visits ceased. When after a long interval Elijah reappeared, he explained that he had stayed away because Joshua had persuaded a fugitive to surrender himself to the authorities. To Joshua's protest that he had acted in accordance with the halakhah, Elijah replied that he should have allowed others to do such a distasteful thing and not done it himself. On another occasion Joshua asked Elijah when the MESSIAH was coming. Elijah told him to go and find the Messiah among the lepers at the gates of Rome and ask him himself. When Joshua did so, the Messiah answered 'today'. At their next meeting, some time later, Joshua informed Elijah that the Messiah was a liar, but Elijah explained that what the Messiah had meant was that any 'today' could be the beginning of the Messianic era if people decided to listen to God's voice. Towards the end of his life, Joshua asked the ANGEL OF DEATH if he could see his place in the Garden of Eden before he died. When the angel agreed, Joshua further asked whether he was allowed to hold the angel's sword in case he slew him en route. The angel lifted Joshua onto the wall of PARADISE, but Joshua jumped straight in and would not return the sword in order to prevent the angel from slaying anyone else. It was only after a heavenly voice commanded him to give back the sword that he did so, but he won the promise that the Angel of Death would not show himself to men before ending their lives. This legend of Joshua Ben Levi was the subject of a poem by Longfellow, 'The Spanish Jew's Tale', in his *Tales of a Wayside Inn*.

Josiah King of Judah in the 7c. BCE who ascended the throne while only eight years old. Josiah's father, Amon, and grandfather, Manasseh, had been very wicked, and God appointed Josiah to purify Israelite religion, giving him a name even before he was born. Josiah undertook a major reform of the Temple ritual

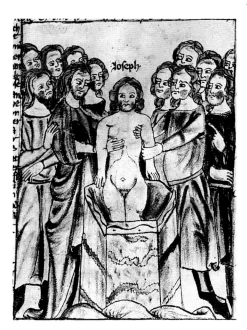

Joseph lowered into the pit by his brothers (14c. German manuscript).

Joshua spares Rahab (Gustave Doré).

when a book of the torah was found, while the Temple was undergoing renovations (II Kings 22). This book was the only remaining copy of the Pentateuch, the others having been destroyed during the antireligious excesses of his father. It contained warnings of dire punishments for idolatry, and Josiah showed it to the prophetess HULDAH. When she made it clear to him that the Temple would indeed be destroyed because of the sins of Israel, he hid the Ark of the Covenant, the jar of manna and other sacred items which will only be retrieved by Elijah in the days of the Messiah. Josiah was thought of as a truly penitent and righteous king (II Kings 23:25). His fate is lamented in the Book of LAMENTATIONS.

Josippon A Hebrew history of the Jews mainly concerned with the period after the Babylonian Captivity until the destruction of the Second Temple. The work was composed in 10c. Italy and was based on a Latin version of the 1c. historian JOSEPHUS. Since medieval Jewish scholars had limited access to historical works, *Josippon* was widely quoted as an authoritative source and believed by them to have been composed by Josephus himself for his co-religionists. Doubts were expressed, however, about some of the stories which were recognized as forgeries even before the growth of modern scholarship. The text exists in a number of different versions and has been translated into Arabic, Yiddish and Ladino.

Jubilee (Hebrew 'yovel', meaning 'ram's horn') Every fiftieth year, at the end of seven SHEMITTAH cycles, a Jubilee year was proclaimed by the blowing of the shofar on yom kippur (Lev. 25). In ancient times this was marked by cessation from agricultural labour, the release of Hebrew slaves and the return of ancestral land to its owners. Inequalities in society were thus rectified every fifty years, and God's ultimate ownership of the land recognized. The laws of the Jubilee only apply when all the Jewish people actually live in the Holy Land, and it has not been in operation since biblical times. The only remaining aspect of the Jubilee year today is the custom of blowing the shofar at the end of every yom kippur to indicate that the fast is over. *See also* SHEMITTOT.

Judah Son of the Patriarch Jacob and his wife Leah. Judah was possessed of remarkable strength, so that he could bend iron with his teeth, and his symbol was the lion, the strongest of animals. When Jacob came to settle in Egypt, he sent Judah ahead to the land of Goshen to establish academies for the study of torah. When the Hebrew tribes split into two groups after the death of King Solomon, the southern tribal area with its capital in Jerusalem was known as the Kingdom of Judah. This was because the descendants of Judah formed a majority there. Jewish history paid Judah the singular honour that all Jews are called by his name, since the Hebrew for Jew, 'yehudi' is derived from Judah, 'yehudah'. His name also contains all four letters of the tetragrammaton in their correct order, indicating that he was fit to lead the Children of Israel. It was from among his descendants that the Davidic line of kings emerged, and he is therefore the ancestor of the Messiah. Despite his great spiritual stature, he was punished for his role in selling his brother JOSEPH

into slavery, and for deceiving his father, by later having to admit publicly that he had had a sexual relationship with his daughter-in-law TAMAR (Gen. 38). He also suffered when his bones rolled around in their coffin during the forty years the Israelites wandered in the wilderness.

Judah Ben Ilai (2c. CE) Mishnaic sage of Galilean origin who flourished in the difficult period after the Bar Kokhba revolt. Judah was responsible for ordering important sections of the *Mishnah* and is referred to as the chief spokesman of the rabbis. He was not universally popular among his colleagues, however, because he praised the Romans for their roads, markets and bathhouses. His extreme poverty meant that he and his wife had to share the only garment they owned, yet he looked well-fed since his face shone, not through wealth but through wisdom. When dressed in his shabbat clothes he looked like one of the angels of the Lord. Judah's outlook favoured moderation, though he was a vegetarian by choice, and he advised people to teach their sons a trade; otherwise, they would be bringing them up to be robbers. He expressed the special character of Israel by use of two biblical images, namely that they would be like the dust of the earth and the stars of the heaven. When they sink, they fall as low as the dust, but when they rise, they ascend to the stars. To Judah we owe a somewhat legendary description of the great synagogue in Alexandria, which was big enough to hold as many Israelites as came out during the Exodus, with its seventy-one thrones of pure gold and a shammash stationed in the centre who waved a flag so that the large congregation, who could not hear the chazzan, could answer 'amen'.

Judah Ha-Chasid (1150–1217) Mystic and leader of the movement of German pietists known as Chasidei Ashkenaz, which introduced an ascetic dimension into Jewish life. Judah's family originated in Italy whence they brought the Eastern mystical traditions of Aaron of Baghdad, whose teachings were highly regarded by Italian Jewry. Judah's own father once saw the heavens open, and he was asked if he had any request to make of God; he replied that he would like sons as gifted as himself. Legend tells how as a youth Judah was ignorant of Judaism and did not even know the prayers. At the age of eighteen he underwent a religious experience which changed his life. He began to fast for six days each week, only eating on the Sabbath, and eventually fasting then, too. He started performing miracles, earning a reputation as a pietist, a chasid. Judah was in contact with bishops and dukes and was reputed by his followers to know the exact year when the Messianic redemption would dawn. The prophet Elijah would attend his Passover seder service. The main literary product of Judah and his circle was the *Sefer* CHASIDIM, which contained a number of teachings at variance with Talmudic lore. While some of these were rejected by later authorities, the book as a whole exerted a great influence on the customs and attitudes of Ashkenazi Jewry.

Judah Halevi (1075–1141) Spanish poet and theologian. Halevi's daughter was married to the great Bible commentator Abraham Ibn Ezra. The marriage came about when Halevi, realizing that his daughter had no suitors, swore that he would give her to the first man who came to his home the next day. When a poorly dressed man entered, Judah Halevi's wife was distraught at the thought of her daughter marrying him, but this pauper turned out to be Ibn Ezra. Halevi's poetry expressed his intoxication with God. Although he was a practising physician, he wrote of his wish to be cured by God alone when ill, rather than by any medicines. His poetry is also characterized by a fervent nationalism and longing for ZION. Halevi's main work was the *Kuzari*, a philosophical dialogue between the king of the Khazars and representatives of Christianity, Islam, Greek philosophy and Judaism, in which the Jewish sage eventually convinced the king that the two 'daughter' religions are really based on Judaism, which is the true religion. Halevi put his own under-standing of Judaism into the mouth of the sage and argued that revealed religion is superior to philosophy, the systems of which are replete with inconsistencies. The public revelation of the torah at Sinai, the biblical miracles and Jewish history all testify to Israel's specially appointed role, namely, that of the heart within the body of the nations. Israel alone has the gift of PROPHECY which is passed on in a hereditary manner to all Jews: it is an inner sense which allows a direct experience of God. At the end of his life Halevi set out for Palestine to fulfil his lifelong dream of living in the Holy Land, despite the efforts of friends to dissuade him. When he arrived in Jerusalem, he bowed down to kiss the ground, was run over by an Arab horseman and died.

Early 19c. Austrian torah breastplate, with the Decalogue flanked by two lions, symbols of the tribe of **Judah**.

Judah Ha-Nasi (135–220 CE) Rabbinic sage descended from Hillel, editor of the MISHNAH and leader (Nasi) of Palestinian Jewry. Judah was on very friendly terms with a Roman emperor, called Antoninus in Rabbinic literature, whose exact identity is unknown. Legend tells that Judah's special relationship with Antoninus developed because, as a baby, he was switched with the son of the Roman empress and grew up in Antoninus' place before his true identity was established. The emperor was impressed that Judah's cold shabbat food tasted better than his own hot food and asked for the recipe. Judah replied that the emperor's food did not lack any herbs or spices but that the missing ingredient was the Sabbath itself. Judah lived in great wealth, but unlike the Roman emperor, he denied himself the delights of this world. He thus earned himself the title of 'Our Holy Rabbi' and received visits from Elijah. When he was dying, he lifted both hands to heaven and said to God: 'Lord of the world, it is known to you that I laboured with all ten fingers in the study of torah, but I did not derive even one finger's worth of pleasure from this world.' On one occasion a calf on its way to be slaughtered escaped and took refuge under Judah's cloak. Judah told it to go, since it was created to be killed and eaten. For this callousness Judah was punished with illness which was only cured when he showed mercy to some mice by saving them from his maidservant who was about to kill them. After his death, Judah appeared to his family on every shabbat eve (*see* AFTERLIFE). See also TANNA.

Judah Loew Ben Bezalel (1525–1609) Theologian and mystic, known as the Maharal of Prague. As a

Title-page of the *Kuzari* by **Judah Halevi** (16c., Venice).

poor student Judah became engaged to a wealthy woman and intended to continue his studies with her family's support. When they became impoverished, however, the marriage was delayed, and his fiancée had to run a food shop. One day a knight passed by and snatched a loaf of bread from the shop on his spear. He explained that he had not eaten for three days and left his cloak, with its lining containing gold coins, as payment. The marriage could thus go ahead, and Judah spent the rest of his life in relative affluence. His financial independence enabled him to be out-spoken in his views. He strongly criticized the neglect of Bible study among his fellow Jews, opposed their artificial methods of Talmudic PILPUL and decried the formulation of halakhah in summary codes like the SHULCHAN ARUKH. Judah maintained that it was better to study the *Talmud* itself, even at the risk of coming to the wrong conclusion about what should be done, than to read the correct answer from a code without understanding the halakhic background. Judah also translated Kabbalistic ideas into more popular termin-ology, evolving a unique system of thought which exerted considerable influence on Jewish thinkers. In the minds of ordinary Jews, however, he was regarded as a Kabbalistic magician and alchemist. Many legends grew up about the artificial creature (*see* GOLEM) which Judah created in Prague to serve the Jewish community. Formed out of dust and brought to life through the insertion of the name of God under its tongue, it obeyed Judah's commands, helping Jews survive anti-Jewish measures and blood libel accusa-tions and serving as a shabbos goi. Eventually, it had to be destroyed because it ran amok on a Friday afternoon during the KABBALAT SHABBAT when Judah forgot to remove the divine name. The remains of the golem were sealed up in the attic of the Altneu Synagogue in Prague. *See also* ALCHEMY.

Judah Maccabee (2c. BCE) Palestinian freedom fighter and member of the priestly family of Hasmoneans. Judah was one of the leaders of the revolt of the MACCABEES against the Seleucid Greek rulers of the Holy Land. He waged a successful guerrilla war against the Seleucid army, using the element of surprise and his knowledge of the physical features of the land. The recapture of Jerusalem by Judah's fighters and their rededication of the Temple led to the institution of the festival of CHANUKKAH. Judah was killed in battle and was buried in his home village of Modiin in the Galilee.

Judaizers Non-Jewish groups or individuals who adopt Judaic ideas and practices. Judaizing tendencies were often found among Christians through the influence of the Hebrew Bible, the Christian 'Old Testament', and sometimes led to practices which the Church regarded as sectarian, such as circumcision, abstention from eating blood, the dietary laws and even not working on Saturday, the Jewish Sabbath. Judaizing sects appeared in Russia from the 15c. onwards and were persecuted by the Russian Ortho-dox Church, their leaders being killed or conscripted into the army and posted to distant parts of the Russian Empire. Fear of the spread of Judaizing heresies increased anti-Semitism in the Russian Church, since Jews were accused of encouraging the Judaizers. The

Inquisition in Spain and Portugal accused some Jewish converts (*see* MARRANO) of the sin of Judaizing, namely, of being Catholics only on the surface but secretly practising Judaism, i.e. crypto-Jews. In modern times it has been claimed that the FALASHAS are not ethnically Jewish but a Judaizing group among the Ethiopian Christian population. Other Judaizing groups today are the urban BLACK JEWS in the USA and the Zionist Christians in Japan.

Judenrein *see* HOLOCAUST

judge *see* DAYYAN

Kabbalah (Hebrew for 'received tradition') General term for the mystical tradition but, more exactly, those esoteric teachings which first began to emerge in Southern France and Spain in the 13c. Kabbalists claimed that their tradition had originally been given to Moses at Sinai together with the torah. Kabbalah may be seen, however, as a development of the earlier mysticism of the MAASEH BERESHIT and MAASEH MERKAVAH, based on the teachings of the *Sefer Ha-Bahir*. Many oral traditions were reworked in the ZOHAR, edited in the late 13c., which came to be regarded as the Bible of the Kabbalists. Kabbalistic theosophy explored the inner workings of the divine in its relationship to man and the theurgic influence of man's actions on God. A number of different Kabbalistic teachings are found in Zoharic literature and in the writings of ecstatic mystics like Abraham Abulafia. Innovations were introduced by Isaac LURIA with his doctrines of TZIMTZUM, the breaking of the divine vessels holding the light of adam kadmon and the need for man's acts of TIKKUN to rectify this. The Chasidic Movement reinterpreted the Kabbalistic tradition in psychological terms. Some Kabbalists emphasized the theosophical exploration of the ten SEFIROT through which the world emerged from the unknowable Godhead by a process of EMANATION. Some stressed the central role played by man (*see* MICROCOSM) in keeping the commandments and the disharmony his sins caused by activating the evil forces of the SITRA ACHRA. Others were more interested in attaining mystical experience through meditational techniques than in building speculative systems. The influence of Kabbalah on exoteric Judaism was wide-ranging, presenting Jews with a powerful set of mystical symbols, spreading the belief in the trans-migration of souls, determining new rituals and cus-toms, influencing halakhah and giving magical prac-tices respectability as elements of practical Kabbalah. Practical Kabbalists, who often tried to create a GOLEM, include JOSEPH DELLA REINA and JUDAH LOEW BEN BEZALEL. *See also* SHARABI, SHALOM.

kabbalat shabbat (Hebrew for 'acceptance of shab-bat') Liturgy for the inauguration of shabbat recited on Friday evenings before sunset. Kabbalat shabbat consists of six Psalms, one for each day of the working week, followed by the LEKHAH DODI hymn, which invites people to greet the Sabbath bride. The next

Psalm (92) begins with the words 'A Psalm for the Sabbath Day', and in reciting it, the community accept the onset of shabbat. One Friday evening Judah Loew Ben Bezalel was praying in the Altneu Synagogue in Prague. The Sabbath Psalm had just been said when he was told that the golem, or artificial man, which he had created had run amok. Without hesitation Judah left the synagogue and removed the magical name of God from the golem's mouth to incapacitate it. When he returned the community recited the Psalm again, and henceforth it became a custom always to repeat Psalm 92 in that synagogue. The origin of kabbalat shabbat goes back to Talmudic times when there were various customs of greeting the arriving shabbat. It was formalized in the liturgy in the 16c. by the Kabbalists of Safed, Palestine, who would dress in white and go out into the fields just before sunset to meet the incoming Sabbath bride with Psalms and hymns.

kaddish (Aramaic for 'holy') Aramaic prayer recited by the chazzan to mark the end of a section of the liturgy and by mourners following the death of a relative or on a yahrzeit. The presence of a MINYAN of ten adult Jewish males is necessary for its recital since it is a public affirmation of God's greatness and holiness. It was composed in Aramaic so that ordinary people, who knew no Hebrew, could say it. LEVI ISAAC OF BERDICHEV added vernacular interpolations to the kaddish. The mystics saw a message in the choice of a secular language for this prayer, namely that the profane world has to be sanctified by using it to express holiness. Many texts attest to the power of the kaddish, which can win forgiveness and a favourable response from heaven. God Himself is said to rejoice at its recital, like a happy king who is praised by his subjects. A child is able to rescue a parent from suffering after death by saying kaddish for eleven months after his or her demise (see AFTERLIFE). The kaddish is not said for the full twelve months, the extent of the MOURNING period, since this would indicate that the parent was regarded as particularly wicked. In the 12c. the Jews of the Yemen included the name of the great sage Moses Maimonides in their kaddish prayers, so highly did they revere him. They asked God to bring about the rule of His kingdom 'in our lifetime and in the lifetime of our teacher Moses the son of Maimon'. At the coming of the Messiah souls suffering in GEHINNOM will be redeemed when they answer AMEN to the kaddish recited in heaven. See also MEMORIAL PRAYERS.

kahal see COMMUNITY

kallah see MARRIAGE

kapote see DRESS

kapparah see ATONEMENT

kapparot (Hebrew for 'atonements') The custom, dating from medieval times, of slaughtering a cockerel or a hen prior to yom kippur, as a vicarious ATONEMENT for a Jew or Jewess. The person for whom the atonement is being made takes the bird and waves it round their head saying: 'This is in exchange for me,

Judah Maccabee (15c. woodcut).

Zodiacal signs thought to have the power to 'govern' the physical universe, from a **Kabbalah** manuscript (17c.–18c.).

this is instead of me, this is my atonement. This cockerel (or hen) shall go to death, and I shall enter in and go to a good, long life and to peace.' The chicken is then slaughtered, its flesh given to the poor, and its innards left out for the birds. There was considerable opposition to this custom in the late Middle Ages (*see* MINHAG), and a number of leading rabbis among the Sephardim abolished it in areas under their control since they regarded it as a pagan practice. Many Ashkenazi halakhic authorities supported it, however, as an established custom. Today, Jews often use money instead of a chicken as kapparot, since this was advocated by those rabbis who continued to oppose the rite. Yiddish speakers will shrug off something bad which happens to them by saying 'may this be oyf kapporos', i.e. an atonement.

kappel *see* HEAD-COVERING

Karaites (from Hebrew 'karaim', meaning 'men of scripture') Jewish sect founded in 8c. Babylonia by ANAN BEN DAVID, who gathered together groups opposed to the Rabbinic tradition including remnants of the Sadducees. Originally, the Ananites, as they were first called, accepted Anan's teachings about the Bible, the TRANSMIGRATION OF SOULS, ascetic practices such as avoiding meat and wine as a sign of mourning for Zion, and opposition to doctors, since God alone heals the sick. Anan told his followers to search the scriptures thoroughly and not to rely simply on his view. In the course of time Karaism considerably modified these teachings, and later Karaites were critical of some of Anan's views. They did, however, maintain his literalistic attitude towards the Bible, rejecting the authority of the ORAL TORAH, and were often stricter than Rabbinic Jews in the application of biblical law. Thus, they would not go out of their homes on shabbat, did not have any fire burning at home and prohibited sexual relations on that day. Their polemics led to a renewed interest in biblical Hebrew and to the textual work of the Masorites (*see* MASORAH). SAADIAH GAON wrote extensively against Ananite-Karaite beliefs and practices. Maimonides was instrumental in eradicating Karaism as a major force in Egypt but was generally conciliatory towards Karaites, even allowing their children to be circumcised on the Sabbath. Karaism in turn borrowed elements from Rabbinic Judaism and formulated its own law codes. The 19c. Karaite, Abraham FIRKOVICH, argued that Karaites were a separate ethnic group from Jews and had no part in the killing of Jesus. This led to the emancipation of Russian Karaites in 1863. The Nazis, too, regarded Karaites as racially different from Jews, so the former escaped persecution. Today there are only a few thousand Karaites left, and many of them live in Israel where they have autonomy to run their own religious affairs.

kasher *see* KOSHER

kashrut *see* DIETARY LAWS

kavvanah (Hebrew for 'inner direction') The mental act of intending to perform a ritual or of focusing on the religious dimension of a prayer. Talmudic literature contains a number of discussions about whether one can perform a MITZVAH without actually intending to do so, e.g. if one is playing with a shofar and accidentally blows a note on rosh ha-shanah. Without kavvanah the COMMANDMENTS are rote actions and are like a body without a soul. On the other hand, once one has done the right action, the intention seems of secondary importance, and commandments ought to be performed even for the wrong reasons. The halakhah rules that prayers said mechanically without any genuine kavvanah do not need to be repeated, as long as there is a basic understanding of the words. Only pietists and mystics raised the importance of inwardness above that of the ritual acts themselves. Thus, early pietists used to meditate for an hour each morning before prayers, so as to focus their minds on God. Kabbalists saw kavvanah as the mystical inner aspect of each prayer. Indeed, a Kabbalistic prayerbook was composed which printed the reference to the relevant part of the structure of the sefirot above each word, so that the mind could hold these in consciousness while the words were uttered. The words thus became symbols for the mystical dimension which lay behind them. These mystical prayers took much longer to recite than the normal prayers, and the Kabbalist Shalom Sharabi set up a special yeshivah in which such prayers were said. A formula, 'leshem yichud' ('for the sake of the unification'), was introduced by Kabbalists and by followers of the Chasidic Movement to be said before performing any ritual act so as to have the correct kavvanah. This addition was opposed by some rabbis who argued that, if one did not have kavvanah for the act or prayer, one could merely recite the formula without thinking about it. *See also* TIKKUN.

kedoshim *see* MARTYRDOM

kedushah (Hebrew for 'holiness') Biblical verses chanted during the chazzan's repetition of the AMIDAH. The kedushah, which is only said in the presence of a minyan, is made up of angelic utterances recorded by the prophets Isaiah and Ezekiel. At its core is the doxology 'Holy, holy, holy is the Lord of Hosts. The whole earth is full of His glory' (Isa. 6:3). According to Rabbinic literature, the world is sustained by the recital of the kedushah, and there are descriptions of the rivers of joy which flow from God's Throne of Glory when the angels and Israel chant its verses. Kedushah must be said standing with the legs together, like the angels who have a 'straight foot' (Ezek. 1:7). It is customary to raise and lower oneself on the toes as the kedushah is said to resemble the angels flying.

kehillah *see* COMMUNITY

kemea *see* AMULETS; MEZUZAH

keneyna hore *see* EVIL EYE

Ketev Meriri *see* DEMONS; THREE WEEKS OF MOURNING

ketubbah (Hebrew for 'document') Aramaic MARRIAGE document, given by the groom to his bride at the wedding, and kept by the wife thereafter. The couple are not allowed to live together as man and wife without their ketubbah, and if it is lost, a new one has to be prepared. The ketubbah sets out the responsibilities of the husband and guarantees the wife support from the husband's estate should he pre-decease her, or a monetary payment from him in the case of DIVORCE. Although there are standard printed ketubbah forms today, couples can still have their ketubbah hand-written by a SCRIBE and illuminated with traditional designs and pictures. Many marriage documents in the past were elaborately decorated (*see* ILLUMINATED MANUSCRIPTS; MICROGRAPHY).

kevurah *see* BURIAL

Khazars People of Turkic origin, located between the Black Sea and the Caspian Sea, whose leaders converted to Judaism in the 8c., perhaps influenced by neigh-bouring MOUNTAIN JEWS. According to legend the king of the Khazars received Christian and Islamic emissaries who came to convert him and decided he would also like to meet representatives of Judaism. When he asked the Christian and Moslem sages which of the other two religions was the best, they both answered 'Judaism', so he decided to become a Jew, taking many of his nobles and some of the common people with him into the new faith. The Khazar king invited Jewish scholars into his kingdom and engaged in correspondence with Hasdai Ibn Shaprut, a high-ranking Jewish official of the Sultan of Cordova. Jewish traders from as far away as Germany and Spain also came to settle among their Khazar co-religionists. This independent Khazar Jewish kingdom came to an end in the 13c. when it could not resist Russian and Mongol invaders. Khazar refugees settled among the Jewish communities of Europe, and some scholars have even made the somewhat exaggerated claim that the Jews of Hungary, and perhaps even the majority of Ashkenazim, were descendants of these Khazar converts. The great Spanish poet and theologian JUDAH HALEVI wrote a philosophical defence of Judaism, the *Kuzari*, set around the questions of the Khazar king and the answers of the Jewish, Christian and Moslem sages.

kibbutz galuyyot *see* INGATHERING OF THE EXILES

kiddush (Hebrew for 'sanctification') The ceremony of reciting prayers and blessings over a cup of WINE at the commencement of SHABBAT and festivals, and once again after the end of the morning service before lunch. The idea behind kiddush is that holy time must be differentiated from profane time by proclaiming its holiness. The Rabbis base the ceremony on the command in the Decalogue: 'Remember the Sabbath day to sanctify it' (Exod. 20:8), which they take to mean 'remember it over wine'. In many communities the evening kiddush is first made in the synagogue itself. Originally, this was for the benefit of any travellers staying in the synagogue, but nowadays the wine is even drunk by children. When a father returns home, he recites kiddush for his family, and this is followed by the evening meal. The lunchtime kiddush is also made at home before the midday meal. In some synagogues a communal kiddush, usually consisting of wine, whisky and cakes, is served for the whole congregation in the synagogue hall.

kiddush ha-shem *see* MARTYRDOM

Group of Crimean **Karaite** merchants (19c., Russia).

19c. Yemenite **ketubbah** decorated with pictures of the holy places in the Land of Israel.

kiddush levanah *see* NEW MOON

kilayim *see* MIXED SPECIES

kinot (Hebrew for 'lamentation dirges') Poems of lamentation recited on the fast of the Ninth of Av (*see* AV, NINTH OF), mourning the destruction of the Temple in Jerusalem and Jewish suffering down the ages. A number of poems by medieval poets expressing their longing for the return to Zion are included in the official collections of kinot. In modern times a kinah has even been composed about the Holocaust of European Jewry under the Nazis, and it has been incorporated in the liturgy of a number of synagogues.

kipah *see* HEAD-COVERING

kishke *see* CHOLENT

Kislev Ninth lunar month of the Hebrew calendar, counting from Nisan, the month of the Exodus, and third month from the New Year festival (rosh ha-shanah). Kislev usually begins in late November or early December, and its zodiacal sign is the bow. On the twenty-fifth of Kislev the festival of CHANUKKAH begins.

kisse ha-kavod *see* THRONE OF GLORY

kitel (Yiddish for 'white garment') A shroud-like gown worn in some communities by men on ROSH HA-SHANAH and YOM KIPPUR, by the CHAZZAN on certain festivals, by the head of the family at the Passover SEDER, by a bridegroom under the CHUPPAH, and by the dead as a burial garment. The kitel has a number of symbolic meanings which help explain its use. The white colour symbolizes purity and divine forgiveness, which are appropriate both to the New Year festival as a day of judgment and to the groom who is forgiven all his sins at the marriage ceremony. It also symbolizes DEW. The kitel is the dress of angels, and on the fast of yom kippur Jews are elevated to the status of ministering angels. It also represents the clothes worn by free men and not by slaves, and Passover is the festival of freedom.

klezmer *see* BADCHAN; MUSIC

kodesh ha-kodashim *see* HOLY OF HOLIES

kohelet *see* ECCLESIASTES

kohen (Hebrew for 'priest') A Jew who is a descendant of Aaron, the first High Priest, through the male line is a PRIEST and has the title 'ha-kohen' appended to his Hebrew name. He is only disqualified from priestly status if a male ancestor entered into an irregular marriage with a divorcee or female proselyte, both of whom are forbidden to priests. The surname Cohen, in its various forms – Cahn, Cohn, Cowan, Kahan, Kahn, Kohn, etc. – usually indicates the priestly descent of the bearer, and because there is no 'h' in Russian, the same is true of Cagan, Kagan, Kaganovitch, etc. There are cases, however, where someone bearing such a surname is a Levite or simply a non-Levitical Israelite. *See also* LEVITE.

kohen gadol *see* HIGH PRIEST

kolel *see* YESHIVAH

kol nidrei (Aramaic for 'all vows') Proclamation of the annulment of religious vows chanted by the chazzan and congregation prior to the maariv service on YOM KIPPUR eve. The synagogue ark is opened and two torah scrolls are carried to the bimah before kol nidrei is chanted to a plaintive tune. The original purpose of the annulment was to remove guilt of unfulfilled vows which had been forgotten and which might be thought still binding on the person concerned. At times of forced conversion to Christianity, Jews associated the formula of kol nidrei with the annulment of vows taken under duress. Christians themselves accused Jews of using kol nidrei to dissolve any undertakings and commitments that Jews had promised to keep and claimed that, therefore, Jews could not be trusted to keep their word. This led various rabbis to emphasize that only religious vows between man and God were included in the proclamation, and indeed, attempts have been made to abolish the whole kol nidrei ritual in some places.

Kook, Abraham Isaac (1865–1935) Chief Rabbi of the Holy Land and mystic. As a young rabbi Kook already showed an independence of spirit. When a plague broke out in the town where he officiated, he publicly stood up in the synagogue on yom kippur, recited the blessings over food and ate to encourage his congregants to do likewise, since it was dangerous to fast. In later life he found halakhic solutions to the problems faced by Palestinian Jewish farmers during the Sabbatical Year (*see* SHEMITTAH), despite the virulent opposition of Ultra-Orthodox opponents, one of whom emptied a chamber-pot on his head. Kook blended Messianic Zionism with Kabbalistic teachings and wrote of the world progressing to a new consciousness. Even the sinners of modern times were inspired to reject religion because of their ideals of socialism and the promotion of social justice. This in itself was indicative of the evolution of mankind, and Kook saw the theory of evolution not as a threat to religious belief but as an expression of the divine purpose for the world. Indeed, all secular knowledge is imbued with an element of the sacred, since reality is a reflection of the divine light. The return of the Jewish People to their ancestral home in the Holy Land was a sign of the Messianic redemption. Despite his Orthodoxy, Kook was tolerant of irreligious Jews, particularly of Zionists engaged in the holy work of resettling the Land of Israel. According to Kook, the more a Jew was rooted in his own traditions and the more he loved his own people and his own land, the more this love overflowed to other peoples and other lands. The Temple was destroyed through the spread of groundless hatred, and the redemption would come about through the spread of groundless love. Kook's theological writings and poetry were written with an intensity which he explained by saying that he did not write because he had to write but because he could not keep silent.

Korah Levite who led a rebellion in the wilderness during the Exodus (Num. 16). Korah questioned the authority of Moses, criticized the tithes given to the priests because they impoverished the people, and claimed that all Israel were on an equal spiritual level. To illustrate this point, he asked whether a garment made entirely of purple wool needed to have fringes (tzitzit) with a purple woolen thread attached to them, or whether a house full of holy books needed to have a parchment with sacred writing (mezuzah) attached to the doorpost. He thus implied that there was no need for Moses and Aaron as prophet and High Priest, since the people were all holy. The rebellion of Korah was not undertaken for purely religious motives, however, but out of jealousy and a desire for a greater role for himself in the cultic hierarchy. He and his followers were punished by being swallowed up by the earth. Thus entombed, they cry out: 'Moses is true and his torah is true' (see RABBAH BAR BAR CHANA). Their cries have continued to resound in the nether-world and were once overheard by a Talmudic rabbi when he chanced upon the place above their underground cavern. According to Kabbalistic teaching, Korah was caught up in the darkness of the powers of evil (sitra achra) and was led to deny that the world was created by God. Korah's sons were not punished, as they repented, and were among the authors of the Book of Psalms. The prophet Samuel was descended from them.

korban *see* SACRIFICE

kosher (Hebrew for 'fit') The most general word for food which is permitted to be eaten according to the regulations of the Jewish DIETARY LAWS. Any food which is not regarded as TEREFAH is kosher. The term is the Ashkenazi pronunciation of the Hebrew 'kasher'. It is found in the Book of Esther: 'if the matter seems fitting [kasher] to the king' (5:5), whence it passed into Rabbinic literature to be used widely about ritual behaviour and about people. A kosher animal is one that has cloven hooves and chews the cud (*see* PIG). A kosher individual may be one who keeps the dietary laws, one who strictly follows the dictates of the halakhah or one who is of a genuinely trustworthy character. In English slang kosher means 'legal' or 'legitimate'. Its main use, however, is for classifying food, and it has produced a series of terms based on it. Thus, 'glatt kosher' indicates that meat is not only kosher but that no doubts have been raised about the slaughtered animal it was taken from (*see* SHECHITAH). As a verb 'to kosher' something is to bring it into a state of ritual fitness, e.g. koshering (salting) meat or koshering (cleansing) pots with boiling water. The general term for rabbinic approval of a food item is 'hekhsher' which has the meaning 'declared as kosher'. Mystics were said to be able to tell whether food was kosher simply by looking at it. In the World to Come (olam haba) all foods will be declared kosher.

kotel ha-maaravi *see* WAILING WALL

Kotsker Rebbe *see* MENACHEM MENDEL OF KOTSK

Kranz, Jacob (1741–1804) Lithuanian preacher popularly known as the Dubno Maggid. Kranz lived as a wandering preacher before settling in Dubno and acting as the chaplain to Elijah the Vilna Gaon. His

Opening phrase of the **kol nidrei** liturgy from an illuminated manuscript.

Photograph of Chief Rabbi Abraham Isaac **Kook**, taken in the early 1930s.

special ability was in explaining biblical and Rabbinic teachings through parables and fables which won him great popularity among the masses. When asked how he was able to find a suitable parable for each sermon, he told the following story. Once a king who was out hunting got lost in a forest and took shelter in the hut of a poor wood-cutter. He was amazed to find outside the hut a series of targets with arrows set in their bull's-eyes. He asked the wood-cutter how he had become such a good shot. The wood-cutter replied that he was not a good shot; he merely fired the arrow first and then drew the target round it after it landed. Thus, Kranz explained, he used parables with which he was acquainted to apply to situations, the parables coming first and the situation or text being made to fit in with it.

Krimchaks Crimean Jews of mixed Tartar and Semitic type who were deported to the Crimea in the early centuries CE. Their culture and dress was Tartar, and they spoke the Tartar language which they wrote in Hebrew characters. Prior to Russian rule the Krimchaks held important positions, even serving as foreign ambassadors. Under the Russians, however, their position seriously deteriorated, and they worked in agricultural pursuits. They were Orthodox Jews who had their own customs. For instance, they all used to gather together in the synagogue courtyard and only enter for prayer when everyone had arrived, maintaining an awed decorum during the service. Weddings took place at dawn, with the bride and groom not standing under a chuppah but covered by a tallit. Cockerels were waved over their heads seven times during the ceremony. From 1867 to 1900 a leading Orthodox rabbi, Chaim Medini, was head of the Krimchak community in the Crimea and helped to raise their educational level. The Nazis exterminated many of the Krimchak Jews while sparing the Crimean Karaites.

Kristalnacht *see* CONCENTRATION CAMPS; HOLO-CAUST

Kuzari see JUDAH HALEVI; KHAZARS

kvater, kvaterin *see* SANDEK

Laban Brother of Rebecca and father of Leah and Rachel. When Laban arranged the marriage of his sister to Abraham's son, Isaac, he was impressed by the presents which Abraham's servant brought. So when Jacob, Abraham's grandson, came to stay and asked to marry Rachel, Laban's younger daughter, he expected him to bring rich gifts. He therefore embraced him at their initial meeting, to see if he could feel the expected jewels secreted on Jacob's body or in his mouth. Finding that he had come with nothing, Laban exploited Jacob's labour and tricked him by marrying his elder daughter Leah to him first. Jacob's presence in Laban's household brought God's blessings, so that Laban's wife bore him sons, and his flocks increased (Gen. 30:27). Instead of feeling gratitude, he still tried to cheat Jacob out of the reward of his labours and to use witchcraft to harm him. Despite the bad reputation Laban has in Rabbinical literature, the blessing which he gave to Rebecca when she left to marry Isaac (Gen. 24:60) is repeated today to brides just before their wedding ceremony.

Ladino Judaeo-Spanish language which developed among Hispanic Jewish exiles (*see* SEPHARDIM) after the expulsions from Spain in the 1490s. A whole literature was produced in Ladino, written in Hebrew characters, from 1510 when the first Ladino work was published in Istanbul. This literature consisted of translations, works for women and those with little Hebrew knowledge, religious and secular poetry, legends and *Me-am Loez*, an encyclopaedic commentary on the Bible. The return of the crypto-Jews (marranos) to the Jewish community after they had escaped from Spain enriched Ladino with Spanish vocabulary. The number of Ladino speakers declined in the modern period which saw the emigration of Sephardi Jews to South America, where Ladino was replaced by Spanish, and the destruction of the Jewish community of Salonika, one of the main centres of Ladino culture, during the Holocaust.

lag ba-omer (Hebrew for 'thirty-third day of the omer') A semi-festive day in the middle of the OMER period, which interrupts the communal mourning associated with this time, lag ba-omer always falls on the eighteenth of Iyyar. It is reputedly the anniversary of the death of SIMEON BAR YOCHAI, the 2c. CE Palestinian mystic to whom the teachings of the *Zohar* are ascribed. Since the death of a saint is understood as a spiritual 'wedding', hillula, when the soul is reunited with its divine source, lag ba-omer is a favourite occasion for weddings. On this festive day people make a pilgrimage to the tomb of Rabbi Simeon in Meron (near Safed in the Galilee) to study the *Zohar*, dance around the tomb and build bonfires into which the HAIR from the first haircut of young boys is cast. The gathering at Meron today has all the hallmarks of a fair, with sheep slaughtered by family groups, much to the consternation of the Israel health authorities.

lamed vavnik (Yiddish for 'one of the thirty-six') There is a belief in Jewish folklore that in each generation there are thirty-six hidden righteous men (*see* TZADDIK) on whose merits the world depends. This belief is based on a Talmudic statement that there are not less than thirty-six righteous people who stand in the presence of the shekhinah every day. One of these humble and unnoticed lamed vavniks is destined to be the Messiah, if the generation is worthy. They wander in exile with their fellow Jews, working as artisans, and only assert themselves when there is danger to the community. After they have acted to save Jews from danger, they revert back to their anonymity. They are forbidden to reveal themselves to others, for if they did so, they would die. Israel Baal Shem Tov was said to know who the lamed vavniks of his generation were and to have given them economic support. Elijah the Vilna Gaon knew of a lamed vavnik called Leib who worked in a distillery. Before he set out on his travels to the Land of Israel,

Elijah wrote to this Leib and asked him to accompany him. When the letter arrived at the distillery, the owner and workmen were surprised to see that the famous sage of Vilna was writing to one of their number, but they were even more surprised to see Leib read the letter and cast it into a furnace. To the man who brought the letter, who needed an answer to take back to his master, all Leib would reply was: 'It's not necessary.' It seems that Leib knew the Vilna Gaon would never actually reach the Holy Land.

Lamentations, Book of (Hebrew 'eikhah') Biblical book written by the prophet JEREMIAH, mourning the destruction of the First TEMPLE and of Jerusalem, and lamenting the fate of the righteous king JOSIAH, 'the anointed of the Lord' (Lam. 4:20). According to Lamentations, it was Israel's sins which led to the destruction and subsequent exile, and therefore repentance will reawaken God's mercy and end the suffering of the people. God Himself recited the Book of Lamentations over the sin of Adam and his expulsion from the Garden of Eden, as well as over the destruction of Jerusalem. Lamentations is one of the Five Scrolls (see MEGILLAH) and is chanted in the synagogue on the fast of Av (see AV, NINTH OF) to a mournful tune.

lamp, Sabbath On Friday evening before sunset two candles are lit in the Jewish home to signal the onset of SHABBAT. The candles represent the two references to the Sabbath in the Decalogue: 'Remember the Sabbath day' (Exod. 20:8) and 'Keep the Sabbath day' (Deut. 5:12). They also symbolize the divine light which descends onto the world on the Sabbath day and the extra soul (see NESHAMAH YETERAH) which shines within each Jew for its duration. It is customary for the wife to light the Sabbath lamps, and if she is negligent in doing so, she is punished with death in childbirth (see BIRTH). After lighting the candles, the woman passes her hands over the flames and covers her eyes; she then makes the benediction and opens her eyes to the light of the Sabbath. This is a time for her to engage in private prayer for her family, a number of Yiddish prayers being especially composed for the occasion. In pre-modern times hanging lamps with oil and wicks were used instead of candles. *See also* REBECCA.

Landau, Ezekiel (1713–93) Rabbi of Prague and leading halakhic authority. Landau lived at a period of great turmoil in Jewish life with the emergence of the Enlightenment in Western Europe and the rise of the CHASIDIC MOVEMENT in the Eastern European lands. As a conservative he tried to arrest modernization, opposing the German Bible translation of Moses Mendelssohn. He also wrote against Chasidic innovations in ritual matters and criticized their indulgence in physical pleasures. It is said that Landau personally supervised the public burning of the first Chasidic book. In his halakhic responsa he forbade a rich Jew from engaging in the hunting of animals for pleasure, since this simply caused suffering to animals. He was also very restrained in his approach to Kabbalistic matters and ensured that the remains of the Prague golem were locked away in a synagogue attic. On one occasion a sick woman was convinced that she could only be cured with the aid of an amulet written

Opening verses of the Book of **Lamentations** with notes of the masorah, showing a Jew wearing a tallit (14c. German).

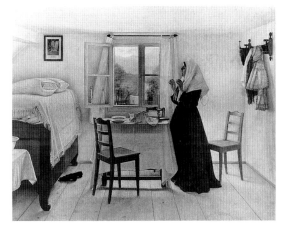

Painting of a woman reciting a prayer after lighting the Sabbath **lamp** by Samuel Hirschenberg (19c.).

by Landau. Under much pressure he had to agree to give her one, so he placed an empty parchment scroll in a case and gave it to her. Landau told her she should wear it for thirty days, and on the thirty-first she should open the case. If the writing had disappeared she would know that the amulet had worked.

lashon ha-ra (Hebrew for 'evil speech') It is forbidden to spread gossip about someone, even though what might be said is essentially true (Lev. 19:16). The punishment for lashon ha-ra is usually LEPROSY although it can also happen that someone who spreads gossip is himself tempted to commit the very sins that he ascribes to others. This happened to the biblical Joseph who told his father about the bad deeds of his brothers and was punished for each sin that he reported by the temptations that beset him in later life. Gossip adversely affects three people: the person who is gossiped about, the one who spreads the gossip and the one who hears it. Since there is little control over the consequences of gossip, which is passed on to ever widening circles of listeners, repentance is very difficult for people who spread it. For this reason they will not merit to be in the presence of God (*see* SHEKHINAH) after death. In order to emphasize the serious nature of the sin of lashon ha-ra, the Rabbis said that gossiping was as bad as the three cardinal sins of idolatry, murder and sexual immorality. Even immoderate praise of a person can lead to gossip because others may respond by saying: 'He is not so marvellous, why he did X or Y.' Lashon ha-ra is allowed, however, if it serves some communal purpose or the information is necessary for the recipient. It is also permitted if the subject is present while he is being talked about. A modern rabbinic authority, ISRAEL MEIR HA-KOHEN, devoted a whole book, *Chafetz Chaim*, to the subject of gossip because he felt that even the most Orthodox Jews took the prohibition about evil speech far too lightly.

Leah Wife of Jacob and one of the MATRIARCHS. Leah was given in marriage to her cousin by her father LABAN in place of her sister RACHEL, because she was the elder daughter. This act of subterfuge was only discovered by Jacob on the morning after the wedding night, because Rachel had cooperated in order not to put her sister to shame. Leah was less beautiful than Rachel, and her eyes were weak from crying since she thought she would have to marry the wicked Esau, the elder of her two cousins. She gave birth to six sons, including Judah and Levi, who were progenitors of the Tribes of Israel, and when she became pregnant for the seventh time, she prayed to God for a daughter, Dinah. She did this because she knew her husband Jacob was destined to have only twelve sons. His concubines had already born him five sons, and she wanted Rachel, the future mother of Joseph, to bear another son. As a reward the Levites and priests were descended from her, as was the Davidic line of kings from whom the future Messiah will come. The Divine Presence, shekhinah, was always in Leah's tent during her lifetime. She lived to the same age as her father, and when she died at forty-five years of age, she was buried in the Cave of Machpelah.

lechaim *see* GREETINGS; TIKKUN; YAHRZEIT

lechem *see* BREAD

Leiner, Gershon *see* TEKHELET

Leiner, Mordechai Joseph *see* FREE WILL; MENACHEM MENDEL OF KOTSK

leket, shikhchah, peah (Hebrew for 'dropped', 'forgotten', 'corner') Agricultural laws allowing paupers and strangers to participate in the harvest (Lev. 19: Deut. 24). Leket refers to those sheaves, dropped one or two at a time during the reaping, which were gleaned by the poor who followed behind the reapers. Shikhchah refers to individual bundles of sheaves which were forgotten in the field when the produce was brought in to the barns. Peah refers to the demand that a farmer leave a corner of each field uncut for the poor. The story of Ruth illustrates how the poor supported themselves on the basis of these laws. The Rabbis stipulated that there should be three times for the poor to collect the peah produce designated for them at the corner of a field: an early collection in the morning for nursing mothers who need food at the start of the day, a later collection around midday for young people who do not get up at the same time as adults and a still later collection in the afternoon for the elderly who arise late. *See also* CHARITY.

Lekhah Dodi (Hebrew for 'go my friend') Hymn sung during KABBALAT SHABBAT on Friday evening to welcome the coming of shabbat. Lekhah dodi was composed by Solomon Alkabetz, a member of the circle of mystics living in Safed in the 16c. The first letters of each paragraph make up an acrostic of the author's name, and the hymn depicts the Sabbath as a bride coming to the marriage ceremony. It contains the hope of the Messianic redemption, when Israel will rise up from the dust of exile, although its terse, poetic language leaves a certain ambiguity about a number of its main features. When singing the last paragraph, the congregation turn away from the synagogue ARK and bow to the door, as they signal the entrance of shabbat with the words 'Come, O bride; come, O bride'. The imagery of lekhah dodi goes back to Talmudic times, when the Sabbath was welcomed as queen and bride, and to the teachings of the Kabbalah about the union of the male and female aspects of God on shabbat. The hymn was composed for the Safed Kabbalists who used to go out into the fields, dressed in white, to welcome the Sabbath bride as the sun began to set on Friday evening.

lekh beshalom, lekh leshalom *see* GREETINGS

leprosy (Hebrew 'tzaraat') Biblical ailment, not specifically identical with true leprosy, which affected skin, hair, clothing and houses. It was variously thought to be a punishment for those who indulged in malicious gossip (*see* LASHON HA-RA) or to afflict children born from sexual relations with a menstruous woman (*see* NIDDAH). 'Lepers' whose ailment had healed had to undergo a process of ritual purification (*see* ANOINTING) before being allowed back into the community (Lev. 13–14). 'Leprosy' was not regarded as straightforwardly contagious, since a groom was allowed seven days of wedding festivities from the time he, his garments or his house developed the symptoms before a PRIEST would examine them, and householders were encouraged to remove items from their dwellings before the priest arrived to declare the house and its contents unclean (Lev. 14:36). There are instances in Jewish literature where leprosy was cured by someone bathing in the river Jordan (*see* NAAMAN) or in MIRIAM'S WELL. It was because Pharaoh suffered from 'leprosy' that he slaughtered Israelite children in order to bathe in their BLOOD. He had been told by his magicians that a twice daily bath in the blood of children would effect a cure. *See also* RABBAH BAR NACHMANI.

levanah *see* MOON

Levi Son of Jacob and Leah, progenitor of the tribe of LEVITES and of the priests. Jacob offered his son Levi as a tithe to God, and Levi was taken up by the angel Michael into heaven. There God blessed him and told him his descendants would be set aside to minister to God on earth as the angels minister to Him in heaven. He was involved with his brother Simeon in the violent revenge against the Canaanites for the rape of his sister Dinah (Gen. 34), and his tendency to zealotry was inherited by his priestly descendant Phinehas.

Leviathan (Hebrew 'livyatan') Biblical sea monster of enormous dimensions and king of all the sea creatures. God slew the female of the species, to prevent the pair breeding and destroying the world, and made clothes for Adam and Eve from her skin. He will eventually have Gabriel slay the male in the age of the Messiah or, according to another version, arrange for the gigantic BEHEMOTH to engage in battle with the Leviathan until they kill each other. At the great Messianic banquet for the righteous, the Leviathan's skin will form a gigantic marquee and its flesh will be eaten. The eyes of the Leviathan light up the sea at night, and water boils up from the hot breath of its mouth. The foul odour of the Leviathan can even overpower the fragrance of the GARDEN OF EDEN, and were its stench to penetrate there, no one would be able to survive. According to the Kabbalistic tradition the Leviathan symbolizes Samael, the prince of evil, who will be destroyed in future times. *See also* JONAH.

Levi Isaac of Berdichev (1740–1810) Polish leader of the Chasidic Movement and disciple of Dov Baer of Mezhirech. Levi Isaac was reputed to be a reincarnation of the Mishnaic sage Rabbi Akiva, and he represented the emotional side of Chasidism. When he prayed, he completely nullified his physical nature and would break into the Yiddish vernacular in the midst of the Hebrew LITURGY. His Yiddish songs to God, in which he depicted the manifestation of the divine 'Thou' in everything, gained great popularity among ordinary Jews. He was also known for the interpolations which he inserted into the kaddish prayer, where he argued with God and asked Him why he let His people Israel suffer and what exactly He wanted of them. Levi Isaac's ecstatic joy when praying made the hairs of those around him stand on end. He carried his state of mystical devotion to God (devekut) out of the synagogue and into the mundane world. In his contacts with people he strove to see the best in them. Levi Isaac once came upon a Jew eating

Leah by Michelangelo.

A 2c. CE Greek bronze coin featuring grape clusters, symbols of the tribe of **Levi**.

on the Fast of Av. He asked him whether he had forgotten what day it was, and the Jew answered, 'No'. 'Do you not know it is forbidden to eat today?' 'No, I know it is a fast day, and it is forbidden to eat today.' 'Maybe you are sick?' 'No, I am not sick.' Levi Isaac then looked up to heaven and said to God; 'You see God, even when they sin your children refuse to lie.'

levirate marriage (Hebrew 'yibbum') The obligation on a man to marry his widowed sister-in-law, if she is childless, and thus to produce children 'to build up the house' of his deceased brother (Deut. 25). If he refuses to marry her, then a ceremony of chalitzah takes place, during which the widow removes the shoe of her brother-in-law and spits in front of him. She is then free to marry someone else. The original purpose of this chalitzah ceremony was to shame the brother for not fulfilling his responsibilities, but today it is standard practice since levirate marriage is not permitted any more. The Kabbalists saw a child born from a levirate marriage as a reincarnation of the dead brother, thus providing a tikkun for his restless soul and enabling it to find rest. The first male child of the levirate union was called by the same name as the deceased. *See also* MARRIAGE; MOUNTAIN JEWS.

Levites Members of the tribe of LEVI who were given the special task of looking after the TABERNACLE and the TEMPLE. The priestly descendants of Aaron (a subgroup of the Levites; *see* PRIEST) actually carried out the sacrificial ritual, while the other Levites were singers, musicians and support personnel. Levites are depicted as the bodyguard of God, His personal legion, who carried the ARK OF THE COVENANT walking barefooted. The Levites were not given a portion in the land of Israel (*see* TRIBES, THE TWELVE) because God was their portion (Josh. 13:14). They lived in Levitical cities scattered throughout the land, each of which served as an additional CITY OF REFUGE and were supported by TITHES. The Levites were chosen for their special role because they had kept faith with the religion of their fathers while in Egypt. In the wilderness they did not worship the GOLDEN CALF but supported Moses, a fellow Levite. During the Babylonian Captivity they refused to sing 'the Lord's song' in a strange land (Ps. 137) and bit off their thumbs so they could not be forced to play as musicians in idolatrous celebrations at the Babylonian court. Today, they have only residual roles in Jewish religion, being called to the torah immediately after a priest and washing the priests' hands before the priestly blessing.

Lilith First wife of ADAM and demon queen of the night. Lilith demanded equality with her husband, but when she found she could not attain equal status, she pronounced the name of God and flew through the air to the Red Sea. Adam complained to God who sent three angels, Sanvi, Sansanvi and Samangelaf, in an unsuccessful attempt to bring her back. The angels did make her promise that, wherever she saw their names, she would not do any harm to humans. Since then she has become the bride of Samael, the master of the evil forces of the sitra achra. Lilith is a seductive figure with long hair who flies like a night owl to attack those who sleep alone, to have demon children from men through nocturnal emissions, to steal children and to harm new-born infants. If she is unable to consume human children, she even eats her own demon progeny. As a protection against her AMULETS, engraved with the words 'Adam and Eve excluding Lilith', used to be attached to the walls of a home in which a woman was about to give BIRTH. The door of the childbirth room had the names of the three angels written on it, and sometimes a circle of burning coals surrounded the room. On the eve of shabbat and the new moon, when a child smiles that is because Lilith is playing with him or her. To prevent any harm, the child should be tapped three times on the nose and an anti-Lilith formula should be said. In the Middle Ages it was considered dangerous to drink water at the solstices and equinoxes because then Lilith's menstrual blood drops down and pollutes exposed liquids. Lilith appeared to Solomon in the guise of the Queen of SHEBA but he suspected that something was wrong so he tricked her into lifting her skirt and showing him her legs. When he saw they were covered with hair, he knew she was a demoness. *See also* DEMONS.

lion King of beasts. The lion is the symbol of the tribe of Judah (Gen. 49:9) and of the Davidic kings from that tribe. King Solomon had lions carved on his throne. It was believed that unless starving the lion did not attack and kill humans. Thus, if someone's husband disappeared and was known to have fallen into a den of lions, this alone was not sufficient evidence of death to allow the woman to remarry. The angel URIEL used to appear in the form of a lion descending from heaven onto the altar and would consume the sacrificial offerings in the Temple. The lion was a favourite motif of synagogue decoration which somehow escaped the censorship on representational art (*see* ARK, HOLY; PAROKHET), and the milk of a lioness was reputed to have healing properties. The Rabbis advised Jews that it was better to be 'a tail to lions than a head to foxes', i.e. better to associate with eminent people even in a subordinate capacity than to be a leader of riff-raff.

Lipkin Salanter, Israel (1810–83) Russian moralist and founder of the MUSAR MOVEMENT. As a young man Israel came under the influence of Joseph Zundel of Salant whom he once overheard recounting his faults to God. Joseph Zundel taught him that the only true way of serving God is through continuous self-examination and self-perfection. Israel was fired by the ideals of his teacher and wandered all over Europe preaching ethics, musar, to Jewish communities and reaching as far as France. He tried to involve the East European yeshivot in musar study as part of their curriculum, but many rabbis objected to their students taking time off from Talmudic texts to spend in self-reflection. Eventually, Israel's own students set up special musar yeshivot. Through these efforts Israel and his disciples rescued Jewish youngsters from the attractions of the secularist Enlightenment and provided the Mitnaggedim with their own tradition of inward spirituality to counterbalance that of the Chasidic Movement. Many stories are told of how Israel emphasized the ethical dimension which should be integrated with Jewish ritual practice. When he was a widower, living with a relative, he always used to wash his hands using the smallest amount of water prescribed by the halakhah. In reply to his host's question of why he did not perform the ritual in a stricter manner, he said: 'The servant has to carry the water a long distance up the hill, and one does not have the right to be pious at other people's expense.' When he lay dying, instead of reciting the deathbed confession, he spent his time persuading the old man with whom he lived that he should not be afraid of being left alone with a dead body. Israel formulated thirteen principles of musar which should be cultivated: truth, energy, decisiveness, honour for others, inner tranquillity, gentle speech, cleanliness, patience, orderliness, humility, righteousness, thrift and silence.

liturgy The formal liturgy of Judaism is modelled on the Temple services and SACRIFICES which came to an end in the 1c. CE. Its central features are the recital of the SHEMA, the AMIDAH prayer and selections from the PSALMS. These are interwoven with verses from the Hebrew Bible, BENEDICTIONS, hymns, PIYYUT, songs and SEFER TORAH readings. It is a duty to pray every day, and there are three public services (*see* SHACHARIT, MINCHAH, MAARIV), additional services for SHABBAT and FESTIVALS (*see* HAFTARAH; MAFTIR; MUSAF; NEILAH), and many shorter liturgies for the SYNAGOGUE and home on special occasions. Although PRAYER may be in any language, since it is the 'service of the heart', public prayer in the presence of a MINYAN is traditionally in Hebrew with some Aramaic additions. New prayers were added to the PRAYER-BOOK and the MACHZOR down the ages, reflecting a response to contemporary events and experiences, while individual prayers in Yiddish or other vernaculars were sometimes published in collections for private use. The leaders of the CHASIDIC MOVEMENT emphasized the value of spontaneous prayer. One of them, LEVI ISAAC OF BERDICHEV, even went so far as to introduce Yiddish dialogue with God into the formal liturgy. In the middle of reciting the KADDISH, he questioned God in Yiddish about the sufferings of the Jewish people. There is considerable variation between the liturgies of different Jewish communities, particularly between the Ashkenazim and the Sephardim. Many of the early disputes between Orthodox Judaism (*see* HIRSCH, SAMSON RAPHAEL) and REFORM JUDAISM were about the introduction of liturgical reforms, such as the shortening of services and the use of European languages for prayers and sermons.

livyatan *see* LEVIATHAN

locusts (Hebrew 'arbeh') Locusts represented a major natural disaster in biblical times. They were one of the Ten PLAGUES brought by God against Egypt, covering the fertile areas and darkening the sky. This plague of locusts is described as being heavier than any which preceded it and than any subsequent swarms (Exod. 10). The prophet Joel describes the attack of a mighty band of locusts on the Land of Israel in terms of a rapacious invading army which could only be removed by repentance and seeking divine mercy. His prophecy has been understood as referring, in fact, to a real army which was depicted as a swarm of locusts because

17c. amulet in the form of a magen david in a circle. The names of the four rivers from the Garden of Eden are on the outside, and the names of the angels which protect humans from **Lilith** are set along the circle and inset in the six-pointed star.

A basalt relief of **lions** fighting, from Hazor, Israel.

Graeco-Roman earthenware lamp with **locust** design.

of the destruction it wrought. Locusts invariably brought famine in their wake, and public fasts would be declared to avert the threat they represented. In general, locusts are symbols of greed and destruction. Some subspecies of locusts are kosher and may be eaten according to the Jewish dietary laws, but in practice they are only eaten by Jews who originate from countries where a tradition of locust-eating is well established, e.g. Morocco or Yemen. The eggs of locusts are described in the *Talmud* as a folk-remedy for curing earache.

Lot *see* DRUNKENNESS; HOSPITALITY; SODOM

luach ha-shanah *see* CALENDAR

Lubavitch Subgroup of the CHASIDIC MOVEMENT founded by SHNEUR ZALMAN OF LYADY in 18c. Russia. His descendants made the small town of Lubavici the centre of their activities, and the members of the group henceforth became known as Lubavitch Chasidim. Lubavitch eschewed the emotional religion of the Polish Chasidim and believed that true DEVEKUT came from the intellectual contemplation of God by means of three of the highest SEFIROT, chokhmah, binah and daat ('wisdom', 'understanding' and 'knowledge', the latter not being one of the official sefirot). Another name for Lubavitch, Chabad, is made up from the initial letters of these three sefirot. Lubavitch headquarters are now in New York where the current Lubavitcher Rebbe, Menachem Mendel Schneerson (b. 1902), the seventh leader of the movement and a direct descendant of the founder, resides. Originally, the TZADDIK in Lubavitch was merely responsible for the spiritual welfare of his followers. In recent times, however, some Lubavitch Chasidim have come to believe that their Rebbe is the Messiah, and they refer all major undertakings to him for his blessing. If, for instance, he does not approve of a proposed marriage, the wedding will not take place. Many visitors attend the gatherings in New York where the Rebbe speaks, particularly on anniversaries of events in Lubavitch history or on the Rebbe's BIRTHDAY. Others listen avidly to him over late-night telephone link-ups. They believe that as a Messianic figure, or at least as the outstanding mystical master of the age, all his teachings are unquestionably true, and he must be obeyed, even if other leading rabbis disagree with him. Unsympathetic critics of the movement (*see* NETUREI KARTA) accuse Lubavitchers of idolizing the Rebbe. Members of the movement are best known today for their missionary work among Jews, accosting people in public places and encouraging them to perform rituals with a zeal born out of their Messianic beliefs.

luck *see* ASTROLOGY; DREAMS

lulav (Hebrew for 'palm branch') One of the FOUR SPECIES shaken together during the festival of sukkot. The lulav is waved to the four directions of the compass, as well as up and down, to acknowledge that God is to be found everywhere. The lulav symbolizes the human spine, which must bend before God. In the Kabbalah the lulav is taken to symbolize the righteous man (tzaddik) who is identified with the masculine dimension of the structure of the sefirot and the male generative organ. It also represents God Himself.

Luria, Isaac (1543–72) Mystic and founder of Lurianic KABBALAH. Luria grew up in Cairo and lived for seven years as a recluse on an island in the Nile studying the *Zohar*. The prophet Elijah communicated secrets to him and told him in 1569 to go to Safed, Palestine. There he attracted the major Kabbalistic figures to him, though some could not absorb his mystical teachings. Joseph Caro, for instance, always fell asleep during Luria's lessons. Luria's ideas were recorded by his pupils, particularly by Chaim VITAL, his main disciple. He taught that, during the emanation of the world from God through the sefirot, some of the vessels holding the divine light (*see* ADAM KADMON) broke and sparks of this light became trapped in the broken pieces. It was man's task to release these trapped sparks, so they could return to their source in God. When this activity of rectifying the world (*see* TIKKUN) was at an end, the Messiah would come. Each individual had his special part to play, and the TRANS-MIGRATION OF SOULS allowed the task to be continued over many lives (*see* DIBBUK). The EXILE of Israel among the nations was to allow Jews to raise the scattered divine sparks throughout the world, since Jews have a higher type of soul than Gentiles and converts to Judaism possess holier souls than other non-Jews. The task of man was fraught with danger, however, because God had withdrawn his essence (*see* TZIMTZUM) so that something other than the divine could come into being, thereby bringing into being the sitra achra which is fed by human sin. Luria introduced new rituals into Judaism and new forms of mystical prayer. He would go out with his disciples every Friday evening into the fields around Safed, dressed in white, to welcome the shabbat bride. Luria was a reincarnation of the soul of Moses; he possessed the Holy Spirit (ruach ha-kodesh) and could tell the state of a person's transmigratory development merely by looking at their forehead.

luz (Hebrew for 'almond tree' or 'almond nut') An indestructible bone, shaped like an almond, at the base of the spine, around which a new body will be formed at the RESURRECTION OF THE DEAD. The bone survives the disintegration of the body after burial, but may be damaged if cremation is practised. In Rabbinic times the luz bone was actually tested by those who doubted the Resurrection and found to be able to withstand fire, water and a severe hammering. Nevertheless, it is claimed that the waters of the Flood at the time of Noah were so strong that they dissolved the luz bone of Adam's skeleton. The bone is sustained only by the food eaten at the MELAVVEH MALKAH ceremony, and those who bow to God in prayer are thought to guarantee themselves a resurrected body because they stimulate the bone when they bend their spine.

Luz is also the name of a city on the borders of the Holy Land built on a site anointed with heavenly oil by the Patriarch Jacob. The city, like the bone, is indestructible and protects its inhabitants from the Angel of Death. The location is hidden from human sight, and it can only be approached via a hollow almond tree which leads to a cave and thence to the city. Those who have grown old in Luz and long to die are placed outside the city walls. It is told how Solomon once discovered that the Angel of Death intended to kill two of his scribes, so he sent them with demons under his control to Luz. The angel in fact had been instructed to kill them at the gate of that city and was surprised when they turned up there.

Luzzatto, Moses Chaim (1707–46) Italian mystic and poet. Luzzatto had a heavenly spirit (maggid) which revealed mystical secrets to him. He also conversed with Adam, the Patriarchs, Elijah and the Messiah, each of whom taught him heavenly knowledge. He formed a Kabbalistic group which sought to hasten the Messianic advent, but he got into trouble with the rabbinic authorities who suspected him of subscribing to the heretical views of Shabbetai Tzevi. Luzzatto had to agree not to promulgate his views and eventually fled from Italy to Amsterdam and then to the Holy Land, having been excommunicated (cherem) by the rabbis of Venice. The importance of Kabbalah for a full religious life was the theme of a number of Luzzatto's works, and he devoted one book to a dialogue between a Kabbalist and a philosopher in which Kabbalah is defended against philosophical criticism. His most important book was a work on ethics, *Mesillat Yesharim* ('*The Path of the Upright*'), which described the ladder of ascent in holiness and self-perfection leading man to the Holy Spirit (ruach ha-kodesh). This work is still widely studied, particularly among followers of the Musar Movement, and the more controversial aspects of Luzzatto's life are now generally forgotten. Elijah the Vilna Gaon said that, if Rabbi Moses Luzzatto were still alive, then he would go on foot to him to learn ethics and morality.

maakeh *see* PARAPET

maariv (Hebrew for 'bringing of evening') The evening prayer, also known as arvit, said to have been instituted by JACOB. Maariv consists of the SHEMA, its benedictions and the AMIDAH. Unlike the two mandatory daily services, shacharit and minchah, the maariv amidah was originally optional because it was not based on any sacrifice. In the course of time, however, it too came to be accepted as obligatory. Maariv is usually said after dark, and its blessings ask for God's protection, so that people may lie down in peace and rise up once again to life, covered by the Tabernacle of divine peace. According to the Jewish mystics, saying the maariv prayer is preparing a bed for God for the night. *See also* LITURGY.

maaseh bereshit (Hebrew for 'work of creation') Early branch of Jewish mysticism concerned with speculation about the CREATION of the world and about the creative power of language. Maaseh bereshit traditions, which are based on the first chapter of Genesis, could only be taught to an individual and not to groups because of their secret nature. They are concerned with the divine utterances which brought the universe into being and how control of these enables man to gain magical power over the world. One of the main literary expressions of maaseh bereshit is the *Sefer* YETZIRAH which details the thirty-two

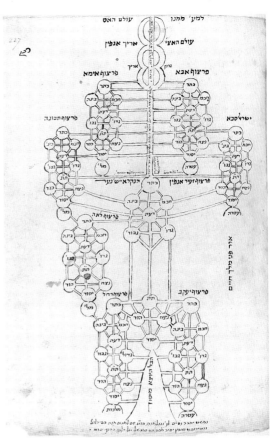

Diagram of the sefirotic structure according to the teachings of Isaac **Luria**, showing the different aspects of the divine (17c.).

Title-page of the first edition of *Mesillat Yesharim* by Moses Chaim **Luzzatto**, published in Amsterdam in 1740.

paths of wisdom underlying the created world. These are made up from the twenty-two letters of the ALPHABET, in various combinations with each other, and the ten sefirot. Letter combination was also an important technique for heavenly ascent in the maaseh merkavah tradition and for inducing mystical experience among the ecstatic mystics. The sefirot later became the backbone of the theosophy of the KABBALAH. The Heikhalot texts, primarily concerned with merkavah mysticism, contain elements of cosmogony describing such things as the garment in which God wrapped Himself prior to the Creation. In general, however, maaseh bereshit was more interested in the inner structure of the cosmos than in the actual chronology of the world's origin. Insight into this structure allowed the adept to manipulate the divine forces inherent in the world, a process which continued in the Middle Ages with the theurgic traditions of practical Kabbalah.

maaseh merkavah (Hebrew for 'work of the chariot') Early mystical practices of heavenly ascent associated with Ezekiel's vision of the divine chariot and the THRONE OF GLORY in heaven. Maaseh Merkavah could only be taught to one student at a time and only then if he was able to understand the teachings from his own inner nature. A part of the merkavah speculation involved the SHIUR KOMAH depictions of the gigantic size of the 'body' of God. The merkavah mystic spent several days preparing himself to ascend to heaven in order to stand in the presence of God, the divine king. He fasted, meditated with his head between his knees, contemplated water in a glass, chanted hymns and songs, used letter combinations of the type found in the *Sefer Yetzirah* and recited complicated angelic and divine names to pass to a vision of the divine throne (*see* MAASEH BERESHIT). HEIKHALOT literature describes the dangers inherent in this journey, during which those who 'descend in the chariot', as the mystics are called, have to pass through seven heavens and through the seven heavenly halls (*see* SANDALFON) guarded by fiery angels, as described, for instance, in the *Sefer Ha-Razin* (*see* RAZIEL). The merkavah mystic was transformed by his experience from man to angel, his hands and feet being spiritually burnt away by the tongues of heavenly fire he had passed through. From his vision of heaven he obtained insight into the divine world and gained magical power over the human world. Jewish liturgy, particularly among the Ashkenazim, was influenced by merkavah hymns and by the angelic songs which the mystics heard in heaven.

maaser *see* TITHES

mabruk *see* GREETINGS

Maccabees The name adopted by JUDAH MACCABEE, the HASMONEAN leader, who was involved in the revolt against the Seleucid rulers of Palestine. The name 'Maccabee' has been variously explained as meaning 'hammer', i.e. as a nickname expressing Judah's valour as a fighter, or as forming an acrostic of the words from a biblical verse (Exod. 15:11) on the Hasmonean banner which asserted the superiority of God over the other gods. The name was eventually extended to all of Judah's family. The Books of the

Maccabees in the Apocrypha tell the story and legends of the Maccabean revolt, but the name 'Maccabee' is not found in early Rabbinic literature. It does appear, however, in later literature in the songs and poetry associated with Maccabean heroism and the festival of CHANUKKAH.

Machpelah, Cave of Ancient burial site acquired by Abraham for the burial of his wife Sarah (Gen. 23). Abraham chose this site because he saw that Adam and Eve were buried there when he entered the cave, and it was pervaded by the odour of Paradise. It was subsequently used as a family sepulchre by his descendants Isaac and Jacob and their wives Rebecca and Leah, thus containing all the Patriarchs and all the Matriarchs except Rachel. The cave is situated in Hebron and is a site of pilgrimage for Jews. It was also said to be the entrance to the Garden of Eden, used by souls departing this life.

machzor (Hebrew for 'yearly cycle') Name given by Ashkenazim to the PRAYER-BOOK used on festivals and by some Sephardim to the daily prayer-book as well. Festival prayer-books differ markedly from country to country because many hymns and religious poems (*see* PIYYUT), reflecting local Jewish culture, were added to the basic liturgy. A handwritten machzor was usually illustrated (*see* ILLUMINATED MANUSCRIPTS) with scenes from the history and ritual of the festival, and even pre-modern printed versions sometimes contained illustrations.

madman *see* MESHUGENER

maftir (Hebrew for 'concluder') The concluding reading from a SEFER TORAH on shabbat and festivals, which usually consists of the last few verses of the weekly Pentateuchal section, sidra, or the special reading relevant to the festival. The role of the maftir in the LITURGY is to enable the person who is called up for the HAFTARAH to first recite the benedictions over a passage from the torah, so that people should not think that the Prophetic reading is equal in importance to the Pentateuchal one. Since the maftir is not one of the obligatory number of torah readings, it can in theory be read by a pre-adult male, and this is the custom in some communities. The practice is not found among Ashkenazim, however, who call a bar mitzvah boy up for an ALIYAH to the maftir to give public expression to the fact that he has reached adulthood.

magen david (Hebrew for 'shield of David') Six-pointed star, or hexagram, made up of two interlocking triangles. The figure is commonly known as 'the star of David', and it is found in Jewish designs and on gravestones and is worn as a pendant by Jews. Although widely recognized as a Jewish symbol today, it does not seem to have played so distinctive a role in the distant past. The star appears on Kabbalistic amulets and is found with other designs in Jewish magical drawings from the Middle Ages. It is believed to possess protective power. The magen david was used by the Nazis to mark out Jews and had to be worn by them as a distinguishing sign sewn on to a coat or jacket (*see* BADGE, JEWISH). It appears on the flag of the State of Israel, and the Israeli first-aid society is known as the Magen David Adom, the Red Magen David, paralleling the Red Cross and the Red Crescent in other countries.

maggid (Hebrew for 'preacher') Title of an itinerant preacher in Eastern European SHTETL culture, who would often earn his living by the fees he collected as he wandered from community to community. Since the community rabbi in pre-modern times was more scholar, teacher and halakhic expert than preacher, the maggid found a ready audience for his long, popular and emotive Yiddish sermons.

The term is also used for a heavenly mentor who communicates with men in visions, dreams, spirit possession, or by speaking out of their mouth for a short period. A number of Jewish mystics possessed a maggid who instructed them in Kabbalah and even dictated some of their works, presumably through a process of automatic writing. Having a maggid was regarded as a sign of high spiritual attainment, but it is reported that Elijah the Vilna Gaon refused the offer of a maggid, since he did not want any knowledge of torah which came without effort on his part. The best-known maggid was the one which communicated with Joseph CARO, speaking with a strange voice through his mouth one shavuot night, to the consternation of those present. Caro recorded some of the revelations of his maggid in a diary published under the title *Maggid Meisharim*. The fact that Caro, a leading scholarly intellectual, should have a spirit mentor shocked some later rationalist thinkers, who denied the authenticity of the work.

Maggid of Mezhirech *see* DOV BAER OF MEZHIRECH

magic The Bible forbids the practice of magic and prescribes the death penalty for witches. A distinction was later drawn between magic and tricks of an illusory nature. Though the latter were prohibited, they were not subject to capital punishment since no forbidden acts were involved. Ordinary Jews were influenced by the magic practices of their neighbours and engaged in sorcery, sometimes on a large scale. Attempts were made to stamp out witchcraft, and it is reported that in the 1c. BCE Simeon Ben Shetach hanged eighty witches in the town of Ashkelon. JESUS is depicted in Jewish literature as a magician who acquired his knowledge of sorcery while in Egypt, the home of black magic. Not all magical practices were forbidden by Jewish teaching, and certain types of white magic, particularly those associated with healing, which did not involve the manipulation of unclean spirits and DEMONS, were allowed or at least not directly outlawed. Indeed, some sages engaged in magical trials of strength with non-Jewish magicians. In the Middle Ages the magical motifs of folk religion were reinforced by the KABBALAH which purported that the world is continuously prey to demonic forces (*see* JOSEPH DELLA REINA). Fear of the EVIL EYE was widespread; AMULETS and MEZUZOT were worn for protection; GEMATRIA determined lucky and unlucky numbers; and ASTROLOGY marked off lucky and unlucky days. Wandering folk-healers (*see* BAAL SHEM) offered magical charms; handbooks prescribed spells and rituals, known as segullot, for every conceivable

The wars of the **Maccabees** (12c. English Bible).

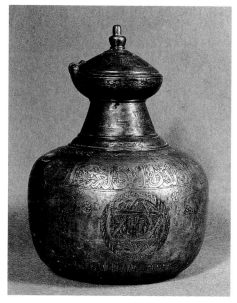

Italian brass vessel with a six-pointed **magen david** design.

ailment and situation; Kabbalists created GOLEMS. Legends about the magical exploits of the tzaddik became a central part of the lore of the Chasidic Movement. The dividing line between 'forbidden Amorite ways', as black magic was called, and the folk magic of Judaism, which penetrated even the framework of the halakhah, thus became blurred in the pre-modern period. *See also* RAZIEL; SUPERSTITION.

Maharal of Prague *see* JUDAH LOEW BEN BEZALEL

mah nishtanah *see* FOUR QUESTIONS

Maid of Ludomir *see* HANNAH RACHEL OF LUDOMIR

Maimonides, Moses (1136–1204) Spanish philosopher and halakhist, commonly known as Rambam. As a child Maimonides fled with his family from Islamic persecution in Spain, eventually settling in Fostat, Egypt. It was even rumoured that his family had been forcibly converted to Islam. Maimonides worked as a physician to the Sultan's court. His reputation as a doctor was great; it was said of him that, if the moon came to him as a patient, he would cure her of her spots. Despite his heavy schedule, he acted as the unofficial head of the Egyptian Jewish community and composed a major halakhic code in Hebrew, the *Mishneh Torah* (1180), and the most important Jewish philosophical work, the *Guide for the Perplexed* (1190), in Arabic. His formulation of the ARTICLES OF FAITH was widely accepted. He also exchanged letters with Jewish communities which sought his advice. The Yemenite Jews, for example, were encouraged by him to withstand Islamic persecution and not to follow a pseudo-Messiah. They came to regard Maimonides as their spiritual mentor, even including a special reference to him in the KADDISH prayer. His *Guide* and code were controversial works, and he was criticized for his reliance on Aristotle, his neglect of the doctrine of bodily RESURRECTION, his condemnation of those who believed in the corporeality of God, his rejection of superstitions and amulets (*see* MEZUZAH), his rational explanations for the commandments, his failure to cite sources and his claim that his own code was all that was needed for practical purposes. His writings were banned by zealots and even today are not studied in certain Orthodox circles. Among Kabbalists it was variously claimed that Maimonides became a mystic at the end of his life or that he was punished for his rationalism by being reborn as a worm. His supporters, however, tell of how Moses came to him in a dream on the night he finished his *Mishneh Torah* and said to him 'Well done!' About Maimonides they would say: 'From Moses to Moses there was none like Moses.' *See also* ANTHROPOMORPHISM; SACRIFICE.

majority opinion A sage must convince his colleagues about his interpretation of the TORAH by the use of logic and by reference to the tradition, unlike a prophet whose claim to authority is based on the divine call he has received. Where there is a dispute among rabbis, the HALAKHAH usually follows the view of the majority. This is based on an interpretation of the verse: 'You shall turn aside after a majority to do good' (Exod. 23:2), which deals with law courts and judges. In a dispute between ELIEZER BEN HYRCANUS and his colleagues, JOSHUA BEN CHANANIAH refused to accept miraculous happenings as evidence for the correctness of Eliezer's view, even rejecting a heavenly voice which supported him. Joshua argued that once the torah had been given to men, religious matters had to be decided, not by God, but by the majority opinion. Although an individual sage was allowed to maintain his own views against the majority opinion of the Sanhedrin, he would have been regarded as a 'rebellious elder', zaken mamre, if he insisted on teaching others to follow such views. Not all rabbinic opinions are of equal worth, however, and often a significant minority view was given preference over a majority view in the post-Talmudic period in determining normative practice.

Malachi *see* PROPHECY

malakh ha-mavet *see* ANGEL OF DEATH

malakhim *see* ANGELS

mama loschen (Yiddish for 'mother tongue') The general, and affectionate, way that Yiddish-speakers refer to the YIDDISH language. In the folk-belief of Yiddish speakers, even Adam and Eve must have spoken the mother tongue because the whole ethos of their Judaism is built into its linguistic expression. Terms like chutzpah, nebich, shlemiel, etc. are untranslatable into other languages and therefore seem to represent the original religious language of God's creation. *See also* SHTETL.

mamzer (pl. mamzerim) A child born as a result of an adulterous (*see* ADULTERY) or incestuous relationship is a mamzer. This term has no English equivalent, and 'bastard' is an unsuitable translation because mamzer does not refer to a child born out of wedlock. A mamzer is a full Jew, a scholarly mamzer being greater than an ignorant High Priest, but he or she cannot intermarry freely with other members of the community, since a mamzer may not enter 'the congregation of the Lord' (Deut. 23:3). Marriage is restricted to others of a similar status or to converts, and the stigma is passed on to any Jewish offspring. Judaism only ascribes mamzer status where the evidence is not amenable to other interpretations. Thus, the children of a married woman with a bad reputation would still be regarded as fathered by her husband, as would those born during his prolonged absence. The child of a married woman who lives with another man, however, is a mamzer. Since the divorce procedures of Reform Judaism are not recognized by Orthodoxy, doubts about the status of some children born into the Reform community make marriage with them problematic for Orthodox Jews. Similar doubts have arisen with Karaites and to a lesser extent with the Bene Israel of India and the Falashas of Ethiopia. In modern Israel, where marriage laws are controlled by the Orthodox Rabbinate, suspicions about the mamzer status of individual citizens have led to a number of *causes célèbres*. The *Talmud* states that money can purify a mamzer, meaning perhaps that wealthy and influential families manage to avoid the stigma because people are afraid to pry too closely into their affairs. In the Messianic age mamzerim will be purified.

Manasseh Wicked king of Judah in the 7c. BCE, and son of HEZEKIAH, who introduced idolatry into Israelite religion and mercilessly shed innocent blood (II Kings 21). According to one view, Manasseh lost his share in the World to Come (olam haba) because of his indulgence in idolatry, blasphemy, immorality, incest and murder. There is a view, however, that he repented and turned back to God at the end of his life (II Chr. 33). Despite the reluctance of the angels to accept his prayers, God opened a small hole under His throne to allow them to enter heaven, and therefore, like all penitents, he was forgiven. He accused the prophet ISAIAH, his maternal grandfather, of teaching heresy and had him killed while he was hiding in a tree.

Manasseh Ben Israel (1604–57) Dutch rabbi of Marrano descent. Manasseh took an interest in the Kabbalistic speculation that the Messiah could only come when the Jews were spread throughout the world, so that they could literally be gathered from the ends of the earth. Reports reached him from Aaron MONTEZINOS, who had returned from Ecuador, about the members of Indian tribes who kept Jewish customs. These were thought to belong to the TEN LOST TRIBES. Manasseh believed that the readmission of the Jews to England was a necessary stage in the Messianic process, for England was 'Angleterre', 'the end of the earth'. He wrote a book on the subject of the Ten Lost Tribes and the Messianic redemption, *The Hope of Israel* (1650), appealing to Puritan interest in the Old Testament. He also journeyed to England in 1655 to meet Cromwell and petition for Jewish readmission, gaining some support from Puritans who hoped the Jews would be converted to Christianity. Although he did not achieve his objective of readmission in his lifetime, his efforts bore fruit after his death.

manna The wonderful food which came, covered with DEW, like 'bread from heaven' (Exod. 16:4) to feed the Israelites during the Exodus. A jar of manna was kept next to the Ark of the Covenant in the HOLY OF HOLIES as a memorial for future generations (Exod. 16:32–4) and was hidden away by King JOSIAH before the Temple was destroyed. It will only reappear in the age of the Messiah. Manna was created on the sixth day of creation at twilight and is the food of the righteous and angels in heaven. It did not fall on the Sabbath. It was entirely absorbed by the body, leaving no waste which had to pass through the digestive system, and tasted like any dish that people wanted. The manna which was not gathered melted and flowed away in streams to be consumed by animals. These animals were then killed and eaten by Gentiles who themselves thus tasted the manna indirectly. The underlying purpose of the daily manna was so that the Israelites could free themselves from economic chores to study torah and learn to depend on God each day for their sustenance.

maoz tzur (Hebrew for 'fortress of rock') Hymn, composed in the 13c., which is sung after the lighting of the CHANUKKAH lights. The rousing tune for maoz

Autograph responsum of Moses **Maimonides** found in the Cairo genizah. The responsum is in a mixture of Hebrew and Arabic written in Hebrew characters.

A 17c. portrait of **Manasseh Ben Israel** (G. Flinck).

tzur goes back to medieval times. The hymn tells how God redeems the People of Israel from suffering and persecution in each age. This redemption was at work when the Israelites were slaves in Egypt and continued to the period of the successful revolt of the Hasmoneans in the 2c. BCE which chanukkah celebrates. In most prayer-books maoz tzur has five stanzas. A sixth stanza, composed sometime after the original, used to be included with the others but was dropped partly under pressure from Christian censorship and partly because some Orthodox and Reform rabbis were embarrassed by it. It calls for God to revenge the blood of His servants shed by a 'wicked nation', a veiled reference to the rule of Christendom, and to usher in the age of the Messiah.

Marcheshvan (also Cheshvan) Eighth lunar month of the Hebrew calendar, counting from Nisan, the month of the Exodus, or second month from the New Year festival (rosh ha-shanah). Marcheshvan usually begins towards the end of October, and its zodiacal sign is the crab. The prefix 'mar' means 'bitter' in other contexts, and it is said that the month is called 'bitter Cheshvan' because no festival falls in it.

maror (Hebrew for 'bitter herbs') Bitter herbs, usually horseradish or lettuce, which are eaten during the Passover seder to remind Jews of the bitter enslavement of the Israelites in Egypt. Maror is dipped in the sweet charoset paste before being eaten, to mask the bitter taste or to kill any worms which may be present in it. Since the charoset has the consistency of mortar, it also serves as a reminder that the bitterness of slavery was related to the building work undertaken by the Israelites in Egypt.

Marrano Spanish name for Jewish converts to Christianity who retained a secret adherence to Judaism. The word has a derogatory sense, usually meaning 'swine', and is often applied to all crypto-Jews but particularly to those of Iberian origin. In 1391 there was a forced conversion of Spanish Jews, but most of the converts retained their Jewish faith. They refrained from eating pork, blew the shofar on rosh ha-shanah in the countryside, and celebrated shabbat and pesach in the secrecy of their homes. Some Marranos used matzah the whole year round, so as not to draw attention to themselves on Passover. Even circumcision, which involved a lifelong danger, was practised. Christians were envious of the wealth of the convert community, and this led to a number of riots against them. Marranos also suffered MARTYRDOM under the INQUISITION, whose introduction into Spain they opposed. The Jews were in fact expelled from the Iberian peninsula in the late 15c. to prevent them from giving support to the Marranos (see SEPHARDIM). The Inquisition hounded Marranos about whom there was the slightest suspicion of Judaizing, torturing them to extract confessions and information about other crypto-Jews. Marranos fled from the oppressive control of the Inquisition to Italy, France, Turkey, Holland and eventually to South America. There, they reverted to Judaism as soon as the opportunity arose (see NASI FAMILY). Those that stayed in Spain and Portugal continued their double existence into the 20c. and maintained residual Jewish practices like lighting candles on Friday night, fasting at yom kippur time and even keeping up the tradition of having a mezuzah in the doorpost of old Marrano homes. Apart from this they were indistinguishable from their Catholic neighbours. There was a revival of Marrano interest in Judaism in Portugal after the Second World War, and some of the Spanish Marrano CHUETAS made an unsuccessful attempt to emigrate from the Balearic Islands to Israel in 1966. See also APOSTACY; MOLCHO, SOLOMON.

marriage It is a duty for a Jew to marry and to procreate. This duty falls primarily on the male and secondarily on the female. The only valid excuse for a man to refrain from marrying is if he wishes to devote his life to the study of torah, but such celibacy is strongly discouraged. God Himself assigns marriage partners, and forty days before a child is formed a heavenly voice (bat kol) decrees who its marriage partner shall be (see SHADKHAN). Before the marriage ceremony begins the groom, chatan, goes to the bridal chamber to view his bride, kallah, before covering her face with a veil. This custom is based on an incident in the Bible where the Patriarch Jacob married the wrong woman because she was already veiled. The wedding service is conducted by the rabbi and chazzan of the synagogue. In some communities the bride performs seven HAKKAFOT around the groom. Blessings are recited over a cup of wine which is handed to the parents of the couple to give to their respective children. Then the groom hands a ring to his bride in front of two witnesses while the couple stand under the wedding canopy, the CHUPPAH. The KETUBBAH is read, and blessings are recited over a second cup of wine. The ceremony ends with the groom breaking a glass to remind everyone of the sadness felt at the destruction of Jerusalem in accordance with Psalm 137. A folk belief has it that, if the groom fails to break the glass at the first attempt, his wife will dominate him. The couple are then led away to spend a few moments together, yichud, which was once the time when the marriage was consummated, although today it is only of symbolic significance. Since marriage is a sacred bond, it can only be dissolved by a religious DIVORCE or death. After the wedding the couple are considered to be born anew, and all their previous sins are forgiven (see ASHAMNU). See also LEVIRATE MARRIAGE; MONOGAMY; SHTREIMEL.

martyrdom (Hebrew 'kiddush ha-shem', meaning 'sanctification of the divine name') Although SUICIDE is normally forbidden by the halakhah, it is a duty for a Jew to sacrifice his or her life rather than worship idols (see IDOLATRY). At times of religious persecution a Jew must prefer martyrdom to abandonment of any detail of Jewish ritual. As the Rabbis put it, a Jew should be prepared to die rather than agree to tie a shoelace in a different way. It is even forbidden for a Jew to publicly deny he is a Jew in order to save his life at such times. A martyr is referred to as a 'holy being', kadosh, and a literature of martyrology holds up the example of martyrs down the ages who died for their faith. These stories include tales about HANNAH AND HER SEVEN SONS, the execution of ten martyr-rabbis by the Romans in 2c. CE Palestine, communities who committed mass suicide during the CRUSADES after reciting a blessing on martyrdom rather than be baptised, the Jews of York who burned themselves alive rather than fall into the hands of a Christian mob and modern stories of martyrdom during the Holocaust. Indeed, all of the Jews who died during the Nazi persecution are referred to as kedoshim, 'holy ones'. Martyrdom was accepted with joy, as exemplified by the Jews of Nordhausen, who on their way to be burnt alive during the Black Death employed musicians to accompany their singing. There are also records of communities who killed their own children rather than allow them to be brought up as Christians, using the AKEDAH story of Abraham offering up his son Isaac to God as a model. Among the crypto-Jews martyrdom took the form of not recanting the Marrano faith under the torture of the Inquisition and eventually being burnt at the stake for Judaizing. Martyrs traditionally recited the SHEMA as death approached, thus affirming their belief in the unity of God.

Masada Ancient hilltop fort, situated at the edge of the Judaean Desert near the Dead Sea, which was made into a citadel by Herod the Great. During the revolt against Rome which culminated in the destruction of the Second Temple (70 CE) Masada became a Zealot stronghold which held out for a further three years. When the Roman garrisons besieging the fort eventually stormed it, they found that the defenders had all committed suicide, preferring to die rather than surrender to Rome. The Zealots destroyed their belongings before killing each other, but they left some grain stocks untouched to show the Romans that they still had supplies and had not died out of desperation. The fall of Masada is described at length by the historian Josephus who claimed that the only survivors of the approximately one thousand defenders of Masada were two women and some children who hid in a cistern. The site of the fort was fully excavated by the modern archaeologist, Yigal Yadin, who found many remains of the Zealot occupation, including ritual baths (mikveh) used for purification. In Israel today the heroism of the Masada Zealots is held up as a paradigm of Jews willing to die for their freedom and independence and, therefore, as a model for the inhabitants of the State of Israel.

mashgiach *see* MUSAR MOVEMENT

mashiach *see* ANOINTING; MESSIAH

masorah (Hebrew for 'tradition') The traditions about the spelling, vocalization, exceptional letters, division into sentences and paragraphs, the musical accents and the general layout of the Hebrew Bible (*see* TENAKH). All these determine the form that a correctly written text should take. The masorah goes back to the members of the Great Synagogue and was the preserve of the SCRIBES, who counted every word and letter of the text and indicated where a word should be read differently from its written form. The text system currently in use is that of the Palestinian school of masoretes active in the 10c. CE. The accepted masoretic text sometimes differs from the biblical quotations referred to in the *Talmud*; nevertheless, it is the former which is read in synagogues. The masorah is thought

Illuminated haggadah manuscript showing the introductory section on **maror**, with a picture of a bitter herb (13c. Spanish).

19c. ring used for the Jewish **marriage** ceremony, with a box for aromatic spices.

Page of an 11c. illuminated biblical manuscript with verses from Isaiah within and the **masorah** around the circumference of the circle.

to be based on the master SEFER TORAH which Moses wrote and deposited in the Ark of the Covenant. *See also* MICROGRAPHY.

masoretes *see* MASORAH; SCRIBE

matchmaker *see* SHADKHAN

matriarchs The four founding mothers of the Jewish people are SARAH, REBECCA, RACHEL and LEAH, the wives of the PATRIARCHS. This list does not include the two wives of Jacob, who were concubines, Bilhah and Zilpah, even though six of the Twelve Tribes are descended from them. The four matriarchs are the most important women of the early period, and it is traditional to refer to them as 'Our mother Sarah', 'Our mother Rebecca', etc.

matzah (Hebrew for 'unleavened bread') The flat bread made out of plain flour and water which is eaten on PESACH, specifically during the SEDER meal, including the AFIKOMEN. Matzah is described as 'bread of affliction' (Deut. 16:3), i.e. the bread eaten by the poor and by slaves. It is a reminder of the slavery of the Israelites in Egypt and of the hurried manner of their Exodus, during which the bread they had prepared did not have time to rise (Exod. 12:39). Matzah must be baked by an adult within eighteen minutes from the time the flour and water are mixed, otherwise the baked product is regarded as leavened bread (*see* CHAMETZ). Matzah symbolizes the humility and purity of a person who is not puffed up with egoism, and the *Zohar* depicts it as the healing agent which encourages true faith. In the Middle Ages Christians falsely accused Jews of using the blood of Christian children in making matzah (*see* BLOOD LIBEL).

matzevah *see* TOMBSTONES

mazal *see* ISRAEL

mazal tov *see* ASTROLOGY; GREETINGS

mechilah *see* FORGIVENESS

mechitzah (Hebrew for 'partition') Men and women in an Orthodox synagogue are seated separately with a formal partition between them. This is known as a mechitzah and represents the division of the synagogue into a male domain, usually the main body of the synagogue, and a female domain, usually a gallery or the back section of the building. In Ultra-Orthodox synagogues the men cannot see the women at all, since the women's section is heavily curtained off. This division of the sexes originated with the separate 'court of women', ezrat nashim, in the Jerusalem Temple and is supported by considerations of the immodest thoughts that would occur during prayers were the two sexes to be sitting together. Reform and Conservative synagogues have abolished both the mechitzah and separate seating, seeing them as discriminating against women. Arguments about the subject between congregations have been very bitter since the early days of Reform, particularly in the USA. The presence or absence of a mechitzah has become the most obvious sign of an Orthodox or Reform congregation.

Megillah (Hebrew for 'scroll') Name applied to five books of the Hebrew Bible (RUTH, SONG OF SONGS, LAMENTATIONS, ECCLESIASTES and ESTHER) because they were once read from separate scrolls written by scribes. The Book of Esther is the only one which is still read from a scroll today in all communities and is thus commonly referred to as the Megillah. On PURIM the Esther scroll is folded back like a letter before being read, since the original was sent out by MORDECAI and Esther as a letter to their co-religionists. During the reading of the Megillah, the congregation hiss, boo and generally make a loud noise whenever the name of the villain Haman is mentioned. This is so 'the name of wicked people should be blotted out'. A Megillah does not have the same sanctity as a sefer torah, and because of this, in the Middle Ages it was often illustrated. Nevertheless, the Book of Esther was believed to have been written through the inspiration of the Holy Spirit (ruach ha-kodesh), and Jewish mystics claimed it was received by Moses with the revelation of the torah. In the age of the Messiah all the books of the Bible, apart from the Pentateuch, will be abolished, but the Esther Megillah will remain.

Meir (2c. CE) Mishnaic sage. Meir was said to be a descendant of the Roman Emperor Nero who converted to Judaism. He was active in rebuilding Jewish life after the ravages of the Bar Kokhba rebellion, and much of the material in the *Mishnah* comes from the original arrangement he made. Where the *Mishnah* quotes a view anonymously, this is regarded as one of Meir's teachings. In general, however, the halakhah does not follow Meir's opinion where there is a disagreement, because his colleagues could not grasp the complex logic behind his views. One of his teachers was ELISHA BEN AVUYAH who became a heretic. Yet Meir continued to study with him to the end of his life, excusing his behaviour by saying that he threw away the indigestible skin (i.e. the heresy) and only ate the fruit of his master's teaching. Meir's wife was BERURYAH, who was known for her wisdom and advised her husband on ethical and religious matters. On one occasion Meir went to Rome to free Beruryah's sister from captivity in a brothel. He managed to do so by bribing the guard and telling him that if he got into trouble he should say: 'The God of Meir help me.' The Romans sought Meir and nearly caught him. He was only saved when Elijah appeared in the form of a prostitute and held him in an embrace, thus convincing his pursuers that the man they were chasing was not the famous Palestinian rabbi. Meir died in Asia Minor and asked to be buried by the sea shore so that the same sea that flowed past the coast of the Holy Land would flow past his tomb. He was later reburied in Tiberias, where his grave became a place of pilgrimage, and Jewish folklore depicted him as 'meir baal ha-nes', 'Meir the miracle-worker'.

melamed *see* CHEDER

melavveh malkah (Hebrew for 'accompanying the queen') Meal eaten on Saturday night to escort the departing shabbat, which is thought of as a queen, and to prolong the Sabbath spirit. The custom is particularly strong among members of the Chasidic Movement and those influenced by the Kabbalah. The meal is traced back to King DAVID who was told by God that he would die on the Sabbath day. So when the Sabbath was past, he would celebrate his survival for another week with a festive meal. The melavveh malkah meal feeds the LUZ bone, from which the body will be reconstituted at the Resurrection and which is the only part of the body that does not disintegrate in the grave. All other organs of the body return to dust as a punishment for having derived benefit from the forbidden fruit eaten by Adam, the first man. Since the luz bone only absorbs the food of the melavveh malkah, it had no part in Adam's sin and is thus indestructible. It is also believed that eating hot food at the melavveh malkah meal prevents sadness, and that women who partake of the meal will not have a difficult labour in childbirth. Hymns are sung at the melavveh malkah to the prophet Elijah who will reappear to herald the age of the Messiah (*see* ZEMIROT). Elijah will not come on the Sabbath, and so Saturday night is the first opportunity to welcome him should the time of redemption be at hand.

memorial prayers (Hebrew 'hazkarat neshamot' or 'hashkavah') PRAYERS for the dead are recited during the first week of MOURNING, on shabbat preceding the YAHRZEIT anniversary of the death of a relative, on the anniversary itself and on certain festivals (*see* YIZKOR). On yom kippur some communities include the names of all those who have died in the past year in their memorial prayers. Prayers for martyred Jewish communities, av ha-rachamim, asking for God's mercy for them and for their eternal rest, are recited at Sabbath services throughout the year. These memorial prayers, and any offerings to charity which accompany them, are thought to effect an atonement for the dead and, like the kaddish, to help release them from punishment in gehinnom.

Menachem Mendel of Kotsk (1787–1859) Chasidic leader known as the Kotsker Rebbe. Menachem Mendel spent his life searching for absolute inner truth, in the belief that the search for truth is the truth itself. In pursuing this search he was very demanding of himself and of his followers and criticized all outward religious show. Man cannot serve God as a matter of habit but must strive for constant renewal. He claimed that while the Mitnaggedim, the opponents of the Chasidic Movement, feared the *Shulchan Arukh*, true Chasidim feared God. He justified the Chasidic practice of praying late on the grounds that it was necessary to prepare oneself for prayer and a labourer is already at work when he is sharpening his tools. He also said that in Kotsk they had a soul and not a clock. Menachem Mendel would ask his disciples: 'Where is God?', and rejecting their conventional replies, he would answer: 'God is where you let Him in.' His fierce independence led him to claim that the only teacher he respected was the one who had taught him the Hebrew alphabet, since he disagreed with all the rest. On a Friday night in 1840 he came to the shabbat table and behaved in a strange way. According to one, unsubstantiated, account he snuffed out the Sabbath candles declaring: 'There is no judgment and no judge.' Whatever actually happened, this incident led some of his followers to desert him and one of his main disciples, Mordechai Joseph Leiner, to set up a rival

Rachel, one of the four **matriarchs** of the Jewish people, by Michelangelo.

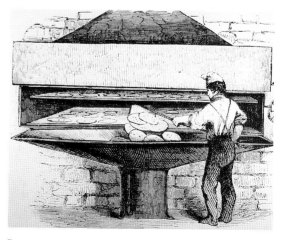

Removing **matzah** from the oven (19c., New York).

Chasidic group. For the next nineteen years Menachem Mendel secluded himself from his community, remaining in a locked room adjacent to his synagogue and only coming out to be called up for the reading of the torah. The bulk of his followers maintained their faith in him and even claimed that the noise made by pigeons on the roof of his room was actually caused by the souls of the dead which came to the Kotsker Rebbe seeking rectification (tikkun) for their past sins.

Mendelssohn, Moses (1729–86) German Jewish sage and leading figure of the Enlightenment. Mendelssohn studied traditional texts in his birthplace Dessau and claimed his hunchback was due to the hours he spent reading Maimonides' *Guide for the Perplexed*. As a young man he travelled on foot to Berlin, where his teacher had recently been appointed rabbi, and thus came into contact with the European culture of the Enlightenment. He taught himself secular subjects, and encouraged by Gotthold Lessing, he began to write literary works in German. One of his essays won a prize in a competition organized by the Prussian Academy of Sciences, beating the entry of the man who was later to become the greatest of German philosophers, Immanuel Kant. Mendelssohn only addressed himself to specifically Jewish issues when challenged by the Swiss pastor J.C. Lavater either to admit the truth of Christianity or to refute arguments put forward to prove its correctness. He replied that he was a Jew by conviction but did not see any benefit in seeking to disprove Christianity. He believed that within Christianity were truths of reason which Judaism regarded as the universal religion for all mankind. Apart from problems with over-zealous Christians, he also found himself in trouble with the rabbinical establishment. His German translation of the Bible in Hebrew characters, with a Hebrew commentary, was regarded as likely to distract students from traditional studies. His privately expressed preference for allowing several days to elapse between death and burial, as desired by at least one state government, was criticized as contrary to the halakhah. In his work *Jerusalem* Mendelssohn argued for the separation of church and society since only actions could be brought under social control and not religious beliefs. Although he remained an Orthodox Jew to the end of his life, all of his grandchildren became baptized Christians after his death. *See also* SHTADLAN.

mene mene tekel ufarsin *see* DANIEL

menorah (Hebrew for 'candelabrum') A seven-branched gold menorah, fuelled by olive oil, was kept burning at all times in the Jerusalem Temple. It symbolized the divine wisdom, the torah being compared to light. The original menorah, made during the time the Israelites wandered in the desert, was of a wonderful design. Moses cast gold into a fire, and the menorah formed itself. An eight-branched menorah is lit during the festival of CHANUKKAH to celebrate the miraculous re-dedication of the Temple candelabrum in the 2c. BCE. Since Temple times the menorah has been one of the main Jewish symbols, occurring on tombstones, synagogue mosaics, and Kabbalistic charts. Three-dimensional representations of the seven-branched menorah are rare, however, since it was forbidden to reproduce any of the Temple implements. A menorah is the emblem of the modern State of Israel. *See also* NER TAMID.

Meshach *see* HANANIAH, MISHAEL AND AZARIAH

meshugener (Yiddish for 'madman') Term often used affectionately of an eccentric but also of someone who is actually mad. The adjective is 'meshuga', as in the comment about a wild course of action: 'That would be a meshuga thing to do.' The noun is 'meshugas' and was used pejoratively in the Yiddish-speaking world of the Eastern European shtetl for anything alien to Jewish culture or anything which could not be understood by people with a small-town mentality. Other cultures or interests were dismissed as merely a meshugas.

meshumad *see* APOSTACY

Messiah (Hebrew 'mashiach', meaning 'anointed') The anointed king of the House of DAVID of BETHLEHEM who will be sent by God to inaugurate the final redemption in the end of days (*see* ESCHATOLOGY). In Jewish folklore the Davidic Messiah will be preceded by a Messianic descendant of Joseph, who will lead the armies of Israel against GOG AND MAGOG but will be killed in the ensuing war. The Davidic Messiah will then finally destroy the evil forces and bring about the INGATHERING OF THE EXILES with the assistance of the prophet ELIJAH. During the reign of the Messiah, the Prince of Peace, there will be a RESURRECTION OF THE DEAD, followed by the great DAY OF JUDGMENT for all mankind. The way to the GARDEN OF EDEN will be revealed. The righteous will join the Messiah in a new world order, OLAM HABA, in which the evil INCLINATION is destroyed. They will feast on the flesh of the Behemoth, the LEVIATHAN and the ZIZ and drink the wine preserved since the six days of Creation. During this banquet Moses will teach the Messianic torah, King David will sing, Miriam will dance and Aaron will recite the Grace. The Temple will descend ready-made from heaven to its site in JERUSALEM. The yearning of oppressed Jews down the ages for the Messianic redemption led to the rise of many MESSIANIC MOVEMENTS with ultimately destructive consequences. Untold misery awaited Jews who had forsaken their possessions to follow a Messianic claimant. In one case, they even walked into the sea, believing that they would be transported to the Land of Israel. Jewish literature is full of warnings not to calculate the Messianic era and not to be easily swayed by pseudo-Messiahs. The *Talmud* tells that JOSHUA BEN LEVI met the Messiah sitting among the lepers at the gates of Rome. When the rabbi asked him when he was coming, the Messiah answered: 'Today'. Later it was explained to the rabbi that the Messiah had not told him a lie but was simply quoting the verse: 'Today, if you harken to His voice' (Ps. 95:7), i.e. any day might be the time of the coming of the Messiah if men only listened to God's voice. *See also* APOCALYPSE; LAMED VAVNIK; OLIVES, MOUNT OF; TREE OF KNOWLEDGE.

Messianic movements The more Jews suffered, the stronger their Messianic belief became since they viewed their sufferings as the 'birth pangs of the Messiah'. The 1c. CE saw the appearance of Jesus and a number of other Messianic claimants, who inspired the revolt against Rome of 67 CE. In the 2c. Simeon BAR KOKHBA won both popular and rabbinic support for his Messianic war against Roman rule. In the post-Talmudic period there was a resurgence of antinomian Messianism in response to the strictures of Islamic rule. Maimonides wrote a letter to the Jews of the Yemen urging them not to follow a false Messiah or calculate the date of the end of days. The Crusades threw up their own batch of Messianic claimants in Europe, and at the same time David ALROY led a militant Messianic movement in Kurdistan. When the latter was eventually killed, his followers believed that he rose from the dead and inhabited an invisible body. The Jewish mystical tradition gave added impetus to Messianism, and a number of leading Kabbalists believed that they were the Messiah of the royal Davidic line or at least the Messiah son of Joseph who would die in preparing the Messianic process. Thus, the mystic Abraham ABULAFIA believed himself to be the Messiah and went to Rome to convert the Pope. The expulsion of the Jews from Spain (1492) led to the strongly Messianic Lurianic Kabbalah (*see* LURIA, ISAAC) which laid the groundwork for the antinomian Messianism of SHAB-BETAI TZEVI and Jacob FRANK. This impetus continued into the Chasidic Movement, and Messianic claims were made about figures like Nachman of Breslov, whose followers continued to believe in him long after his death. LUBAVITCH Chasidim today ascribe Messianic qualities to their leader. The Holocaust and the State of Israel raised Messianic hopes among religious Zionists, but no individual figures have yet arisen to spearhead a contemporary Zionist Messianic movement. *See also* MANASSEH BEN ISRAEL; MOLCHO, SOLOMON; NACHMANIDES, MOSES; NETUREI KARTA.

Metatron Heavenly being who is the transfigured form of the biblical ENOCH. Enoch 'walked with God' (Gen. 5:22) and was taken up into heaven while still alive to be transformed into one of the angels. Although Metatron is called a youth, he is the Prince of the Divine Countenance and also the Prince of this World who acts as a heavenly scribe recording the deeds of Israel. He is an angelic High Priest who serves in the Temple on high and is keeper of the heavenly treasures. His importance is indicated by the fact that he is depicted as the little God, a bearer of the divine name, for God's name is in him. The mystics of the maaseh merkavah tradition were granted a vision of Metatron after they made a heavenly ascent, and one 2c. CE sage, Elisha Ben Avuyah, became a heretic when he saw Metatron sitting in heaven. This led him to the belief in two deities. Attempts have been made to explain the origin of the name Metatron from Latin or Greek roots meaning 'the guide' or 'the one behind the divine throne'. Metatron is sometimes identified with Raziel.

Methusaleh *see* ALCHEMY

mezuzah (Hebrew for 'doorpost'; pl. 'mezuzot') Parchment scroll made by a scribe containing the hand-written text of the first two paragraphs of the SHEMA, which is fixed in a case to the right side of doorposts

Lavater and Lessing at the home of Moses **Mendelssohn**.

Menorah on a column capital from a 5c. synagogue in Caesarea.

in the home. The mezuzah is a literal fulfilment of the command to write God's words upon 'the doorposts of your house' (Deut. 6:9, 11:20). It is customary to kiss the mezuzah on entering or leaving the house, and it serves as a reminder to man not to sin. It also guarantees a fine home and long life. Indeed, the *Talmud* remarks that a human king has a contingent of soldiers to guard him, but God, the Divine King, guards his subjects with the mezuzah. Under the influence of Kabbalah, many Jews regard the mezuzah as a talisman, the divine name written on the outside of the parchment being regarded as an abbreviation of the Hebrew words meaning 'guardian of the doors of Israel'. Some rabbis stipulated appropriate times, determined by astrology, when mezuzot, like amulets, should be written. Demons and a DIBBUK cannot inhabit a house which has a mezuzah, and evil spirits which haunt a house are said to depart once a mezuzah is put up (*see* EXORCISM). There are even reports from the Middle Ages of Christians asking Jews for mezuzot to protect their homes and castles. When plague, catastrophe or tragedy came upon a community or family, they would examine their mezuzot to check that the text had not deteriorated. Today, this practice is still common among members of the Chasidic Movement. During the Second World War Jewish soldiers would carry mezuzot in their pockets to ward off bullets, and it is customary for people to wear a little mezuzah on a chain round their necks as a kemea, or AMULET. This magical attitude to the mezuzah was criticized by the medieval theologian Maimonides. He objected to the writing of angelic names on the mezuzah parchment because it turned a command- ment, whose purpose was to enhance man's conscious- ness of God, into a form of base magic.

Michael Highest in rank of the archangels, Prince of Water and angel of silver. In the biblical period Michael announced to Sarah that she would give birth to Isaac, he called out to Abraham at the akedah not to sacrifice his son, he wrestled with JACOB and led the Israelites during their wandering in the desert. Michael is the heavenly Prince of Israel who acts as advocate for the Jewish people and presents man's prayer before God. His position is to the right of the Throne of Glory and at the right hand of man on earth. He is associated with GABRIEL, RAPHAEL and URIEL but is superior to them because he flies to perform his tasks in one movement rather than two. His main foe is Samael, a fallen angel who leads the evil forces of the SITRA ACHRA and accuses Israel in heaven. It is Michael who accompanies the pious after death into heaven and offers up their souls on the heavenly altar. Indeed, according to one view it is Michael, not Metatron, who is the heavenly High Priest, and in the age of the Messiah he, not ELIJAH, will sound the shofar at the Resurrection of the Dead.

microcosm The idea that man contains within himself a mirror image of the cosmos. The *Sefer* YETZIRAH sees reality reflected on three levels: the universe (i.e. space), the year (i.e. time) and the soul (i.e. the individual person). Man is thus a small version of the macrocosm, and just as a man's soul gives life to man, so God is the soul of the universe giving life to it. The importance of the microcosm idea lay in the attempts

of Jewish mystics to discover the world and God by knowing themselves through meditation and inner contemplation. The mystic, as microcosm, can look into himself and see the cosmos. In the words of the ZOHAR, both the upper and lower worlds are united in human beings. Behind the microcosm idea is the teaching of Kabbalah that adam kadmon, the supernal form of man, was actually an integral structure of the Creation.

micrography Pictures made up of minute writing. Sometimes the opening page of a religious work was laid out in a floral geometric design, known as a carpet page, formed out of the text itself written in miniature. Commentaries were written out in the form of pictures of holy places or grotesque animals. In ILLUMINATED MANUSCRIPTS of the Bible, the masorah notes were incorporated in micrographic designs, and authors might be pictured by a drawing consisting of one of their works. Thus, a famous portrait of Shneur Zalman of Lyady is made out of his most popular work, the *Tanya*. Today, techniques of micrography are still used in the decoration of marriage contracts (ketubbah).

midrash (Hebrew for 'searching out') Homiletic method of biblical interpretation in which the text is explained differently from its literal meaning (*see* PESHAT). Midrash is also the name given to various collections of such Bible commentaries compiled from the ORAL TORAH. The nature of midrash is explained by the image of a hammer, which splits the rock of torah into many pieces. Since midrash often makes fantastic claims about biblical characters and events, midrashic teachings are not treated literally. Neverthe- less, both Sadducees and Karaites were highly critical of some of the bizarre pronouncements found in midrash. An example is the claim that Jacob did not actually die, despite the fact that he was embalmed by the Egyptians and buried in the Land of Israel by his sons. His continued existence is midrashically derived from the words of God's promise about the return of the Israelites from exile: 'Therefore fear not, Jacob my servant, ... for I will save you from afar and your seed from the land of their captivity' (Jer. 30:10). Midrash was used to reconcile contradictions in scrip- ture, to express theological ideas in an imaginative way and to bring a contemporary message from the biblical text to ordinary people. *See also* PARDES; TARGUM.

mikra *see* TENAKH

mikveh (Hebrew for 'gathering') A pool of 'living' water, gathered together from rain or from a spring, which is used for ritual purification and ABLUTION. Once a mikveh is constituted out of the minimum amount of natural water, then piped water may be added. In Temple times many impurities were removed by the use of the mikveh, but today it has a more restricted function. Proselytes bathe in a mikveh, tevilah, as part of their conversion to Judaism, this being the origin of the Christian baptism. Married women use the mikveh after menstruation (*see* NID- DAH) before resuming sexual relations with their husbands. Cooking utensils bought from a Gentile are dipped in a mikveh, tevilat kelim, before being used in the preparation of food. Men bathe in a mikveh prior to the yom kippur fast, so as to face God in a state of purity, and those influenced by Kabbalistic teaching bathe there on the eve of shabbat or, in the case of members of the Chasidic Movement, every day before prayers. What a woman sees on emerging from her post-menstrual bath in a mikveh will influence the child she conceives during conjugal relations that night. If she meets a dog, the child will have an ugly, dog-like face; if an ass, it will be stupid; and if an ignorant man, it will be ignorant. In such cases the woman might return and bathe again. There are even reports of women being led home blindfold from the mikveh, so they could think only of meeting a pious man. If, however, the woman meets a horse, that is a good sign and she will have a happy child who rejoices in the torah, or if she meets a scholar, that too is a good sign. The *Talmud* tells how Rabbi Yochanan, a Palestinian sage of handsome appearance, used to sit at the entrance to the mikveh, so that women would see him and have beautiful children like him. To those who questioned his behaviour, he answered that he was not troubled by unchaste thoughts on seeing the women emerge, for to him they were like white swans. *See also* TAHARAT HA-MISHPACHAH.

minchah (Hebrew for 'offering') The afternoon PRAYER, consisting of the AMIDAH accompanied by Psalms and short prayers, based on the offerings brought into the Temple before evening. On shabbat and fast days there is also a brief reading from the torah during the minchah service. The prayer is said to have been instituted by the Patriarch ISAAC who went out 'to meditate in the field towards evening' (Gen. 24:63). Since it is a prayer that sometimes has to be said in the middle of the working day, when one must 'direct one's heart to heaven' amidst secular activity, God is more receptive then than at any other time. Indeed, Elijah in his confrontation with the idolatrous prophets of Baal on Mount Carmel was only answered by God at minchah time (I Kings 18). Kabbalists recommended that one should devote the greatest concentration to the minchah prayer, and some did not attend synagogue to pray with a minyan but preferred to say the prayer in the privacy of their homes. *See also* LITURGY.

minhag (Hebrew for 'custom') Customs were important elements in determining the HALAKHAH and were often collected in minhag books or codified in legal texts. Folk practice is thought to reflect the will of God for 'if the people themselves are not prophets, they are the sons of prophets'. A visitor to a place is, therefore, bound to respect the local minhag. This is exemplified by the three angels who came to visit Abraham, for although they did not normally consume food, they 'ate' the meal prepared by him. Similarly, Moses did not eat for forty days when he went up to heaven to receive the Decalogue. In the past, communities had the power to punish members who refused to conform to established customs by fining or even flogging them, since they were guilty of 'moving landmarks' (Prov. 22:28). In some respects custom is more powerful than halakhah, since it acts as a conservative force in the community. New

Jacob Epstein's sculpture of the archangel **Michael** vanquishing Satan.

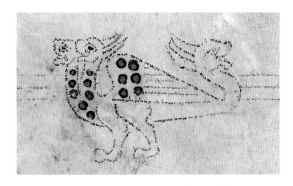

Fabulous creature made up from the **micrography** of the masorah notes in a 14c. Spanish Bible.

customs emerged under the influence of Kabbalah and the belief in demons. Thus, in the Middle Ages many communities forbade the drinking of water at the equinox or solstice because it was believed that demons contaminated it with drops of poison. These customs were so powerful in the popular consciousness that they became firmly entrenched, even when they clashed with established ritual. Superstitious customs were often opposed by rabbis, but they were not always successful in eradicating them. For example, the practice of KAPPAROT was fiercely attacked by some medieval halakhic authorities, but it has survived in many areas. Those who opposed the power of customs to undermine legal precedents remarked that minhag spelt backwards becomes gehinnom or hell. The customs of the Ashkenazim, who lived in Christian countries in the Middle Ages, and the Sephardim, who lived under Islamic rule, often differed markedly.

minyan (Hebrew for 'number') Quorum of ten Jewish males over the age of thirteen, who constitute a community necessary for public acts of worship and for sefer torah readings. There is a custom to count a pre-bar mitzvah boy holding a Hebrew Bible as a tenth man in situations where it is difficult to assemble the full quorum. Prayer with a minyan is preferable to private prayer because the shekhinah is present in a congregation and angels come to join the minyan in prayer. There are various derivations of the minimum number for a minyan. One of them relates to Abraham's intercession on behalf of the doomed city of Sodom (Gen. 18). In his plea to God to forgive the people of the city, he bargained about how many righteous inhabitants would suffice to save Sodom from destruction. Abraham started with fifty men, but when he reached the number ten, he stopped bargaining because less than ten righteous men would not even constitute a mini-community in that wicked city. Some synagogues actually pay 'minyan men' to attend services to guarantee a quorum for those wanting to say KADDISH. Orthodox congregations do not count women to a minyan, but they are counted as part of the quorum in most non-Orthodox synagogues. It is not actually allowed to count human beings *per se*, because they cannot be depersonalized as numbers and because such counting may conjure up the evil eye to harm them. A minyan has, therefore, to be counted using a verse which has ten words in it or by using expressions like 'not one, not two, not three ... not ten.' See also BATLAN; LITURGY.

miracles (Hebrew 'nissim', meaning 'signs') The Hebrew Bible, particularly the Pentateuch, tells of the many miracles which represent God's intervention in the history of Israel. These range from personal miracles, such as the birth of Isaac to Sarah, who was long past the age of childbearing (Gen. 21), to national miracles, such as the extraordinary events associated with the Exodus and the crossing of the RED SEA (Exod. 14). The Rabbinic tradition enhances these stories of biblical miracles. Indeed, there is hardly a biblical event or character about whom there are not elaborate accounts of wonderful happenings. For the Rabbis the whole biblical past was literally full of the supernatural, since anything coming into contact with the divine must somehow transcend its mundane

nature. Thus, the *Talmud* tells how the Tabernacle built in the wilderness existed in a miraculous space where the ARK OF THE COVENANT and the bodies of the golden cherubim had physical form but were miraculously dimensionless. At the close of the biblical period, miracles became less common, or if they did occur, they were less obvious, and the Rabbis warned people not to rely on miracles happening. Nevertheless, many accounts of miracles, and especially of wonder-working saints (*see* BAAL SHEM, LAMED VAVNIK, TZADDIK) are found in Jewish literature and folklore. Thus, for instance, the *Talmud* tells of a man whose wife died and who grew breasts so that he could suckle his child. The return of the Jews to the Holy Land and the rebirth of the modern State of Israel are regarded as miraculous acts of God by many Jews today. *See also* DEVEKUT; TABLETS OF THE DECALOGUE.

Miriam Older sister of Moses who watched over him when, as a baby, he was put into the Nile in a basket (Exod. 2). As a reward the whole people waited for her when she was stricken by leprosy during the wandering of the Israelites in the wilderness. It was Miriam who persuaded her father not to refrain from procreating when, faced by the Egyptian policy of killing all male Israelite babies, he decided that there was no point in having children. She prophesied to him that he would have a son who would save Israel, and thus she was indirectly responsible for the birth of Moses. Miriam is considered a prophetess, and she sang a song of triumph with the Israelite women after the crossing of the Red Sea (Exod. 15:20). A miraculous well accompanied the Israelites in the wilderness because of her merits. When she died, MIRIAM'S WELL was transferred to the Sea of Galilee, where its healing waters are still to be found. At the great banquet, in the time of the Messiah, Miriam will dance before the righteous.

Miriam's Well A miraculous well of water, flowing out from a stone, which accompanied the Israelites on their wanderings through the wilderness after the Exodus. When they encamped, the stone halted, and when they travelled on, it did too. The well was created by God at twilight on the first Friday night of the Creation, just before shabbat began. It was this same well which the Patriarchs dug in their search for water in the Land of Israel, and it was at this well that Eliezer, Abraham's servant, stopped when looking for a wife for Isaac, his master's son. The water of the well would flow when the elders of the Twelve Tribes came and sang to it. It tasted like wine, milk and honey. The well is named after MIRIAM because it existed for nearly forty years in the desert because of her merits. When she died, the well ceased to give its plentiful supply of water. At the entrance to the Holy Land it disappeared and was hidden by God in the Sea of Galilee, where it can sometimes still be seen from a high vantage point. Once a leper was bathing nearby, and he was cured of his leprosy when he inadvertently touched the well. Mystics believed that the water of Miriam's Well helped refine the body, and those who drank from it were thus able to understand the teachings of the Kabbalah. Isaac Luria initiated his disciple Chaim VITAL into his Kabbalistic teachings by giving him a cupful of water from a certain part of the Sea of Galilee. In the days of the Messiah the prophet Elijah will restore the well with its healing waters to the people of Israel.

mishkan *see* TABERNACLE

mishle *see* PROVERBS, BOOK OF

mishloach manot *see* PURIM

Mishnah Earliest surviving work of Rabbinic literature, edited by Judah Ha-Nasi and completed by members of his circle after his death in the early 3c. CE. The six divisions of the *Mishnah*, known by the abbreviation 'Shas', are mainly concerned with HALAKHAH and include elements from compilations of the ORAL TORAH collected by Judah's predecessors. Although not a legal code, since it cites different opinions on many subjects, the *Mishnah* was regarded as authoritative by later generations and became the basis of the whole halakhic tradition. The TALMUD is essentially an extended commentary on the *Mishnah*, though it ranges far beyond the original Mishnaic agenda. The publication of the Hebrew text of the *Mishnah* was effected either in writing or in an oral form memorized by professional memorizers (*see* TANNA). *Mishnah* became a favourite subject of study by laymen, while the yeshivah academies concentrated on the more intellectually taxing text of the *Talmud*. Under the influence of the mystical tradition, it became customary to study a section of the *Mishnah* at services in a house of mourning, since the rearranged letters of the word '*Mishnah*' spell 'neshamah', which means 'soul'. Rabbi Joseph CARO was a devoted student of the *Mishnah* and came to be possessed by its spirit (maggid) which spoke through his mouth and conveyed messages to him.

mishpachah (Yiddish 'mishpochoh') *see* FAMILY; SHTETL

Mitnaggedim (Hebrew for 'opponents') Orthodox Jews, mainly from Lithuania and White Russia, who were opposed to the CHASIDIC MOVEMENT. The Mitnaggedim suspected the Chasidim of following the heretical teachings of Shabbetai Tzevi whose followers had gone underground after his apostasy. This led the spiritual head of the Mitnaggedim, ELIJAH THE VILNA GAON, to sign excommunication orders (cherem) against the new sect, despite his reluctance to involve himself in public affairs. Chasidic innovations which aroused the ire of these 'opponents' were changes in the liturgy, laxity about times of prayer, neglect of torah studies, widespread use of alcohol and particularly adulation of the Chasidic master (tzaddik). CHAIM OF VOLOZHIN, the main disciple of the Vilna Gaon, claimed that any such worship of holy men was itself a form of idolatry. The Mitnaggedim outlawed the Chasidim, forbade intermarriage with them, would not eat their ritual slaughter (shechitah) and in a few instances had their leaders imprisoned by the secular authorities. It is sometimes wrongly assumed that the Mitnaggedim were anti-mystical and the Chasidim were mystically-minded, but this does not accord with the original situation, since both the Vilna Gaon and Chaim of Volozhin were Kabbalists. It is true, however, that, while Chasidism promoted a very

A painting by John Martin of Joshua performing a **miracle** by making the sun stand still.

The dance of **Miriam** (from a 14c. Spanish illuminated haggadah).

emotional form of religion, the Mitnaggedim were more intellectual and developed a system of analytic torah study (pilpul) in their yeshivot. The Mitnaggedic world-view also gave birth to the MUSAR MOVEMENT as a spiritual counter to Chasidism (see LIPKIN SALANTER, ISRAEL). Today, many of the bitter disputes of the past between Chasidim and Mitnaggedim are forgotten, but there is still some rivalry between them. In the Agudat Israel religious party in Israel, there is an ongoing struggle for power between Chasidic members and Mitnaggedic members who have even accused Chasidic subgroups, like Lubavitch, of continuing to perpetuate Shabbatean heresies.

mitzvah (Hebrew for 'commandment'; pl. 'mitzvot') A term originally used of divine commands in the Bible but which eventually came to refer to any good deed. There are 613 COMMANDMENTS in the torah, divided between positive and negative ones, or between those between man and God and those between man and man. There are also numerous Rabbinic mitzvot and seven biblical commandments for Gentiles known as the NOACHIDE LAWS. In general women are excused from positive mitzvot which must be performed at a specific time, though they have a small number of commandments which apply to them and not to men (see NIDDAH). At the age of twelve or thirteen girls and boys have to keep the commandments and are thus known as bat mitzvah and bar mitzvah respectively. Though no benefit is to be derived from a mitzvah, a person is protected from bodily harm while engaged in fulfilling a commandment. It is therefore customary to hand a coin to someone setting out on a journey, to be given to CHARITY on their arrival at their destination. They are thus engaged in a mitzvah while travelling and will arrive safely. Many reasons for the commandments were put forward by Jewish thinkers in terms of their medical, social or theological functions. There is, however, a view in the *Talmud* that the sole purpose of the mitzvot is to refine man's nature, disciplining him to serve God rather than follow his own desires. That is why the intention to perform a mitzvah (see KAVVANAH), even if one is unable to do it, is considered by God as equivalent to its performance. In the Messianic Age, when human nature will be perfected, the commandments will cease to be operational. *See also* GOLDEN RULE; MOHEL.

mixed species (Hebrew 'kilayim') It is forbidden to cross-breed species of animals, to graft different plants together, to sow two kinds of seeds in a field or vineyard, to yoke different animals together behind a plough or even to wear garments woven of wool and linen (see SHAATNEZ) (Lev. 19:19, Deut. 22:9–11). These laws prohibiting any change in the order of Creation were regarded as divine decrees, incomprehensible to man. Nevertheless, they were explained by Maimonides as means of avoiding certain idolatrous practices associated with agriculture and the natural world.

mizbeach *see* ALTAR

mizrach (Hebrew for 'rising sun', 'east') The direction of prayer for Jews living in the western world, who turn towards Jerusalem while reciting the AMIDAH. Since the vast majority of Jews lived in the west, the term mizrach came to be associated with Zion, and indeed, the religious faction within Zionism took the name Mizrachi. Many Jewish homes have a decorated mizrach plaque on the eastern wall. This may include a picture of Jerusalem or a verse like 'From the rising (mimizrach) of the sun until its setting the name of the Lord is praised' (Ps. 113:3). In the synagogue the seats along the mizrach wall are reserved for elders of the community. If someone does not know the correct direction of prayer, he should direct his heart to Jerusalem, whether he is facing mizrach or not.

modeh ani (Hebrew for 'I give thanks') Short prayer said immediately on awakening: 'I give thanks before you, living and established King, for having returned my soul unto me with compassion. Great is your faithfulness.' Modeh ani may be said even before the hands are washed because it does not actually contain the name of God. The prayer is based on the idea that, when people go to sleep, their souls leave their bodies and are given into God's hands for safekeeping. The body is left like a corpse, sleep being one sixtieth part of death, and so on awakening, God is thanked for reviving the dead.

Modena, Leone (1571–1648) Italian scholar and poet. As a young man Modena wrote a work condemning card playing, yet he was addicted to gambling and blamed this addiction on astrological influences. Though he tried several times to reform his ways, he was unsuccessful and eventually lost all his money through gambling. Modena's life was also beset by personal tragedies. His wife went mad; two of his sons died in his lifetime, while his third son never returned from Brazil. When the leaders of the Venice community issued an edict of excommunication (cherem) against those who participated in games of chance, Modena, who was the rabbi of Venice, opposed them and wrote a responsum on the subject saying excommunication was far too severe a punishment. At times he adopted a highly critical approach to traditional Judaism, objecting to aspects of the Kabbalah, to belief in the transmigration of souls and to aspects of the oral torah. He advocated changes to the liturgy and to certain Jewish rituals, arguing that some of the biblical commandments were meant metaphorically.

moed *see* FESTIVALS

mohel (Hebrew for 'circumcisor') A trained ritual circumcisor who removes the foreskins of Jewish babies, usually on the eighth day after birth, and of male proselytes prior to conversion to Judaism. Since CIRCUMCISION is a mitzvah, the mohel is not supposed to take payment for his services, though he may have his expenses reimbursed. The mohel must be a male Jewish adult. A Gentile or a Jewess is not allowed to perform the rite in normal circumstances. In the past a mohel was often also a shochet who performed ritual slaughter (shechitah) for the community since he needed to have dexterity with a knife. As part of the ritual, the halakhah insists that the mohel must suck blood from the penis to ensure that there is no infection of the wound. In the past Jewish communities were shaken by scandal when children were found to be suffering from a disease like syphilis which, it was believed, they had contracted from the mohel who circumcised them. This led to the introduction of a glass pipette to draw blood, thus avoiding direct contact with the mouth. Many traditional circumcisors have resisted this halakhic innovation, however, and continue to suck the blood out directly.

molad *see* CHAIM OF VOLOZHIN; NEW MOON

Molcho, Solomon (1500–32) Portuguese Marrano and pseudo-Messiah. Molcho was brought up as a Christian, but under the influence of the Messianic ideas spread by David REUVENI, he circumcised himself and emigrated so he could live openly as a Jew. He studied Kabbalah, had visions, preached the coming of the Messianic kingdom in 1540 and proclaimed himself the Messiah, although JOSEPH OF ROSHEIM tried to dissuade him. Molcho wandered around for a while spreading his teachings and then came to Italy where, in an act of Messianic identification, he spent thirty days among the sick beggars of Rome on the banks of the Tiber. While in Italy he was reported to the church authorities who sentenced him to death or recantation. Molcho chose a martyr's death, which made a deep impression on those who knew him. Rabbi Joseph CARO, who met him in the Levant, dearly wanted to be martyred like him. Many of his followers did not believe he had been killed, since he had correctly predicted a flood in Rome in 1530 and an earthquake in Portugal in 1531. Molcho's reputation for saintliness survived him. His garments were kept as relics by the Jewish community of Prague and were exhibited in great awe. Only his fringed undergarment (tallit) was considered too holy to be exhibited. A beadle of the Prague synagogue where these garments were kept copied the divine names embroidered on this undergarment, and the rabbi of the community in turn made a copy of this document, but the papers have since been lost.

monogamy According to biblical law, a man may practise polygamy, having several wives and CONCUBINES, while a woman can only have one husband at a time. Even with men, however, monogamous elements seemed to have been prevalent in MARRIAGE from early times. Thus, the story of the creation of Eve as a helpmeet for Adam concludes with the statement that a man will leave his father and his mother and cleave to his wife, the two of them becoming one flesh (Gen. 2:24). Noah and his sons during the Flood only had one wife each, as did the biblical High Priest. The poem in praise of the woman of virtue in the Book of PROVERBS depicts a monogamous situation (Prov. 31). There is also little evidence of polygamy amongst Talmudic rabbis, some of whom seem to have opposed the practice. The general view of the *Talmud* was to allow up to four wives if the economic condition of the husband meant that he could support them. In the post-Talmudic period, some of the Babylonian geonim (gaon) insisted that the wife had to give her consent before her husband took a second wife, and indeed, at various times we find women who had a 'no bigamy' clause

Mizrach plaque showing the Hebrew word 'mizrach' in the centre under the Decalogue, surrounded by biblical scenes.

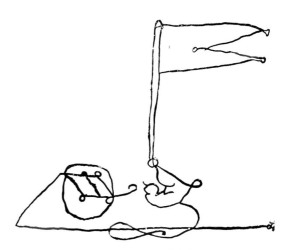

Autograph of the 16c. pseudo-Messiah Solomon **Molcho** (from a manuscript of the Alliance Israélite Universelle).

written into their marriage contract (ketubbah). In the early 11c. the leading rabbi of German Jewry, Rabbenu GERSHOM, is reputed to have called together a Rabbinical Council which forbade polygamy to Ashkenazim. Anyone breaking this decree was subject to excommunication (*see* CHEREM). This became the rule for most Jews in Christian lands throughout the Middle Ages, and though it was only meant to be valid for a limited period, it has now become normative halakhah and is incorporated into modern Israeli law. It is still possible for Sephardim to practise polygamy and for an Ashkenazi Jew to take a second wife if he is unable to DIVORCE his first wife because she has become insane. It is also possible in other circumstances if he can obtain the agreement of one hundred rabbis. *See also* ADULTERY.

monotheism The belief in one God is central to the Bible and *Talmud*, to Maimonides' formulation of his Thirteen ARTICLES OF FAITH, and to the main liturgical affirmation of faith, the SHEMA: 'Hear O Israel . . . the Lord is one' (Deut. 6:4). According to Jewish tradition it was ABRAHAM, the founder of the Hebrew people, who first recognized the unity of God while reflecting on the unity of the world. There are different levels of understanding the divine unity exemplified in various biblical characters. Thus, Jethro recognized that God was 'greater than all gods' (Exod. 18:11), but he still believed in other gods. Naaman accepted that there was no other god 'in all the earth but in Israel' (II Kings 5:15) but allowed for other gods in heaven. It was Moses, however, who exemplified the most comprehensive monotheism, for he asserted that the Lord was 'God in heaven above, and on the earth beneath, there is none else' (Deut. 4:39). A similar expression is contained in the words of Isaiah 'I am the first and I am the last, and beside Me there is no God' (46:6). Biblical monotheism emphasized that both GOOD AND EVIL were created by the one deity (Isa. 45:7), in contrast to the dualistic belief in a separate god who brought evil into the world. With the rise of Christian doctrine, Jewish thinkers emphasized that true monotheism must deny any idea of a trinitarian God. Though the Kabbalah deals with the different substructures emanating from the Godhead, the mystics were careful to stress that the SEFIROT must not be understood as implying a negation of monotheism.

Montefiore, Sir Moses (1784–1885) British Sephardi philanthropist, community leader and shtadlan. Montefiore, who was related to the Rothschild family by marriage, made a fortune on the stock exchange and retired at the age of forty to devote himself to helping his co-religionists. He travelled widely with his wife Judith, taking his own ritual slaughterer (shochet) with him so that he could eat kosher food. The Jews he visited regarded him as an influential and wealthy benefactor who brought hope and comfort to them and who could intercede on their behalf. Such intercession was the purpose of his seven visits to the Holy Land and his visits to Russia, Syria, Morocco and Romania. Montefiore survived adventures with highwaymen, wolves and treacherous ice on his travels, as well as facing a hostile mob in Romania. His visit to Damascus in 1840 helped secure the release of Jews subject to a blood libel accusation that they had killed

a Franciscan friar. Montefiore was not always so successful, and his efforts in 1858 to bring about the return to his family of the MORTARA boy, who was taken away by the Church in Italy, were in vain.

Montezinos, Aaron (17c.) Marrano explorer. Montezinos claimed to have found members of the TEN LOST TRIBES in Ecuador in 1642. These South American Indians could recite the shema prayer and belonged to the tribes of Reuben and Levi. On his return to the Netherlands, Montezinos swore to the truth of his claims and convinced MANASSEH BEN ISRAEL who wrote about them in his book, *The Hope of Israel*.

moon (Hebrew 'levanah') The Hebrew CALENDAR is lunar, the year containing twelve or thirteen lunar months, each of which begins with the NEW MOON. At the creation of the world, the moon was as bright as the SUN, but since there could not be two great lights in heaven, the moon's light was diminished. The moon symbolizes the People of Israel, whose fortunes also wax and wane. Just as the light of the moon will become as bright as the sun once again in the age of the Messiah, so too Israel will emerge from its lowly position to its former glory. An eclipse of the moon is thought to be unlucky for Jews, and when the moon wanes the forces of evil increase. Sleeping by the light of the moon is considered dangerous because of the demoness, Agrat Bat Mahalat, who stalks the earth in search of her prey. It is also prohibited, according to the Jewish mystics, even to look at the moon, although one is permitted to glance at it casually when the kiddush levanah blessing of the new moon is recited.

Mordecai Prophetic leader of the Jewish exiles in the Persian empire and descendant of King Saul. Mordecai is the hero of the purim story, and his activities are recorded in the Book of ESTHER. His refusal to bow down to HAMAN and worship him as a deity led to the latter's plot to exterminate the Jews. This plot was frustrated by the intercession of Mordecai's cousin, Esther, the Persian queen, whom he had persuaded to marry the king with some such eventuality in mind. As a member of the Sanhedrin, Mordecai could speak seventy languages. He was thus able to understand the little-known dialect used by two of the royal bodyguards as they plotted against King Ahasuerus, and he reported the plot to the king. As a reward for his loyalty, and because of his family connections with the queen, Mordecai was eventually appointed vizier to the Persian court. Not all his co-religionists approved of him accepting office, however, because this meant he had less time for torah study.

Moriah, Mount (Hebrew 'har ha-moriyyah') Site of the Temple and the place where Abraham was to have offered up his son Isaac to God (akedah) (Gen. 22:2). The later sacrifices were thus effective in their atonement because of the devotion of the first Patriarch at that location. The name of the mount is understood to come from the Hebrew word for teaching, because the mount had housed the academy of Shem and Eber in Patriarchal times and it was in the Temple precincts that the Sanhedrin sat. The sanctity of Mount Moriah goes back to the beginning of time, for on it is the foundation stone of the world (*see* HOLY OF HOLIES).

Adam, the first man, was created from the dust of Mount Moriah, and when he was expelled from the Garden of Eden, it was onto Mount Moriah that he first stepped, because the entrance to Paradise is nearby. *See also* SINAI, MOUNT.

Mortara Case Edward Mortara was an Italian Jewish boy who had been secretly baptized by his Catholic nurse. When she reported this to the Church, the Catholic authorities abducted the six-year-old boy in 1858 and refused to return him to his parents. There was much protest and a public outcry about the case. Sir Moses MONTEFIORE travelled on an unsuccessful mission to Rome to persuade the Catholic Church to release him, but Pope Pius IX refused. The boy was brought up as a Catholic, and at the age of eighteen was free to return to his family, but he refused to go back and eventually became a professor of theology. The case shocked the Jewish world and led to the founding of educational organizations, like the Alliance Israélite Universelle, to help safeguard Jewish life.

Moses (Hebrew 'moshe rabbenu', literally 'Moses our teacher') The greatest of the prophets who saw God through a clear glass, while the other prophets saw Him through a darkened glass. He was born circumcised and the Divine Presence was with him. As a baby, he was placed in a basket in the Nile, where he was found by Pharaoh's daughter. As a child he was tested by Pharaoh, to see whether he was a future troublemaker, by having glowing coals and gold brought before him. He wanted to reach out for the gold, but the angel GABRIEL pushed his hand onto the coals. Moses immediately put his hand into his mouth, and the hot coal remnants caused him to develop a stutter. He had to flee from Egypt after killing an Egyptian taskmaster and spent some years as a military leader in Ethiopia before becoming a shepherd in Midian. One day while pasturing his sheep in the wilderness, he scrambled up the side of Mount SINAI to recover a lamb that had strayed. God decided that Moses was the man to care for the 'lost sheep of Israel' and revealed Himself to him in a BURNING BUSH. Moses led the EXODUS and when he brought the Israelites to Mount Sinai, he went up the mountain to heaven to receive the TABLETS OF THE DECALOGUE and the ORAL TORAH. During the forty days he spent there he did not eat, since one must follow local custom (minhag) and the angels abstain from all food. While in heaven he was shown how the torah would be taught in a future time by Rabbi Akiva, finding himself at the back of Akiva's class in the 2c. CE and not understanding what they were studying. When he came down from the top of Mount Sinai, his face shone because he had touched his head with his writing quill which had some miraculous ink on it. Moses died on his birthday, seventh of Adar, at the age of 120 years with his strength undiminished. He was buried by God and the angels in an unknown grave on Mount Nebo, so that Jews would not turn his burial place into a site of pilgrimage and Gentiles would not turn it into an idolatrous shrine. The day of his death is kept as a special day by members of Jewish burial societies (chevra kaddisha). *See also* AMALEK; BIBLE; BRAZEN SERPENT; GOLDEN CALF; MENORAH; ORAL TORAH; PLAGUES, THE TEN; PROPHECY; TETRAGRAMMATON.

Portrait of Sir Moses and Lady Judith **Montefiore** entering Jerusalem, 1839.

The Finding of **Moses** by Sir Lawrence Alma-Tadema.

Moses de Leon (1240–1305) Spanish Kabbalist and presumed author of the ZOHAR. Moses graduated from an interest in philosophy, particularly Maimonides' *Guide for the Perplexed*, to the study of mysticism. He seems to have begun writing the *Zohar*, perhaps under the influence of an automatic writing technique, a little after 1280 and to have circulated individual sections of the work among his fellow Kabbalists. He promised to show Isaac of Acre the original ancient manuscript of the *Zohar*, which he said was at his home, but died before Isaac was able to visit him. After his death a rich Jew made a very generous offer for the original text, but Moses' wife, though impoverished, denied that it existed. She said Moses wrote the whole work himself but ascribed it to the 2c. CE sage Simeon Bar Yochai so as to be able to sell copies. In fact, there were several explanations from de Leon of how he came into possession of the work: it was found hidden in a cave in Palestine and sent to Spain by Nachmanides; or it was first found by a Moslem boy digging for treasure, and when Moslem savants did not know what it was, it was handed over to Jewish scholars; or it was discovered among the plunder taken away from a great library containing many ancient texts.

Mountain Jews Jewish tribes living in the Soviet Caucasus who claim to originate with the Ten Lost Tribes and to have arrived there around the time of the destruction of the First Temple. The Mountain Jews speak their own dialect of Judeo-Tat, which they write in Hebrew script. These Jewish Tats may have helped introduce Judaism to their KHAZAR neighbours in the 8c. They are the heirs to a military tradition, carrying daggers, swords and guns with them even into the synagogue, and they engage in vendettas. Although they sent their sons to yeshivot in Eastern Europe in the 19c., they preserved customs not found among other Jews. They have continued to practise levirate marriage, as have some of the Gentile tribes of the area who originally converted from Judaism and preserved Judaic customs, long after such marriage had ceased in other Jewish communities. The girls of the Mountain Jews' community go out to dance on hoshana rabba when God seals the fate of the world at the end of the High Holiday period. Family life is very strong among the Mountain Jews. They practise polygamy and celebrate the Passover seder together in the house of the eldest male member of the extended family. Their religion contains many folk-beliefs associated with demons; for instance, they believe in a constant battle between good and evil spirits, which seems to indicate Persian influence.

mourning (Hebrew 'avelut') After the death of a near relative, a Jew has to keep a period of mourning which varies in length and severity according to the relationship to the deceased. The mourner, avel, whether a child, parent, spouse or sibling of the deceased, keeps seven days of intense mourning, shivah, after the burial. During this time an avel sits at home on a low stool wearing a rent garment, does not wear leather shoes, cut the hair or wash properly, and is visited by members of the community who express their condolences. Services are usually held at home, and MEMORIAL PRAYERS for the deceased are recited.

The only interruption in the shivah is for shabbat or festivals, when no public mourning is allowed. At the end of seven days, a less severe period of mourning, called sheloshim, begins which lasts for thirty days from the day of death. Children have to continue their mourning for the first twelve months after a parent's demise, which includes sons reciting the KADDISH for eleven months. There are a number of mourning customs, of folk origin, which are meant to protect the family of the deceased from demonic forces. Any water in a house in which someone dies has to be poured out, since the poison from the sword of the Angel of Death may have fallen into it. It is customary in some communities to stop seven times on the way back from a funeral to confuse the demons. The hands are washed on leaving the cemetery before re-entering a house to eradicate the impure spirits which cling to them. All mirrors in a house of mourning are covered during the shivah, thus protecting the reflection of a person, i.e. his soul, from potential threat from demons.

mumar *see* APOSTACY

musaf (Hebrew for 'addition') Additional AMIDAH said on the new moon, shabbat and festivals, based on the additional sacrifices offered on these occasions. The central section of musaf recounts the details of these sacrifices and expresses the hope that God will rebuild the Temple so that offerings can be brought once more in love and joy. Various extra prayers and rituals, such as the priestly blessing, the blowing of the shofar, and seasonal prayers for rain and dew, are included in musaf on certain festivals. Modern negative attitudes to the sacrificial system have led some Orthodox synagogues to shorten the chazzan's repetition of the musaf amidah and most Reform synagogues simply to omit the prayer altogether.

Musar Movement Movement stressing the ethical side of Judaism founded among the MITNAGGEDIM by Israel LIPKIN SALANTER in the late 19c. The Hebrew word 'musar' means 'ethical instruction', and the followers of the movement are known as Musarniks. Lipkin Salanter originally wanted to persuade ordinary householders to bring ethical considerations into their service of God and to become aware of their economic sins as well as their lapses in purely ritual matters. He visited Jewish communities far and wide, but he had only limited success among lay people. The movement eventually concentrated on YESHIVAH students who were more amenable to the harsh demands of musar self-perfection. His followers spread their master's teaching throughout Eastern Europe but met strong opposition from rabbis who felt musar distracted students from Talmudic studies and claimed that there was already sufficient ethical content in the *Talmud* for everyone's needs. To circumvent this opposition, the Musarniks founded their own musar academies, where the students met together for group sessions to confess their failings to each other, where they spent hours studying musar literature in a soulful tune and where the ethical superviser, mashgiach, gave a weekly talk, or musar shmues. Musarniks, however, influenced non-musar yeshivot to introduce a mandatory half-hour a day of musar studies. After Lipkin's death the movement split up into different subgroups of Musar, the most extreme of which was the Novaredok school founded by Joseph Josel HORWITZ, who laid down a series of musar exercises for his students to foster inner moral strength. *See also* ELUL; LUZZATTO, MOSES CHAIM.

music Jewish music in synagogue ceremonial and at rituals in the home originated with the musical tradition of the LEVITES in the Temple. Due to the dispersion of Jewish communities in many lands with different musical cultures, the chants and songs preserved from Temple times have undergone many transformations and adaptions. Musical instruments were discouraged after the destruction of the Temple as an expression of mourning, and the organ is the only instrument used today in Orthodox synagogues, and only for weddings. Reform congregations have introduced a number of instruments as part of the shabbat and festival liturgy. Outside the synagogue proper Jewish bands, known as klezmer, used to entertain at weddings in the Eastern European shtetl, but they were never more than a folk phenomenon (*see* BADCHAN). Most liturgical music is vocal, either the cantorial music of the CHAZZAN and synagogue choir, the tunes used for chanting the prayers, the torah and other biblical books, or the songs sung in the home (*see* ZEMIROT) and at community gatherings. The mystics thought that each aspect of nature and each creature sang its own song to God, and they ascribed a collection of biblical verses to them in the work PEREK SHIRAH. They also saw the redemption from exile as coming about through song. The CHASIDIC MOVEMENT used music as a means of awakening the soul to devekut, or cleaving to God, through joy. The song without words, or niggun, was thought to penetrate to the deepest levels of religious consciousness. *See also* CHAD GADYA; DAVID; ZION.

Naaman Syrian general who was cured of leprosy by bathing in the Jordan seven times, according to the instructions of the prophet ELISHA. Naaman, who as an ordinary soldier had killed the Israelite King Ahab, was afflicted by leprosy as punishment for arrogance and for keeping an Israelite maidservant. Indeed, it was this maidservant who first suggested he visit Elisha (II Kings 5:3). After his miraculous cure, Naaman accepted God as the only deity in the Land of Israel, although he recognized the power of other gods elsewhere.

nachash *see* BRAZEN SERPENT; SERPENT

Nachmanides, Moses (1194–1270) Spanish mystic and Bible commentator, commonly known as Ramban. Nachmanides is best known for his popular commentary on the Pentateuch in which he put forward a mystical perspective, describing the torah as one long combination of the names of God and bringing in the belief in transmigration of souls. He tended to take the biblical stories literally and saw them as prophetic hints foreshadowing later events of Jewish history. He believed that the Messiah would appear in 1358 and brought proofs from biblical texts

Donating money to charity at a funeral as an act of **mourning**, thereby hoping to stave off the Angel of Death (18c. Czech painting).

Pottery figurines of two female **musicians** playing the tambourine, 9c.–7c. BCE (Azkir).

for this date. He was highly critical of Maimonides' philosophical approach to Judaism, yet he defended the latter against those who launched personal attacks on him. While he objected to Maimonides' *Guide for the Perplexed*, he allowed his code to be used. Nachmanides was first encouraged to study Kabbalah by one of his teachers, who showed him the value of its teachings. This teacher was sentenced to be burnt at the stake by the Catholic Church but escaped through the use of Kabbalistic formulae. Nachmanides himself was forced to participate in the DISPUTATION at Barcelona (1263) where he had to defend Judaism in the face of Christian truth claims. He did so successfully, winning the respect of King James of Aragon, but his Dominican opponents complained about his anti-Christian remarks, and he thought it prudent to emigrate to the Holy Land. Before leaving he told his Spanish co-religionists that, when he departed this life, his parents' tomb would split apart and the form of a candelabrum would appear. When this indeed happened, they knew that Nachmanides had died. He was buried on the road which the Messiah will take on his march into Jerusalem. Although he earned his living as a physician, he actually believed that faithful Jews should turn to God for healing and not to doctors. The true work of physicians was preventative medicine or to help those of little faith. *See also* MOSES DE LEON; ZOHAR.

Nachman of Breslov (1772–1811) Leader of the Chasidic Movement and descendant of Israel Baal Shem Tov. As a youth Nachman practised extreme asceticism, swallowed his food without chewing it, so as to avoid physical pleasure, and kept the name of God in the forefront of his thoughts. He undertook a hazardous PILGRIMAGE to the Holy Land, behaving en route like a holy fool. In Breslov he attracted many followers to his special brand of mysticism, although they were derided by other Chasidim as heretics. He promised his persecuted disciples that in the age of the Messiah all men would be Breslov Chasidim. Nachman taught the supreme value of joy and said that no one should despair as they crossed over the 'very narrow bridge of life'. Man should talk to God each day in Yiddish and recite the PSALMS which help him overcome sexual desire. Creation is singing to God, and man's faith is strengthened by spending time in the midst of Nature's song, in fields and forests. Indeed, faith is the only way across the abyss which separates the human and divine worlds, and this has to be mediated by faith in the Chasidic tzaddik. Conventional medicine should be avoided, since God alone is the true healer and doctors are simply agents of the Angel of Death, who is too busy to kill everyone himself so he enlists their help. Some of Nachman's ideas were expressed through mystical fairy stories in order to awaken people from their spiritual sleep. His teachings were recorded by Nathan of Nemirov, who also composed prayers based on his master's ideas. Before Nachman died, he told his followers that he would always be with them and if necessary would pull them out of gehinnom by their earlocks (*see* PEOT). Since their master is still alive to them, they never appointed a successor to him, earning them the nickname of 'Dead Chasidim'. They used to travel *en masse* on pilgrimage to his grave in the Ukrainian city

of Uman to be with him during the festival of rosh ha-shanah.

Nachshon Chief of the tribe of Judah during the Exodus who brought about the splitting of the RED SEA by jumping in while all the other Israelites hesitated. As a reward for this daring act of faith, King David was one of Nachshon's descendants and the future Messiah will be of his line.

Nachum of Gimzu (1c.–2c. CE) Mishnaic sage. The *Talmud*, in a play on his name, refers to him as a 'man of gamzu', because whatever happened to him he would accept it and declare 'gam zu letovah', meaning 'this also is for the best'. Once when Nachum was journeying to Rome with a gift of jewels for the emperor, he was robbed and the jewels were replaced by earth. When the emperor discovered what had been brought for him, he wanted to kill the bearer in order to avenge the insult. Nachum merely said; 'This too is for the best.' At the last moment Elijah the prophet appeared in the guise of a Roman senator and suggested that the earth might indeed be a fitting gift, since it must be magical earth which destroys one's enemies. The earth was tested and indeed found to be possessed of a magical potency, so Nachum was saved and his optimism justified. Towards the end of his life, he went blind and lost the use of his limbs. He accepted his condition as a punishment from God because he once delayed feeding a starving man, who died before Nachum could help him.

Naomi Mother-in-law of RUTH, whose story is told in the Book of Ruth. After the death of her husband and sons in Moab, Naomi was informed by God that the famine in the Land of Israel had ended, and she decided to return to her hometown of Bethlehem. She also encouraged her daughters-in-law Ruth and Orpah to return to their homes. Orpah did so, but Ruth was determined to accompany Naomi, despite the hardships entailed by conversion to Judaism. When she saw that she could not dissuade her, Naomi taught her daughter-in-law about Judaism and helped her to become a proselyte. Ruth's descendant King Solomon had Naomi in mind when he wrote in the Book of Proverbs that 'the woman of valour . . . stretches forth her hand to the needy' (Prov. 31:20), for Naomi had helped Ruth to find shelter 'under the wings of the shekhinah'.

Napoleon *see* ASSEMBLY OF JEWISH NOTABLES; ORTHODOX JUDAISM

Nasi (Hebrew for 'prince') In the Bible the head of each of the Twelve Tribes was called a Nasi. The term came into prominence, however, in the early centuries CE as the title of the head of Palestinian Jewry, parallel to that of the EXILARCH in Babylonia, and head of the Sanhedrin. The Nasi had to be of the House of David, and the position came to be the preserve of Hillel and his descendants, who were the highest-ranking religious and secular Jewish officials of the Holy Land. At the death of a Nasi the whole of the Jewish people went into public mourning. Perhaps the most famous member of the family of Hillel who actually used the title in his name was Judah Ha-Nasi, the editor of the

Mishnah. The importance of the title may be seen from the fact that the 2c. military leader Bar Kokhba, who led a major revolt against Roman rule, used the designation 'Nasi' on his coins. The term Nasi was used in later times for the head of a Jewish community, and today it is the title of the President of the State of Israel.

Nasi family (16c.) Marrano family which left Portugal so that the family members could live openly as Jews in Italy and Turkey. The matriarch of the family was Gracia Nasi (1510–69), who used her influence with the Turkish Sultan and her many business contacts to help Marranos escape to religious freedom from Portugal. She even tried to organize a trade boycott of those places which persecuted Marranos seeking refuge. Her efforts on behalf of her co-religionists, her philanthropic support for synagogues and Talmudic academies (yeshivot) and her charity to poor Marranos earned her the praise of the rabbis, who referred to her as 'the heart of her people'. Her nephew and eventual son-in-law, Joseph Nasi (1524–79), fled Portugal for Istanbul where he had himself circumcised. As a banker and statesman he was on friendly terms with European kings and was also an adviser to the Sultan who made him Duke of Naxos. Joseph and Gracia were granted control of the city of Tiberias, in Palestine, and encouraged Jews to settle there. *See also* SHTADLAN.

Nathan admonishing David (Rembrandt).

Nathan Court prophet during the reign of King David. Nathan was the teacher of David's son Solomon. He stood up to the abuses of David and rebuked his royal master for having taken BATHSHEBA from her husband and arranging his death because he wished to marry her (II Sam. 15). David's men kept continuous watch on Nathan to ensure that he did not divulge the details of the king's sin to others.

Nathan of Gaza (1643–80) Shabbetean prophet. Nathan studied Kabbalah, practised asceticism and communicated with the souls of the dead. In 1665 he had a vision of God which lasted a whole day, during which time he remained in a trance with his hair standing on end and his knees knocking together. In the vision an angel revealed to him that the Messianic age was about to dawn, and Nathan discovered that SHABBETAI TZEVI was the Messiah, when he saw his name engraved on the Throne of Glory. Thus, when Shabbetai Tzevi came to Nathan seeking a Kabbalistic cure for his strange psychological condition and desiring to know the root of his soul, the latter convinced him of his Messianic destiny. He later claimed that he had found an ancient manuscript in which Shabbetai Tzevi's name appeared as the Messiah. It was through Nathan's efforts that the Shabbetean Movement became a mass movement. He spread its propaganda in letters, in visits to Jewish communities as far away as India and in Kabbalistic works. He even went to Rome to engage in Kabbalistic rites against the Pope. Nathan proclaimed 1666 as the year when the Messianic age would begin, and he called upon people to repent in order to hasten the end, declaring that the Fast of Av was now a Messianic feast. When Shabbetai Tzevi was converted to Islam, Nathan justified this act of apostasy on the grounds that the Messiah needed to

Portrait of **Nathan of Gaza**, prophet of the Shabbetean Movement.

descend into the depths of evil in order to redeem the holiness trapped there. After Shabbetai Tzevi's death, Nathan proclaimed that he had only disappeared and would reappear later. He said that the souls of those who continued to believe in Shabbetai Tzevi contained an element of the soul of King David, while Nathan himself was thought to be a reincarnation of Isaac Luria.

Nazirite Person who in biblical times took a vow of abstention from wine, cutting the hair and contact with the dead. At the end of the period of the Nazirite vow, a sin offering was brought to atone for having given up the pleasures of God's world. In special cases the Nazirite vow could last a lifetime, as with SAMSON (Judg. 13). One acceptable reason for becoming a Nazirite was in response to seeing the evil effect of drink on a person's behaviour, as for example in the case of women suspected of adultery. Today Nazirite vows are only practised among the FALASHAS. *See also* ABSALOM; SIMON THE RIGHTEOUS.

nebich (Yiddish for 'poor thing', or as an exclamation, 'how unfortunate') Someone who consistently fails in his undertakings, however hard he tries to succeed, is a nebich. The term is related to a group of Yiddish terms for unfortunate people, yet differs from them in attitude. Referring to someone as a SHLEMIEL or a shlimazel ('bad luck person') is implicitly critical, whereas calling someone a nebich is intended to evoke pity. A nebich is an ordinary person who is faced by a bad situation, and a description of his lot is usually accompanied by the exclamation 'how unfortunate'. For example, 'Mr Cohen, nebich, left his prize-winning lottery ticket in his trousers when he sent them to the dry cleaners.' Nebichs are favourite characters of Yiddish literature such as the 'hero' of I.L. Peretz's short story, 'Bonze Zweig'. During his lifetime everything goes wrong for Bonze Zweig, but he accepts it with resignation. When he dies and goes to heaven, the whole heavenly court greets him and because of his saintliness he is offered anything he wants. All he can think of, however, is that he would like a bun and butter every day for breakfast. Nebich.

Nebuchadnezzar *see* BEN SIRA; SHEBA, QUEEN OF

Nehemiah *see* BIBLE; EZRA

neilah (Hebrew for 'closing') Prayer which concludes the yom kippur liturgy. Neilah is recited as the SUN begins to set and its name signifies that the gates of heaven are closing. This prayer is thus the last opportunity for the Jew to turn in repentance to God and effect atonement before the 'book of destiny' for the coming year is sealed. For most of neilah, the synagogue ark is left open and the congregation stand. The traditional tunes and confessional prayers give the service a numinous and highly charged emotional quality. At the end of neilah, kaddish is recited in a joyous, vibrant tune, and the shofar is sounded to mark the completion of the fast.

ner tamid (Hebrew for 'eternal lamp') Lamp hanging in the synagogue above the ARK which is kept alight even when the synagogue is empty or closed. The ner tamid is modelled on the menorah in the Temple which always had one flame of its seven branches miraculously still burning while the others were being cleaned, despite the fact that they all had the same amount of oil. The synagogue is thought of as a 'little temple', and the eternal flame represents the idea that God is always present in the world.

neshamah *see* MISHNAH; SOUL

neshamah yeterah (Hebrew for 'additional soul') The extra soul which descends on every Jew for the duration of the Sabbath and which is symbolized by the Sabbath LAMP. This enables the Jew to celebrate the day with great joy and even to eat more than he is capable of during the week. On Saturday night when shabbat ends, SPICES are used in the havdalah ritual to revive the body after the departure of the neshamah yeterah. According to the *Zohar* this extra soul comes from the heavenly Tree of Life, and it is the type of soul that man will possess after the Resurrection of the Dead.

Neturei Karta (Aramaic for 'guardians of the city') Extremist religious group centred in Jerusalem, who are opposed to the existence of the State of Israel and to modern Zionism, both of which they regard as anti-religious. The members of the Neturei Karta believe that Jews must wait for the coming of the Messiah before they gain political independence. The founders of the Neturei Karta broke away from the Agudat Israel party in 1935, since it was considered too mild in its negation of Zionism. Followers of the Neturei Karta recognize the head of the Satmar Chasidic sect as their religious mentor, and they follow the Satmar Chasidim in rejecting modernity. They live in a world separate from the secular ethos of Israeli society and refuse to pay taxes, vote in elections or carry an Israeli passport. Those rabbis who cooperate with Zionism or with the State of Israel are bitterly attacked by the Neturei Karta, and their orthodoxy is impugned. In New York Neturei Karta sympathizers have burnt an effigy of the leader of the Lubavitch Chasidim, who is suspected of Zionist leanings, and shaved off half the beard of Lubavitch Chasidim who have strayed into their territory. They have also attacked religious institutions run by the Belz Chasidim because the latter accept financial support from the Israeli government. The more politically active members of the Neturei Karta support the Palestine Liberation Organisation, hold anti-Israel demonstrations and advertise their views in the press, in order to cause as much embarrassment as possible to the Zionist State of Israel.

new moon (Hebrew 'rosh chodesh', meaning 'head of the month') The beginning of each lunar month is a minor festive period of one or two days, when the HALLEL Psalms and a MUSAF are added to the normal liturgy. On the preceding shabbat a special prayer, composed by Rav, is recited, asking for God's blessing and redemption and announcing the name of the month and the day or days of rosh chodesh (but *see* TISHRI). It is also customary to inform the congregation of the exact moment when the molad ('birth') of the new moon takes place. After the third day from the molad, if the MOON can be seen in the night sky, a ceremony of sanctifying the moon, kiddush levanah, takes place out of doors, usually on a Saturday night. During the recital of the prayers at this ceremony, each person greets three others with the words 'shalom aleikhem', meaning 'peace be upon you' (see GREET-INGS), to indicate that the request for God's punishment of one's enemies is not meant to apply to anyone present. If a person wishes to avoid toothache in the month ahead, it is recommended that he should add the phrase 'and I shall have no toothache' to the thrice repeated request that enemies should not be able to do any harm. The ritual expresses the hope that God will restore the light of the moon to its former glory, and Israel to its former greatness. For in the age of the Messiah the moon will shine as a full moon throughout the month. *See also* CALENDAR.

New Year *see* ROSH HA-SHANAH

New Year for Trees *see* TU BI-SHEVAT

niddah (Hebrew for 'menstruating woman') During her monthly period and after childbirth a woman is ritually unclean, and in the Temple period even contact with objects touched by her was avoided (Lev. 15:19–24). There is evidence that a special house was set aside for her during this time, a practice still found among Falashas. A niddah is not allowed to have physical contact with her husband during menstruation (Lev. 20:18), and a week later she purifies herself by bathing in a MIKVEH. When sexual relations are resumed, it is like a renewal of the marriage (*see* TAHARAT HA-MISHPACHAH). Menstrual bleeding is Eve's punishment for 'shedding Adam's blood', i.e. causing his death by tempting him to eat the forbidden fruit. During their forty years in the wilderness, Israelite women did not menstruate. Keeping the menstrual regulations is one of the specific commandments affecting women, and a woman who disregards them may be punished by death in childbirth. A child born from sexual relations with a niddah is of tainted origin and likely to be arrogant or afflicted with leprosy. The determination of exactly which types of secretion are to be considered menstrual blood occupies a large part of the literature about niddah. King David was said to spend his spare time examining female discharges, so as to enable women to resume relations with their husbands. It was believed that, if a niddah looked into a mirror, spots of blood would appear on the glass, and if she passed between two men at the beginning of her period, one of them would die. If she did so at the end of her menstrual cycle, then the men would quarrel. A man who passes between two menstrual women will be punished. In Christian legend Jewish men, identified as followers of the Devil, were thought to suffer regular monthly bleeding and to need Christian blood as a remedy, leading to blood libel accusations. There is, indeed, a Jewish belief that men originally menstruated, and this only ceased at the time of the Matriarch Rachel. *See also* LILITH.

niddui *see* CHEREM

niggun *see* MUSIC

Illuminated page of the **neilah** service, from the Leipzig Machzor.

Orthodox Jews in the Mea Shearim quarter of Jerusalem, wearing the dress characteristic of members of the **Neturei Karta**.

Nisan First lunar month of the Hebrew calendar, counting from the period of the Exodus from Egypt, or seventh month from the New Year festival (rosh ha-shanah). Nisan is the month associated with spring and with the new barley crop and usually begins in late March or early April. Its zodiacal sign is the ram. The first day of Nisan is regarded as the beginning of the new year for the cycle of the festivals and for dating the reign of kings. There is also a view in the *Talmud* that the world was created in Nisan. Every twenty-eight years at the beginning of Nisan a ceremony of blessing the SUN, birkat ha-chammah, takes place, representing the return of the heavens to their position at the Creation of the world. The festival of PESACH falls in the second half of the month.

nittel *see* GAMBLING

Noachide Laws (Hebrew 'sheva mitzvot benei noach') The seven laws which GENTILES have to keep, based on the Rabbinic interpretation of the command to Adam (Gen. 2:16) and the covenant with NOAH after the Flood (Gen. 9:4). Though there are differing versions of these laws, it is generally accepted that the Sons of Noah must not practise idolatry, blasphemy, murder, sexual immorality, robbery, or eat a limb torn from a living animal. They must also establish a system of justice. If Gentiles transgress these laws, they could, in theory, be punished by the death penalty. The other laws of the torah are only binding on Jews, not on Gentiles, although the latter may practise them if they wish, except for observance of the shabbat and torah study, both of which are prohibited to non-Jews. A Gentile who keeps these Noachide regulations is to be considered a resident alien, ger toshav, to whom the Jewish community should extend support. He is also considered among the RIGHTEOUS GENTILES who will have a portion in OLAM HABA. The great medieval theologian Maimonides insisted that a 'pious Gentile' was someone who kept these laws because he believed they were revealed in the Bible. Other Jewish thinkers, like Moses Mendelssohn, disagreed and maintained that it was sufficient for a Gentile to keep the Noachide Laws because they seem rational and moral. In general, Moslems have been regarded as followers of the Noachide Laws, but doubts have been expressed about Christian worship of Jesus, which is regarded as idolatrous.

Noah Biblical character who survived the FLOOD together with his family in Noah's ARK (Gen. 6–8). Noah was born circumcised and was saved by God because of his righteousness. There is a dispute as to whether this righteousness only seemed extraordinary because his generation was so wicked or whether, having managed to avoid the bad influences of his age, he would have been even more righteous in a less corrupt period such as that of Abraham. Support for the former view is contained in the criticism of Noah for not pleading with God to spare his contemporaries. He thus showed that he lacked the compassionate qualities of Abraham, who pleaded for the people of Sodom to be saved. During the Flood, Noah was kept very busy trying to feed and control the animals in the ark, and the lion actually attacked him on one occasion. Noah also had to feed the giant Og, who

clung onto the top of the ark during the Flood, by passing food to him through a hole in the roof. While in the ark, Noah was not able to sleep at all because of his many responsibilities. Noah sent out a DOVE to see if the waters were receding. *See also* ALCOHOL; DRUNKENNESS; RAINBOW; RAZIEL.

nochri *see* GENTILE

Nostradamus (1503–66) French astrologer of Jewish origin. His grandparents converted to Catholicism to avoid anti-Jewish persecution, and Nostradamus (literally 'Our Lady') was brought up as a devout Christian. Although he was educated as a physician, he became interested in ASTROLOGY, the occult and Kabbalah. His fame rests on the works of astrological prediction which he published, written in a cryptic style. Some of the predictions were thought to have come true in his lifetime, such as the death of the French king, while others looked ahead far into the future and are regarded as referring to events which have happened since the 16c. Nostradamus fell out of favour with the Catholic Church, and his prophetic writings were banned and put on the Index of Prohibited Books.

Oath More Judaica A special oath which European Jews had to take in the Middle Ages before giving testimony in a law court. The purpose of the oath was to humiliate Jews, as is apparent from the different ways it was administered. It had to be taken standing barefoot on a sow's skin or wearing a special hat while standing on a stool or standing in water while wearing a crown of thorns, or a Jew might be forced to pronounce the name of God while bareheaded (*see* HEAD-COVERING). The oath sometimes referred to the death of Jesus and the responsibility of all Jews for deicide and would often contain curses against those who uttered false testimony. With the emancipation of the Jews in the 19c. the oath disappeared.

Og, king of Bashan *see* ARK OF NOAH; NOAH

olam haba (Hebrew for 'World to Come') The new order of being, coming into existence after the advent of the MESSIAH, which no mortal eye has seen and no human can imagine (*see* ESCHATOLOGY). The ordinary world of everyday affairs is depicted as a corridor before olam haba in which man has to prepare himself before entering the main hall. Every Israelite (*see* COVENANT) has a portion reserved for him in this World to Come, if he is worthy, as do the RIGHTEOUS GENTILES. The Rabbis held out the promise of olam haba to many categories of people, ranging from those who were humble to those who at any time walked four cubits in the Holy Land. They also warned people that they would lose their share in the World to Come if they put people to shame in public, uttered the tetragrammaton in public, read the books of the Apocrypha in place of scripture, walked behind a woman, or became a scribe or a doctor because of the great responsibilities of these professions. An apikoros also has no portion in olam haba. In olam haba the world will be full of the knowledge of the Lord, like the waters cover the sea (Isa. 11:9). There will be no eating or drinking, no procreation or business dealings, no jealousy, hate or competitiveness, but the righteous will sit with crowns on their heads sustained in bliss by the light of the shekhinah. Since there were differences of opinion about the meaning and relative importance of doctrines of IMMORTALITY, the AFTER-LIFE, the RESURRECTION OF THE DEAD and the trans-migration of souls, olam haba is a somewhat ambiguous concept. It is widely used, for instance, to refer to the spiritual world of the soul after death in the heavenly Garden of Eden (see TREE OF LIFE) and many of the teachings about the World to Come could be taken to refer not to the post-Messianic world of redemption but to the *post-mortem* world of existence with God. It is also used by mystics to refer to a level of spiritual existence available to the adept while he is still alive.

Old Testament *see* BIBLE; JUDAIZERS

olive (Hebrew 'zayit') Olives were among the seven products of the Holy Land in Bible times (Deut. 8:8), and a special blessing is said after they are eaten. The importance of olives for everyday life is shown by the use of 'the size of an olive' as a standard of halakhic measurement. An olive branch figures as the first item found by the DOVE which Noah sent out from the ark after the Flood (see OLIVES, MOUNT OF). There are also many references to olive oil in the Bible and *Talmud*. This oil was used in the Temple candelabrum (see MENORAH), as fuel for the Sabbath LAMP and as the choicest oil for the lights kindled on the festival of CHANUKKAH. Israel itself is compared to the olive. Just as an olive needs to be crushed to give out its oil, so the People of Israel will only be brought to repentance and to the fulfilment of its destiny as a holy people through being crushed by persecution and suffering.

Olives, Mount of (Hebrew 'har ha-zeitim') Mount near Jerusalem from which the dove, sent out of the ark by Noah, brought back an olive branch symbolizing the end of the Flood. At the coming of the Messianic Day of the Lord, God will reveal Himself on the mount (Zech. 14). The Messiah will begin his triumphal entry into Jerusalem from there, with the sounding of the great shofar by Elijah and the Resurrection of the Dead. In Temple times the RED HEIFER was burnt on the Mount of Olives, and the ashes were taken to the Temple along a connecting bridge. It was also the place on which the first beacons announcing the sighting of the new moon were lit (see CALENDAR). Today, the Mount of Olives is best known for its cemetery, the most important cemetery in the Land of Israel, since those buried there are closest to the place of the RESURRECTION, and their bodies will not have to roll along subterranean passages before they arise from the ground. *See also* INGATHERING OF THE EXILES.

omer, counting of (Hebrew 'sefirat ha-omer') A sheaf, or omer, of the new barley harvest was offered up in the Temple on the second day of PESACH, the

Venetian mosaic of **Noah** bringing the birds into the ark.

Traditional portrait of **Nostradamus**.

Kibbutz children holding the first ears of barley during celebrations of the **omer** festivities.

'day after the Sabbath' (Lev. 23:11). This offering allowed the new cereal crop to be eaten. For the next seven weeks, each day was counted till SHAVUOT, which falls on the fiftieth day. This practice of counting, which is still maintained, was understood as representing the ascent by the Israelites of the forty-nine steps from the depths of spiritual impurity in Egypt. They eventually reached the level of purity represented by the giving of the torah on Mount Sinai, which took place on shavuot. The period became one of semi-mourning in the Middle Ages, ostensibly because the pupils of Akiva died in the 2c. CE at this time. It took on greater significance because of the post-Easter massacres of Jewish communities by the Crusaders which took place during the omer period. The mourning is interrupted in the middle of the omer by LAG BA-OMER.

Onan see BIRTH CONTROL

Onkelos An aristocratic Roman proselyte who composed the most popular Aramaic translation of the Bible, the TARGUM Onkelos. Before Onkelos converted to Judaism he consulted various biblical and post-biblical characters, whom he called back from the dead so that he could ask them about the Jewish people. Jesus answered him that whenever anyone harms the Jews, it is as if he harmed his own eyeball. When the news of his conversion reached his uncle, the Roman Emperor, the latter sent three bands of soldiers to apprehend him, but they became convinced of the truth of Judaism through his arguments and also converted. The fourth band were instructed not to talk to Onkelos but simply to capture him and bring him to the emperor. As they were leaving his house, Onkelos kissed the mezuzah on his doorpost. The soldiers asked him what this was, and his answer so impressed them that they too converted to Judaism. He composed his Targum, under instruction from Eliezer Ben Hyrcanus and Joshua Ben Chananiah, for the masses who could not understand Hebrew and whose vernacular was Aramaic. It is a literal translation, but it paraphrases anthropomorphisms and generally follows the Rabbinic interpretation of the text. The Targum Onkelos was highly regarded as an inspired work, and Jews were instructed to read the weekly portion, sidra, twice in the Hebrew original and once in the translation of Onkelos. This practice has continued, although many people now use the Hebrew commentary of Rashi, instead of Onkelos, because they no longer understand Aramaic.

Oppenheimer, Joseph Suess (1698–1738) German COURT JEW. Joseph came from a wealthy and influential family and was known to be lax in his religious practice; indeed, his sister and brother converted to Christianity. After working for various German states, Joseph became financial controller to the Duke of Württemberg. He was very successful in improving the Duke's finances, but his opulent life-style, his tight fiscal control of state taxes, his support for the Catholic ruler of an essentially Protestant state and his help to his co-religionists to settle in the Duke's domains gained him many enemies. When the Duke died in 1737, Joseph was arrested and imprisoned. While awaiting sentence, he took a renewed interest in

Judaism, keeping rituals he had long neglected and refusing to be baptized to save his life. He was eventually hanged in a cage in public, in the sight of a large crowd of jeering onlookers. Joseph died with the shema on his lips and was mourned as a martyr by the German Jewish communities. His story was told in the historical novel *Jew Suess* by the German Jewish writer, Lion Feuchtwanger.

oral torah (Hebrew 'torah she-baal peh') The oral traditions of Judaism which were received by Moses during the forty days and nights he spent on Mount Sinai and handed down to the elders and prophets. The general principles of the development of the oral torah, including the questions and comments of wise pupils in future times, were also revealed to Moses. Even the contradictory views of different sages were thought to be part of this revealed teaching and were all valued as 'words of the living God'. The oral torah was originally not allowed to be written down but was memorized and expounded by masters (see TANNA) to their pupils. Only when Roman persecution of Jews in Palestine threatened to wipe out the sages, who were repositories of the oral tradition (see PHARISEES), was this prohibition lifted. The literature of the early Rabbinic period, MISHNAH, MIDRASH and TALMUD, encapsulates oral teachings which are believed to go back to the Mosaic period. The SADDUCEES, Karaites and Reform Judaism, however, all rejected this idea of an authoritative oral teaching. The oral torah is depicted as the soul of the written torah, because its explanations bring the text to life, and without them many laws and teachings would be incomprehensible. Indeed, the explanations given in the oral tradition sometimes differ markedly from the literal meaning (peshat) of the biblical text.

ordination see SEMIKHAH

orel, orelte see GENTILE

original sin There is a well-attested belief in Jewish literature that each individual has FREE WILL to choose between good and bad, subject only to his ability to resist his evil INCLINATION. Nevertheless, the sin of ADAM left its mark on future generations, so that individuals eventually die whether they are sinless or not, for Adam's sin brought DEATH into the world. The *Talmud* tells how the SERPENT in the Garden of Eden had sexual relations with EVE and injected its filth into her, which affected all her descendants. The mystics understood this to reflect a fissure in the divine unity. The Satanic forces of the SITRA ACHRA, strengthened by human sin, replace the divine male principle and couple with the divine female principle, shekhinah. It was only the experience of receiving the torah at Sinai which removed the filth of the serpent from Israel.

Orpah see INTERMARRIAGE; NAOMI

Orthodox Judaism Umbrella term describing traditionalists who rejected the religious reforms of the 18c. The term was first used in a Jewish context in 1795 and today is applied to those who do not share the modernist beliefs and practices of CONSERVATIVE or

REFORM JUDAISM. It has been suggested that an alternative term, 'Orthoprax', would be a more suitable designation for those who share a common commitment to the halakhah. As it is, Orthodox Jews have to be divided into two main subgroups, usually called 'Modern Orthodox' and 'Ultra-Orthodox'. The former, while subscribing to codes like the *Shulchan Arukh*, maintain a modern life-style, wear modern dress, believe in secular education and have sermons in the vernacular. They base their outlook on the Neo-Orthodox Movement founded by Samson Raphael HIRSCH in 19c. Germany, which took a positive view of the secular world while preserving a commitment to halakhic norms. The difference between Modern Orthodox Jews and members of non-Orthodox communities is sometimes only a matter of degree, since many members of Orthodox communities are only nominally Orthodox. One of the most obvious signs of an Orthodox community is the presence of a MECHITZAH in the synagogue. Ultra-Orthodox Jews reject the values of modernity, wearing a ghetto style of clothing to symbolize this, and often only speak Yiddish. They differentiate themselves totally from non-Orthodox Jews and even from Modern Orthodoxy. Their attitudes go back to the fight against Moses Mendelssohn and the Enlightenment. Thus, in the 19c. Shneur Zalman of Lyady supported the regime of the Russian Czar against Napoleon because he opposed the liberalizing policies of the latter. The Hungarian rabbi Moses Sofer (1762–1839) forbade the introduction of anything new into Judaism in order to preserve Jewish tradition. The State of Israel officially recognizes only Orthodox rabbis as representatives of Jewish religion, and some of the fiercest power struggles within Orthodoxy have taken place there.

The **Original Sin** (Michelangelo).

Ostropoler, Hershele (18c.) Jewish badchan and wit who served the Chasidic leader Rabbi Baruch of Tulchin, the grandson of Israel Baal Shem Tov, as a court jester. Hershele was at one time the ritual slaughterer (shochet) in the Polish town of Ostropol, hence his surname. When he was dismissed from this post, he began wandering from community to community in great poverty, telling jokes and amusing people. At the court of Rabbi Baruch he found employment as a professional wit and jester, but he went too far when he made the tzaddik the butt of his jokes. Eventually, Baruch had Hershele physically thrown out by his Chasidim. It was Hershele's lack of respect for eminent persons that led to his sacking, both from Ostropol and from Rabbi Baruch's court, yet it was precisely this characteristic that turned him into a hero of Jewish folklore. It is told that, when thieves once broke into Hershele's home, he got out of bed and, grabbing one by the arm, said to him excitedly, 'Maybe if we search my house together we'll find something.' Another time a friend suggested to Hershele that it would be a good idea if rich and poor pooled their resources and then gave everyone what they actually needed from a community storehouse. 'Fine', said Hershele, 'I'll tell you what. I'll get the agreement of the poor; you persuade the rich.'

Group of **Orthodox Jewish** boys in the Mea Shearim quarter of Jerusalem.

oved kochavim umazalot *see* AKKUM

oyf kapporos *see* KAPPAROT

Pale of Settlement Restricted area of Jewish settlement in Czarist Russia stretching in a wide belt from the Baltic to the Black Sea. When the Russian Empire absorbed parts of Poland in 1791, it brought in a large Jewish population. These Jews were segregated in the Pale of Settlement, and during the 19c. only those who had special rights because of wealth, medical qualifications, university training or because they had served in the Russian army as CANTONISTS were allowed to live outside the Pale. At the end of the 19c. there were close to five million Jews in the Pale of Settlement, living in SHTETL communities and speaking Yiddish. From this concentration of Ashkenazim, waves of migrants left for Western Europe and North America from the 1880s onwards. They were escaping from large-scale persecutions (*see* POGROM), some of which were government inspired, and from the poverty and overcrowding which characterized the extended GHETTO of the Pale. The Pale of Settlement came to an end with the Russian Revolution of 1917.

panentheism The doctrine, found in certain schools of Kabbalah, that all reality exists in God and that the world is therefore part of the divine. While pantheism simply identifies the world with the divine, panentheism sees divinity behind mundane reality. As the *Zohar* puts it, God is in everything and everything is in Him, since He clothes Himself in the world. This continuity of substance between the world and God is a consequence of the doctrine of EMANATION, which is thought of as the unfolding of the Godhead through different levels. Since the world exists within God, and at the same time God exists within the world, part of the task of the mystic is to discover the divine underlay behind everyday phenomena. Rabbinic literature commenting on the use of makom ('place'), as a name of God, states: 'He is the place of the world, but the world is not His place'. *See also* TZIMTZUM.

Paradise (Hebrew from the Persian 'pardes', 'orchard') The heavenly abode of the righteous after death (*see* AFTERLIFE), identified with the biblical GARDEN OF EDEN. It is also possible to enter Paradise while still alive. Among the biblical characters who did so were Jonah, ENOCH and ELIJAH. Four Talmudic sages once went on a mystical journey to Paradise, but only Akiva came out unharmed. Of the other three, SIMEON BEN AZZAI died, Simeon Ben Zoma went mad and ELISHA BEN AVUYAH became a heretic. There are a number of stories about another Talmudic sage, JOSHUA BEN LEVI, who was able to visit Paradise to see what awaited him after death. He subsequently sent a letter with the Angel of Death to his rabbinic colleagues describing the wonders of Paradise. The term PARDES was also used as an acronym of the four traditional methods of Biblical interpretation. *See also* BEHEMOTH; TREE OF LIFE.

parah adumah *see* RED HEIFER

parapet (Hebrew 'maakeh') A flat roof must have a parapet built around it to prevent people who use the roof from falling off (Deut. 22:8). A synagogue does not need such a parapet since its roof should not be used. The rule about parapets was extended to include responsibility for fencing in pits and wells and for keeping any fierce animals away from people.

Pardes Word of Persian origin which in Hebrew literature is used to mean 'garden' or 'orchard', and subsequently 'Paradise'. The four consonantal letters of the word (p–r–d–s) are also used as a mnemonic for the four basic categories of biblical interpretation: PESHAT (the simple and often the literal meaning), remez (the meaning hinted at in the text), derush (the midrashic (*see* MIDRASH) or homiletic meaning), and sod (secret or mystical meaning). Each category has equal validity in its own area, since the Bible is like a rock which can be split into many pieces under the hammer of interpretation. There is, however, always a special importance given to the simple meaning of a biblical verse.

parents Jewish descent is passed on through the mother, but tribal and priestly status is derived from the father (*see* FAMILY). There are three partners in the formation of CHILDREN, the parents who provide the physical make-up and God who provides the soul. Just as respect is to be shown to God, so parents too are to be honoured, as stated explicitly in the Decalogue. A child should not contradict his parents, not call them by their first names and not sit in a seat reserved for them. Parents should be supported by their children, even if they have to beg to do so. They must be provided with food, drink and clothing and taken out or brought in. After death, they must be buried and the KADDISH prayers should be recited by a son. Respect for parents also extends to step-parents and even grandparents. Where parents ask their children to break God's commandments, however, they are not to be obeyed. The *Talmud* describes the extent to which some of the sages went in honouring their parents. Rabbi Tarfon, for instance, used to bend down so that his mother could step on him as she got into or out of bed. It also tells of a heathen whose respect for his father was exemplary. Though he was offered a large sum of money for some gems, he refused to conclude the deal because his father was asleep and the key to the gem casket was under his pillow. This heathen was later rewarded when a Red Heifer was born among his cattle, and he was able to sell it to the Jewish authorities at considerable profit. Parents have responsibility for educating their children, but they should not beat a mature child who has misbehaved; otherwise the child may respond violently, and this would constitute 'putting a stumbling block before the blind'. Neither should parents favour one child over the others, since it was such favouritism shown by JACOB for his son JOSEPH that led to jealousy and rivalry among his children.

pargod *see* PAROKHET

parnas (Hebrew for 'official') Elected synagogue official who is the senior lay leader of the COMMUNITY, the name originally meaning someone who 'provided food' for the poor. The *Talmud* forbad the appointment of a parnas without the agreement of the community and insisted that to prevent him becoming too arrogant in wielding power he should have at least one skeleton in the cupboard. He could thus always be reminded of his own blemishes if his haughtiness became unbearable.

parokhet (Hebrew for 'curtain') Curtain hanging in front of the synagogue ARK, modelled on the decorative curtain which screened the Holy of Holies, with the Ark of the Covenant inside, from the rest of the Temple. The curtain is often decorated with woven lions and Tablets of the Decalogue. In many communities the magen david hexagram is also used as a motif, but this was regarded by certain groups within the Chasidic Movement as basically a non-Jewish design. The parokhet is usually changed for ROSH HA-SHANAH to a white colour signifying forgiveness, since this is a festival of repentance. The parokhet symbolizes the division between the holy and the profane. There is also a spiritual curtain between the human and divine worlds, known as a pargod, which keeps the two separate. Those who manage to penetrate the pargod or to overhear voices conversing on the other side of it, are able to find out what is in store for the world in the future. *See also* PETICHAH.

parve (Yiddish for 'neutral'; also 'parev') Food which is classified by the Jewish DIETARY LAWS as neither meat nor dairy, e.g. fish, eggs and vegetables. Parve food can be eaten with either meat or milk dishes, except for fish, which cannot be eaten together with meat, since this is considered unhealthy. The term is also used to describe a somewhat nondescript person who has no distinctive characteristics. The origin of the word is unclear.

Pascal Lamb *see* AFIKOMEN; FALASHAS; PESACH; SAMA-RITANS

Passover *see* PESACH

Patriarchs The three founding fathers of the Jewish religion, ABRAHAM, ISAAC and JACOB, whose main wives are known as the MATRIARCHS. The daily prayers were instituted by the Patriarchs, and each one understood God in a slightly different way. Thus Abraham referred to the place of God as a 'mount' (Gen. 22:14), Isaac referred to it as a 'field' (Gen. 24:63) and Jacob referred to it as a 'house' (Gen. 28:17). It was Jacob's understanding of God which was felt to be most complete. The Patriarchs are religious role models, and the events of their lives foreshadow the future history of the Jewish people. They are even identified with the divine chariot of Ezekiel's vision of heaven, for they are the carriers of God's teaching here on earth. The Patriarchs kept the torah before it was actually given. They are buried in the Cave of Machpelah, and the merit of their faith in God, known as 'the merit of the fathers' (*see* ZEKHUT AVOT), benefits their descendants.

Pentateuch *see* CHUMASH

Pentecost *see* SHAVUOT

People of the Book *see* DHIMMA

Elisha watching Elijah ascend to **Paradise** (Gustave Doré).

18c. German **parokhet** for a synagogue ark.

peot (Hebrew for 'corners') The sidelocks worn by some Ultra-Orthodox men in front or behind the ears as a fulfilment of the biblical requirement 'not to cut around the corners of the head' (Lev. 19:27). Although most traditional Jews simply stop short of removing all the HAIR beside the ear, those influenced by Kabbalistic and Chasidic teaching allow the peot to grow completely uncut. Indeed, some young boys have their first haircut on the minor festival of LAG BA-OMER, after their third birthday, when all the hair of their head is removed except for that at the side of the ear. Wearing peot has come to symbolize the rejection of modernity, and an attempt was made as early as 1845 by Czar Nicholas I to prohibit it. The reason for the commandment not to cut off the hair at the corners of the head is unknown. Maimonides believed it was to distinguish Jews from idolators, who shaved the whole head as part of a pagan rite. The Chasidic mystic NACHMAN OF BRESLOV saw the peot as spiritual vehicles for draining off the excess of the imagination. Today peot have the function of markedly distinguishing Jews from their Gentile neighbours.

Perek Shirah (Hebrew for 'Chapter of Song') A short work containing the biblical verses sung by nature, by insects, birds and animals in praise of God. The work was composed by King David who, when he wrote the Psalms, felt that no other creature had recited more praises to God than he. These feelings were short-lived when he met a frog who told him not to be so proud since even he, a mere frog, had uttered more songs than David. In response David composed Perek Shirah. According to another legend, the work was written by David's son Solomon, who knew the language of birds and animals. In fact the idea that animals and nature sing to God is associated with the maaseh merkavah mystical tradition. Its texts tell how trees and animals sing when mystical secrets are expounded. There are also Talmudic accounts of how the grain sings during the harvest month of Nisan, how the cows that pulled the Ark of the Covenant sang and how, when Joshua made the sun and the moon stand still (Josh. 10), they stopped singing and Joshua sang in their place. The army of Sennacherib was defeated outside Jerusalem when his soldiers heard the beasts of the field singing and died. The story is told of one Talmudic sage who fasted and prayed so that dogs should be allowed to sing God's praises. An angel appeared to him and told him his fasting was unnecessary, for dogs were specially favoured by God since they did not bark when the Israelites left Egypt. The song sung by dogs in fact ends Perek Shirah. Criticism was directed against Perek Shirah by Karaites, who made fun of the idea that donkeys sing to God. The work, which is incorporated in some prayer-books, is divided into six chapters so that a chapter may be said each day of the week. Those who recite Perek Shirah daily will be saved from the power of the evil inclination while alive and from punishment in gehinnom after death. They are also guaranteed a portion in the World to Come (olam haba) in the age of the Messiah.

pesach (Hebrew for 'Passover') One of the three PILGRIM FESTIVALS or HARVEST FESTIVALS. Pesach is the festival of freedom, commemorating the redemption of the Israelite slaves from Egypt and pointing ahead to the final redemption of the world in the age of the Messiah. It is also the time of the barley harvest (see OMER) and the end of the rainy season. The lunar CALENDAR must be adjusted by the addition of an extra month, where necessary, so that pesach always falls in the spring. No leavened bread (see CHAMETZ) may be eaten for the whole festival, and a day before pesach begins, all leaven is cleared out of the home after a search for any crumbs that may be hidden in nooks and crannies (see BEDIKAT CHAMETZ). The festival lasts for seven days (eight days in the diaspora) beginning on the evening before the fifteenth of Nisan, the night of the EXODUS, with a ritual family SEDER meal. MATZAH is eaten at the seder to remind the participants of the bread of slavery eaten in Egypt, and pesach is also known as 'chag ha-matzot', 'the festival of unleavened bread'. The end of pesach is the time when the Israelites crossed over the Red Sea, and because their rescue involved the drowning of the Egyptians, only the shortened form of the HALLEL Psalms is recited. The Song of Songs is also read. The mystics saw pesach as a celebration of the marriage of the Community of Israel, symbolizing the female aspect of God, with Her husband the male aspect. The name of the festival originates in the last of the ten PLAGUES, when the Egyptian firstborn children were slain by God, who 'passed over' the houses of the Israelites, which had the blood of the Pascal lamb smeared on their doorposts, and spared their firstborn (Exod. 12:27). See also CHOL HA-MOED; DEW; SIYYUM.

pesach sheni see IYYAR

peshat (Hebrew for 'plain') The straightforward, though not always literal, meaning of a biblical verse. Peshat is contrasted with other methods of interpretation (see PARDES) and specifically with MIDRASH, which usually explains verses in ways which conflict with their plain meaning. While there may be many different and contradictory midrashic interpretations, there can only be one peshat to a verse. A minority of the classical Bible commentators favoured peshat and sometimes criticized the excesses of midrash. There is a Talmudic rule that 'a verse never deserts its plain meaning', although one sage remarked that, having studied until the age of eighteen, he never knew about it.

Petaachiah of Regensburg (12c.) German Jewish traveller who left an account of his journey from Prague through Poland, Russia, Armenia, Khazaria, Persia, Babylonia and Syria on a pilgrimage to the Holy Land. Petaachiah is the source of many legends about the Jewish communities he visited. He described how there were only Karaite Jews in the Crimea, where meat was warmed by being placed on a horse's back under the saddle. He heard the story of the king of the Khazars who had a dream that he should adopt the religion of Moses or else his land would be destroyed, so he sent to the Babylonian rabbis for instruction. In Babylonia he came across a red stone set in the walls of a synagogue which was one of the original stones of the First Temple. In Baghdad he found a girl, the only child of a rabbi, who used to teach male pupils from the window of her home, thus preserving her modesty since they could not see her. Nearby was EZEKIEL's tomb, holy to both Jews and Moslems, where people setting out on a journey would leave bundles of their money for safekeeping. Petaachiah saw some of these disintegrating since the travellers had not returned after a long absence. In former times a pillar of fire had hovered over the tomb. He also saw the tomb of DANIEL suspended over a river since the Jews on both banks had wanted him buried in their domain to improve their harvest. Under this tomb swam fish with gold rings attached to their heads. Petaachiah found a well in the Holy Land which only gave water for six days but was dry on the shabbat. He saw the tree, split into three parts, under which the three angels who visited Abraham had sat, the fruit of which was 'very sweet. He also saw the enormous stone over the well at Haran which Jacob had lifted but which took forty men to remove. At Jerusalem, which was under Crusader rule, he only found one co-religionist – a Jewish dyer.

petichah (Hebrew for 'opening') Ceremonial opening of the synagogue ARK so that a sefer torah may be taken out and carried to the bimah to be read. When the parokhet curtain is drawn and the doors of the ark are opened, the congregation stand and sing: 'When the ark would travel Moses used to say: Rise up, O Lord, and let Your enemies be scattered' (Num. 10:35). Petichah is also performed during important parts of the liturgy, when no scroll is removed. It used to be customary for someone who wished to protest against the actions of a member of the congregation to hold up the synagogue service until he gained satisfaction for his grievances. He would stand before the open ark after petichah, thus preventing a scroll from being taken out, and complain to the assembled worshippers. This action obviously put pressure on the congregation to deal with his case. Those who abused this privilege were warned that after death the torah itself would remonstrate with their souls for the indignity it had suffered during their protest and would not allow them to rest in peace. There was also a similar method of protest to God Himself about some wrong. This involved standing before the open ark, when the community were not at prayer, and expressing one's grievances to God. The open ark and the presence of the torah scrolls were thought to make this an effective way of gaining justice from heaven.

Pharaoh Name of the kings of Egypt in biblical times, particularly used to refer to the Egyptian ruler during the enslavement and Exodus of the Israelites. This Pharaoh suffered from LEPROSY and was advised to kill Israelite babes, so that he could bathe in their blood to relieve his condition. Despite this he passed himself off to his people as a divinity who did not have any ordinary human weaknesses. That is why MOSES met him in the early morning by the banks of the Nile where he used to go secretly to perform his toilet. Pharaoh alone escaped from the drowning of the Egyptian army in the Red Sea and, after undergoing punishment for his sins, was installed as king of Nineveh. When the prophet Jonah came to that city with a message from God, Pharaoh, now a changed man, led the people in penitence. He did not die but

Orthodox Jews in the Mea Shearim quarter of Jerusalem with shtetl garb and **peot**.

19c. Italian plate used for the **pesach** seder meal.

The Egyptian **pharaoh** Rameses II.

remains at the gates of hell to instruct the kings of the Gentiles who come there in a true understanding of God's ways. *See also* JETHRO; JOSEPH.

Pharisees (Hebrew 'perushim', meaning 'separatists' or 'interpreters') Members of a group within Judaism at the end of the Second Temple period who opposed the biblical literalism of the more aristocratic priestly Sadducees and the asceticism of the Essenes. After the destruction of the Jerusalem Temple in 70 CE, the two latter groups virtually disappeared, and the oral teachings of the Pharisees shaped the Rabbinic Judaism which emerged from the council of sages at Jabneh (*see* ORAL TORAH). Though Pharisaism is depicted negatively in the New Testament, the Pharisees themselves were highly critical of hypocrisy among their own members. There is some dispute among scholars as to whether the original Pharisees were minimalists, who were mainly concerned with the laws of ritual purity of food and with tithes, or were maximalists, who applied the rituals of the Temple to the home and synagogue, upheld popular traditions and made the study and interpretation of the torah the centre of religious life. The very name of the group has been variously explained as meaning those 'who kept themselves separate' from ritual defilement, or as those 'who interpreted' the written text of the torah, thus developing the Rabbinic Tradition. *See also* SIMEON BEN SHETACH.

Philo Judaeus (20 BCE–50 CE) Egyptian Jewish philosopher. Philo lived in Alexandria and reinterpreted Judaism for those Egyptian Jews whose culture was more Greek than Hebraic. He wrote in Greek about the Bible, its characters and stories which he explained in Platonic and Stoic terms as expressing philosophical truths. Philo's allegorical and symbolic exegesis had some influence on Rabbinic thought, but in the main his teachings were unknown to his Aramaic-speaking co-religionists in Palestine and, indeed, were in conflict with the Rabbinic ethos. While Judaism did not preserve his works, they owe their survival to the Christian Church which was particularly attracted to the doctrine of the Logos, developed by Philo to explain biblical language about God. *See also* ARISTEAS, LETTER OF.

Phinehas Biblical High Priest and grandson of Aaron who was renowned for his zealotry. When Zimri, an Israelite leader, behaved immorally with a Midianite woman, Moses felt unable to interfere because he himself had married a Midianite wife. Phinehas, however, did not hesitate, and taking the law into his own hands, he killed Zimri and the woman with a spear. Although he is generally commended for this action, some rabbis expressed reservations about it. Phinehas is variously identified with the prophet Elijah, also known for his zealotry, and with one of the two spies sent by Joshua to spy out the Land of Canaan, who was able to make himself invisible by magical means. Phinehas was still alive some three hundred years later when Jephthah took a vow to offer up to God the first thing coming out of his house if he was victorious in battle. Unfortunately, Jephthah's daughter came out of his house to greet her father first (Judg. 11:34).

Phinehas' reluctance to go to Jephthah and release him from this vow was partly responsible for her death.

Phinehas Ben Yair (2c. CE) Mishnaic sage. Phinehas was known as a saint who was very strict about giving the priestly and Levitical tithes before he would eat food. Once his donkey was stolen, but the thieves were unable to feed it because it would not eat their untithed food, and they had to turn it loose. The *Talmud* comments on this incident that, if God does not allow the animals of the righteous to commit an unintentional sin, how much more so does He protect the righteous themselves. Phinehas' care not to offend others was rewarded with special powers, and when he travelled to redeem Jewish captives, he was able to miraculously cross over rivers on dry ground. He formulated a ladder of holiness enumerating those qualities which lead one to be possessed by the Holy Spirit (ruach ha-kodesh).

phoenix *see* TREE OF KNOWLEDGE

phylacteries *see* TEFILLIN

pidyon ha-ben (Hebrew for 'redemption of the son') The ceremony of redeeming a FIRSTBORN son takes place after the child is thirty days old. A priest asks the father whether he would prefer to have his child or to keep the five silver coins necessary for its redemption. The father naturally agrees to pay the priest the redemption money. He makes two blessings and hands over the money. The priest pronounces the son redeemed and blesses him with the priestly blessing. A party is then held to celebrate the occasion. The father does not have to redeem his child if either parent comes from priestly or Levite stock. The firstborn must be the first child of his mother's womb, and therefore if he is preceded by a sister, or a miscarriage, or if he is born by section, he does not have a redemption ceremony. The origin of the redemption goes back to the priestly role of the firstborn in ancient times. Since that role was taken over by the Levitical priests, they redeem a firstborn from his residual priestly status. It is told of one great 18c. scholar, Elijah the Vilna Gaon, that he continued to go through the ceremony with every priest he met, since he was in doubt about their authenticity as priests.

pig (Hebrew 'chazir') The pig is an unclean animal prohibited by the Jewish DIETARY LAWS (Lev. 11:7; Deut. 14:8). Although it possesses one of the two signs of a KOSHER animal, the pig has come to exemplify non-kosher food *par excellence*. It conjures up an image of filth and was described as a mobile toilet. The very name was avoided, a pig sometimes being referred to as 'the other thing', and people were warned not to walk between two pigs. Calling a fellow human being a 'chazir' is a terrible insult indicating bestial behaviour. The pig is said by the *Talmud* to be the only animal which has cloven hooves but does not chew the cud. It thus represents the spirit of hypocrisy since it can put its feet forward and claim to be kosher, while on the inside it lacks the other necessary sign of a clean animal. Many Jews, even though they do not keep the dietary laws very strictly, regard eating pork or

157

bacon as a final break with the Jewish tradition. Nevertheless, a person should not say: 'I do not like pork'; he should say: 'I would like to eat pork, but what can I do since the torah forbids it.' Attempts to undermine Judaism often involved forcing Jews to eat pork. It is believed that eating pig meat blocks up the soul, generates animal lusts and prevents someone attaining holiness. Pigs are thought to have certain internal organs similar to human beings, so when disease spreads among pigs, Jews would declare a fast since this might portend an epidemic in the community. A merchant must not deal in pork, and the religious authorities forbid Jews to breed pigs in the Land of Israel, even if not for their own consumption, out of respect for the holiness of the land. The breeding of pigs by secularists in modern Israel causes offence to religious Jews, some of whom have tried to have it banned and the consumption of pork outlawed. In the days of the Messiah, pigs will chew the cud and their flesh will be allowed.

pikkuach nefesh (Hebrew for 'saving life') Where a danger to life exists, the laws of the torah may be broken in order to save a Jewish person from death, since one must not stand idly by when a neighbour's blood is being shed (Lev. 19:16). The term pikkuach nefesh literally means 'an opening for a life' and comes from the situation where a house has collapsed on SHABBAT and it is necessary to dig an opening in the rubble to rescue anyone trapped. One must continue digging until one reaches the nostrils of the survivors, to see if they are still breathing. The law of pikkuach nefesh is derived from the mitzvah of circumcision. For if the Sabbath may be broken by an operation on one organ of the human body, how much more so may it be broken for the sake of a whole human life. This idea is expressed in a different context as follows: it is better to put out the shabbat light, thus breaking the Sabbath, than to put out the light of God, i.e. a human life. One breaks shabbat so that the person whose life is saved can himself keep many Sabbaths, and this rule is held to apply by most authorities even if the person is critically ill and may not survive until the next week. There are three prohibitions, however, which may not be transgressed in order to save life or to cure a sick person. They are murder, idolatry and sexual immorality (i.e. incest and adultery). In cases of pikkuach nefesh speed is of the essence, and it is not necessary, or may even be forbidden, to seek rabbinic endorsement before acting where there is a clear case of an emergency.

pilgrimage (Hebrew 'aliyah le-regel') The three main festivals, pesach, shavuot and sukkot, were PILGRIM FESTIVALS in the period of the Temple. Indeed, they are still known as the shalosh regalim, the 'three foot-festivals'. JERUSALEM was full of pilgrims from all over the Land of Israel, and from many parts of the diaspora. The local Jewish population was forbidden to charge the visitors rent, and yet, according to Jewish tradition, nobody complained that they could not find a bed in Jerusalem overnight. The Temple courtyard was crowded, with people standing shoulder to shoulder during the festivals. When the moment came for the crowd of pilgrims to prostrate themselves, a miracle occurred: the courtyard expanded, and everyone had

Ceremonial dish of silver gilt showing the angel saving Isaac from the akedah sacrifice by his father Abraham. It was used in the **pidyon ha-ben** ceremony for the redeeming of a firstborn son.

Pilgrimage to Jerusalem in 1897 by followers of the Zionist Movement.

enough space to stretch themselves out on the ground. This was later interpreted to mean that people only feel confined when they are erect and proud, but when they humble themselves before God, there is always enough room. After the Second Temple was destroyed and the major Jewish population centres shifted outside the Holy Land, pilgrims continued to make their way to visit such holy sites as the Wailing Wall, the burial site of the Patriarchs in Hebron, and the tombs of biblical characters, such as RACHEL, and wonder-working rabbis, such as Meir. Under Kabbalistic influence many graves of saintly characters from the past became centres of pilgrimage, since it was believed that messages left there would be conveyed straight to God by the soul of the deceased. Mystic masters even used their intuitive insight to rediscover the forgotten graves of biblical and post-biblical figures. The tomb of Simeon Bar Yochai in Meron is a popular venue for pilgrims on LAG BA-OMER, the day of his death. Sepulchres of leaders (tzaddik) of the Chasidic Movement are also important pilgrimage centres. Nachman of Breslov instructed his Chasidim to come and spend rosh ha-shanah with him at his graveside in the Ukrainian town of Uman. *See also* TOMBSTONE.

pilgrim festivals (Hebrew 'shalosh regalim', meaning 'three foot-festivals') The three HARVEST FESTIVALS, PESACH, SHAVUOT and SUKKOT, were times of PILGRIM-AGE when Jews would flock to the Temple in Jerusalem (*see* CHERUB) in accordance with the biblical recommendation (Deut. 16:16). The pilgrims would sing Psalms as they went up to the Holy City. Since these are agricultural festivals associated with the various harvests in the Holy Land, the pilgrims brought the produce of the land as gifts to be offered to the Temple. At Passover time the number of pilgrims was particularly large, but even then there was always enough room to house what has been estimated as several million pilgrims.

pillar of cloud and of fire During the wanderings of the Israelites in the wilderness after the EXODUS, they were led by two miraculous guides, a pillar of cloud by day and a pillar of fire by night (Exod. 13:21–2). The cloud provided shelter for the people, and this is celebrated each year on the festival of SUKKOT, when Jews move out of their homes to live in makeshift booths. The cloud also protected the Israelites from the pursuing Egyptians (Exod. 14:24), from over-exposure to the heat of the sun and from rain, while the fire provided light in the darkness. When there was a valley or a hill in their path, the cloud would alter the terrain, raising or lowering the ground so they could travel on a smooth path. Its magical properties prevented their clothes from wearing out.

pilpul (Hebrew for 'peppery') A casuistic method of Rabbinic interpretation in which diverse subject matters are brought together and compared and new formulations achieved by analogy. Much of the Rabbinic tradition depends on the use of pilpul. Indeed, the TALMUD tells how, after the death of Moses, the Israelites forgot a large part of the tradition, and it was reconstructed by one of their leaders through his own intellect and the application of pilpul.

Members of the Sanhedrin had to have the ability to use pilpul to argue convincingly that reptiles were ritually pure animals, even though the torah declares them impure. Pilpul was regarded as a useful means of sharpening the minds of students in YESHIVAH academies, but its more extreme forms were criticized for introducing hair-splitting distinctions and for distracting students from the study of the sources themselves. Those sages who were masters of the tradition, known as 'Sinai', were generally preferred to those who were masters of pilpul, called 'uprooters of mountains'. The analytic ability of the latter could lead to fundamental mistakes if there was too much reliance on the sharpness of the intellect. Concentration on pilpul alone was dismissed as a waste of time, and JUDAH LOEW BEN BEZALEL said it was better to study carpentry. One of the greatest exponents of pilpul was the 16c. Polish sage Rabbi Jacob Pollak. It is told how once, before he gave a lecture in his yeshivah, his pupils cut out several pages of the *Talmud* text he used. Pollak did not notice the missing pages and carried on with his lecture, relating one topic with a very different one several pages later by means of pilpul.

piyyut (Hebrew for 'poem'; pl. piyyutim) Synagogue poems and hymns many of which were composed during the Middle Ages and incorporated into the LITURGY. Piyyutim often reflect historical events such as the Crusades, persecutions, martyrdom and the expulsion of Jews from districts or whole countries. Some poems also deal with ritual or purely spiritual matters. Different liturgies adopted piyyutim into their festival services, particularly those poems which have local relevance. This practice was opposed by a number of leading rabbis who thought it wrong to add extraneous material to the traditional prayer-book or machzor. Nevertheless, the recital of such poems and hymns has continued in many communities, despite the fact that few worshippers understand the subtle allusions and the intricate language of medieval Hebrew poetry.

Plagues, The Ten The punishments brought upon the Egyptians by God through Moses so that the Israelite slaves could go into the desert in the EXODUS and serve God (Exod. 7–11). The first plague, in which the waters of Egypt turned to blood, was mainly directed against the Nile, which the Egyptians worshipped as a deity and which had been used to drown new-born Hebrew babies. The plagues did not affect the Israelites. Thus, during the thick darkness of the ninth plague the Egyptians could neither see nor move about. The Israelites, however, not only had light in Goshen, where they lived, but were able to see when they went into Egyptian homes. Those Israelites who were unworthy to be redeemed from slavery, about four-fifths of the population, died while the Egyptians were in darkness, so that the latter should not know of their fate and rejoice. During the Passover seder a little wine is spilled from the cup of each participant during the recital of the Ten Plagues to remember that freedom was only acquired through the suffering of the Egyptians. The Passover HAGGADAH multiplies the number of plagues to show the terrifying power of God to punish those who refuse to obey His commands. *See also* LOCUSTS.

pogrom (Russian for 'destruction') Term used specifically of attacks on Jews or on the Jewish quarter of towns or villages (*see* GHETTO; PALE OF SETTLEMENT). The Czarist government encouraged pogroms to force SHTETL Jews to emigrate and to provide a scapegoat for a dissatisfied populace. The anti-Jewish feelings of ordinary Russians who took part in these attacks were based on economic resentment and were inspired by Christian anti-Semitism. The series of pogroms which led to the mass exodus of Russian Jews to the West began in 1881 in Kiev, after the assassination of Czar Alexander II and reached their peak in the Kishinev massacres in 1903. Jewish self-defence groups were set up by members of the BUND and by socialist Zionists in response to these attacks, and the pogroms led to the strengthening of aspirations of ZIONISM among Russian Jewry. Pogroms were an all too frequent part of Jewish experience in pre-Nazi Eastern Europe, and indeed, even after the Holocaust Jewish refugees returning to their homes were massacred by local Gentiles in the Polish town of Kielce in 1946.

Potiphar *see* JOSEPH

Potocki, Count Valentine *see* PROSELYTE

prayer Jewish LITURGY began to achieve its fixed shape in the centuries after the destruction of the Second Temple, although the PRAYER-BOOK only took on its classical form in the Middle Ages. Spontaneous prayers are found throughout the Hebrew Bible (tenakh), such as the emotive prayer of the barren HANNAH asking God for a child (I Sam. 1), which was taken as a model of prayer in Talmudic times. More formal prayers, like the singing of Psalms by the Levites, were associated with Temple SACRIFICE. In the Rabbinic period the AMIDAH came to be regarded as the centrepiece of the SHACHARIT, MINCHAH, MAARIV, MUSAF and NEILAH services. It is believed that angels carry men's prayers to heaven and that the righteous can more effectively intercede with God than ordinary mortals. The sole ultimate focus of prayer, however, must be God Himself. While it may be legitimate to ask 'angels of mercy' to act as agents of man, bringing his prayers before the Throne of Glory, or to request righteous individuals to pray for someone, it is never permitted to pray to the angels or to holy men themselves. A number of prayers, seemingly directed to angels, which found their way into the liturgy came close to infringing this prohibition, as did the reverence paid to the tzaddik in the CHASIDIC MOVEMENT. Various rabbis protested against these 'dangerous' practices. Ideally, prayers should be said with a MINYAN in synagogue using the Hebrew and ARAMAIC forms of prayer fixed by liturgical custom, but they can also be said privately in the home. In either case prayer has to be the 'worship of the heart' (*see* KAVVANAH) and not mere lip service. To emphasize the value and power of prayer, the *Talmud*, in a series of daring anthropomorphic images, depicts God Himself as praying, wrapped in a TALLIT and wearing TEFILLIN. *See also* ALEINU LE-SHABBEACH; AMEN; HAVDALAH; KADDISH; LAMP, SABBATH; MEMORIAL PRAYERS; MODEH ANI; NEILAH; SANDALFON; SWAYING IN PRAYER; YIGDAL.

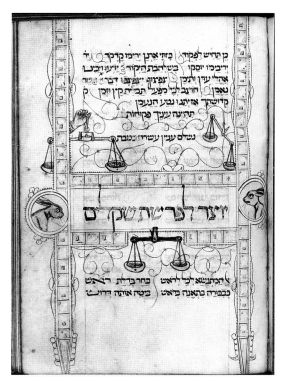

Page from a 14c. prayer-book containing a **piyyut** for the fast of the tenth of Tevet and for shabbat shekalim. The scales indicate that man's sins and good deeds are weighed up in heaven.

Memorial to the **pogrom** in Kishinev in 1903 (E.M. Lilien).

prayer-book (Hebrew 'siddur', meaning 'order') The Hebrew and Aramaic text of the daily prayer-book evolved slowly from the early LITURGY, which was fixed in the centuries after the destruction of the Second Temple. Considerable variation in forms of PRAYER and liturgical customs between communities led to the development of markedly different prayer-books and versions of the festival MACHZOR. The two most general types are those which follow the rites of the SEPHARDIM and those which follow the rites of the ASHKENAZIM, but there are also many varieties of these rites. Modern movements have produced their own prayer-books, with REFORM and Conservative communities introducing changes to the traditional liturgy and incorporating new prayers. The prayer-book is a mirror of popular Jewish experience. It reflects the suffering of the Jewish People down the ages, their understanding of God and their hopes for redemption with the coming of the Messiah. It is used not merely for public prayers in synagogue but for the many rituals of the home where prayers, GRACE AFTER MEALS and BENEDICTIONS are recited. *See also* MAOZ TZUR; PEREK SHIRAH; PIYYUT; SHARABI, SHALOM.

priest (Hebrew 'kohen') In Temple times priests officiated at the sacrificial offerings, in the determination of leprosy and in a number of ritual and social roles (*see* DAYYAN; SOTAH). They were supported by gifts and agricultural tithes. Today, priests have only a minor role in the ritual of the synagogue. They pronounce the PRIESTLY BLESSING, are called first for an ALIYAH to the torah and officiate at a PIDYON HA-BEN ceremony. They still have to preserve some of the restrictions affecting the Temple priesthood. Thus, a priest cannot marry a convert, a divorcee or even remarry his own divorced wife (*see* DIVORCE). He must not come into the defiling presence of a dead body (*see* TOMBSTONE), except in the case of close relatives, and must leave a building if someone dies there, since he is forbidden to be under the same roof as a corpse. In Jewish cemeteries there is a separate section for priests, so that members of their families do not have to come within four cubits of the other graves. People of priestly stock had the reputation of being quick-tempered, arrogant and energetic. In the Temple they used to compete in races to see who could get to the ALTAR first to claim the right to officiate. Modern surnames which are variants of the Hebrew word KOHEN (particularly the name Cohen) usually indicate that the bearer is of priestly descent. *See also* ANOINTING; HIGH PRIEST.

priestly blessing (Hebrew 'birkat kohanim') The three biblical verses with which a PRIEST blesses the people: 'The Lord bless you and keep you. The Lord shine His face upon you and be gracious unto you. The Lord lift His face to you and grant you peace' (Num. 6:24–6). The priest himself is not the actual source of the blessings. He only directs the BENEDIC-TION to the congregation, since it is God who asks him to put His name (*see* TETRAGRAMMATON) on the Children of Israel and He will bless them (Num. 6:27). The priestly blessing is pronounced in synagogue each day, each shabbat or on festivals, depending on local custom. Before going up to stand in front of the synagogue ARK, the priest removes his shoes and has

his hands washed (*see* ABLUTION) by one of the LEVITES. He chants the blessing word by word after the chazzan with the fingers of his hands spread out in groups of two, the thumbs being held together. There is a popular belief, supported by mystical texts, that anyone looking at the hands of the priest will be blinded by the light of God, which rests on his fingertips while he makes the blessing. To avoid this, priests cover their head and outstretched arms with a tallit during the blessing, and members of the congregation, who stand in front of them, look down or cover their own heads with a tallit. Some people even turn their backs, although this is disapproved of because it shows lack of respect for the priests and for the ritual. The priestly blessing is also used by parents to bless their children on Friday evenings, in the EXORCISM ritual, and by rabbis to bless the bride and groom under the chuppah and to bless boys and girls on their bar mitzvah and bat mitzvah. *See also* TOMBSTONE.

prophecy (Hebrew 'nevuah') The communication of a divine message to especially appointed prophets, inspired by the Holy Spirit (*see* RUACH HA-KODESH), who were charged with the task of passing it on to others. The BIBLE is the record of prophetic teachings of lasting value, but there were many more transient prophetic messages which were not written down. Moses was the greatest of the Hebrew prophets, to whom God spoke 'mouth to mouth' (Num. 12:8), while He appeared to other prophets in DREAMS or visions: the latter saw God through a clouded glass, and Moses saw Him through a clear glass. Each prophet expressed his message in a different personal style. Prophecy came to an end with the prophet Malachi, and from the time of the destruction of the First Temple prophecy is only to be found in the utterances of fools and children. The Jewish sage (*see* CHAKHAM), however, has taken over the prophet's mantle and is, indeed, considered greater than the prophet. According to the medieval theologian JUDAH HALEVI, the whole People of Israel is elevated above all other peoples by possessing the gift of prophecy, although there have been great individual Gentiles in the past, like Balaam who was ranked as a prophet on a par with Moses. There were altogether forty-eight prophets and seven prophetesses in the Hebrew scriptures, whose teachings were only elaborations of Mosaic prophecy since their prophetic messages were proclaimed together with the Mosaic revelation at Mount Sinai. *See also* BAT KOL; HAFTARAH; SANDALFON.

proselyte (Hebrew 'ger') A convert to the Jewish faith is known as a ger tzedek, or 'righteous stranger', and conversion involves circumcision for a man and bathing in a mikveh for both sexes in the presence of three judges (dayyan) of a bet din. Proselytes are considered to be born anew, children of Abraham and Sarah who have come under the 'wings of the Divine Presence' (shekhinah). All their sins are forgiven them. They take on a new identity and a new name, usually Ruth or Sarah for a woman and Abraham for a man, and it is forbidden to remind them of their previous life. The would-be convert should be 'discouraged with the left hand while the right hand draws him near'. Thus, conversion should be refused on the first three occasions, but then the proselyte should be accepted. In practice, however, because many proselytes wish to convert in order to marry Jews, they may have to wait for several years before conversion. Priests cannot marry proselyte women, and proselytes will not be accepted in the age of the Messiah. In Christian lands in the Middle Ages Jews were forbidden to accept proselytes, although there are records of individual Christian laymen and clergy converting, including an Italian bishop in the 11c. Maimonides wrote a letter to one such proselyte allowing him to say the words 'God of our fathers' in the prayers even though his own ancestors had not been Jews. Some of these Christian proselytes fled to Islamic countries to escape persecution, while others suffered martyrdom.

In the 18c. a Polish aristocrat, Count Valentine Potocki, was taught about Judaism by an old Jew he met in Paris and subsequently converted from Catholicism in Amsterdam. Some time after he returned to Poland, Potocki was reported to the Christian authorities by a Jewish tailor, whose son he had insulted. Although he was tortured, he refused to recant the faith of Israel and was burned at the stake in Vilna on the second day of shavuot 1749. Before he died, he cursed the informer and his descendants, and visitors to the shtetl near Vilna where the tailor had lived reported as late as 1930 that members of his family were all lame, deaf or dumb. While most of the Jewish community remained indoors, one Jew, who had shaved off his beard and dressed himself as a Christian, managed to collect some of Potocki's ashes by bribing an official, and they were buried in the Jewish cemetery in Vilna. A large tree which looked like a man, with its branches forming hands and feet, grew beside his grave, and the last resting place of this martyred proselyte became a centre of pilgrimage. The Jewish community of Vilna recited kaddish for Potocki, who had adopted the Hebrew name of Abraham Ben Abraham. They were unsuccessful, however, in their efforts to protect his grave from Polish vandals who cut off the branches of the tree and destroyed the building with its Hebrew inscription which was subsequently erected on the spot.

prosbul see HILLEL; SHEMITTAH

prost see YICHUS

Proverbs, Book of (Hebrew 'mishle') One of the Wisdom books of the Bible, written by Solomon in his middle age. The wisdom which is praised in the book refers to the torah, through which God created the world (Prov. 3:19). The torah is indeed the blueprint of the Creation. The last twenty-two verses of the book are about the woman of valour, eshet chayil, who labours long hours in caring for her family and household. This section praising the ideal woman, inspired by NAOMI, is sung by the father and children every Friday night in the Jewish home in appreciation of their wife and mother and also in praise of the shekhinah, the feminine aspect of God. It is also recited at the funeral of a woman and at a girl's bat mitzvah ceremony.

Psalms, Book of (Hebrew 'tehillim') Biblical book of 150 psalms composed by David, with additions from nine other authors, which were sung by the

Page from a 15c. German illuminated **prayer-book** showing a group of Jewish musicians.

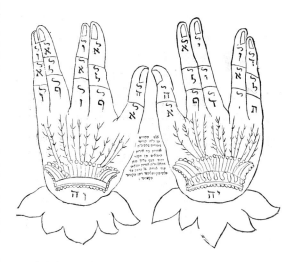

Hands held together in the form of the **priestly blessing** showing signs of the Kabbalah, two letters of the tetragrammaton on each hand (18c.).

Levites in the Temple. David wrote his psalms, inspired by the Holy Spirit (ruach ha-kodesh), when the harp which hung over his bed was played at midnight by a north wind. The strings of this harp came from the ram offered as a sacrifice to God by Abraham at the akedah. David asked God to consider those who read the Psalms as meritorious as those who studied the torah itself. The Book of Psalms is the most widely used biblical book in the liturgy, and people are encouraged to recite psalms when faced by sickness, hardship or some crisis in life. A dream about the Book of Psalms is a sign that one is growing in piety. There are ten different musical types of psalm, and according to the Chasidic master Rabbi Nachman of Breslov, each type is effective in nullifying an aspect of the power of evil. Nachman therefore recommended the recital of a selection of ten psalms, one from each type, on the day after a nocturnal emission as a tikkun to rectify the loss of semen to the sitra achra. The recital of these ten psalms also has the effect of developing a chaste character. *See also* HALLEL; PRAYER.

purim (Hebrew, from the Persian for 'casting of lots') A minor festival on the fourteenth of ADAR celebrating the story of the Book of ESTHER, which is read from a hand-written scroll (*see* MEGILLAH). A festive meal is eaten in the late afternoon to celebrate the victory of the Jews over their Persian enemies, and intoxicating beverages are drunk (*see* ADE-LO-YADA). On purim charity must be given to at least two poor people and indeed to any pauper who asks for a donation. It is also mandatory to send food gifts to at least one friend (mishloach manot, or in Yiddish, shlach monos). Favourite purim foods include three-cornered buns known as hamantaschen which are taken to represent Haman's ears. The festival takes its name from the lot (pur) cast by HAMAN to determine the best time to attack the Jews, although as it turned out this was an unlucky time for him and his followers. The message behind the name is that God, and not fate, determines what will happen. To show that things are not what they seem and that God works in mysterious ways, it is customary to wear fancy dress on purim and to act out parodies of established authority (*see* PURIM SHPIEL). This is carried even to the point of lampooning Jewish teaching. Yeshivah students elect one of their number to be the purim rabbi who makes fun of the mannerisms of the yeshivah head. Purim is very much a folk festival, held in such high regard that it is said that yom kippur, the holiest day of the Jewish year, is modelled on purim (a play on the Hebrew 'yom kippurim' which can mean 'a day like purim'). There is a paradoxical teaching that in the Messianic age all festivals will be abolished except for purim, and it is even said that the light of the divine wisdom shines more brightly on purim than on shabbat. Many Jewish communities and families celebrate their own special purim which commemorates escape from some past persecution or danger.

purim shpiel (Yiddish for 'purim play') On the festival of PURIM it is customary for children, and sometimes adults as well, to dress up in fancy dress. Originally these 'purim shpielers' would put on amateur dramatics for the community, perhaps a parody

version of the ESTHER story, or would go around from house to house and perform a short sketch, which might be rewarded by the householder with a donation to charity and some refreshment for the revellers. In modern times, traditional purim shpiels continue to be in vogue, and fancy-dress parties for children are also organized. The usual proprieties of dress are relaxed for the duration of the festival, and people are allowed to dress up as members of the opposite sex.

Rabad *see* ABRAHAM BEN DAVID OF POSQUIERES

Rabbah Bar Bar Chana (3c. CE) Babylonian Talmudic sage. Rabbah is the source of a number of bizarre and fabulous traveller's tales recorded in the *Talmud*. He once passed the place where Korah and his followers were swallowed up by the earth, and he heard voices saying 'Moses is true and his torah is true, and we are liars.' Rabbah saw the bodies of the dead Israelites who came out from Egypt lying in the desert. It was possible for a camel and its rider holding an upright spear to pass under their bent legs. He came across a gigantic fish, which was so big that the sailors thought they had arrived at an island and started cooking a meal on its back when the heat made it turn over. Another fish of enormous dimensions died and was washed up on the sea-shore. In the process it destroyed sixty harbour towns, and one eye of the fish supplied three hundred jars of oil. Yet another fish of this type had two fins which were set so far apart that it took a ship three days to sail from one fin to the other while the fish itself was swimming in the opposite direction.

Rabbah Bar Nachmani (3c.–4c. CE) Babylonian Talmudic sage. Rabbah was a popular teacher who always began his lectures with a joke. He was exiled by the Babylonian authorities after they received complaints that his teaching distracted people from work and thus diminished the state taxes. A strange legend is told of how Rabbah died. An argument was going on in the Academy on High between God and the souls of the dead sages. The sages declared that a certain case of leprous defilement was impure while God declared it pure. They needed someone who was an expert in the matter to come and adjudicate. Since Rabbah was the greatest living authority on leprosy, he was summoned to the Heavenly Academy, and as he died he called out: 'Pure, pure.' The expression 'called to the Heavenly Academy' was subsequently used euphemistically for the death of a sage.

rabbi (Hebrew for 'my master') Ordained scholar who is traditionally licensed to decide on questions of Jewish ritual, usually associated with the DIETARY LAWS. This ordination is known as SEMIKHAH. Rabbis are also known as rav ('master') or CHAKHAM ('sage'). Since it is forbidden to take payment for teaching or issuing rulings about HALAKHAH, rabbis in the past were not paid for their activities and had to support themselves. Today, they are salaried synagogue officials, with wide preaching and pastoral duties. Officially, they are not paid for their religious role, however, but are financially compensated for not being able to work in another profession because of their rabbinic commitments. Women have been ordained as rabbis by REFORM and CONSERVATIVE seminaries, but ORTHODOX JUDAISM has strongly opposed the ordination of women. *See also* MAGGID.

Rachel Favourite wife of JACOB and one of the MATRIARCHS. Rachel's father, LABAN, would not allow her to marry Jacob before her older sister Leah. So he tricked his son-in-law by substituting Leah for Rachel. In order for the ruse to work, Rachel had to co-operate, and she helped her sister by telling her how to convince Jacob that she was really Rachel. She did this, despite wanting to marry Jacob herself, so as not to embarrass her sister. Rachel married Jacob after Leah. While giving birth to her second son, Benjamin, Rachel died and was buried near Bethlehem. Her tomb became a site of pilgrimage particularly popular with barren women, since Rachel herself had been barren for some time before giving birth to her first son, Joseph. Her grave was also strategically placed so that the Judaeans going into exile to Babylonia would pass by, and in heaven she asked God to bring them back. The prophet Jeremiah conveyed a message to Rachel, who was weeping for her children and refusing to be comforted. 'Thus says the Lord: Refrain your voice from weeping and your eyes from tears ... They shall come back from the land of the enemy ... Your children shall return to their own border' (Jer. 31:15–17).

Rahab *see* HOSPITALITY; JEREMIAH; JOSHUA

rain (Hebrew 'geshem') Rain plays a major role in Judaism, particularly in the liturgy, reflecting the agricultural base of religion in the Holy Land. If the rains were delayed, the community would hold a public fast and recite penitential prayers, since shortage of rain was regarded as punishment for sins such as theft and the non-payment of money set aside for charity. In the past saintly men who were able to influence the rainfall, like Choni Ha-Meaggel, were resorted to when drought threatened (*see* ABBA). The column of smoke from the altar at the end of the festival of sukkot was regarded as an indicator of the rains to come. If the column drifted northwards, the poor were happy because the coming year would have a heavy rainfall and produce would have to be sold quickly and cheaply to prevent it rotting. If it drifted southwards, the landowners were happy because there would be little rain and produce could be stored and sold for higher profits. If it drifted westward or eastward, then everyone was either sad because it meant drought or happy because it meant a reasonable season. The best nights for rain were Wednesday and Friday nights when everyone was indoors. *See also* MUSAF.

rainbow The sign of God's covenant with the descendants of Noah that He would never again destroy the world by flood (Gen. 9:11–14). The rainbow is a reflection of the divine glory and should therefore not be looked at for any length of time. When it is

17c. Syrian wine jug for **purim**.

*A Jewish **Rabbi*** by Rembrandt.

observed, however, a benediction is said praising God for remembering His covenant and being faithful to it. Since the merits of outstandingly righteous people protect their generation from the threat of destruction, it is unnecessary for a rainbow to appear in their lifetime. Indeed, the occurrence of a rainbow indicates that there are no such righteous persons in the world.

Rambam see MAIMONIDES, MOSES

Ramban see NACHMANIDES, MOSES

Raphael Archangel who specializes in healing, as his name ('God is healing') indicates. References to Raphael are included on amulets used for healing and in preventing sickness. His position is behind the Throne of Glory and at the back of man. Raphael is one of the four Angels of the Divine Presence, the others being GABRIEL, MICHAEL and URIEL. On his chest he has a tablet engraved with God's name; his symbol is a serpent, and he journeys on the wings of the wind. When God was about to create Adam and some angels opposed this, Raphael supported the idea. It was Raphael who visited Abraham to heal him after his circumcision.

Rashba see ADRET, SOLOMON

Rashi (1040–1105) Acronym of Rabbi Solomon (Ben) Isaac, a French scholar of Davidic descent, who wrote standard commentaries on major Jewish texts. Rashi's father refused to sell a jewel he owned as a decoration for a statue of the Madonna. Although the local Christians were willing to pay a great price for it, he preferred to throw it away rather than see it become part of idolatrous worship. As a reward he was granted a son of the calibre of Rashi, who became a living spiritual 'jewel'. One day when Rashi's mother was pregnant with him, she was almost run down by a Crusader horseman, but a niche opened up miraculously in a nearby wall and she was able to shelter there. This wall later became a well-known landmark. Rashi was the founder of a whole school of textual exegesis in Northern France, and his descendants continued his methods. He is reported to have spent the last years of his life in the town of Worms. There the small 'Rashi Synagogue' survived until its destruction during the Nazi era and after the war was rebuilt by the German government. Rashi's commentaries on most of the Bible and much of the Babylonian *Talmud* made these texts available to ordinary laymen, and his Bible commentary in particular was thought to be inspired. Indeed, Rashi himself occasionally makes the claim that an interpretation of his came neither from his teachers nor from Jewish tradition but was revealed to him from heaven. His special talent lay in the ability to express an exegetical point in just a few words of commentary, working homiletical comments into his literal and grammatical explanations. He did not refrain, however, from adding sometimes: 'I do not know what this means.' Rashi had three daughters, scholars in their own right, who helped their father with his writings. At least one of his daughters was reputed to have worn tefillin when she recited the morning prayers, indicating a high level of piety. See also DEW.

Rav (3c. CE) Babylonian Talmudic sage whose real name was Abba or Abba the Tall. Rav studied with Judah Ha-Nasi in Palestine and was regarded as having the same authority as a Mishnaic sage although he belonged to the post-Mishnaic era. He explained the commandments not as rites of a quasi-magical nature but as means of refining man in obedience to God. What difference does it make to God, for instance, exactly how an animal is slaughtered (shechitah). Although he was inclined to mysticism, he encouraged a positive attitude to the enjoyment of this world, saying that man will have to give an account after death for all those pleasures he denied himself in this world. He defined a true child of Abraham as someone who has pity on his fellow, since a cruel person shows himself not to have inherited the compassion of the first Patriarch. Rav was instrumental in spreading Rabbinic studies in Babylonia. The academy at Sura which he founded lasted for eight hundred years and at one time had a student enrolment of more than a thousand. A number of Rav's liturgical compositions found their way into the prayer-book, such as the aleinu said at the end of every service and the supplication recited on the shabbat before the NEW MOON. As he was a man of saintly character, his grave became a place of pilgrimage, and its dust was reputed to have a magical healing power. See also SAMUEL, MAR.

Rava (3c.–4c. CE) Babylonian Talmudic sage. Rava advocated logical analysis of the subject matter as the best method of torah study and engaged in many disputes with his colleague, Abaye. These disputes became a paradigm of Talmudic argumentation, and the halakhah was decided in Rava's favour in all but six of the cases. He claimed that torah study was superior to prayer because prayer was concerned with this-worldly matters while torah was connected with man's eternal life. A person involved in torah study was thus even greater than the High Priest, who alone was allowed to enter the Holy of Holies in the Temple ritual. Despite his positive attitude to the logical study of texts, Rava was a pietist who recognized that God desires people's hearts to be directed toward Him. He sometimes took a very strict approach to ritual, as well. Thus, for instance, he fasted for two days during yom kippur instead of the customary one day. Rava had some influence with the Persian court, being friendly with the mother of the Persian king, Shapur II, and encouraging her interest in Judaism. He used his considerable wealth to bribe Persian court officials so that Judaism was allowed to flourish without too much interference. It is said of Rava that he created an artificial man (golem) through mystical techniques.

Raziel Angel who reveals heavenly secrets and knowledge of the future to man, as indicated by his name which means 'secrets of God'. Raziel conveyed a book of secret magic to Adam and another book to Noah. When he wishes to inform man about some future event, he instructs Elijah who comes down to earth to communicate with humans. The books of Raziel's teachings, originally engraved on sapphire, are thought to have a special sanctity, so that keeping them in the house protects the home from fire and calamity. *Sefer Raziel*, the book of secrets revealed to Adam, contains remedies for ailments and speculations on mystical subjects such as the *Shiur Komah*. The book of secrets revealed to Noah, *Sefer Ha-Razin*, contains information about charms, segullot and amulets, as well as descriptions of the seven heavens through which the maaseh merkavah mystic makes his ascent. Raziel is sometimes identified with other angels such as Metatron or Uriel.

Rebecca Sister of LABAN, wife of ISAAC and one of the MATRIARCHS. Rebecca was chosen at the age of three as the future spouse of Isaac because of her kindness. She offered water to Eliezer, Abraham's servant, and to his camels when he came to find a wife for his master's son. Eliezer saw the water of the well rising to meet her, indicating that she was possessed of special holiness. After her marriage she lived in the tent of her late mother-in-law, Sarah, and the tent was once again blessed with a cloud of glory which hovered overhead. Miraculous shabbat candles, whose light lasted from one Friday evening to the next, burnt for her as they had for Sarah. Rebecca had a difficult pregnancy with the twins she was carrying. Every time she passed a house of idolatry Esau kicked and tried to get out, and every time she passed an academy of torah study Jacob did the same. In later life Jacob was her favourite child, and she helped him win his father's blessing which should have gone to his older brother (Gen. 27). She was buried in the Cave of MACHPELAH.

rebellious son (Hebrew 'ben sorer umoreh') A son who rebelled against his parents, living a depraved and self-indulgent life, could be brought before the city elders and stoned to death (Deut. 21:18–21). This law was never actually implemented because it applied only to the first three months after the bar mitzvah of a son and demanded that his parents act completely in unison. The boy also had to indulge himself in enormous quantities of meat and wine in order to be found guilty. Its purpose, however, was to warn the community of the dangers of allowing a child to develop in a totally undisciplined way. If a child like the rebellious son were ever to exist, he would deserve to die since he would simply become a gangster in later life. It would, as it were, be better for him to die innocent than to die guilty.

Reconstructionism An offshoot of CONSERVATIVE JUDAISM in North America which was founded by Mordecai Kaplan in 1922. Reconstructionism promotes a non-supernaturalist religion based on Judaism as an evolving civilization, with a major concern for social justice but no doctrine of transcendent revelation, no belief in Jews as the Chosen People, or in the Messiah. Kaplan expressed his ideas in his main work, *Judaism as a Civilization* (1934), where Judaism is viewed as the aggregate of the literature, folk-ways, history, ethics and ideals of the Jewish People. Zionism and the State of Israel came to play major roles in Reconstructionist thought. Despite the radical nature of Reconstructionism and its use of a separate prayer-book, it retained affiliation with the Conservative Movement for a long time, only starting its own rabbinical seminary in 1967. Kaplan wished to reconstruct Judaism for modern man, combining religious

Angelic names, magen david stars and mystical signs for use in amulets, from the *Book of* **Raziel**

Rebecca and Eliezer at the well (Paolo Veronese).

and non-religious aspects of Jewish life. Reconstructionism does not have a large following, but because it appeals to intellectuals, its influence is disproportionate to its numerical strength.

red heifer (Hebrew 'parah adumah') Red cow, having at most one hair of another colour, which was burnt and its ashes, mixed with water, used for ritual purification. The red heifer was regarded as a rite having no rational explanation, whose real meaning will only be revealed in the Messianic age. One of its paradoxical features was that, although it purified those with a high degree of impurity, it also caused minor impurity to the priests involved in its preparation. The first red heifer was burnt in the time of Moses, and some of its ashes were mingled with the other eight cows which were prepared, up to the destruction of the Second Temple. In future times the Messiah will supervise the burning of the tenth red heifer, or according to another view, God Himself will purify the People of Israel. *See also* OLIVES, MOUNT OF.

Red Sea, crossing of (Hebrew 'keriyat yam suf', meaning 'crossing of the Reed Sea') When the Israelites were fleeing from the Egyptian army during the EXODUS they were saved by being able to cross a sea of reeds, which mistakenly came to be identified as the Red Sea. The waters of the sea miraculously receded leaving dry land, and NACHSHON led them across it. After the last Israelite had emerged on the other side, the waters returned, drowning the Egyptians who followed them; only PHARAOH was saved. The angels were prevented from singing a song of victory in heaven by God, who silenced them since it was not appropriate to sing when His creatures were drowning (*see* HALLEL). The Israelites, however, were able to see the dead Egyptians washed up on the shore and to convince themselves that their pursuers were a threat no more. They sang a great hymn to the victorious power of God (Exod. 15). *See also* TETRAGRAMMATON; URIEL; ZEKHUT AVOT.

Reform Judaism Modernist movement which arose after the 18c. Enlightenment made European culture available to Jews. The movement began with a new type of synagogue, known as a 'temple', whose amended liturgy sought to appeal to Jews alienated from traditional Judaism. The reformers justified their innovations on traditional grounds, although they also took the church service as a model for their vernacular prayers and sermons, choirs, organs and ultimately mixed seating. A number of doctrines were rejected as antiquated, e.g. belief in a personal Messiah, the Resurrection of the Dead, the return to the Holy Land, the rebuilding of the Temple and the eventual reintroduction of sacrifices. They also rejected the authority of the oral torah. At the German Rabbinical Conferences held in the 1840s, there was a split among the university-educated Reform rabbis between a minority who wanted radical reform and the more traditional majority. The former wished to dispense with circumcision and dietary laws and to move the Sabbath from Saturday to Sunday. While these extreme measures met with only limited approval, Reform practice has diverged from ORTHODOX JUDA-

ISM on a number of major issues, a recent example being the ordination of women as rabbis. Orthodoxy does not recognize the authority of Reform rabbis and refuses to accept proselytes converted by them as Jews. Indeed, there are cases where Orthodox rabbis do not recognize Reform marriages as valid. They argue that where the clergy and all the guests dined on non-kosher food, there were no religiously reliable witnesses present. Those married in such ceremonies, therefore, do not need a religious divorce (*see* GET) before remarrying (*see* MAMZER). Since the Holocaust, Reform Judaism has become more supportive of Zionism and has also taken a renewed interest in ritual. The main centre of Reform today is the USA, while in the State of Israel it has no official existence, since only Orthodox rabbis are recognized there as religious functionaries.

repentance (Hebrew 'teshuvah', meaning 'returning') Since SIN involves straying from God, repentance is literally 'returning' to Him, as expressed by the prophets: 'Return, O Israel, to the Lord your God' (Hosea 14:2). Repentance was created before the world, and the gates of repentance are always open. If, however, one sins with the intention of repenting afterwards, then such repentance will not win divine FORGIVENESS. One should repent the day before one dies, and the prayers for a dying person include a confession of sins (*see* ASHAMNU). Since, however, one does not actually know the day of one's death, one should repent every day. This is particularly true of the month of Elul and of the Ten Days of Penitence, which are periods devoted to repentance culminating in yom kippur. For true repentance to take place, the sinner must resist the same temptation in a similar situation, and if he repents because of his love of God, his sins are turned into merits. King David, who was rebuked by the prophet Nathan for his sin with Bathsheba, was regarded as a model for penitents, and the story of Jonah, where the Gentile inhabitants of Nineveh were forgiven after they repented, is read on yom kippur as an example to the community. Under Kabbalistic influence many ascetic practices were introduced into the process of penitence, including rolling in the snow and prolonged fasting, in order to prepare humanity for the coming of the Messiah through personal and communal rectification (tikkun). *See also* ATONEMENT; LASHON HA-RA.

resh galuta *see* EXILARCH

Resh Lakish *see* SIMEON BEN LAKISH

responsa (Hebrew 'she-elot u-teshuvot', meaning 'questions and answers') Collections of replies to specific questions addressed to rabbinic authorities which became a major source of HALAKHAH. These responsa began after the editing of the Babylonian *Talmud* when the geonic sages of Babylonia (*see* GAON) received written requests for explanations of obscure passages in the *Talmud* and for rulings on matters of practical import. Since that time there have been thousands of such responsa collections, sometimes published by the authors themselves, sometimes by pupils who have gathered the scattered replies of their teachers from their many correspondents. Responsa deal mostly with matters of ritual and Jewish law, in the form of simple statements in the early responsa or long, learned disquisitions in later ones. Every subject of Jewish life is dealt with, including modern scientific developments like transplants and transsexual surgery. There are also references to matters of theology, historical movements, Kabbalah and religious controversy. One collection of responsa, entitled *Responsa From Heaven* by JACOB OF MARGEVE, consists of replies which came in dreams to questions posed by means of mystical techniques.

Resurrection of the Dead (Hebrew 'techiyyat ha-metim') In the age of the MESSIAH the dead will rise from their graves and come back to life to be judged on the DAY OF JUDGMENT by God (*see* ESCHATOLOGY). The resurrection will be brought about by Elijah who will blow the great shofar on the Mount of OLIVES summoning the dead to arise. DEW, made of the light which was present at the Creation but has been hidden away ever since, will be used by God as the revivifying agent. Even those whose bodies have decomposed will be reconstructed from the LUZ bone in their spine, which is indestructible. The resurrection will take place in the land of Israel after the INGATHERING OF THE EXILES from the CEMETERIES of the diaspora (*see* BURIAL). Maimonides included the belief in resurrection as one of his Thirteen ARTICLES OF FAITH, and those who deny the Resurrection of the Dead will not come back to life nor will they have a portion in OLAM HABA. The central prayer of every liturgy, the amidah, contains a benediction which begins 'You are faithful to revive the dead'. In a morning prayer said on awakening, the resurrection is compared to the return of the soul to the dead and unconscious body after sleep (*see* NESHAMAH YETERAH). The state of the post-resurrection world is a kind of ultimate Sabbath, of which the weekly shabbat is merely a reflection. Reform Judaism rejected the belief in the Resurrection of the Dead.

Reuveni, David (15c.–16c.) Messianic pretender. Reuveni claimed to be a prince from an independent Jewish kingdom in Arabia near the River Sambatyon. He said that he came from the tribe of Reuben, one of the Ten Lost Tribes, hence his surname. His real origin is unknown, but it is assumed that he was indeed from Arabia or Ethiopia. During his extensive travels, he disseminated his Messianic propaganda, parading with a flag and attendants as befitted someone who had been sent on a mission by his brother, the king. Reuveni managed to win some support from rich and influential Jews. He arrived in Rome in 1524, riding on a white horse, and had an audience with the Pope, suggesting a pact between his Jewish kingdom and Christendom against the Moslems. The Pope gave him a letter of introduction to the King of Portugal, where his presence led to expectations among the crypto-Jews that the Messiah was about to usher in the period of redemption. At least one Marrano, Solomon MOLCHO, was influenced by Reuveni's appearance to adopt Judaism openly. The excitement he caused was unacceptable to the Portuguese authorities, and he was arrested for a short time. He was imprisoned once again in Italy, before being transported to Spain where he died. Reuveni left a

The crossing of the **Red Sea**, from a 4c. CE Roman sarcophagus.

Interior of a Cologne synagogue affiliated with **Reform Judaism** (E. Zwirner).

A depiction of the **Resurrection of the Dead** by the anthropomorphic hand of God in Ezekiel's vision of the valley of the dry bones (3c. CE, Dura Europos).

diary of his travels, and it seems that he passed himself off as a descendant of Mohammed while journeying through Moslem lands. He is described by eyewitnesses as small, dark-skinned and thin from much fasting and ascetic practices.

righteous Gentiles (Hebrew 'chasidei umot ha-olam') A GENTILE who keeps the NOACHIDE LAWS, believing that God has commanded them in the torah, is considered a righteous, or pious, Gentile who has a portion in the World to Come (olam haba) at the time of the Messiah. In each generation there are thirty righteous Gentiles through whose merit all non-Jews exist, since righteousness atones for Gentiles, just as sacrifice used to atone for Israel in Temple times. There is an Avenue of Righteous Gentiles at the Yad Vashem Centre, in Jerusalem, where trees are planted in honour of those non-Jews who risked their lives to save Jews from Nazi genocide during the Holocaust.

Righteous Men, The Thirty-Six *see* LAMED VAVNIK; SHEKHINAH; TZADDIK

rosh chodesh *see* CALENDAR; NEW MOON

rosh ha-shanah (Hebrew for 'head of the year', i.e. the New Year festival) The Jewish year begins on the first of TISHRI, and the first and second of Tishri are celebrated as the New Year festival. This is the date on which God created Adam, the first man. Rosh ha-shanah, also called the Day of Judgment, initiates a time of judgment for mankind, ending on HOSHANA RABBA, when God the heavenly king sits on His throne and determines the destiny of each individual in the year ahead. Three books are open in heaven, one for the truly righteous, one for the truly wicked and one for those who fall into neither category. The prayers and repentance characteristic of the TEN DAYS OF PENITENCE, which begin with rosh ha-shanah, are meant to ensure that one's name is included in the book of the righteous who will survive the year and not be punished for their sins. Even the dead pray for mercy for the living. It is customary for Jews to greet one another with the words: 'May you be written down for a good year.' In order to show trust in God's compassion, Jews dress in their best for the festival and celebrate it in joy. White, signifying purity, is the dominant colour in the synagogue, the chazzan and rabbi wearing a white KITEL. The shofar is blown (Lev. 23:24) to awaken sinners to repentance and also to confuse Satan, who will therefore be unable to act in his role as accuser of Israel. The special foods eaten on the festival are chosen because of their positive symbolism and are harbingers of good luck for the coming year (*see* BREAD; HONEY). The head of an animal or fish is eaten, so that the person concerned will be a 'head' and not a 'tail' in the coming year. On the afternoon of the first day of rosh ha-shanah, a ceremony of casting away sins (*see* TASHLIKH) takes place beside a stream.

rosh yeshivah *see* YESHIVAH

ruach ha-kodesh (Hebrew for 'the Holy Spirit') The spirit of God, representing His activity in the mundane world, but also occasionally used as a synonym for God Himself. Ruach ha-kodesh guided the Patriarchs, inspired the prophets (*see* PROPHECY) and the authors of the biblical books and continues to guide the whole People of Israel. The power of ruach ha-kodesh can be passed on from master to disciple as happened to Elijah and Elisha (II Kings 2:9–10). Inspiration can come to people through ecstatic rituals like those of the WATER DRAWING FESTIVITIES where it was said that ruach ha-kodesh was drawn up with the water. The Kabbalah prescribed methods for attaining the Holy Spirit, and the medieval mystic and halakhic authority, Abraham Ben David of Posquières, claimed that ruach ha-kodesh had appeared in his academy. Followers of the Chasidic Movement revered their leaders (tzaddik), claiming they possessed the Holy Spirit and the SHEKHINAH spoke out of their mouths. Chaim of Volozhin objected to these claims and maintained that even to worship ruach ha-kodesh in a man is idolatry. It was believed that a person would glow when ruach ha-kodesh rested on him. In the time of the Messiah all people, Jews and Gentiles alike, will be filled with the Holy Spirit (Joel 3). *See also* LUZZATTO, MOSES CHAIM.

Ruth Moabite heroine of the biblical book of Ruth and ancestress of King David. Ruth, who was a daughter of the king of Moab, married an Israelite living with his family in Moab. When her husband died, her mother-in-law NAOMI encouraged her to return home. Ruth, however, refused to leave the aged Naomi, promising to go with her and to accept her people and her God (Ruth 1:16). Naomi then instructed her in the tenets and practices of Judaism, and Ruth became a righteous convert (*see* PROSELYTE). After living for a while in great poverty in Bethlehem, during which time Ruth supported her mother-in-law by gleaning after the reapers at harvest time (*see* LEKET, SHIKHCHAH, PEAH), she eventually married Boaz, a relative of her late husband. Ruth was forty years old when she married Boaz, while he was eighty at the time and his first wife had only recently died. Although Ruth was physically unable to have children, God performed a miracle for her and she conceived on her wedding night. Boaz died the day after the wedding, while Ruth survived until the reign of her great-great-grandson Solomon. *See also* MEGILLAH.

Saadiah Gaon (882–942) Philosopher and halakhic authority. Saadiah was born in Egypt and moved to Babylonia to become the gaon of the academy at Sura. He was active in the disputes between Babylonian and Palestinian Jewry over the calendar, wrote polemical works against the teachings of the Karaites and engaged in a bitter personal vendetta with the Babylonian Exilarch David Ben Zakkai. The latter excommunicated (cherem) Saadiah and deposed him from his position, only to find that Saadiah in turn had excommunicated him and appointed another exilarch in his place. Eventually, an uneasy peace was achieved, and Saadiah actually adopted the exilarch's grandson after he became an orphan and brought him up in his own home. Saadiah wrote the first major work of Jewish philosophy in the Middle Ages, the *Book of Beliefs and Opinions* in Arabic. He confronted the problems posed by reason for Judaism as a revealed religion and posited two paths to truth to resolve them. In so doing he criticized Christian Trinitarianism, the belief in the transmigration of souls and Islamic teachings. Saadiah was a controversial figure who was denigrated by his opponents as a man from an ignorant background or descended from converts. Yet the later Kabbalistic tradition claimed him as a mystic, and works on Kabbalah were ascribed to him. On one occasion he jokingly asked a tailor how many stitches he had sewn that day. The tailor replied by asking how many words there were in the Bible, and Saadiah had to reply that he did not know. That night in a dream an angel came and revealed the number to him, so he composed a poem on the letters and words of the Bible.

Sabbath *see* SHABBAT

sacrifice (Hebrew 'korban') The sacrificial cult of the biblical period, administered by the priests and by the High Priest, involved regular daily offerings, special offerings for shabbat and festivals, and a variety of obligatory and voluntary offerings for special occasions. Despite the centrality of sacrifice for Israelite religion, there were prophets who spoke out against the corrupt practices it engendered and against those who brought fatted animals to the TEMPLE while disregarding God's teaching. Since the destruction of the Second Temple, Jews have prayed every day for the reintroduction of sacrifices, and they have modelled the LITURGY and the amidah prayers on the daily, Sabbath and festival offerings. Yet, there are statements asserting that PRAYER is really greater than sacrifice and that the hospitality shown in inviting poor people to dine at one's table turns the table into an altar and the meal into an ATONEMENT. The great 12c. theologian Maimonides expressed the controversial view that the sacrificial system was meant to wean the Israelites away from the idolatrous practices of surrounding cultures. Instead of sacrificing to idols, they were to sacrifice to God. The many biblical prescriptions about sacrifice were thus merely concessions to forms of worship current in the ancient world. Although there is some precedent for Maimonides' view in midrashic literature, it was attacked by those who regarded the sacrificial system as expressing the highest religious and mystical ideas. *See also* AKEDAH; RED HEIFER; SALT; SUKKOT; TIKKUN; URIEL.

Sadducees Priestly sect at the end of the Second Temple period. The Sadducees did not accept the oral traditions (oral torah) of the Pharisees and interpreted the torah very literally. They denied the belief in immortality and in the Resurrection, interpreted 'an eye for an eye' (Exod. 21:25) literally and had their own calendar. According to the Rabbinic tradition, the Sadducees began when some students of a 2c. BCE rabbi understood his statement that 'one should not serve God in order to receive any reward' to mean that there was no reward and punishment after death. The Sadducees were thought by the Pharisees to live

Avenue of the **Righteous Gentiles** at the Yad Vashem Centre in Jerusalem, commemorating those Gentiles who risked their lives to save Jews during the Holocaust.

Ruth gleaning corn in the fields of Boaz (Hans Holbein).

*The **Sacrifice** of Noah* by Michelangelo.

a life of self-indulgence and luxury, and the name 'Sadducee' came to mean 'a heretic'. Although the Sadducees disappeared when the Jerusalem Temple was destroyed in 70 CE, their teachings resurfaced among the Karaites, who broke away from Rabbinic Judaism in the 8c. *See also* SIMEON BEN SHETACH.

sage *see* CHAKHAM

salamander A reptile like a large spider or a small mouse which lives in fire, breeds in water but dies if left in air. The fire most suitable for producing the reptile is one made out of myrtle which has burnt for seven days, or seven years, or even seventy years. The blood of the salamander is a protection against fire, when smeared on humans. The biblical King Hezekiah was cast as a child into the fire of Moloch by his father, the evil King Ahaz. He was saved from death since he had been smeared with salamander blood. This protective quality of the salamander is used as an image for the torah scholar, who is not affected by the fires of hell since he is protected by the power of the divine torah which itself is all fire. The same is true of the souls of the righteous, made from the fire of the Throne of Glory, which are washed in the heavenly river of fire, just as the salamander is washed in fire. The story is told of Christian priests who claimed that they possessed a garment of Jesus which did not burn when exposed to fire, thus proving its genuineness and saintliness. A wise Jew realized that it had been dipped in salamander blood, so he washed it in soap and vinegar and was able to burn it.

Salanter, Israel *see* LIPKIN SALANTER, ISRAEL

salt was offered up with every sacrifice in the Temple (Lev. 2:13) and represented the eternal covenant between God and Israel, since it does not decompose. This sacrificial symbolism continued in the use of salt with bread at meals in the Jewish home, because after the destruction of the Jerusalem Temple, the home became a sanctuary and the table became an altar. It is recommended that salt be eaten at all meals to prevent illness and a bad smell in the mouth. In the Middle Ages considerable care was taken about the way salt was handled. It was believed that, if a person used his thumb to handle salt, his children would die; if he used his little finger, he would become a pauper; and if he used his index finger, he would become a murderer. The only safe way was to use the other two fingers. Although these regulations made their way into the *Shulchan Arukh*, the most authoritative code of Jewish law, they eventually fell into disuse on the grounds that the nature of things had changed and salt had become relatively innocuous. Some people still maintain the tradition of washing the hands after a meal to prevent rubbing any salt remaining on their fingers into their eyes. This hand washing was encouraged by the Kabbalah as a propitiatory offering to the powers of evil (sitra achra). Bread and salt would be the first things brought into a new home and were also used to greet visitors. Salt is thought to provide protection from Satanic influences. Its protective power is particularly efficacious against the evil eye, and it is often put in the pockets of children or hung in a little packet around their neck. In the Jewish dietary laws, salt is used to remove blood from meat before it can be eaten.

Samael Prince of DEMONS, leader of the angels who were expelled from heaven, head of the forces of the SITRA ACHRA and husband of Lilith. Samael is dark complexioned and has horns. He is identified with SATAN and the evil inclination and is the main accuser of Israel in heaven, where he is opposed by Michael, the guardian angel of Israel. It was Samael who sent the SERPENT to seduce Eve in the Garden of Eden. He is active at night (*see* DAY AND NIGHT) and tempts men into sin. When they do sin, they increase Samael's power and allow him to gain temporary control over the SHEKHINAH, bringing calamity to the world. In order to keep him in check the Kabbalah recommends that certain rituals be offered as bribes to Samael, just as the biblical scapegoat sent out into the wilderness on yom kippur was an offering to him. Since he symbolizes all that is evil and unclean, his very name, which means 'poison of God', is avoided and he is either referred to euphemistically or in an abbreviated manner. Kabbalistic tradition associates him with the Leviathan. On shabbat and festivals he has no power over the world. *See also* JOSEPH DELLA REINA.

Samaritans Members of a Jewish sect in the Holy Land who originated near ancient Samaria, hence their name. Samaritans claimed descent from tribes of the Northern Kingdom of Israel, but according to the Bible, they were the descendants of the foreign peoples brought there after the exile of the Northern Kingdom in 721 BCE. The Jewish status of these foreigners was considered doubtful by some rabbis of the Talmudic period, who accused them of worshipping doves, and intermarriage between Jews and Samaritans was forbidden. Today, a small community of around one thousand Samaritans is concentrated in two centres in Israel. It is still led by a priestly hierarchy, and on PESACH the Pascal lamb is sacrificed at the Samaritan holy site of Mount Gerizim, near Nablus. Samaritans possess their own version of the Pentateuch, which they interpret literally, and though they do not regard the Prophets and Hagiographa as scripture, they believe in the Messiah and the Resurrection. Like later sectarians such as the Sadducees and the Karaites, they have their own calendar. Some of their rituals differ markedly from Jewish ones, e.g. the Samaritans have the custom of building a sukkah inside their houses rather than under the open sky.

Sambatyon Legendary river which flows strongly for six days carrying rocks and stones and only rests on the shabbat, its name being based on the Greek form of Sabbath. Some of the Ten Lost Tribes are thought to be exiled beyond the Sambatyon. They cannot cross it during weekdays, when the river is flowing powerfully, and they will not cross it when it is quiescent because of restrictions on Sabbath travel. There have been various attempts to locate the river in Ethiopia (*see* ELDAD HA-DANI), India, China, Arabia (*see* REUVENI, DAVID) and near the Caspian Sea. According to some versions of the legend, the Israelite tribes were carried away into exile by a PILLAR OF CLOUD, and the river Sambatyon started flowing out of Paradise behind them. On Saturdays the river is always covered in cloud, but at its narrowest parts, it is possible to communicate with those across the river. Traders leave their goods beside the river bank on Fridays and return on Sundays to collect their pay. The water of the Sambatyon has curative powers, and if some of it is kept in a jar, it will move around in a turbulent manner for six days and only be still on the Sabbath.

Samson Israelite leader during the biblical period of the Judges (12c.–11c BCE). Samson was a NAZIRITE from birth, his mother having been told by the angel URIEL that she would have a son who should be dedicated to God, since he would save Israel from Philistine oppression (Judg. 13:3–5). Though gifted with superhuman strength (*see* HAIR AND BEARD), Samson was also the slave to powerful sexual passions. He was eventually captured by the Philistines through the intrigues of his mistress Delilah, who sold her lover for silver. He was blinded by the Philistines, and this was understood as a punishment because he had followed after the temptation of his eyes in indulging his lust. While Samson was a blind prisoner in Gaza, Philistine women came to visit him for sexual relations since he had lost none of his physical attraction. They also wanted children by him who would be possessed of his strength and stature. Samson's self-inflicted death, when he brought about the collapse of the Philistine temple with the cry 'Let me die with the Philistines' (Judg. 16:30), was regarded not as SUICIDE, but as selfless martyrdom.

The Blinding of **Samson** *by* Rembrandt.

Samuel Israelite prophet whose life was devoted to the service of God by his mother, Hannah, when God answered her prayers for a child. Samuel, who was a descendant of the rebellious Korah, grew up under the tutelage of ELI, the High Priest of the sanctuary at Shiloh. Even as a youngster Samuel was outspoken enough to show Eli and the priests that they were ignorant of aspects of ritual law. He was only saved from punishment for his disrespect by the intercession of his mother. When King Saul persuaded the witch of ENDOR to call Samuel up from the dead, so that he could seek his advice, Samuel thought he had been summoned to the Resurrection and the Day of Judgment. He anointed both Saul and King David. Samuel is regarded by some as a prophet on a par with Moses, or even superior in some respects, for while Moses had to enter the Tabernacle for God to communicate with him, Samuel was spoken to outside. *See also* SHMUEL BUKH.

Samuel, Mar (2c.–3c. CE) Babylonian Talmudic sage and astronomer. Before his birth Samuel's father was told by a woman that she had overheard the birds talking about the son he was going to have, who would be great in wisdom. Samuel grew up to become the head of the academy at Nehardea and, together with his colleague Rav, helped make Babylonia into the main centre for torah studies. He had a considerable knowledge of medicine, preferring to take an empirical approach to disease rather than to regard it as a consequence of the EVIL EYE. His astronomical interest earned him the nickname Samuel Yarchinaah, 'Samuel the Moon', and he did important work on the

The prophet **Samuel** anointing David as king in a fresco from the Dura Europos synagogue (3c. CE).

determination of the Jewish lunar calendar. He said he was as familiar with the courses of the stars in heaven as with the streets of Nehardea. Samuel's halakhic expertise was in the area of civil law, whereas in ritual matters the views of Rav were preferred by later authorities. In acting as a judge, he was careful not to show any bias to plaintiff or defendant and on one occasion refused to try a case of someone who had helped him across the bridge over a river. He formulated the important principle that 'The secular law of a country is law', i.e. that Jews must obey the laws of the land they inhabit. One of his rulings restricted the power of merchants to make large profits on their goods, and he showed particular concern for the poor, for orphans, for women and for slaves. Yet he did not advocate asceticism and told his followers to enjoy themselves: 'Snatch and eat, snatch and drink, for this world is like a wedding feast.' According to Samuel the only difference the coming of the Messiah would make to ordinary life would be the cessation of Gentile dominion over Israel.

Sandalfon Angel in charge of prayer. Sandalfon is keeper of the keys to the gates of heaven which he opens to allow prayers in, and he then translates human requests to God. He is taller than the other angels and stands behind the Divine Chariot making crowns for God out of the prayers of Israel. Sandalfon is also the guardian angel of birds; he forms children in the womb and is responsible for the effectiveness of the shofar blasts on rosh ha-shanah. He is mentioned frequently in the literature of the maaseh merkavah as an angel of fire whom the mystic comes across in the seventh hall at the end of his heavenly ascent. It is Sandalfon who enables prophets to gain divine inspiration from the Holy Spirit (ruach ha-kodesh) by wrapping them in clothing of fire. Sandalfon is identified with the prophet Elijah, who lives in heaven as an angel only returning to earth from time to time to instruct people and help mankind.

sandek (Of Greek origin, meaning 'godfather') The man who holds the child on his knees during the CIRCUMCISION ceremony. It is a great honour to be asked to serve in this role, and usually a grandfather, the rabbi or a respected elder of the community is chosen. The sandek is like an altar on which the child is offered up to God as he enters the covenant of circumcision. The reward for acting as a sandek is to be blessed with riches, and any gifts which he subsequently gives the child are in recognition of this enrichment. In some communities it is considered unlucky for the same person to act as sandek twice for the same family. For reasons of modesty, women do not normally serve as sandek. Additional godparents, known among Ashkenazi Jews as kvater (male) and kvaterin (female), bring the baby into the room and hand it over to the mohel. A childless couple are often assigned this task, since it is supposed to promote childbearing.

Sanhedrin (Hebrew, from the Greek 'council') The supreme religious council consisting of seventy or seventy-one elders, which was situated in the Chamber of Hewn Stone on the Temple mount in Jerusalem. Its origin goes back to the appointment by Moses of a council of seventy elders (Num. 11:16). The most

serious cases were brought before the great Sanhedrin, but smaller Sanhedrin courts, consisting of twenty-three members, dealt with capital cases (see CAPITAL PUNISHMENT). The Sanhedrin also determined the religious calendar. The Sanhedrin sat in a semi-circle, with the president of the court, the Nasi, in the centre, so that the judges could see each other during their debates. The views of the most junior judges (see DAYYAN) were canvassed first, so that they would not be afraid to express an independent opinion which disagreed with that of senior colleagues (see MAJORITY OPINION). Members of the Sanhedrin were supposed to know foreign languages so they need not rely on translators, to be adept at PILPUL and to be experts in magical practices in case they had to try wizards and sorcerers. After the destruction of the Second Temple, the Sanhedrin moved to Jabneh and then to the Galilee, before it eventually ceased existence in the early 5c. In the 16c. an unsuccessful attempt was made by Jewish refugees from Spain, under the leadership of Rabbi Jacob Berab, to revive ordination (see SEMIKHAH) and reconstitute the Sanhedrin in Palestine because they believed the age of the Messiah was dawning. Napoleon called together a French Sanhedrin in 1807 as a follow-up to the ASSEMBLY OF JEWISH NOTABLES before granting the Jews emancipation. See also SOTAH.

Sanvi, Sansanvi and Samangelaf see AMULETS; LILITH

Saphir, Jacob (1822–86) Jewish traveller sent as an emissary to raise funds for the community in Jerusalem. Jacob left a written record, *Even Sappir*, recounting his adventures and describing the Jews he met in the East and in the Southern Hemisphere. He set off originally to collect money to rebuild the Churvah Synagogue in Jerusalem and hoped he would uncover evidence of the Ten Lost Tribes en route. His journeys took him via Egypt, Yemen, Aden, India, Singapore and Java to Australia, New Zealand and Ceylon. While he was impressed with the quality of Jewish life in the Yemen, he found Judaism in the antipodes rather lax. Some Jews in Australia were salting non-kosher meat, since they had no one who could perform ritual slaughter (shechitah) for them. During his stay in Australia, he converted a woman to Judaism, outraging the local religious authorities for interfering in their affairs and being reported to the Chief Rabbinate in London. He also helped solve the problem of a deserted wife when he found a Jew in Melbourne who had run away from Russia, leaving behind his wife who was unable to remarry (agunah). In Dunedin, New Zealand, he discovered that the community did not have a megillah to use for the festival of purim, so he wrote one out for them from memory in two days.

Sarah Wife of ABRAHAM and first of the biblical MATRIARCHS. Sarah was Abraham's niece and became his lifelong companion, following him on his travels in response to God's call (Gen. 12). She helped him spread the belief in monotheism by instructing the women she came into contact with while he instructed the men. Indeed, she was more gifted in prophecy than her husband. She was an old woman when she eventually gave birth to her son Isaac, yet she proved that she was his real mother by suckling the babes of her neighbours, who doubted that she had indeed given birth. Sarah died of a broken heart at the age of 127 when she was misinformed that her husband had offered Isaac up as a sacrifice to God (*see* AKEDAH). It was said of her that at the age of one hundred she was as beautiful as at twenty, and as sinless at twenty as at seven. Abraham bought the cave of MACHPELAH in Hebron as her burial place.

Satan Heavenly prosecutor in the Bible (e.g. Job 1 and 2), whose name means 'the accuser'. Later Satan came to be regarded as the king of demons who had rebelled against God and was expelled from heaven. In his exile from heaven, he took with him a host of fallen angels and became their leader. The rebellion began when Satan, the greatest of the angels with twice their number of wings, refused to pay homage to ADAM. The latter was a mere creature made out of dust, while Satan was formed out of the splendour of God Himself. Satan became jealous of Adam's status and desired EVE for himself. Satan was behind the sin of Adam in the Garden of Eden. Through the SERPENT he had sexual intercourse with Eve and fathered CAIN; he helped Noah become intoxicated with wine and tried to persuade Abraham not to obey God during the akedah episode. He also deceived the Israelites into believing Moses was dead and thus induced them to worship the GOLDEN CALF. The *Talmud* tells how on one occasion the great AKIVA stripped off his clothes and began to climb a palm tree when Satan appeared as a naked woman seductively perched in its branches. A 15c. Kabbalist, JOSEPH DELLA REINA, tried to overcome Satan but was defeated and tragically forced to submit to the Satanic realm. Satan came to be regarded as the personification of wickedness, known under a number of different names, the most important of which is SAMAEL. As the evil INCLINATION he tempts man to sin, and no one, however saintly, is free from his wiles, for he can appear in many different forms. He is most active at times of danger, and people who talk about evil things are said to be 'opening their mouths to Satan', giving him an opportunity to bring that very evil about. Some liturgical prayers have the purpose of keeping Satan away from man, and the SHOFAR blown on rosh ha-shanah is meant to confuse him so he will not remind God of Israel's sins. He has no power on yom kippur when Jews engage in prayer and repentance. *See also* JOB.

Satmar Chasidim *see* NETUREI KARTA

Saul First king of Israel who was anointed by the prophet SAMUEL (I Sam. 10). Kingship was taken away from him because he was too kind-hearted. He was unable to slay Agag, the king of AMALEK, and the Amalekite women and children, as God had commanded. Saul himself was very modest. Although subject to fits of depression and jealousy, it was mainly the false rumours spread in his court and the instigation of jealous advisers that led to his antagonism towards DAVID, a one-time favourite. Despite his failings, Saul is highly regarded in Jewish literature, and his choice of a suicidal death by falling on his sword on the battlefield rather than fall captive to the Philistines is not condemned by the halakhah. In the World to

Satan conducting souls to hell (English sculpture).

*David Playing the Harp for **Saul*** by Rembrandt.

Come (olam haba) he is granted a position of honour with the prophet Samuel. *See also* ENDOR, WITCH OF.

Saul of Tarsus *see* GAMALIEL

scapegoat *see* AZAZEL; SAMAEL; YOM KIPPUR

Schneerson, Menachem Mendel *see* LUBAVITCH

schnorer (Yiddish for 'beggar') The life-style of the professional schnorer involved manipulating potential donors by playing on their gullibility and sympathy. Every Jewish settlement, however small, had its schnorers, who survived even in the most impoverished SHTETL through the use of chutzpah. For example, if a regular donor explained to his local schnorer that he would have to cut down his donation, as his daughter was getting married and he promised to support his son-in-law, the schnorer might reply: 'But why do it with my money?' Schnorers were regarded as part of the community and would go from house to house eating meals, living by their wits and exposing the vanity of others. Their main meeting-point was at the doors of the synagogue, where they could catch congregants as they arrived for prayers or as they were about to depart. They were also to be found at weddings or other celebrations, and the host would sometimes pay them not to molest the guests. Schnorers became heroes of Jewish folklore, beloved for their eccentricities. When they were given money which they felt was insufficient, they would drop it on the ground and walk off, thus leaving the donor with a feeling of guilt. They were renowned for their repartee and were highly inventive in the curses they used against those they considered stingy or unresponsive. To a man who criticized a schnorer for begging, when he looked healthy and was in possession of all his limbs, the beggar might reply: 'Do you expect me to cut off an arm just for the small change you might give me?' The schnorer, despite his reputation, was considered a valuable member of the community, because he enabled the Jewish householder to fulfil the duty of giving charity.

scribe (Hebrew 'sofer'; pl. 'soferim') The early Pharisaic teachers of the TORAH were called scribes because they were the guardians of the canonical Bible text, whose very letters they counted. Several textual features are ascribed to tikkun soferim, 'emendation of the scribes', which may refer either to changes in the text or to rules about its orthography (*see* MASORAH) and interpretation. In more modern usage the term 'scribe' refers to those responsible for writing a mezuzah, tefillin, get, KETUBBAH, SEFER TORAH or megillah. A scribe has to be trained very carefully in the preparation of the parchment and in the use of special ink and a quill pen. Before writing the tetragrammaton, he bathes in a mikveh to purify himself. Each sizeable community should have its own scribe, and so important was his work considered, that it was said one should not live in a town which did not have both a scribe and a doctor. Nevertheless, someone who becomes a scribe is likely to lose his portion in olam haba because he will be held responsible for any scribal errors he makes. The Men of the Great Synagogue fasted and prayed that scribes should

never become rich so they would not cease to do their work. Some scribes were great craftsmen, and a beautiful and clear script was much in demand. The *Talmud* mentions one scribe who could write with four pens in one hand at the same time but who refused to teach others his technique. The angel Metatron acts as the heavenly scribe recording the deeds of Israel.

secret Jew *see* MARRANO

seder (Hebrew for 'order') The ritual meal eaten at home on the first night of the festival of PESACH (in the diaspora on the first two nights). The family meal is accompanied by the retelling of the story of the Exodus from a HAGGADAH text, during which the youngest child asks FOUR QUESTIONS of the head of the household. Each person is encouraged to think of himself as if he had actually been redeemed from Egypt, and the seder has a number of features to educate children in understanding the message of the Exodus (*see* EGG). Special types of food and drink are arranged on the table and included in this Passover meal, among the most important of which are the FOUR CUPS of wine, the unleavened bread, MATZAH, and the bitter herbs, MAROR, which are dipped in CHAROSET. It is customary to recline on one's left side during the seder, since this was once the manner in which free men ate. A cup of WINE is poured out for the prophet Elijah (*see* ELIJAH, CUP OF), and the door of the house is opened so that he may enter. At the end of the meal the piece of matzah which symbolizes the Pascal offering (*see* AFIKOMEN) is the last thing eaten. The evening ends with HALLEL Psalms, the singing of hymns and songs (*see* CHAD GADYA), and the declaration: 'Next year in Jerusalem.' The seder night is regarded as a time of divine protection for Israel, and the demonic forces at work in the world need not be feared. *See also* HOSPITALITY; KITEL; PLAGUES, THE TEN.

sefer torah (Hebrew for 'torah scroll') The scroll of the Hebrew text of the Pentateuch. A sefer torah must be handwritten by a SCRIBE on the parchment of a kosher animal, using special ink applied with a quill pen in accordance with the orthographic rules of the MASORAH. The scribe must be an adult male Jew. The scroll is kept in the holy ARK of the synagogue usually covered with a decorative mantle, a silver breastplate and a crown with bells at its top (*see* PETICHAH). When it is carried to and from the BIMAH, people stand and kiss it as it passes. The parchment should not be touched by the naked hand, and a pointer (*see* YAD) is used by the reader to indicate the place to those called up for an ALIYAH to the torah. If the scroll is dropped on the ground, that is an ill omen and the whole congregation has to fast for a day. On SIMCHAT TORAH all the scrolls are carried seven times around the synagogue with singing and dancing to celebrate the completion of the Pentateuchal readings. Every Jew has a duty to write at least one torah scroll. Today, this is usually done by contributing towards the cost of a new sefer torah and helping to ink in some letters at its end. When such a new scroll is brought into the synagogue for the first time, it is carried under a wedding canopy (chuppah) accompanied by singing and dancing congregants. The sanctity of a sefer torah relates to the word of God it contains, and one rabbi criticized Jews for showing respect for the physical scroll but not for the sages who are living embodiments of torah. Chananiah Ben Teradyon, who was martyred in 2c. CE, was burnt alive wrapt in a sefer torah. As he was dying, his pupils asked him what he could see, and he answered: 'I see the parchment burning and the letters flying up into the air.' This was understood by later generations to mean that divine revelation cannot be destroyed, even though scrolls and books of the torah are the first things desecrated during times of persecution. *See also* GELILAH; HAGBAHAH; MAFTIR; SIYYUM.

sefirat ha-omer *see* OMER, COUNTING OF

sefirot The ten divine structures which bring the world into being through EMANATION and make up the different levels of reality. Sefirot are mentioned in the *Sefer* YETZIRAH, developed in the *Sefer Ha-*BAHIR and reach their full expression in the ZOHAR under different designations and in the Lurianic KABBALAH. The ten sefirot form a unity and should not be thought of as separate entities. The highest sefirah is keter, the 'crown', which is the primal divine will and sometimes identified with the unknowable Godhead, en sof. Keter is situated in the centre, at the top of the sefirotic pattern, and the nine lower sefirot are in the form of structures of the right side, the left side and the centre. Their most common names are: chokhmah, 'wisdom' (right); binah, 'understanding' (left); chesed, 'love' (right); gevurah, 'power' (left); tiferet, 'beauty' (centre); netzach, 'victory' (right); hod, 'glory' (left); yesod, 'foundation' (centre); and malkhut, 'kingdom', or SHEKHINAH, 'divine presence' (centre). Those sefirot on the right side are male, because they convey the flow of the divine energy in an undifferentiated form, while those on the left are female, because they receive and shape that flow. The last sefirah, malkhut, is female with regard to the group of six sefirot above it. When the ten sefirot interrelate in dynamic harmony, and the male and female aspects are united, then the world itself benefits. When, however, the sin of man divides malkhut from those sefirot above and allows the evil power of the SITRA ACHRA to control it, the world is beset by calamities. The pattern of the sefirot is often depicted as making up a human body or a tree linking heaven and earth. Apart from these sefirot of holiness, the sitra achra has its own sefirot of evil and impurity. There was considerable disagreement between Kabbalistic schools as to whether the sefirot were actually part of the divinity or merely vehicles for the divine to flow through. *See also* SHEMITTOT; TZADDIK; TZIMTZUM; USHPIZIN.

segullah, segullot *see* MAGIC; RAZIEL

selichah *see* FORGIVENESS

semikhah (Hebrew for 'ordination') The transference of spiritual authority which originated with Moses, who was told to lay his hands (the actual meaning of the word 'semikhah') on his successor Joshua (Num. 27). Such ordination was only practised in the Holy

A **scribe** from Jerusalem at work.

An open **sefer torah**.

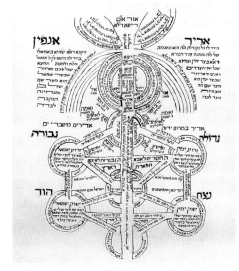

A diagram from a Kabbalah manuscript showing how the **sefirot** combine to form the structure of adam kadmon.

Land and allowed the ordinand to be elected to the Sanhedrin and to act as a judge (dayyan). The chain of ordination ceased sometime in the 3c. or 4c. when Jewish life in Palestine deteriorated under persecution. Since then the semikhah which a RABBI receives has lacked the authority of the divine spirit passed on by Moses and is merely permission from a master for his disciple to teach and decide matters of Jewish law (see YESHIVAH). In 1538 an attempt was made by Rabbi Jacob Berab in Safed, Palestine, to revive the original semikhah, but it failed because of the opposition of the rabbis of Jerusalem (see also CARO, JOSEPH). Berab, who was an exile from Spain, based himself on a teaching of Maimonides that the rabbis of the Holy Land acting together could ordain someone with a valid semikhah. He had himself ordained in the belief that the age of the Messiah was about to dawn and the Sanhedrin would be reconstituted.

Sephardim (Hebrew for 'Spaniards') Jews of Spanish and Portuguese origin who spread throughout North Africa, the Ottoman Empire, parts of South America, Italy and Holland after the expulsion of Jews from the Iberian peninsula at the end of the 15c. It is estimated that approximately a quarter of a million Jews left Spain and Portugal at this time. The Sephardim brought with them a highly developed Jewish and general culture, as well as their own customs, liturgy and musical traditions to the Jewish communities among whom they settled. Later waves of Sephardi refugees were made up of crypto-Jews (see MARRANO), who had been forcibly converted to Christianity and, when the opportunity arose, escaped from the clutches of the Inquisition to profess their religion openly. The Sephardim eventually merged with the native Jews, imposing Sephardi culture on much of North African and Oriental Jewry, but some families of pure Sephardi stock still put two Hebrew letters after their name which stand for the words 'pure Sephardi'. The first Jews to settle in North America were Sephardim who arrived in New Amsterdam (i.e. New York) in 1654, as were the first Jews to return to England in the 17c. The Sephardim and the ASHKENAZIM represent the two main divisions of Jewry, differing in their customs, pronunciation of Hebrew, liturgical practices and attitudes towards Kabbalah and philosophy. Despite these differences, Ashkenazim study the works of the great Sephardi rabbis, such as Maimonides and Joseph CARO, with reverence. Sephardim have retained their separate communal identity, some continuing to speak LADINO among themselves. Although in the past they tended to oppose intermarriage with Ashkenazim, whom they looked down upon, such marriages are now quite common. See also MONOGAMY.

Septuagint *see* ARISTEAS, LETTER OF; TEVET

serpent (Hebrew 'nachash') The biblical serpent was king of the beasts. It was a crafty animal, walking upright on two legs, talking and eating the same food as man. When the serpent saw how the angels honoured Adam, it grew jealous of him, and the sight of the first couple engaging in sexual intercourse awoke the serpent's desire for EVE. At the instigation of SATAN or SAMAEL, or according to some views possessed by him, the serpent persuaded Eve to eat the forbidden fruit and seduced her. As a punishment its hands and legs were cut off, so it had to crawl on its belly, all food it ate tasted of dust, and it became the eternal enemy of man. Since the serpent was identified with Satan, it came to symbolize the power of evil. When it had sexual relations with Eve, it injected its filth into her and into all her descendants (see ORIGINAL SIN). This filth was only removed from the People of Israel when they stood at Mount Sinai and received the torah. Gentiles, however, have never been cleansed of this serpentine impurity. The Rabbis recommended that the best of serpents should have their brains crushed, according to one view even on the Sabbath. A serpent will not attack, however, if not interfered with, and therefore if someone is praying the amidah and a serpent coils itself around his ankles, he should not interrupt his prayers. Liquid left exposed overnight was forbidden in case a snake had drunk from it and deposited some of its venom. Someone bitten by a serpent was recommended to eat some of its flesh as an antidote to its poison, and a BRAZEN SERPENT was erected by Moses in the wilderness in order to act as an antidote to snake bite. One of the miracles which took place in the period of the Temple was that no one was ever bitten by a snake in Jerusalem. Despite the fact that the Angel of Death is said to have a serpent's face, seeing a serpent in a dream was considered a good omen.

seudah shlishit (Hebrew for 'third meal', Yiddish 'shalosh sudos') Three meals must be eaten on SHABBAT, to differentiate the Sabbath from the rest of the week. The normal practice is to have an evening meal on Friday night and a mid-morning meal on Saturday, as on working days. Seudah shlishit, the extra meal on Saturday, is usually added late on Saturday afternoon. Unlike the two main meals of shabbat, the third meal is not preceded by kiddush and is usually a light repast, often comprising challah, herring and beer. At seudah shlishit ZEMIROT are sung, and 'The Lord is my Shepherd' (Ps. 23) is often chanted to a haunting tune. It is said that those who fulfil the commandment of eating three meals on shabbat are spared from three troubles: from the birth pangs of the Messiah, from the pre-Messianic war of Gog and Magog and from descent into gehinnom. Mystics have emphasized the importance of eating the three meals in joy, saying that anyone who does not eat a third meal is not among the courtiers of the heavenly king. Since the souls of the dead, who suffer in gehinnom, are released from their torments for the duration of the Sabbath, some communities extend the seudah shlishit past nightfall. This delays the return of these souls to hell.

Seven Faithful Shepherds *see* AARON; USHPIZIN

shaatnez Cloth made from wool and linen threads, which must not be worn because of the laws of MIXED SPECIES (Lev. 19:19; Deut. 22:11). Shaatnez was found in the garments used by a priest while officiating in the Temple and was also theoretically permissible where a linen garment had woolen tzitzit attached, but it was prohibited in the secular clothing of lay people and only allowed for shrouds for the dead. Even if a person found that he was wearing shaatnez clothes in the street, he would have to remove them

immediately. The name 'shaatnez' is of unknown
origin, and the shaatnez law was considered an incomprehensible divine decree. Its bizarre character leads
the evil inclination to raise questions about it, which
sow doubt in the minds of the faithful. Attempts were
made to explain the origins of the prohibition in terms
of the clothing used in idolatrous cults, which Jews
were meant to avoid. A connection was also found
between shaatnez and the story of Cain and Abel.
Cain was a tiller of the ground whose offerings to
God were of flax, while Abel was a shepherd who
offered up wool (Gen. 4). According to the Kabbalah
these two sons of Adam were totally different types;
the former represented the evil power of the sitra
achra, while the latter represented the power of
holiness. The combination of the brothers in their
mother's womb led to the tragedy of fratricide.
Similarly, anyone wearing the linen–wool combination is likely to come to harm. God has instituted a
world order which man must respect. The law of
shaatnez conveys the message that everything in God's
creation has its own place and must not be interfered
with by man.

shabbat (Hebrew for 'Sabbath') The Jewish Sabbath
lasts from Friday evening to Saturday night. It is the
day which God blessed, having rested from the work
of Creation which He performed in six days. A Jew
must imitate God (*see* IMITATIO DEI) by resting on
shabbat from all work which manifests human control
over nature. Prohibitions on working are suspended,
however, when danger to life is involved. Shabbat is
also a day of celebration. The mother lights two
candles (*see* LAMP, SABBATH) on Friday evening to
bring added light into the home. The liturgy welcomes
the Sabbath queen, and when the head of the household
returns home from synagogue, he is accompanied by
two angels, who come to inspect whether the shabbat
preparations have been made. The family sing a song,
'Shalom Aleikhem', to these visiting angels before
reciting the evening kiddush over wine. Three meals
must be eaten (*see* SEUDAH SHLISHIT), at which special
foods like the challah bread and a hot CHOLENT stew
are served, and ZEMIROT are sung. The end of the
holy day is marked by the HAVDALAH ceremony. The
importance of shabbat is shown by its inclusion in the
Decalogue, where it also commemorates the Exodus
from Egypt and freedom from slavery. Nature itself
rests on the Sabbath, as evidenced by the cessation of
the manna on that day and by the legendary river
Sambatyon, which flows with torrents of rocks the
whole week but is quiescent on Saturday. Jews receive
an extra soul (*see* NESHAMAH YETERAH) for its duration,
and the fires of gehinnom are cooled down. The day
is a foretaste of the World to Come (olam haba) in
the Messianic age, when the peace and tranquillity of
shabbat will characterize the whole world. If all the
Jews were able to keep a Sabbath day completely, the
Messiah would come. The mystics saw the union of
the male and female aspects of God as taking place on
shabbat, which is therefore an auspicious time for
sexual union between husband and wife. It is a day of
cosmic harmony when the forces of evil (sitra achra)
have no control. *See also* ERUV; FALASHAS; KABBALAT
SHABBAT; LITURGY; MELAVVEH MALKAH; PIKKUACH
NEFESH; SHABBOS GOI.

The staff of Moses turned into a **serpent**, from a
14c. Spanish haggadah.

Closing up a shop in the Mea Shearim quarter of
Jerusalem on Friday afternoon before the onset of
shabbat.

Shabbetai Tzevi (1626–76) Turkish pseudo-Messiah whose following extended at one time throughout the Jewish world. As a young man Shabbetai Tzevi studied the Kabbalah of Isaac Luria and was subject to strange states of ecstasy, during which he behaved in an antinomian manner. He declared himself the Messiah, but nobody took him seriously, since he was regarded as mentally unstable. In 1664 he married Sarah, a young girl with a reputation for loose living, and a year later went to see NATHAN OF GAZA to seek a spiritual cure for his psychological condition. Nathan persuaded him that he was indeed the Messiah and undertook to spread the beliefs of the new movement. The Messianic news caught on (*see* GLUEKEL OF HAMELN); people started prophesying and experiencing ecstatic trances, and the year 1666 was expected to be the onset of the Messianic era. Believers in Shabbetai Tzevi put social and physical pressure on those who doubted his Messianic claims. As a troublemaker Shabbetai Tzevi was put into prison by the Turkish Sultan, where he began to describe himself as a divine incarnation. He was subsequently forced to choose between conversion to Islam or death. Shabbetai Tzevi, at the time in a state of severe depression, allowed himself to be converted and was subsequently exiled to Albania. A number of Shabbetean believers followed his example, and like him, they remained secret Jews, later constituting the DOENMEH sect. Nathan explained this shocking apostasy in Kabbalistic terms as the descent of the Messiah to the depths of evil in order to redeem the holiness entrapped there. Orthodox opposition to the movement and its heretical doctrines grew, and many Shabbeteans were forced to go underground, living ostensibly as ordinary Jews.

shabbos goi (Yiddish for 'Sabbath Gentile') Since Jews are forbidden to work on the SHABBAT, a Gentile is sometimes employed to help perform necessary tasks. In theory a Jew is not allowed to ask a non-Jew to do something for him on the Sabbath which he himself is prohibited from doing. The only exceptions to this rule are lighting fires for warmth, since everyone is considered a sick person when it comes to suffering from the cold, attending to communal needs and helping with the performance of a mitzvah. People evaded these restrictions by asking the Gentile indirectly if he could do something for them. In the Middle Ages a shabbos goi was used to warm food, and Christian musicians even played at Jewish wedding feasts on the Sabbath. It is reported that the Spanish rabbi Solomon Adret objected to the custom, approved by some French rabbis, of using a shabbos goi to light fires. When Adret's own Christian maidservant kindled the oven on the Sabbath, he put a lock on it and hid the key. The stories of the GOLEM created by Judah Loew of Prague show that this artificial creature was used as a shabbos goi for the Jewish community there. The Russian writer Maxim Gorky acted as a shabbos goi in his youth.

shacharit (Hebrew for 'dawn') Daily morning prayers, based on the morning sacrifice brought to the Temple. Shacharit was instituted by Abraham when he 'got up early in the morning to the place where he stood before the Lord' (Gen. 19:27). It is the longest prayer of the day consisting of benedictions, psalms,

the shema and hymns, with the amidah at its centre. The Jew begins the day by taking upon himself 'the yoke of the kingdom of heaven'. Adult males wear the TALLIT and TEFILLIN for shacharit prayers on weekdays, and on Mondays and Thursdays there is a short torah reading during the service. One is not allowed to eat before shacharit since, as the mystics put it, one must first provide God with the morning prayers which are His spiritual breakfast food and only then can man indulge his own needs.

shadkhan (Aramaic for 'matchmaker') Among traditional Jews it is considered immodest for young men and women to court each other in the process of finding a future spouse. Instead, an arranged marriage, shiddukh, is set up by a shadkhan who knows both families and considers the future couple to be well matched. The boy and girl are introduced and will be expected to decide whether they wish to marry each other after a number of further meetings. The shadkhan was a well-known community figure in the past, often sporting a distinctive item of clothing, such as a red and white spotted handkerchief, and his exaggeration of the merits of potential marriage partners was a byword of Jewish folklore, since he was only paid if he produced results. He appears as a figure of fun in many humorous stories. *See also* YICHUS.

Shadrach, Meshach and Abed-nego *see* HANANIAH, MISHAEL AND AZARIAH

shaigetz *see* GENTILE

shaimos *see* GENIZAH

shalom (Hebrew for 'peace') Peace, truth and justice are the three pillars on which the world is established. In order to preserve peace between husband and wife, it is even allowed to erase the name of God in the ritual of the wife suspected of adultery (sotah) or to tell white lies, as God did on occasion in the Bible. The most usual form of GREETING between Jews is 'Peace be upon you', to which the reply is 'Upon you be peace'. On the Sabbath one of the common forms of greeting is 'shabbat shalom', 'a Sabbath of peace'. Since 'shalom' is one of the names of God, it should not be used as a greeting in an unseemly place, such as a toilet or a bathhouse. One of the principles of the halakhah is that society should be ordered 'according to the ways of peace', and in a war there is a duty to seek a peaceful outcome first before engaging in hostilities.

shalom aleikhem *see* GREETINGS; NEW MOON

Shalom Aleikhem *see* ANGELS; SHABBAT

shalosh seudos *see* SEUDAH SHLISHIT

shamir A miraculous worm that could break even the hardest stone. The shamir was formed by God at twilight on the sixth day of Creation just before the onset of shabbat. It was as big as a grain of barley and was created for the sole purpose of helping with the building of the Temple, where metal tools were forbidden as they were also instruments of war. King Solomon, the builder of the First Temple, learnt from the demon ASMODEUS that the shamir had been brought from Paradise by a bird and was being kept hidden. So he covered all birds' nests with glass, and when the bird brought out the shamir to break the covering over its nest he managed to capture the worm. Thereafter, he kept it wrapped in wool in a lead box and used it not only for hewing stones but also for engraving the precious stones of the Urim and Thummim on the High Priest's breastplate.

Shammai (1c. CE) Mishnaic sage. Shammai, a builder by trade, had a number of major disputes with his colleague HILLEL in most of which he took a stricter attitude to the halakhah. He was a literalist in his interpretation of the Bible and opposed any innovation in Judaism. While Hillel was of patient disposition, Shammai could not stand fools. In a number of stories told about the two sages, it is always Shammai who drives away those he does not consider serious in their inquiries. Thus, a would-be convert who sought his aid on condition that he taught him the torah while he stood on one leg, or one who only wanted to learn about the written torah or another whose reason for becoming a Jew was in order to be appointed High Priest were angrily rebuked and turned out by Shammai, who even threatened them with his builder's tools. Yet they were all eventually accepted as converts by Hillel. Despite this attitude, Shammai used to say that every person should be received with a pleasant countenance. In the generations after Hillel and Shammai, their schools, Bet Hillel and Bet Shammai, continued the different approaches to Rabbinic Judaism of their respective masters. It has been argued that these differences emerged from the different social classes of the two groups: the traditions of Shammai represented the conservative aristocracy, while those of Hillel represented the plebian values of ordinary Jews. Though the views of Hillel and his school were adopted in most instances, it was said that the Hillelite teachings were for this world, while the Shammaite ones were for the World to Come (olam haba) in the days of the Messiah. *See also* DIVORCE.

shammash (Hebrew for 'beadle') Synagogue official whose role is usually to keep the synagogue clean, put prayer-books in order, prepare the torah scrolls and support the rabbi and chazzan in their duties. In the pre-modern communities of Eastern Europe the shammash used to go around knocking on the houses of community members in the early morning to rouse the men for prayers. He would also make the announcements in synagogue about births and deaths in the community and times of prayer services. Although in Talmudic and medieval times the synagogue shammash was a respected individual, he became something of a figure of fun in later Jewish folklore, as a ne'er-do-well, a nebich. *See also* CHELM.

Sharabi, Shalom (1720–77) Yemenite mystic who headed a yeshivah of Kabbalists in Jerusalem. Before Sharabi came to Palestine, he earned his living as a pedlar in the Yemenite town of Sana. One day a Moslem lady, who had fallen in love with him and wanted to seduce him, closed the door behind him

A picture of **Shabbetai Tzevi**, the counterfeit Messiah.

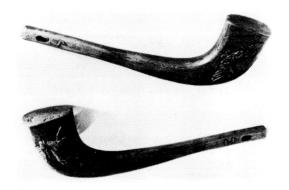

Shulklapper mallet used by the **shammash** in Eastern Europe to knock on house shutters and awaken people for morning prayers.

when he came into her house to show his wares. Sharabi realized what was happening and jumped straight out of the window, fleeing Yemen for Damascus and eventually arriving in Jerusalem. There, he did not want people to know of his Kabbalistic learning, so he pretended to be an ignoramus and obtained the position of servant to Rabbi Gedaliah Chayon, who was head of a Kabbalistic yeshivah. His employer, however, discovered Sharabi's greatness and when he died left a will in which he requested that his servant should be appointed his successor. Sharabi gained a reputation for holiness and was visited by the prophet Elijah, who revealed mystical secrets to him. Every night, at midnight, Sharabi used to make his way to the Wailing Wall to recite the tikkun chatzot prayers remembering the destruction of the Temple. Although the area of the Wailing Wall was prohibited to Jews, he was never caught or turned back because he had the ability of making himself invisible to the Moslem guards who were on duty there. He knew all of the writings of Isaac Luria by heart and was thought to be a reincarnation of him. The mystical prayer-book he wrote, with its emphasis on KAVVANAH and detailed Lurianic meditations for each part of the liturgy, is still used by Kabbalists in Jerusalem, and his grave on the Mount of Olives is a place of pilgrimage.

Shas see MISHNAH

shavuot (Hebrew for 'Pentecost'; literally 'weeks') One of the three PILGRIM FESTIVALS or HARVEST FESTIVALS which falls on the sixth, and in the diaspora also on the seventh, of Sivan. This is at the end of seven weeks after the second day of Passover (see OMER), hence the festival's name. There was a dispute between supporters of the Rabbinic tradition and sectarians, like the Karaites, who fixed the date of shavuot always on a Sunday, according to a literal interpretation of shavuot as falling fifty days after 'the day after the Sabbath' (Lev. 23:15). Shavuot is the festival of the wheat harvest but is celebrated today mainly as the time when the Decalogue was revealed to Moses and the Israelites on Mount Sinai. The Decalogue is read in synagogue, and during the reading, the congregation stand. Synagogues are decorated with flowers and plants, recalling that Mount Sinai, a dry, desert mountain, burst into flower on the occasion of God's revelation. There is a widespread custom of staying awake all night on shavuot studying torah. This is based on a Midrashic story which tells how at Mount Sinai all the Israelites overslept and had to be woken by Moses. The Kabbalah emphasized the importance of this all-night ritual, known as tikkun leil shavuot, and there are even accounts of mystic revelations which took place during this vigil. The Kabbalists saw it as the preparation of the wedding clothes for the spiritual marriage between Israel and God implicit in the covenant established at Mount Sinai. The Book of Ruth is read in synagogue on shavuot, because it is set at harvest time. It tells how Ruth freely accepted Judaism and became a convert, just as the Israelites accepted the torah, and mentions King David, a descendant of Ruth, who died on shavuot. Milk and CHEESE foods, including cheesecake, are characteristic of the festival.

Sheba, Queen of Royal visitor from Ethiopia or Arabia to the court of King Solomon (I Kings 10). Solomon had originally been told of the kingdom of Sheba and of its queen by a bird, whose language he understood. Sheba was a peaceful country, full of gold and silver, whose plants were watered by the rivers of Paradise. He very much wanted to meet the queen because he had heard of her wonderful land. She wanted to meet him because he had a reputation for wisdom, and she wanted to question him about magic and sorcery. When she arrived, she found him sitting in a house of glass, which she thought was water, so she raised her skirt revealing very hairy legs. These indicated that she herself was a sorceress, and she has even been identified as LILITH. Nevertheless, Solomon married her and prepared a potion that would remove her leg hair. The royal house of Ethiopia claimed to be descended from their union, and the black Jews of Ethiopia, the Falashas, trace their own origin to the Israelites whom Solomon sent back with her. Another descendant of their union was Nebuchadnezzar, who became king of Babylon. A rather different tradition denies that it was a queen who came to visit Solomon, asserting instead that it was the king of Sheba.

shechitah (Hebrew for 'slaughter') Method of ritual killing of animals and birds by drawing a sharp knife quickly across the front of the throat. Shechitah is prescribed by the DIETARY LAWS in order for the meat to be kosher. It is performed by a trained slaughterer, or shochet, who must be an adult male Jew accredited by a rabbinic authority with a certificate of trustworthiness. There are cases, however, of women serving as slaughterers among Jewish communities in the Yemen. The shochet must first examine the knife, usually with his fingernail, to ensure that it is perfectly smooth and without notches, and the local rabbi also examines the knife for nicks which might invalidate the shechitah. Before cutting the windpipe and gullet, the shochet makes a blessing, and after slaughter has taken place, the blood of non-domesticated animals and birds is covered with earth. The internal organs are then examined to see that there are no perforations, signs of disease or lesions on the lungs which would make the animal TEREFAH. Any live young found in the bodies of slaughtered animals are considered to have been ritually slaughtered and can be killed in any way and eaten. There is a Kabbalistic belief that the souls of sinners have reincarnated into the bodies of animals and they are released from the process of transmigration of souls by being killed in the holy act of shechitah. The view was expressed in the *Talmud* that, although it may not make any difference to God how an animal is killed, the purpose of shechitah is to refine and purify man. See also MOHEL; TIKKUN.

Shechter, Solomon see BEN SIRA; CONSERVATIVE JUDAISM; GENIZAH

she-elot u-teshuvot see RESPONSA

sheitel (Yiddish for 'wig') Wigs are used by married women who are not allowed to expose their hair to anyone but their husbands. The practice of covering the hair is thought to go back to biblical times and is a sign of shame and guilt for the sin of Eve. It is told

of the mother of seven sons, each of whom in turn
became High Priest, that her children attained this
honour through her merit, for she always covered her
hair so that even the beams of the house never saw
her uncovered head (*see* HEAD-COVERING). Originally,
married women cut off their hair and wore a scarf to
cover their head, a custom still found among certain
Jewish groups like the Ultra-Orthodox Neturei Karta
in Israel. In the 19c. the use of sheitels by married
women became widespread and was opposed by some
rabbis as an immodest way of circumventing the
covering of the hair, since wigs could be even more
attractive than natural hair. Wigs are common among
Ashkenazim in the diaspora today, although most
Modern Orthodox women only cover their hair
during synagogue attendance, usually with a hat, and
not at other times.

shekhinah (Hebrew for 'indwelling') The divine
presence or immanence of God. Shekhinah is often
used merely as a synonym for God, but it was regarded
by some Jewish philosophers as a separate entity, a
created being of light, with which man comes into
contact. The Tabernacle in the wilderness and the First
Temple at Jerusalem were dwelling places of the
shekhinah, but God did not dwell in the Second
Temple. The exile of Israel caused the shekhinah itself
to go into exile, for it dwells with the community of
Israel even in their uncleanliness. The shekhinah rests
on the People of Israel and also inspires individuals,
particularly those who serve God with joy. In this
regard the shekhinah and RUACH HA-KODESH are
interchangeable. There are thirty-six righteous men
(*see* LAMED VAVNIK) who receive the face of the
shekhinah each day. The sins of Israel, particularly
pride, push away the shekhinah, while the study of
torah and the performance of God's will cause the
divine presence to draw near. Proselytes to Judaism
are said to come under the 'wings of the shekhinah'
(*see* DOVE). The shekhinah is situated in the West, and
like the setting sun, its divine rays are everywhere. In
the imagery of the Kabbalah the shekhinah is the most
overtly female sefirah, the last of the ten SEFIROT,
referred to imaginatively as 'the daughter of God'.
The state of devekut with the shekhinah is depicted
in sexual imagery, and there are reports of Kabbalists
who saw her in the form of a woman mourning at
the WAILING WALL in Jerusalem. The harmonious
relationship between the female shekhinah and the six
sefirot which precede her causes the world itself to be
sustained by the flow of divine energy. She is like the
moon reflecting the divine light into the world. When,
however, the sins of man give power to SAMAEL, the
shekhinah is taken over by the forces of the SITRA
ACHRA (*see* ORIGINAL SIN). The flow of energy to the
world then comes via the depths of evil, and calamity
ensues for mankind. *See also* AFTERLIFE; MINYAN; OLAM
HABA.

shekoach *see* GREETINGS

sheliach tzibbur *see* CHAZZAN

Shem *see* JACOB; MORIAH, MOUNT

shema (Hebrew for 'hear') The three biblical paragraphs (Deut. 6:4–9, 11:13–21; Num. 15:37–41) which

Visit of the Queen of **Sheba** to King Solomon
(13c. stained glass).

A Jewish Marriage by Marc Chagall. The angel
above the couple represents the **shekhinah** which
rests on the bride and groom.

are recited in the shacharit and maariv prayers each morning and evening. The name comes from the opening line: 'Hear [shema], O Israel, the Lord is our God, the Lord is one.' The shema is an affirmation of MONOTHEISM and demands that man should love God with all his heart, soul and might. It requires him to bind God's words on his hand and head (see TEFILLIN), write them on the doorposts of his house (see MEZUZAH) and wear fringes (see TZITZIT) as a reminder of God's COMMANDMENTS. The third paragraph also mentions the Exodus from Egypt. In reciting the shema, the Jew takes upon himself 'the yoke of the Kingdom of Heaven' and 'the yoke of the commandments'. The shema is also recited just before going to sleep to keep away demons which may attack the unconscious body. It is recited by a dying person and by martyrs who wish to die with the words 'the Lord is one' on their lips, since loving God 'with all your soul' is understood to mean 'even if He takes away your soul'. It is reported that the martyred sage Akiva smiled as he recited the shema while being tortured, because he felt he could at last love God with all his soul. The first line of the shema is the best-known verse of the LITURGY and is supposed to be engraved on the battle standards of the Ten Lost Tribes. It was the only surviving piece of Hebrew among the BENE ISRAEL of India, who had been cut off from contact with other Jews for centuries. When a Jewish visitor to their community heard them recite the first line of the shema, he realized they were Jews and so re-established contact between them and the wider Jewish community.

shemesh *see* SUN

shem ha-meforash *see* TETRAGRAMMATON

shemini atzeret (Hebrew for 'eighth day of convocation') The festival which falls on the eighth day of SUKKOT. Shemini atzeret is regarded as a separate festival on which the practices specific to sukkot, e.g. living in the sukkah and shaking the four species, are discontinued. Its main content is the celebration at the end of reading the torah cycle, and the commencement of the Book of Genesis once again, known as SIMCHAT TORAH.

shemittah (Hebrew for 'Sabbatical year') Agricultural work on Jewish-owned land in Israel is forbidden during the Sabbatical year, the last year of each seven-year cycle, and also during the JUBILEE year, after seven such cycles (Exod. 23, Lev. 25, Deut. 15). The produce of fields, vineyards and orchards can be gathered for immediate use but not harvested; it has to be treated as holy and made available to the poor and to beasts. Debts are remitted at the end of shemittah, and a special prosbul document was introduced by HILLEL in the 1c. BCE guaranteeing loans so that the poor would still find lenders as the Sabbatical year approached. The religious message conveyed by these institutions is that the land and commerce belong to God, not to man, and all members of the community, including debtors and the landless, are equal before God. The punishment for not respecting the Sabbatical year is exile from the land. The laws of shemittah still apply today, as a Rabbinical ordinance, and land in the modern State of Israel is sold to an Arab sheikh, so that it is not technically Jewish-owned land and may therefore be worked. Some religious settlements which do not wish to rely on this controversial sale have introduced hydroponic agriculture, which is based on water rather than on land. *See also* KOOK, ABRAHAM ISAAC; SHEMITTOT; TITHES

shemittot (Hebrew for 'Sabbatical periods') Cosmic cycles in each of which the world comes under a new spiritual influence. The idea is an application to the historical plane of the agricultural SHEMITTAH cycle in which the land of Israel is left fallow every seventh year. An embryonic doctrine of shemittot is found in views on the date of the Messianic era in the *Talmud*. There it is said that the world will last for six thousand years, the first two thousand ruled by chaos, the next two thousand under the control of torah and the last two thousand during which the Messiah will come. This will be followed by a thousand years of rest. Versions of this teaching in the Kabbalah hold that the world is under the sway of each of the seven lower sefirot for a mini-cycle or shemittah lasting seven thousand years, during the last part of which the world is at rest. When seven of these cycles have passed, the Jubilee age dawns after which the whole process starts again. A new revelation of torah takes place in each shemittah, when the same torah is read differently. The current shemittah is one of judgment, full of commandments and restrictions. The torah has one letter of the Hebrew alphabet missing or possibly one whole book of the torah has disappeared. The previous shemittah was one of grace, with no such restrictions, and the next one will be one where there is no evil inclination in man. The doctrine of shemittot was not favoured by the *Zohar* and the Lurianic Kabbalah because the idea that the torah changes with time lent itself to antinomianism.

shemoneh esreh *see* AMIDAH

shemot *see* CHUMASH; GENIZAH

shenei luchot ha-berit *see* TABLETS OF THE DECALOGUE

sheva mitzvot benei noach *see* NOACHIDE LAWS

Shevat Eleventh lunar month of the Hebrew calendar, counting from Nisan the month of the Exodus, or fifth month from the New Year festival (rosh ha-shanah). Shevat usually begins in the second half of January, and its zodiacal sign is the water carrier. The fifteenth of Shevat is the New Year for Trees (see TU BI-SHEVAT). In the Middle Ages it was believed that anyone who slaughtered geese during the months of Tevet and Shevat was in mortal danger, unless the slaughterer (shochet) himself ate part of the animal he had killed. This was because geese were associated with witchcraft, and there was a specific moment of time during these two months when demons would attack anyone who slaughtered a goose. Since this moment was not actually known, the whole period was regarded as a time of danger.

shevirat ha-kelim *see* ADAM KADMON; TIKKUN

shiddukh *see* SHADKHAN

shikor *see* DRUNKENNESS

shikse *see* GENTILE

Shir Ha-shirim *see* SONG OF SONGS

shiur, shiurim *see* SHUL; YESHIVAH

Shiur Komah (Hebrew for '*Measure of Stature*') Text of the MAASEH MERKAVAH tradition which speculates on the size of the 'body' of God seen by the mystic at the end of his journey into heaven. The merkavah mystics possessed secret names for each organ of the *Shiur Komah*, and even angels were not granted this vision of the enormous dimensions of the divine stature. The knowledge of the *Shiur Komah* measurements was considered an important achievement for the mystic and guaranteed him a place in the World to Come (olam haba) at the time of the Messiah. The physical imagery of the *Shiur Komah* was criticized by philosophically minded thinkers. Saadiah Gaon expressed doubts about the authenticity of the text, and the mature judgment of Maimonides was that the *Shiur Komah* was a heretical work, written under Hellenistic influence, and should be destroyed. Others explained it as a description of the garment in which God wraps Himself, so as to appear to man, or as a non-literal expression (*see* ANTHROPOMORPHISM) of the mystic's sense of the greatness of God, based on Ezekiel's vision of a man-like figure on the Throne of Glory (Ezek. 1:26). *See also* RAZIEL.

shivah *see* APOSTACY; MOURNING

shivah asar be-tammuz *see* TAMMUZ, SEVENTEENTH OF

shivviti A plaque with the words: 'I have set [shivviti] the Lord before me always' (Ps. 16:8). Such decorative plaques are hung on the walls of Jewish homes and placed in front of the chazzan's desk in the synagogue. Many other verses and motifs are interwoven with this verse from Psalms on the plaques, such as Kabbalistic images, a seven-branched candlestick, the shape of a hand to ward off demons, and lions. Sometimes the shivviti is in the form of a papercut, and it might be combined with the MIZRACH sign which indicates the direction of Jerusalem. The idea behind such plaques is the need to keep God always before one's mind, the four letters of the tetragrammaton usually occupying a prominent place on the shivviti plaque. Certain pietists endeavoured to keep the image of the name of God literally in their mind's eye at all times, but for ordinary mortals the shivviti acts as a reminder of the divine presence.

shlach monos *see* PURIM

shlemiel (Yiddish for 'fool', 'born loser') According to a Yiddish proverb a shlemiel is the type of person who, when he falls on his back, damages his nose. As a personality type the shlemiel is born a shlemiel, not made into one by circumstances, and once a shlemiel always a shlemiel. He figures prominently in Yiddish

The month of **Shevat**, represented by the zodiacal sign of the water carrier, from a synagogue mosaic at Hammath, Tiberias.

Shivviti plaque showing the tetragrammaton surrounded by divine and angelic names, with a menorah at the bottom.

literature and Jewish folklore and represents an amalgam of all those Eastern European Jewish characters who were simply unable to make a go of the life of the shtetl. The people of CHELM represent a special type of shlemiel, bringing a mad wisdom to their crazy attempts to cope with a complex reality. The story is told of how an angel was given the task of distributing wise and foolish souls in equal numbers throughout the earth. When the angel got to Chelm he tripped, and only the foolish souls fell out. The shlemiel is related to the NEBICH but should be distinguished from the shlimazel. The latter is an unlucky person who may have talent but is unfortunate. The shlemiel is not unlucky, just inept. It is said that when a shlemiel carrying a bowl of soup stumbles, he pours the hot liquid down the neck of a shlimazel.

shlimazel *see* NEBICH; SHLEMIEL

Shmuel Bukh (Yiddish for '*Samuel Book*') A Yiddish epic in rhyme, modelled on medieval German ballads, about the prophet Samuel, King Saul and King David. The *Shmuel Bukh* was written in the 15c. and is the first major YIDDISH epic. It retells the biblical stories in the light of midrash and Talmudic legend, with descriptions of battle scenes and acts of heroism. King David is depicted in glowing terms, and the weaknesses and sins ascribed to him in the Bible are glossed over. The book was very popular and had considerable influence on the development of Yiddish literature. Its poetry was sung to a special tune.

Shneur Zalman of Lyady (1747–1813) Chasidic leader and founder of the Chabad (*see* LUBAVITCH) branch of the Chasidic Movement. At the age of eighteen Shneur Zalman went to study with Dov Baer of Mezhirech to learn how to serve God. Eventually, he became one of the leaders of the Chasidim in White Russia, introducing a more intellectual approach to religion than the emotive form favoured by his Polish colleagues. He believed that the contemplation of the greatness of God should be an essential part of Chasidic piety, although he encouraged song and dance among his followers and used to pray in ecstasy, banging his hand against the wall without noticing the blood that trickled down. His devotion to God is expressed in his saying: 'I do not want Your afterlife or Your Garden of Eden – I want only You.' In 1796 he published his *Tanya* in which he explained how the brain should rule the heart and how meditation raises man's lower instincts. He also emphasized the difference between Jews, who possess a divine soul, and Gentiles, who only possess an animal soul. The book has since become a classic and is studied daily by his followers. In order to annul the decree of excommunication (cherem), which Elijah the Vilna Gaon had proclaimed against Chasidism, Shneur Zalman visited Vilna to try to persuade the Gaon to change his mind. The latter would not even see his Chasidic visitor, however, and so nothing came of these peace moves. The Mitnaggedim, opponents of Chasidism, were incensed by the behaviour of Shneur Zalman's disciples when they rejoiced at the death of the Vilna Gaon. Shneur Zalman was denounced to the Czarist authorities, was twice arrested and interrogated but each time was found innocent. His descendants,

who succeeded him in the leadership of Chabad Chasidism, were gifted scholars and mystics. One son, however, rebelled against the Jewish tradition, became an irreligious drunk and it was even rumoured that he converted to Christianity. *See also* MICROGRAPHY.

shochet *see* SHECHITAH

shofar (Hebrew for 'horn') Ancient instrument blown on rosh ha-shanah (Num. 29:1) to awaken people from their spiritual slumber and summon them to repentance. The most commonly used shofar is made from a hollowed-out ram's horn, which serves as a reminder of the ram that was substituted as a sacrifice for Isaac in the story of the akedah. There are three basic sounds for the shofar blowing: tekiah, a long plain note; shevarim, three broken notes; and teruah, a series of short trumpet notes. A hundred shofar sounds are blown in the synagogue as part of the rosh ha-shanah liturgy (*see* SANDALFON). The blowing is divided into two parts in order to confuse Satan, who may be led to think that the second shofar blowing heralds the DAY OF JUDGMENT, when Elijah will blow the great shofar to inaugurate the ingathering of the exiles and the Resurrection of the Dead. In some communities the shofar is blown briefly each morning during the month of Elul, leading up to rosh ha-shanah, and at the end of the yom kippur fast. It is also used in the EXORCISM ritual and when someone is excommunicated by the community (*see* CHEREM).

shokelin *see* SWAYING IN PRAYER

shtadlan (Aramaic for 'intercessor') Jew who represents the Jewish community to the secular authorities. The shtadlan would try to ensure that Jews gained permission to reside in certain areas, that they were not expelled, that taxes on Jews were not excessive, that the community was protected from mob violence or from religiously inspired anti-Semitism, and that Jewish prisoners were released after payment of a ransom. A well-organized Jewish community would employ a professional shtadlan to act as a one-man Jewish pressure group, since Jews had no basic rights until modern times. The shtadlan's task could also be undertaken by any Jew who happened to be in a position to help. COURT JEWS, Jews in government service, merchants who might have social contacts with officials and rabbis who were in touch with the Church hierarchy all acted in the role of shtadlan when the need arose. Thus Gracia Nasi and members of the NASI FAMILY influenced the Turkish Sultan to support the Marrano cause in the mid-16c.; Saul Wahl, whom legend depicts as having been appointed King of Poland for one day, helped the community of Brest-Litovsk win the right to try lawsuits between Jews in 1593; Moses MENDELSSOHN, the great German-Jewish savant, interceded with the Duke of Schwerin on behalf of the local Jewish community and was also active in the campaign for the emancipation of German Jewry in the 18c.; Moses MONTEFIORE acted as a shtadlan for the Russian Jewish masses, for the Damascus community during a blood libel accusation and in the Mortara Case in Italy in the 19c. In modern times Theodor HERZL, the founder of political Zionism, devoted the latter part of his life to persuading leading statesmen to support the cause of establishing a Jewish homeland.

shtetl (Yiddish for 'little town') Small provincial community of Jews in pre-modern Eastern Europe (i.e. Russia, Poland, Lithuania and the eastern part of the Austro-Hungarian Empire). Most of the Jews in the PALE OF SETTLEMENT lived in shtetl-type towns or villages, where the Jews often constituted the majority population. In some few cases the town was wholly Jewish in make-up. The shtetl was the main demographic centre of the Ashkenazim in the 19c. where the lingua franca was YIDDISH, which Jews referred to as mama loschen, the 'mother tongue'. Judaism was known as yiddishkeyt, and turned around the intimate synagogue, known as a SHUL or shtibl. At the core of shtetl life lay the extended family, mishpochoh, with its many branches and large numbers of children. Education for boys took place in cheder and then at a more advanced level in yeshivah. Status came from learning as well as wealth, and families were proud of illustrious ancestors (yichus) who guaranteed better marriage prospects through the assistance of a marriage broker (shadkhan). The shtetl had a number of welfare schemes to support those in particularly difficult circumstances. Everyone was expected to contribute to charity. Local beggars (*see* SCHNORER) were an integral part of community life. Although there was tension between Jews and non-Jews in the shtetl, occasionally leading to the outbreak of a POGROM, the two communities interrelated with each other, and a Gentile might act as a shabbos goi for his Jewish neighbours. *See also* MAGGID; SHLEMIEL.

shtibl (Yiddish for 'little room') Small synagogue favoured by communities within the Chasidic Movement because of its informal atmosphere. A shtibl is usually a converted house in which an ark and a makeshift bimah are set up, but since there are no pews, the congregants sit around tables. Ritual meals, like seudah shlishit on Saturday afternoons, are eaten in the shtibl, and groups meet there to study the torah. The services are led by laymen, there being no salaried officials, and the style of prayer is emotional with singing, dancing and hand-clapping. Each Chasidic subgroup usually has its own shtibl, if the members can muster a minyan, where they run the services according to their special customs. The shtibl involves much less expense than a purpose-built synagogue, and so is within the means of a small, often impoverished, community.

shtreimel Wide-brimmed hat once common among East European Jews but now worn mostly by members of the Chasidic Movement on shabbat and festivals. The hat is round in shape, with a black centre surrounded by thirteen brown sable furs. Certain Chasidic groups wear a spodak, a high conical fur hat, instead of a shtreimel. Under the shtreimel/spodak a small skullcap, or yarmulke, is worn (*see* HEAD-COVERING). The shtreimel was once an item of clothing worn by Poles and was adopted by Jews when Western dress became the norm in Russia and Poland. By retaining this older form of headgear, Jews preserved a separate identity from Polish Gentiles, and thus it attained a certain sanctity as a feature of specifically

Interior of a small Polish wooden **shtibl** painted in the traditional manner.

Jewish merchants in mid-19c. Odessa, showing the dress of the shtetl and fur **shtreimel** hats.

ᅟ

Jewish dress. The shtreimel is put on for the first time by a bridegroom at his marriage, and today it distinguishes the Chasid from other Orthodox Jews, most of whom wear ordinary hats.

shul (Yiddish for 'school') Common name for a synagogue among Ashkenazim, originally applied to a bet ha-midrash which was used both for prayer and for study, hence the name 'school'. The East European shul was a meeting place for the community, and the atmosphere even during prayers was informal. With regular study groups, shiurim, each evening, the menfolk of the community spent much of their free time there. Shul politics were the life-blood of the shtetl community. They involved competition among individuals and factions for positions of power in the synagogue and in-fighting between those who supported the rabbi and those who opposed him.

Shulchan Arukh (Hebrew for 'Prepared Table') The most authoritative code of HALAKHAH, written in the 16c. by Joseph CARO as a manual for laymen and young students. Caro based his decisions in the *Shulchan Arukh* on the majority opinion of three of his predecessors, two of whom were Sephardim. He often followed the language and formulation of Maimonides, one of the greatest Sephardi codifiers. Since the code neglected the traditions of the Ashkenazim and their customs, Moses ISSERLES, a Polish contemporary of Caro, wrote his own glosses to the work representing the Ashkenazi position. The two parts of the work, known as the 'Prepared Table' and the 'Tablecloth', were subsequently printed together, making the joint code widely acceptable to most sections of Jewry. It did not achieve its position of pre-eminence, however, without controversy, since its very strengths as a popular code were considered a major defect by certain rabbis. It was feared that the *Shulchan Arukh* would lead people to regard the views of Caro or Isserles as more authoritative than those of the *Talmud* itself and would discourage people from going back to the sources. One eminent critic was JUDAH LOEW BEN BEZALEL.

siddur *see* PRAYER-BOOK

sidra *see* MAFTIR; ONKELOS

siman tov *see* GREETINGS

simchat bet ha-shoevah *see* WATER DRAWING FESTIVITIES

simchat torah (Hebrew for 'rejoicing of the torah') The ceremonials associated with the conclusion of the annual torah reading which take place in Israel on SHEMINI ATZERET and in the diaspora on the next day, the ninth day of sukkot. In the evening all sefer torah scrolls are taken out of the ark, and a candle is left in their place to signify the light of torah which continues to burn. The male congregants carry the scrolls as they parade around the synagogue with singing and dancing. There are seven HAKKAFOT in all, and the celebrations sometimes go on for several hours (*see* SIYYUM). Children carry flags, on the top of which

are lighted candles inserted into apples. The ritual is repeated the next morning. At the end of the evening hakkafot, a short torah reading takes place, and in the morning the last section of Deuteronomy and the first section of Genesis are read for specially appointed BRIDEGROOMS OF THE TORAH, chatan torah and chatan bereshit. Before these bridegrooms are called up, each adult male in the synagogue takes his turn for an aliyah to recite the benedictions over the torah. An adult also gathers all the children together under a tallit on the bimah to repeat the benedictions after him. It is customary for the two bridegrooms to host a simchat torah party for the whole congregation.

Simeon Bar Yochai (2c. CE) Mishnaic sage and mystic. Simeon, who was a pupil of Akiva, shared his master's antagonism to the Romans and even denigrated their achievements. He used to say: 'The best of heathens deserves to be put to death.' To escape arrest by the Roman authorities and a possible death sentence, he and his son went into hiding in a cave for thirteen years. They were able to survive because a carob tree and a spring of water miraculously appeared. Father and son used to sit buried in the sand during the day, so that their clothes would not wear out, while the prophet Elijah visited them and taught them heavenly secrets. When the Roman emperor who had sought to punish Simeon died, he and his son returned to civilization. Simeon grew very angry, however, when he found how much ordinary Jews were now disregarding the study of torah, and his fiery gaze burnt up the world around him. To stop this destruction, Simeon was made to return to the cave for a further twelve months. At the end of that period he resumed his role as teacher, gathering around him a group of companions to whom he revealed mystic teachings. A protective fire burnt around his academy, not allowing those unworthy of receiving his instruction to enter. When Simeon went on a journey, nature itself would respond to him: birds hovered overhead to keep the sun away, and trees spread out their branches for shade. The ZOHAR is thought by Kabbalists to record these secret teachings of the master. During Simeon's lifetime, no rainbow appeared since his merits were sufficient to protect the world, and in heaven even the Messiah studies at his academy. Simeon died on LAG BA-OMER.

Simeon Ben Azzai (2c. CE) Mishnaic sage. Simeon was one of the few rabbinic figures who never married because he devoted his life to the study of TORAH. He used to excuse himself by saying: 'My soul desires only the torah.' According to one view he was actually betrothed to Akiva's daughter for some time, although he never consummated the marriage. Simeon was one of the four sages who went on a mystical journey to PARADISE, but as a bachelor he was not stable enough for such an experience so he 'gazed on the plants and died'. Simeon believed that the reward for keeping the commandments was the ability to keep further commandments, and the punishment for sin was further sinning. It is said that seeing Ben Azzai in a dream is an omen of spiritual growth.

Simeon Ben Lakish (3c. CE) Palestinian Talmudic sage, commonly known as Resh Lakish. As a young

man Simeon left respectable society to become a
gladiator and a robber. He was brought back to a life
of torah, repeating his studies forty times till he
memorized them, and became one of the leading
scholars of his generation. He still preserved some
of his anti-establishment views, expressed opinions
independent of his colleagues and was even critical of
the Nasi. So careful was he about the company he
kept that it was said that anybody with whom Simeon
was seen in public conversation could be lent money
without any security, since they were bound to be
respectable. The tough quality of his early life inclined
him to asceticism, and he taught his students to be
prepared to sacrifice their lives for the torah, so that
its words would penetrate through to them. He himself
was able to sleep on the ground, since he was
short and corpulent and his fat protected him from
discomfort. He also warned people that adultery could
be committed with the eyes and mind as well as
physically. Man's natural condition is not to sin, but
he sins when a foolish spirit enters into him. At the
end of his life Simeon suffered greatly when he was
reminded of his unsavoury past. In a dispute about
swords and their ritual impurity, he was once upset
by a colleague who remarked to him that 'the robber
knows his tools'.

Simeon Ben Shetach (1c. BCE) Pharisaic sage, President of the Sanhedrin and brother of Queen Salome,
the wife of King Alexander Yannai. Simeon was an
outspoken proponent of his views and no respecter of
persons. He lost the sympathy of his brother-in-law,
who favoured the Sadducees, but on the latter's death
Salome became ruler and allowed the Pharisees to
dominate Jewish life in Palestine and oust the Sadducees. Simeon was an uncompromising leader and once
had eighty witches executed in Ashkelon. When his
son was arraigned on false charges by the witches'
families and eventually executed, he refused to inter-
vene because he did not wish to undermine the judicial
system. He introduced legislation to safeguard wives in
divorce cases and brought about educational reforms,
appointing professional teachers for children, who
previously had been taught by their parents. On one
occasion Simeon bought an ass from a Gentile and
found a precious stone around its neck. He returned
the gem because he had only bought an ass, not a
jewel, and the heathen praised the God of Simeon Ben
Shetach.

Simon the Righteous (3c.–2c. BCE) Early Pharisaic
leader who was one of the last members of the Great
Synagogue. Simon was High Priest for forty years, and
when Alexander the Great passed through Palestine,
Simon met him dressed in his full high-priestly regalia.
He impressed Alexander and won his support against
the Samaritans. Simon objected to people taking the
Nazirite vow. Once, however, he met a beautiful
Nazirite who had taken the vow when he saw his
reflection in water and became enamoured with his
own beauty. The Nazirite said to himself: 'You wicked
fellow, why are you so arrogant? One day you will
be worms.' He then took the Nazirite vow. When he
heard this, Simon kissed him on his forehead and said:
'May there be many Nazirites like you in Israel.' His
priestly reign was accompanied by a number of

The interior of the Altneu **shul** in Prague, one of
the oldest Ashkenazi synagogues in Europe.

A synagogue in Livorno on the festival of **simchat
torah** when all the torah scrolls are carried in
procession around the bimah (Solomon Hart).

miracles. The lights of the Temple never went out, and the red thread around the scapegoat sent to Azazel on yom kippur always turned white, indicating that the sins of Israel were forgiven. Simon knew the year of his death because he was always accompanied by an angelic figure in white when he entered the Holy of Holies on yom kippur. During the last year of his life, he was accompanied by a figure dressed in black.

sin (Hebrew 'chet') One of the meanings of sin in the Bible is missing the mark, straying from the path, and thus REPENTANCE is literally returning to God. Since man has FREE WILL, he is always responsible for his actions, so in ancient times he had to atone even for unintentional sins by bringing a sin offering. No man in fact sins unless a spirit of foolishness enters into him. There are three Cardinal Sins: idolatry, murder and sexual immorality, which must not be committed even to save life. Gossiping (*see* LASHON HA-RA) is also regarded as a particularly bad sin. It is also particularly evil to cause others to sin. The saintly Chanina Ben Dosa was once asked to rid a village of a poisonous reptile. He did so by placing his foot over the reptile's lair. When it bit him, the reptile died, and Chanina commented that it was not the bite of a reptile which kills people but sin. The intention to sin is not counted as a sin itself, with the exception of idolatrous thoughts which are already part of the sin of idolatry. God punishes sin, and even repentance and the penitential fast of YOM KIPPUR is not always sufficient to win FORGIVENESS without further punishment. Sin makes the divine presence (*see* SHEKHINAH) depart and increases the power of the SITRA ACHRA, and according to the Kabbalah, it leaves its impression on the forehead, on which the record of a person's sins can be read. Converts to Judaism and couples at their MARRIAGE are considered to be like new born children, and all their sins are forgiven them. *See also* ASHAMNU; CHILLUL HA-SHEM; GOOD AND EVIL; INCLINATION; ORIGINAL SIN; TASHLIKH.

Sinai, Mount (also called Horeb) Desert mountain where God appeared to MOSES in a BURNING BUSH (Exod. 3) and where the DECALOGUE and ORAL TORAH were revealed to the people of Israel after the Exodus (Exod. 19,20). God chose this mountain because it was the lowliest of mountains, to show how much He valued humility and to teach the lesson that no part of Creation is beneath His consideration. It was also chosen because Sinai had once been part of Mount Moriah on which the akedah, or sacrifice of Isaac, was to have taken place. Sinai separated itself from the Temple Mount in Jerusalem and went into the wilderness. At the giving of the torah, the bare mountain burst into flower and greenery, and at SHAVUOT synagogues are decorated with flowers and plants to commemorate this. When the Israelites were gathered at Mount Sinai, God raised the mount above their heads. He threatened them that, if they did not accept the torah, they would be buried there because their whole existence as a people depended on their vocation as the bearers of divine revelation (*see* COVENANT). *See also* DEW; PILPUL.

Sisera *see* DEBORAH; JAEL

sitra achra (Aramaic for 'other side') The generic name for demonic powers (*see* DEMONS), structured in the form of SEFIROT of impurity, which play a central role in the KABBALAH. The sitra achra came into being as part of the process of emanation because of the necessity of self-limitation within the Godhead, so that a world of finite entities could have an existence separate from the divine. It is thus a product of TZIMTZUM and of the constricting justice of the fifth sefirah (gevurah) which balances the overflowing divine love. The home of the sitra achra is on the left-hand side, in the hole of the great abyss ruled over by SAMAEL and Lilith. The sitra achra has no energy of its own and is parasitic on the divine light for its activity. Man's sins provide the sitra achra with sufficient energy to divide the SHEKHINAH from her divine husband and force her to enter into an adulterous relationship with Samael, thus bringing catastrophe to the world (*see* ORIGINAL SIN). Although the sitra achra is not an independent entity opposed to God but a waste by-product of emanation, to all intents and purposes it frustrates the spiritual development of God's world. As the evil inclination, it leads man into sin and covers holiness like a shell, kelippah, covers a fruit. On shabbat the forces of evil have to relinquish any control they have over the world, and the demons of the sitra achra slink back into the great abyss. The world of the sitra achra is depicted as a kind of anti-matter, reflecting the sefirotic realm through a distorting mirror like a monkey represents a distorted image of a man. In the age of the Messiah the sitra achra will cease to disrupt the harmony of creation. According to some Kabbalists Samael himself will be captured by the angel Michael and brought to the People of Israel in iron chains. After the evil has been purged from him, he will be transformed into an agent of holiness, and the divine light will illumine the sitra achra. *See also* DIETARY LAWS; ESAU.

Sivan Third lunar month of the Hebrew calendar, counting from Nisan the month of the Exodus, or ninth month from the New Year festival (rosh hashanah). Sivan usually begins sometime in late May or early June, and its zodiacal sign is the twins. The festival of SHAVUOT falls on the sixth of Sivan (and in the diaspora also on the seventh).

siyyum (Hebrew for 'conclusion') The completion of the study of a religious text, or of the writing of a sefer torah, which is usually followed by a party to mark the occasion. The whole community has such a party every year on simchat torah when the cycle of weekly readings of the torah is completed and begun again. It is also customary to complete the study of a text on the eve of Passover so that firstborn children, who should fast on that day, can break their fast by participating in the meal. The most common siyyum is when a study group completes a Talmudic tractate. Scholars give learned discourses, the HADRAN is recited, the ten sons of Rabbi Papa are mentioned, since their names are thought to help the memory, and a celebratory meal is served. It is permitted to eat meat and drink wine at a siyyum even at times of national mourning, such as the nine days preceding the Fast of Av. Since 1923 there has been a programme of study of one page of the *Talmud* every day, known as daf ha-yomi, undertaken by Jews all over the world. This involves a major siyyum ever seven years or so, when the whole of the Babylonian *Talmud* is completed.

slaughter *see* SHECHITAH

Sodom City by the Dead Sea which was destroyed because of the wickedness of its inhabitants (Gen. 19). The people of Sodom hated strangers since they suspected all outsiders of having come to gain possession of the riches of the area. They used to subject all strangers, even the males, to sexual abuse. They kept Procrustean beds for visitors on which they would stretch them, if they were too short, or cut off their legs if they were too long. One girl of Sodom was punished for feeding a beggar. She was dipped in .honey and then exposed to be consumed by bees. When they did have a system of law and order, they only followed the letter of the law, refusing to help others when the law did not demand it, even though it cost them nothing to do so. Only Lot, his wife and two of his daughters were saved from destruction by the angel to whom they had offered hospitality. While escaping, Lot's family were told not to look back, but his wife could not resist the temptation to see what was happening to the doomed city. When she glanced behind her, she was turned into a pillar of salt, which was still known as a landmark in the Middle Ages (*see* BENJAMIN OF TUDELA). *See also* MINYAN.

sofer, soferim *see* SCRIBE

Sofer, Moses *see* HAIR AND BEARD; ORTHODOX JUDAISM

Solomon Third king of Israel and son of David and Bathsheba. Solomon was offered one gift by God and asked for wisdom, since everything else depends on it. With divine help Solomon came to know the language of animals and birds and gained a reputation as the wisest of men (I Kings 5). His renown extended as far as the Land of SHEBA whose queen came to visit him to obtain knowledge of sorcery. Yet his wisdom misled him into believing he could ignore the warnings against a king amassing wealth and horses, and taking many wives (Deut. 17), as well as several hundred concubines. His confidence in himself was unfounded, and at the end of his life his wives led him astray. Solomon built the First TEMPLE in Jerusalem with the help of angels and demons, over whom he had some control, and used the miraculous SHAMIR worm to split rocks for the Temple and altar. Solomon managed to capture ASMODEUS, the king of demons, but he was tricked by him and had to go into exile, leaving Asmodeus impersonating him on his throne. He remained away for three years, wandering great distances on the back of an eagle. He visited the mountains of darkness where the fallen angels, Aza and Azazel, were bound. There he learnt secrets by means of a magical plate on which the name of God was engraved. He was eventually able to return to his kingdom when he managed to convince people that the occupant of his throne was an imposter and that he was the real Solomon. Solomon had the gift of prophecy and wrote the SONG OF SONGS in his youth, PROVERBS when middle aged and ECCLESIASTES as an old man. *See also* ALCHEMY; LUZ.

Rock formation known as 'Lot's wife', near the Dead Sea on the site of the biblical **Sodom**.

The Judgment of **Solomon**, detail of relief on a silver casket of Italian origin.

Song of Songs (Hebrew 'Shir Ha-shirim') Biblical book written by King Solomon in the form of a series of love poems, also known as the Song of Solomon and Canticles. The book is generally interpreted allegorically to depict the love between God and the People of Israel. Questions were raised in the 2c. CE about whether the book should be regarded as inspired or as a secular composition, since the name of God does not appear in it. Rabbi Akiva defended the Song of Songs against its detractors with the words: 'All the scriptures are holy but the Song of Songs is the holy of holies.' The Song of Songs is read in the synagogue on Passover, the festival of the Exodus, because Pharaoh's chariot is mentioned in the book (1:9). Kabbalists introduced the custom of reading the work on Friday before the onset of shabbat, since the Sabbath is depicted as a bride, and on the Sabbath eve the male and female aspects of the divine come together in loving union. Friday night is thus a time when sexual relations between husband and wife are encouraged in mystical *imitatio dei*. *See also* MEGILLAH.

sotah (Hebrew for 'woman who has turned away') A wife suspected of ADULTERY, who underwent a trial by ordeal, drinking a bowl of 'bitter water' to prove her guilt or innocence. If her husband had warned her against consorting with a certain man and she was found to have been alone with him, then the husband brought her to the Temple in Jerusalem. There the Sanhedrin tried to persuade her to admit her guilt, so as not to undergo the ordeal, in which case she would be divorced by her husband. If she maintained her innocence, a priest took dust from the sanctuary floor, sprinkled it onto water into which he then dissolved a text with the curses against the sotah (Num. 8) and gave it to her to drink. If she was guilty, her face lost its colour, her eyes bulged, her stomach swelled, and she died. At the same time God also punished the person who had committed adultery with her, and he died. If her husband had himself committed adultery, the waters had no effect upon her, nor did they have any effect on an innocent woman who emerged from the ordeal with her reputation intact and with God's blessing that she would have many children. Though the ritual ceased after the destruction of the Temple, the lesson learnt from it was the importance of making peace between husband and wife, for God was willing to have His name erased from a Bible text to achieve that purpose.

soul (Hebrew 'nefesh', 'neshamah') The soul of man represents the divine part of the human being, the image of God in man, and is described as the lamp of God. God breathes the soul into each man as he did into Adam, the first man. At death man's soul leaves him (*see* AFTERLIFE), just as it does each night in sleep, and will return once again to a physical form at the Resurrection of the Dead. The body is to be washed and treated respectfully because it acts as host to the soul, and it is for God alone to decide when He wishes to take back what He has given. Suicide is therefore forbidden. On the Sabbath each Jew receives an extra soul (*see* NESHAMAH YETERAH) which brings him the extra holiness associated with the day. According to the Kabbalah each soul originates from a combination of male and female soul elements which split up on

coming into the world. Heterosexual love between husband and wife is seen as the attempt of the male and female souls to reunite as one whole. Individual souls are made up of different parts. Among these soul subdivisions, there is the animal soul which all humans have and the divine soul which is only possessed by the People of Israel. Beyond the level of the divine soul, there are further structures, including the soul of the soul through which the mystical apprehension of the divine is achieved. The Lurianic Kabbalah specialized in being able to tell which soul aspects from the past had transmigrated (*see* TRANSMIGRATION OF SOULS) into contemporary bodies. *See also* SPICES; TIKKUN.

spices (Hebrew 'besamim') Spices were used in the Jerusalem Temple for incense offerings. It was believed that the sound of the chant used while grinding the spices actually improved the quality of the incense. So powerful was the aroma of the incense that it wafted as far as Jericho, and the *Talmud* reports that brides in Jerusalem did not need to perfume themselves before marriage because its sweet smell was sufficient. In the HAVDALAH ceremony on Saturday night, which marks the transition from the holy shabbat to profane time, spices are used. These spices are meant to comfort and stimulate the ordinary weekday soul which remains after the extra soul (neshamah yeterah), which each Jew possesses for the duration of the Sabbath, leaves. It was considered shameful for a scholar to go out in public smelling of perfume or spices.

spodak *see* SHTREIMEL

Star of David *see* BADGE, JEWISH; MAGEN DAVID

suicide It is forbidden to take innocent human life, including one's own, and a suicide was thought to lose his portion in the World to Come (olam haba). The 2c. martyr Rabbi Chananiah Ben Teradyon even refused to hasten his own death when he was burnt alive by the Romans, because it was up to God to take his life away. In the past, suicides would be buried at the outer extremity of a Jewish cemetery, and no mourning rites would take place in their honour. Today, however, suicides are assumed not to be responsible for their actions and are treated like other people. There are several circumstances where suicide is permitted or prescribed. For instance, one should be prepared to die, even by one's own hand, rather than transgress the three cardinal sins of idolatry, sexual immorality (*see* HANNAH AND HER SEVEN SONS) and homicide. Martyrs should prefer death to forced conversion to another faith (*see* MARTYRDOM). The suicide of SAMSON, who killed himself with the Philistines, of SAUL, who fell on his own sword to avoid degradation and death at the hands of his enemies, of the inhabitants of MASADA, who killed each other rather than be captured by the Romans, or of the Jews of York, who burned themselves alive rather than be converted to Christianity, have all been held up as exemplary (*see also* JOSEPHUS FLAVIUS). A dispute raged in the Middle Ages about whether it was permissible to kill children at times of anti-Jewish persecution to prevent them being forcibly baptized. In one tragic incident, a rabbi had the children of his community killed at a time of persecution, basing himself on the story of the akedah when Abraham offered up his son to God. The anti-Jewish measures subsided, however, and the community escaped forced conversion. A colleague of the rabbi called him a murderer and uttered a curse that he would die a strange and terrible death. This indeed happened when the rabbi was later captured by a Christian mob who skinned him alive and put sand under his skin.

sukkah (Hebrew for 'tabernacle') During the festival of SUKKOT Jews transfer their living quarters from the house to a sukkah, which is a makeshift booth whose roof is of branches or vegetation thin enough to let the rain in. People eat in the sukkah, and many pious Jews even sleep there. The sukkah is meant to remind Jews of the booths in which their ancestors dwelt when they wandered in the wilderness during the Exodus (Lev. 23:43) and of the clouds of glory which surrounded them. They were protected by God from the elements, and by remembering this, Jews are reminded that it is not the brick and mortar of the house which affords ultimate protection but God Himself. Although the Exodus took place in spring, the festival of sukkot is celebrated in the autumn, since people naturally move out of their homes into cooler accommodation in the spring, and the significance of dwelling in booths would be lost. Autumn is also the end of harvest season when the granaries are full. Moving into a simple dwelling thus serves to remind rich farmers of the plight of the poor. Each evening of the festival, seven biblical characters are invited to the sukkah as spiritual guests (*see* USHPIZIN). Each one in turn is the special guest for an evening, the others coming to accompany him, and if the host does not also invite poor people to join him for the meal, the spiritual guests depart in disgust at this lack of hospitality. The mystics identified the sukkah with the Divine Presence, shekhinah, within whose being the whole universe dwells, and they thus understood living in the sukkah as an affirmation of faith. *See also* SAMARITANS.

sukkot (Hebrew for 'Tabernacles') One of the three PILGRIM FESTIVALS or HARVEST FESTIVALS. Sukkot is a seven-day festival, beginning on the fifteenth of Tishri after the ingathering of the yearly harvest, and is the happiest of the biblical festivals. It celebrates God's bounty in nature and God's protection, symbolized by the fragile booths in which the Israelites dwelt in the wilderness. During sukkot Jews eat and live in such booths or tabernacles (*see* SUKKAH) which give the festival its name and its distinctive character. The FOUR SPECIES, representing the agricultural world, are waved together during the recitation of HALLEL each day of sukkot, except on shabbat, and the bimah in the synagogue is circumambulated with them (*see* HAKKAFOT). From the second night on, there are minor celebrations based on the WATER DRAWING FESTIVITIES in the Temple, and the seventh day is HOSHANA RABBA when the synagogue is circumambulated seven times and willow branches are beaten on the ground. At the end of sukkot there is a separate festival, SHEMINI ATZERET. According to the Rabbis sukkot is also a festival involving Gentiles, and seventy bullocks were offered up in the Temple for the seventy

Box for havdalah **spices** (Bohemian).

Interior of the New Synagogue, London, showing the celebration of the festival of **sukkot**.

SUN

192

nations of the world. The mystics explain that, because of God's love for Israel, He wished to give something of His offerings to the guardian angels of each nation, thus encouraging them to love Israel, also. In the Messianic age all nations will come up to Jerusalem to celebrate sukkot, as an affirmation of faith in God's guidance of the world. *See also* CHOL HA-MOED.

sun (Hebrew 'chammah', 'shemesh') The MOON is thought to symbolize the Jewish people, with its lunar CALENDAR and its periods of waning and waxing, while the sun symbolizes the Gentile nations. Thus, an eclipse of the sun is a token of bad luck for the Gentiles. Nevertheless, there is a ceremony of blessing the sun, birkat ha-chammah, every twenty-eight years at the beginning of Nisan when it returns to the position in the sky which it occupied when first created. In the Messianic era God will remove the sun from the covering which masks it, and its heat will burn up the wicked but will heal the sick among the righteous. This is based on the words of the prophet Malachi that there will be healing on the wings of the sun of righteousness when it rises (3:20). According to one Talmudic view, the sun is essentially white in colour, but it appears red because in the morning its rays are reflected through the rose leaves of the Garden of Eden as it rises, and in the evening they are reflected through the fires of gehinnom as it sets. The sun symbolizes the essentially masculine aspect of the Creation, since it gives its heat and light, while the moon symbolizes the receiving, feminine aspect. Thus, someone born while the sun shines will be able to support himself and not have to receive his sustenance from others.

superstition Superstitious practices were prohibited in the Bible on the basis of the verse, 'You shall be perfect with the Lord your God' (Deut. 18:9), which forbids competing beliefs to intrude into Israel's monotheism. Yet, despite the proscription of certain types of behaviour as 'Amorite ways', a whole series of superstitious practices found their way into Jewish lore. These involved activities associated with healing, which even some rationalists allowed because if people believed in them they were effective, beliefs about lucky or unlucky times, ways of behaviour which might attract the attention of DEMONS and many quasi-magical practices which were supported by popular forms of KABBALAH. In the course of time some of the more obscure superstitions associated with ASTROLOGY and MAGIC were jettisoned on the grounds that times had changed and such forces were not operative any more. Folk beliefs like the EVIL EYE, which gained a firm place in the halakhah, retained their hold on people's imagination. Other beliefs were upheld on religious, rather than superstitious, grounds. Lucky days were reinterpreted as relating to the differences between the days of the week in the Creation story. Tuesday, for instance, is twice referred to as a day on which God saw that His work was good and is therefore a 'lucky' day. There were many attempts by rabbis to eradicate superstitious practices which they felt were alien to Judaism. These attempts had only limited success, either because other rabbis approved of the practices or because they were so deeply entrenched in the consciousness of the ordinary Jew

that any opposition to them appeared heretical. Whole areas of ritual, such as those associated with DEATH and BURIAL, or with BIRTH, were structured as much around superstitious and magical beliefs as around biblical and Talmudic teachings. *See also* CHUKKAT HA-GOI.

swaying in prayer (Yiddish 'shokelin') It is common for Jews to sway back and forth while praying and while studying torah. A variety of different explanations have been proffered to explain this. The *Talmud* suggests that it is an expression of ecstacy in line with the verse from Psalms (35:10), 'All my bones shall say: "Lord, who is like You." ' The mystics saw it as a reflection of the flickering light of the Jewish soul, a spark from the holy light of God, in communion with its source. The philosopher Judah Halevi offered the more pragmatic opinion that it originated in the scarcity of religious texts, so that people had to sway forward to read and backward to enable others to read in their turn. It has also been maintained that swaying is an aid to inflaming the heart with devotion, or that it is used to shake off profane thoughts which arise during prayer, or that it symbolizes the union between man and God, the spiritual counterpart of the sexual union which involves a swaying action, or that it helps keep people awake, or that it has remained from the time that Jews were nomads and swayed on their camels, or that it provides much-needed exercise for scholars who spend most of their day sitting and studying. From time to time leading rabbis opposed swaying in prayer as an unseemly response to God, but the custom has persisted in traditional communities despite this criticism. It is only in Reform, Conservative and some more modern Orthodox congregations that prayers are conducted without overt bodily movements.

synagogue (from the Greek for 'place of gathering') The synagogue is assumed to have begun as an institution sometime during the Babylonian Captivity, after the destruction of the First Temple. According to Jewish tradition, however, it is much older, and synagogues already existed at the time of the Patriarch Jacob who as a child in his mother's womb tried to get out every time she passed one. Moses is said to have instructed the Israelites on how to pray in synagogues. When the Babylonian exiles returned to the Holy Land, they brought the use of synagogues back with them, and these continued side by side with the sacrificial cult of the Second Temple. The synagogue set the pattern for the organization of all future diaspora communities and came into its own after the destruction of the Second Temple in 70 CE. Wherever Jews settled, they built a synagogue for prayer, for torah reading and for conducting community affairs. It was used as a COMMUNITY meeting-place, hence both its Greek name and its Hebrew name, bet ha-keneset ('meeting house'). It was forbidden for a Jew to live in a town where there was no synagogue, which was also used by travellers as a lodging-house, where one could always find a place to sleep on a spare bench or in a corner. Often these synagogues of the BET HA-MIDRASH type were simple buildings and were used as much for study as for prayer. Occasionally they were large, elaborate buildings with frescos and mosaics (*see* ART, RELIGIOUS). The great synagogue in Alexandria, Egypt, in the 1c. CE was so large that the worshippers at the back could not hear the chazzan leading the prayers (*see* JUDAH BEN ILAI). A synagogue is built facing towards the site of the Temple in Jerusalem, and although it is a lay institution with priests playing only a minor role, it is referred to as a 'little sanctuary' (based on Ezek. 11:16). In the age of the Messiah all the synagogues of the diaspora will be uprooted and replanted in the land of Israel. *See also* ARK, HOLY; BIMAH; CHAZZAN; GABBAI; MECHITZAH; NER TAMID; RABBI; SEFER TORAH; SHAMMASH; SHTIBL; SHUL; TALLIT.

Synagogue, The Great (Hebrew 'anshei keneset ha-gedolah', meaning 'Men of the Great Assembly') Religious body said to have governed Jewry at the end of the prophetic period and to have included some of the prophets as its members. The councils of the Great Synagogue, consisting of 120 members, were called together by EZRA and the Scribes to deal with issues faced by the Jews returning from Babylonian exile. The institution of the Great Synagogue came to an end sometime in the 2c. BCE. Much of the ritual and liturgy of Rabbinic Judaism goes back to the enactments of the Great Synagogue, whose members were responsible for the authorship of certain biblical works and for undertaking the major task of determining the biblical canon.

A Polish wooden **synagogue** in Ludow.

taanit *see* FAST DAYS

taanit ester *see* ESTHER, FAST OF

Tabernacle (Hebrew 'mishkan') The portable sanctuary which was erected in the wilderness and accompanied the Israelites on their wanderings after the Exodus. It was attended by the LEVITES. Inside the Tabernacle was the HOLY OF HOLIES, containing the ARK OF THE COVENANT and the Tablets of the Decalogue, separated off by a curtain from the rest of the structure. The Tabernacle represented the indwelling of God in the midst of the community (shekhinah) and was modelled on the heavenly sanctuary. Its layout symbolized the Creation, the structure of the cosmos and the future history of the People of Israel up to the Messianic Age. The architect of the Tabernacle was BEZALEL but in fact it built itself. On one occasion when the Israelites were dying from plague, Aaron, the HIGH PRIEST, managed to stop the epidemic by dragging the Angel of Death into the Tabernacle and locking him in. The Tabernacle was replaced by the Temple in the time of Solomon.

Tabernacles *see* SUKKOT

Tablets of the Decalogue (Hebrew 'shenei luchot ha-berit', meaning 'two tablets of the Covenant') The two stones, taken from the Throne of Glory, on which the DECALOGUE was engraved. MOSES broke the first set of tablets, engraved by the finger of God, when he found the Israelites worshipping the Golden Calf

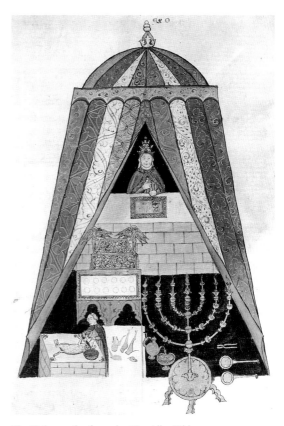

The **Tabernacle**, from the 15c. Alba Bible (Spanish).

on his descent from Mount Sinai. The divinely engraved text was lighter than air and supported the weight of the stone, thus enabling Moses to carry the tablets unaided. Confronted by the sin of the Israelites, the letters departed, and Moses dropped the stone which was now too heavy for him. He had to return to the top of Mount Sinai and carve a new set of tablets himself (see YOM KIPPUR). The first tablets contained the text of the Decalogue in Exodus (Exod. 20) and the second set contained the slightly different version in Deuteronomy (Deut. 5). The second set of tablets and the pieces of the first set were both kept in the ARK OF THE COVENANT, thus teaching the lesson that aged scholars who had forgotten their learning should, like the broken tablets, still be respected. The tablets were engraved right through in a wonderful manner and could be read from both sides. The circular letters were not supported by contact with the rest of the stone and maintained their position through a miracle.

taharah see BURIAL; CHEVRA KADDISHA

taharat ha-mishpachah (Hebrew for 'family purity') The proscription against sexual relations between a menstruating woman (see NIDDAH) and her husband during the time of her monthly bleeding, a minimum of five days, and for seven days afterwards. When she subsequently bathes in a MIKVEH, marital relations are resumed. Although children born to parents who do not practise family purity are not illegitimate (see MAMZER), they do carry a minor stigma and will grow into arrogant and unruly people. Sanctified sex was thought to lead to sanctified children and also enabled the husband and wife to be like a bride and groom again after twelve days of separation.

tal see DEW

tallit (Hebrew for 'cloak') Four-cornered prayer shawl with TZITZIT worn by males during morning prayers (shacharit). The tallit is usually made of white wool, silk or cotton, with black or purple stripes in memory of the blue TEKHELET thread which was once included in the fringes. The source of the custom of wearing a tallit is the biblical prescription: 'They shall make fringes on the corners of their garments ... that you may remember the commandments of the Lord and perform them.' A smaller version of the tallit in the form of a four-cornered vest, known as a tallit katan ('little tallit'), is worn by traditional Jews under their clothes throughout the day. Wearing such a tallit vest protects one from the evil eye and from demons. In many communities today all adult males wear a tallit in synagogue, although in the past there were places where scholars wore one and other Jews wore the fringed vest under their clothes. There are still communities among the Ashkenazim where only married men wear a prayer shawl, with the consequence that bachelors in the congregation are easily recognized. It is said that a Jew wrapped in a tallit is like an angel of the Lord of Hosts, and many Orthodox Jews of the old school wear their tallit over their heads as an expression of awe in the presence of God. A dead person is buried in his tallit, but the fringes of one corner are cut. Burying someone in a kosher tallit

would be regarded as mocking the dead, since they can no longer keep the commandments. In recent times a number of Jewish women have taken to wearing a tallit in synagogue, but this practice is not approved of by most Orthodox rabbis. The Krimchaks and some Sephardi communities use a tallit instead of a chuppah in their wedding ceremonies. See also MOLCHO, SOLOMON; PRIESTLY BLESSING; SIMCHAT TORAH.

talmid chakham see CHAKHAM

Talmud (Hebrew for 'study') The most important work of the ORAL TORAH, edited in the form of a long Aramaic commentary on sections of the MISHNAH. The Talmud is also known by the Aramaic name, Gemara, which came to be widely used to avoid the criticism by Christian censors of the Talmud as a foolish and revolting anti-Christian work. Ignorance of the Talmud, exemplified by the writer who referred to it as 'Rabbi Talmud', and the belief that it was the main obstacle to the conversion of the Jews, led to Talmud copies being burnt on a number of occasions by Christian authorities in medieval Europe. The Talmud was redacted in a Palestinian version (Yerushalmi, literally 'Jerusalem') in approximately 400 CE and in a more authoritative Babylonian version (Bavli) a hundred years later (see GAON). The two recensions of the Talmud reflect differences in social conditions and outlook between the communities of the Holy Land and of Babylonia. Agricultural laws relevant to Palestinian Jewish farmers occupy a prominent place in the Palestinian Talmud but not in the Babylonian. The latter has a much more highly developed tradition of demonology, reflecting Babylonian culture, than the former. Both Talmuds deal mainly with halakhah, but about one-third of the Bavli and one-sixth of the Yerushalmi focus on aggadah which involves not only theology but also midrash, folklore, medicine, astrology, magic, proverbs and stories about the Talmudic rabbis (see AMORA). The study of the Bible must be undertaken in a serious frame of mind, but the Talmud should be approached in a bright and lively mood and the text studied in a singsong manner using traditional melodies. The Babylonian Talmud is the main subject of study in YESHIVAH academies, where teachers often use a dialectical method of exegesis (see PILPUL) in their ventures into what is called the 'Sea of the Talmud'. Prominent among commentaries on the Talmud are those of Rashi. See also RESPONSA.

Tam, Jacob (1100–71) French rabbi whose real name was Jacob Ben Meir. He was given the nickname Tam, 'perfect', because of his saintliness and because this title was used of the biblical Jacob (Gen. 25:27). Tam was the grandson of Rashi and the greatest of the Tosafist school of Talmud commentators. In 1147 he had a narrow escape when a Crusader band broke into his home and destroyed his property. They wounded him, but he was miraculously saved by a Gentile nobleman, who managed to persuade them to leave when he indicated that, if they did not kill Jacob, he would convert him to Christianity. Tam was wealthy and on good terms with the French aristocracy, even

with the king of France. His halakhic rulings were of
an independent nature, sometimes being quite lenient,
and he tried to establish his bet din as the authoritative
law court for all Europe. Jacob Tam's poetry was
highly praised by his friend Abraham Ibn Ezra.

Tamar Daughter-in-law of JUDAH. Tamar dearly
wanted a child, so she disguised herself as a prostitute
and waited at a place that Judah would pass by to
entice him into having sexual relations with her (Gen.
38). He did not recognize her, because she was very
modest at home and her face was always covered.
When she was found to be pregnant, she showed great
strength of character in not revealing that Judah was
the father of her child, although she faced the death
penalty for her immoral behaviour. She merely sent
back the pledges, which Judah had left with her in
lieu of payment for her services as a prostitute, asking
him to identify them. When she was looking for these
pledges, Samael, the Prince of Demons, hid them from
her hoping she would indeed be executed, but the
angel Gabriel returned them. As a reward for her
behaviour in not embarrassing her father-in-law, she
became the ancestress of King David and of the
Messiah.

Tammuz Fourth lunar month of the Hebrew calendar, counting from Nisan the month of the Exodus,
or tenth month from the New Year festival (rosh ha-
shanah). Tammuz usually begins in late June or early
July, and its zodiacal sign is the crab. It is proverbial
as the hottest month of the year, and there is a folk-
saying quoted in the *Talmud* that 'asses feel cold even
in the month of Tammuz'. Although originally meant
literally, this was later taken to mean that fools
are never satisfied. The period of THREE WEEKS OF
MOURNING for the destruction of the Temple in
Jerusalem begins on the seventeenth of Tammuz (*see*
TAMMUZ, SEVENTEENTH OF).

A torah reader, wrapped in a **tallit**, reading from a
scroll, from a 14c. German illuminated Chumash
manuscript.

Tammuz, Seventeenth of (Hebrew 'shivah asar be-
tammuz') The beginning of the destruction of the
First and Second Temples is thought to have taken
place on the seventeenth of Tammuz, when the walls
of Jerusalem were breached. This is commemorated
by a FAST DAY which initiates a period of THREE WEEKS
OF MOURNING leading up to a fast on the Ninth of
Av, when the Temples themselves were destroyed.
According to the biblical version, the walls of Jerusalem
were breached in First Temple times on the ninth of
Tammuz (Jer. 52:6), but one Talmudic view dismisses
this as an inaccurate date due to the confusion following
the Temple's destruction. Other catastrophic events in
Jewish history are said to have taken place on the
seventeenth of Tammuz. These include the breaking
of the two Tablets of the Decalogue by Moses when
he found the Israelites worshipping the Golden Calf.
In the Messianic era this sad fast day will be turned
into a day of rejoicing.

tanna (Aramaic for 'teacher') A term, literally meaning
a 'repeater' of a text, which was originally used of
memorizers of the ORAL TORAH, who could provide
encyclopaedic recall, even though they may not have
understood what they were saying. Eventually 'tanna'
was used to refer to a sage from the period of the

A group of elderly Jews studying the *Talmud* in a
Jerusalem synagogue.

Mishnah in contrast to an AMORA from the Talmudic era. Judah Ha-Nasi was essentially the last tanna, although some of his pupils are referred to as having tannaitic authority to disagree with views expressed in the Mishnaic corpus.

Tanya *see* MICROGRAPHY; SHNEUR ZALMAN OF LYADY

Targum (Aramaic for 'translation') An Aramaic translation-commentary on the Bible. A Targum may be quite literal, like that of ONKELOS, or may involve a considerable amount of midrash, like *Targum Sheni* to the Book of Esther. Translations of the torah were originally made orally, line by line, by professional translators, as the Pentateuch was read in the synagogue. This was to enable Aramaic-speaking Jews, who did not know Hebrew, to understand the text. Certain sections of the Bible were left untranslated because they were felt not to be suitable for ordinary people. There was opposition to writing down these translations since, if they were too literal, they would not convey the correct exegesis of scripture, and if they were too midrashic, they would be a blasphemous addition to revelation. The *Talmud* tells how Gamaliel the Elder had a Targum of Job taken out of circulation and bricked up in a wall genizah.

taryag mitzvot *see* COMMANDMENTS, THE 613

tashlikh (Hebrew for 'you shall cast away') On the first day of ROSH HA-SHANAH, or on the second day if the first is a shabbat, it is customary to go to a river, the sea-shore or other place of flowing water where FISH are found and symbolically cast away one's sins. Various Psalms, biblical passages and prayers are recited, and people turn out their empty pockets into the water. There is a widespread custom for people to empty BREAD crumbs out of their pockets for the fish, the bread representing their sins. Although this custom has persisted, medieval Rabbinic authorities strongly objected to it. The name of the ceremony is taken from the words of the prophet Micah who speaks of 'casting away sins in the depths of the sea' (7:19).

techiyyat ha-metim *see* RESURRECTION OF THE DEAD

tefillin (Hebrew for 'prayer objects', or Aramaic for 'ornaments') The two black leather boxes containing four biblical passages (Exod. 13:1–10, 11–16; Deut. 6:4–9, 11:13–21) written by a scribe which are attached by leather straps to the left arm and upper forehead. Tefillin are worn by adult males during the weekday shacharit service, since God's words must be 'bound as a sign on your arm and they shall be as frontlets between your eyes' (Deut. 6:8). They are not worn on shabbat or festivals since these days are themselves a sign (*see* CHOL HA-MOED). Tefillin are thought to inculcate humility, and the reward for wearing them is long life. They are referred to in English as phylacteries, meaning 'amulets', but though there are stories in Jewish literature about the protective powers of tefillin, they are not regarded primarily as magical charms. In the meditation before putting them on, the tefillin of the hand are understood as a reminder of God's outstretched arm when he took the Israelites out of Egypt (*see* HOSEA), and they are placed opposite the

heart to subjugate the desires of the heart to God. The head tefillin are meant to subjugate the senses and thoughts of the brain to God. To emphasize the importance of the ritual, the *Talmud* even depicts God Himself as wearing tefillin. Women do not wear tefillin, although there are records of saintly women who did so in the past, and some feminists have begun to wear them in synagogue services.

tehillim *see* PSALMS

tekhelet (Hebrew for 'blue-purple') The dye used for one of the threads of the TZITZIT attached to each corner of the tallit (Num. 15:38). It was made from a sea creature, the chilazon, which was believed to surface from the deep only once every seventy years. The identity of the chilazon, and the methods of preparing the dye, were lost after Jewish life in Palestine deteriorated during the Talmudic period, and today only plain white threads are used for the tzitzit. A leader of the Chasidic Movement in the 19c., Rabbi Gershon Leiner, claimed he had rediscovered the dye. He identified a species of cuttlefish as the chilazon and made a dye from its secretions which he and his followers used for colouring the threads. Most scholars who subjected his claims to critical scrutiny rejected his arguments. One of his critics, Rabbi Isaac Herzog, later to become the first Ashkenazi Chief Rabbi of Israel, was awarded a doctorate in 1919 from London University for his thesis on 'The Dyeing of Purple in Ancient Israel'. The *Talmud* explains that the tekhelet resembles the colour of heaven and thus reminds the Jew of God and His commandments. In general tekhelet was regarded as the colour of divine justice, and the mystics warned that it was a bad omen if one saw this blue-purple colour in one's dreams.

Temple (Hebrew 'bet ha-mikdash') Central building of the sacrificial cult (*see* SACRIFICE), situated in Jerusalem and looked after by the priests and LEVITES. The First Temple was built by Solomon to replace the Tabernacle, using angels and demons as his builders and hewing out the stone with the help of the SHAMIR, a rock-breaking worm. Solomon also planted gold-bearing trees in the Temple courtyard. The First Temple was destroyed by the Babylonians as a divine punishment for the sins of bloodshed, sexual immorality and idolatry committed by the people (*see* JEREMIAH). It was rebuilt by EZRA after the Babylonian Captivity. The Second Temple was destroyed by the Romans but this time for the sin of causeless hatred which was rampant among the Jews. The Rabbis drew the lesson from this that causeless hatred was to be regarded as an unmitigated evil. The Temple mount was known as Mount MORIAH. Inside the Temple, in the HOLY OF HOLIES, was the foundation stone of the world, the even shetiyyah, and the Ark of the Covenant rested on it. Cherubim were woven onto the curtain before the Holy of Holies and carved onto the Temple doors. Jews should tear their garments when they see the place of the Temple for the first time or after an interval of thirty days, and as a memorial to the destruction of the Temple, a patch of wall should be left undecorated in the home. The Jewish year has a period of THREE WEEKS OF MOURNING preceding the fast of the Ninth of Av (*see* AV, NINTH OF) which recalls the destruction of both Temples. The Third Temple will descend ready-made from heaven in the Messianic era. See also ALTAR; HIGH PRIEST; JUDAH MACCABEE; LAMENTATIONS; MENORAH; PILGRIMAGE; PILGRIM FESTIVALS; PRIEST; TAMMUZ, SEVENTEENTH OF; WAILING WALL; WATER DRAWING FESTIVITIES; ZION.

tenakh (also mikra, 'that which is read' and kitvei ha-kodesh, 'the holy writings') Most general term for the Hebrew BIBLE, made up of the initial letters of the tripartite division of scripture: torah, neviim and ketuvim – the Pentateuch, the• Prophets and the Hagiographa or Writings. There are twenty-four separate books in the tenakh, five in the Pentateuch (see CHUMASH), eight in the former and latter Prophets (the twelve minor prophets being counted as one book), and eleven in the Hagiographa. The torah is the holiest part of the threefold division, for it was given directly by God. Next in holiness are the Prophets, written by men inspired by PROPHECY, even though some of the books in this second section are more obviously historical than records of prophetic utterances. Last is the Hagiographa, written down under the inspiration of the Holy Spirit (ruach ha-kodesh). See also MASORAH; SAMARITANS.

Ten Commandments see DECALOGUE

Ten Days of Penitence (Hebrew 'aseret yemai teshuvah') The ten-day period from the first of Tishri (see ROSH HA-SHANAH) to the tenth of Tishri (see YOM KIPPUR) is one of penitence and soul searching. Jews have to be stricter in their ritual practice during this period, since they are judged at this time. God is described in the liturgy during these ten days as a king sitting on His throne of judgment. Additions are made to the regular prayers (see AVINU MALKENU) which include the confession of sins (see ASHAMNU) and a request to be written down by God in the book of life. See also REPENTANCE.

Ten Lost Tribes After having broken with Judah under JEROBOAM to form the Northern Kingdom of ISRAEL, the tribes of Reuben, Simeon, Issachar, Zebulun, Dan, Naphtali, Gad, Asher, Ephraim and Manasseh were carried away (II Kings 17:6, 18:11) into captivity by the Assyrians in 722 BCE. They are believed to be still in the land of their exile, either maintaining their Judaism intact or living outwardly as Gentiles. Some of them exist beyond the river SAMBATYON which Jews cannot cross. At various times individuals have appeared claiming to come from one of the Ten Lost Tribes (see REUVENI, DAVID), and reports have reached travellers to Ethiopia, Arabia and Persia about independent Jewish kingdoms in inaccessible areas across deserts or mountains (see ELDAD HA-DANI). The remnants of the Ten Lost Tribes have purportedly been found among the high-caste Hindus of India and among the Shinto priests of Japan, whose practices seemed to indicate a biblical origin. The first Japanese king is traced back to 730 BCE, the period of the captivity, and Japanese Israelites are assumed to have crossed to their new home on rafts. The Karaite Jews of the Crimea claimed descent from the lost tribes, as did certain Danes who interpreted the name of their country, Denmark, as coming from the tribe

Palestinian **Targum** to Genesis. The Aramaic text follows the first few Hebrew words of each sentence.

Marc Chagall's painting of a Jew praying while wearing a tallit and **tefillin**.

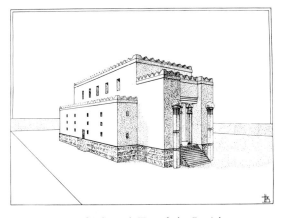

Reconstruction of Solomon's **Temple** by Bursink.

of Dan. A similar linguistic association was made by British Israelites who saw 'British' as the two Hebrew words 'berit ish', meaning 'the covenant of man'. The Stone of Scone was similarly thought to be the stone on which Jacob laid his head when he dreamed of a ladder reaching into heaven (Gen. 28) which the Israelite exiles brought with them. Travellers to South America claimed that the Indians found there were from the Ten Lost Tribes (see MONTEZINOS, AARON) and retained Jewish practices like levirate marriage and tearing their garments in mourning. Claims were also made for Kurdish tribes, Australian aboriginals, North American Indians, Mexicans, the Masai of Kenya, and for inhabitants of Afghanistan, China, Bokhara, the Caucasus (see MOUNTAIN JEWS), Burma, and Soviet Georgia. In the Age of the Messiah the lost tribes will return to the Holy Land to be reunited with their brethren. See also FALASHAS; SHEMA; TRIBES, THE TWELVE.

terefah (Hebrew for 'torn') General term for a blemished KOSHER animal whose meat is prohibited by the DIETARY LAWS. The term is nowadays used widely to refer to non-kosher food, but it originally referred only to an animal that had been torn by a beast of prey (Exod. 22:30). After an animal is slaughtered (see SHECHITAH) it is carefully examined for any missing, defective or perforated internal organs, particular attention being paid to lesions on the lungs. The types of blemishes enumerated in the *Talmud* have remained the basis for the rules of terefah, but the general rule of thumb is that a blemish which would prevent the animal surviving for twelve months makes it terefah. In the 18c. a controversy arose when a rabbi decided that a chicken, in which no heart was found, was not terefah on the grounds that the heart must have been mislaid when the chicken was opened. Other rabbis disagreed and claimed that the chicken was not kosher since a missing major organ like a heart makes it terefah.

teshuvah *see* REPENTANCE

tetragrammaton (Hebrew 'shem ha-meforash') The four-letter name of God which nowadays is never enunciated, the Hebrew word a-do-nai ('my Lord') being used instead. The name Jehovah, found in some English translations of the Bible, is based on a misreading of the text, where the Hebrew letters of the tetragrammaton are usually written with the vowel points of a-do-nai. Of all the various names of God, the tetragrammaton alone is thought of as a true name, the others being descriptions. So sacred is the name that even a-do-nai is only used in prayer, otherwise it is referred to as ha-shem ('the name') because of the prohibition of taking God's name in vain. Today, the correct pronunciation of the tetragrammaton has been forgotten, but it was used in the Temple during the priestly blessing and by the High Priest in the ritual of yom kippur. Rabbis would teach it to their senior students once in seven years, but they threatened those who made public use of it with the loss of their portion in the World to Come (olam haba) as punishment (see BLACK JEWS). The tetragrammaton was revealed to Moses (Exod. 6) when he was told of the divine plans for rescuing the Israelites from bondage in Egypt,

since the name signifies the compassionate aspect of God. According to the Kabbalists, God gives life to the whole world through the tetragrammaton, and its healing and magic potencies can be controlled by those who know how to master the name (see DEVEKUT). It was used by Moses to slay an Egyptian taskmaster; it was carved on the rod of Aaron with which the Red Sea was split; it was engraved on the magic ring of Solomon; and it is written in amulets and on SHIVVITI plaques. David Alroy in the 12c. is said to have journeyed long distances in a very short time by means of its power.

tevah *see* ARK, HOLY; ARK OF NOAH

Tevet Tenth lunar month of the Hebrew calendar, counting from Nisan the month of the Exodus, or fourth month from the New Year festival (rosh ha-shanah). Tevet usually begins in the second half of December, and its zodiacal sign is the goat. The festival of CHANUKKAH extends into the first few days of Tevet. On the eighth of the month the translation of the Bible into Greek by seventy-two elders was completed (see ARISTEAS, LETTER OF). This was considered a great tragedy by the Rabbis, since they regarded the translation as merely an inaccurate paraphrase suitable for Gentile use. The tenth of Tevet is a public fast day commemorating the beginning of the seige of Jerusalem by the Babylonians, which eventually led to the destruction of the first Temple. This is the only fast day that occurs on a Friday. In the Middle Ages there was a reluctance to slaughter geese during the months of Tevet and SHEVAT.

tevilah *see* ABLUTION; MIKVEH

tevilat kelim *see* MIKVEH

Thirty-six Righteous Men *see* LAMED VAVNIK; SHEKHINAH; TZADDIK

Three Weeks of Mourning (Hebrew 'bein ha-metzarim', meaning 'between the straits') The period of three weeks between the fast on the seventeenth of Tammuz (see TAMMUZ, SEVENTEENTH OF) and that on the ninth of Av (see AV, NINTH OF) is one of national mourning for the destruction of the two Temples in Jerusalem. No weddings are held, no music is played, and Orthodox Jews do not buy new garments during this time. It is customary in many communities not to have a haircut or shave for these three weeks and not to eat meat or drink wine for the last nine days of this period. Because of the association of these three weeks with tragedies in Jewish history, they came to be regarded as times of bad luck when Jews should avoid disputes with Gentiles, particularly in courts of law, since they were unlikely to win. It was recommended that people should not go out alone between the fourth and ninth hours of the day, during this time, since a demon called Ketev Meriri (see DEMONS) is active then. This demon, which lurks between sun and shade, has a hairy body and is full of eyes. If one looks upon the eye fixed over its heart, one immediately falls down dead.

Throne of Glory (Hebrew 'kisse ha-kavod') The throne upon which God sits in heaven. Only God may be seated in heaven, while the angels and other heavenly creatures have to stand. The image of the throne is based on the court of an earthly king and goes back to the vision of the prophet Ezekiel (Ezek. 1:26) who saw a human form on a throne above the angelic hosts when the heavens opened. The mystics of the MAASEH MERKAVAH tradition regarded a vision of the Throne of Glory as the goal of their ascent into heaven. They brought back reports of the songs sung by the angels who bear the throne, and these appear in HEIKHALOT literature. The *Talmud* states that the throne was created before the world and that the souls of the righteous are stored under it. The overt ANTHROPOMORPHISM of God sitting on the Throne of Glory embarrassed Jewish philosophers, who treated it as an allegory or interpreted the form on the throne as a heavenly being of light created by God. The angels of the Divine Presence, GABRIEL, MICHAEL, RAPHAEL and URIEL, are positioned around the Throne. *See also* KEDUSHAH; SALAMANDER; TABLETS OF THE DECALOGUE.

tikkun (Hebrew for 'rectification') Kabbalistic teaching about the need for man to rectify the world. During the process of emanation, sparks of the divine creative light making up ADAM KADMON became trapped in the pieces of the vessels which were meant to contain them, but proved inadequate for the task and broke (shevirat ha-kelim). It is up to man, through carrying out the commandments with mystical kavanah, to reunite these sparks with their divine source. Man can thus remove the alienation within the sphere of the holy which the entrapment of the sparks represents. The Messianic redemption comes when this tikkun is completed. The collection of passages to be studied throughout the night on the eve of the festival of SHAVUOT was known as tikkun leil shavuot, and the midnight ritual of mourning for the destruction of the Temple was known as tikkun chatzot (*see* SHARABI, SHALOM). A different but related form of tikkun affects individuals in their own spiritual evolution, where failures in the process of TRANSMIGRATION OF SOULS need to be rectified (*see* LEVIRATE MARRIAGE). In Temple times a soul incarnated in the body of an animal could receive rectification when the animal was offered as a sacrifice to God. Today, this can be effected when the animal is killed through ritual slaughter (shechitah). There is therefore some opposition to vegetarianism among adherents of the Kabbalah since this would deprive such souls of tikkun. Kabbalistic masters could read a person's past sins by looking at their forehead and were able to suggest acts of tikkun to remedy their situation. Isaac LURIA released souls entrapped in stones which addressed him seeking tikkun, and Israel BAAL SHEM TOV released the soul of a scholar which, as a punishment, had been reincarnated as a frog. Members of the Chasidic Movement introduced the custom of making a tikkun for dead relatives on their YAHRZEIT. This involved someone offering alcohol after morning prayers for a 'lechaim' to be drunk for the soul of the departed. *See also* TZIMTZUM.

tikkun soferim *see* SCRIBE

tisha be-av *see* AV, NINTH OF

The month of **Tevet**, represented by the zodiacal sign of the goat, from a synagogue mosaic at Hammath, Tiberias.

The **Throne of Glory** in Ezekiel's vision (Bear Bible).

Tishri Seventh lunar month of the Hebrew calendar, counting from Nisan the month of the Exodus, or first month of the year reckoning from the New Year festival (rosh ha-shanah). Tishri usually begins in mid-September, and its zodiacal sign is the balance, which aptly fits its character as a month in which man is judged and his good and bad deeds weighed. According to one Talmudic view, the world was created in Tishri, the Patriarchs were each born in this month, and the future Messianic redemption will take place in it. The first and second of Tishri are ROSH HA-SHANAH, the third is the Fast of GEDALIAH, the first ten days of the month are the TEN DAYS OF PENITENCE, the tenth is YOM KIPPUR, the festival of SUKKOT begins on the fifteenth, HOSHANA RABBA is on the twenty-first, and SHEMINI ATZERET begins on the twenty-second. Tishri differs from the other months, for no blessing for the new moon is recited before it begins, since the new-moon day of Tishri is itself a festival.

tithes (Hebrew 'maaser') In biblical times a number of different tithes were taken from the produce of the Holy Land (Num. 18:21–6; Deut. 14:2–9, 18:3–4). These went to the priest, to the Levites or to the poor in different years of the shemittah cycle, while other tithes were taken to be eaten in Jerusalem. From the end of the Babylonian exile the Levitical tithes were not offered, since Levites refused to join Ezra in returning to the Land of Israel. God rewards tithing with riches, and the giver of tithes escapes from hell, while neglecting tithes leads to drought. Jews are encouraged to test God by giving tithes and seeing whether he does indeed reward people. Today, it is customary to give one-tenth of one's income to charity as an extension of these agricultural tithing laws. *See also* CHALLAH; KORAH; PHINEHAS BEN YAIR; TU BI-SHEVAT.

tombstones (Hebrew 'matzevah') Jewish graves are marked with a tombstone bearing the Hebrew name of the deceased, his or her date of death and an inscription. Although these stones are mostly simple slabs, they do occasionally have a carved emblem indicating the status or profession of the person concerned. Thus, priests might have two outstretched hands, the sign of the priestly blessing; Levites might have a carving of a vessel with water, since one of their tasks was to wash the priests' hands; and scholars might have a torah scroll or an open book. Important people often have more elaborate structures erected over their graves. Those with a reputation for special piety and the ability to work miracles might even have a building erected above their graves for pilgrims who come seeking their help and miraculous cures. It is customary today to indicate Jewish tombstones with a hexagram, a MAGEN DAVID, although in ancient times a candelabrum, MENORAH, was commonly used instead. The original purpose of the stone was to indicate that there was a grave there to be avoided by priests, lest they become defiled by contact with the dead, and by farmers who were working the land. The erection of a stone was considered by the Kabbalists as an aid to the soul of the deceased in attaining rest. The *Talmud* warns people against reading tombstone inscriptions, since this makes one forget one's learning. *See also* CEMETERY.

torah (Hebrew for 'teaching') One of the central concepts of Judaism which may refer to the Jewish teaching of the Pentateuch (*see* CHUMASH) or the Hebrew Bible (*see* TENAKH), or in its widest sense to the whole of the Jewish tradition. God studies the torah in heaven, where it is written in black fire upon white fire (*see* ACADEMY ON HIGH). The torah existed before the world came into being and was used by God as the blueprint and instrument of the Creation. The Patriarchs kept the torah before it was actually given. In the revelation to MOSES and the Israelites at Mount SINAI, God gave the torah to man (*see* ORAL TORAH), thus removing the filth of the SERPENT from Israel. Had the Israelites not accepted it, the world would have ceased to exist, since the Creation was conditional on this happening (*see* COVENANT). The torah given to man is masked in the form of stories and COMMANDMENTS. The inner meaning of the torah, its 'soul', is only available to those who penetrate its mystical symbolism. Ultimately, a full revelation of the inner meaning of torah must await the coming of the Messiah. The Talmudic rabbis saw it as their task to study and expound the torah, and where there was disagreement on an issue, they followed the MAJORITY OPINION in determining the practical HALAKHAH. Various attempts were made to sum up the essential core of torah teaching. Hillel told a would-be convert to Judaism that the whole of Jewish teaching was a commentary on the idea of not doing to one's fellow what was hateful to oneself. The verse 'love your neighbour as yourself' (Lev. 19:18) was said by Rabbi Akiva, following Hillel, to be the great principle of the torah, while his colleague Simeon Ben Azzai claimed it was the verse 'This is the book of the generation of man, on the day God created man He made him in the image of God' (Gen. 5:1). Ben Azzai's position may well reflect a more universal standpoint which recognizes that all humans are made in God's image, in contrast to the narrower interpretation of 'neighbour' as applying just to Jews in the GOLDEN RULE. The torah is the antidote to the evil INCLINATION in man, and the Angel of Death is powerless against someone engaged in torah study. *See also* ALIYAH; BATLAN; BIBLE; SIMCHAT TORAH; TARGUM; ZOHAR.

torah im derekh eretz *see* HIRSCH, SAMSON RAPHAEL

torah scroll *see* SEFER TORAH

torah she-baal peh *see* ORAL TORAH

tov ve-ra *see* GOOD AND EVIL

transmigration of souls (Hebrew 'gilgul neshamot') The belief that after death the SOUL is reincarnated in a new physical form, whether human, animal or inanimate. Transmigration was taught by Anan Ben David, the founder of the Karaites, but his view was criticized by Jewish philosophers as alien to Orthodox belief. Nevertheless, it became part of the Kabbalah, appearing first in the *Sefer Ha-*BAHIR. Transmigration gave a new meaning to many aspects of life. The dead husband literally came alive again in the child born to his wife and brother in a LEVIRATE MARRIAGE. The deaths of young children were less tragic, since they were being punished for previous sins and would be reborn in a new life. Wicked people were happy in this world because they had done good in some previous existence. Proselytes to Judaism were Jewish souls which had been incarnated in Gentile bodies. It also allowed for the gradual perfection of the individual soul through different lives. Under the influence of Isaac LURIA, the whole framework expanded. Mystics viewed each other as possessing elements of the souls of biblical and Talmudic characters, Luria claiming to be a reincarnation of part of the soul of Moses. The souls of the dead may be reincarnated in animals, and ritual slaughter (see SHECHITAH) frees them to undertake their spiritual journey. Many 'naked' souls are unable to find a new body, so they may become a DIBBUK or just need rectificatory help (see TIKKUN) to continue their development. Luria himself released souls trapped in stones. A mystic master could read the stage of a person's transmigration from marks on the forehead. Good deeds lead to rebirth as a human, bad deeds to rebirth as an animal, depending on the sins involved. Proud people transmigrated into bees, adulterers into asses and cruel people into crows. If a fly or a moth attaches itself to a group of people, this means it is a gilgul of someone who was associated with one of the group in the past or in a previous life. See also AFTERLIFE; IMMORTALITY; ZOHAR.

Tombstones from a Jewish cemetery showing Hebrew inscriptions and engravings.

Tree of Knowledge (Hebrew 'etz ha-daat') Tree in the GARDEN OF EDEN, described as the Tree of the Knowledge of Good and Evil. Adam and EVE were forbidden to eat the fruit of this tree, because if they did so, they would die (Gen. 2,3). The Serpent managed to persuade Eve to eat the fruit, and she not only gave it to Adam but also to all the birds and animals except for one bird. As a result this bird, the phoenix, never dies. The forbidden fruit was variously identified as a fig, a grape, an ETROG, a nut and even as wheat, which originally grew on stalks as tall as trees. Adam and Eve were expelled from Eden before they could eat from the TREE OF LIFE which shared a common root with the Tree of Knowledge. Many different explanations have been given about the Tree of Knowledge. It was held to symbolize the ability to choose between good and evil (see FREE WILL) or to represent sexual experience, the forbidden tree signifying woman, or to indicate the evil inclination, the serpent having injected its poison into the fruit, or it was a metaphor for man forsaking nature in pursuit of self-indulgence and luxury, or for the ability to tell lies, or for the exploitation of nature and the mixing of natural types which were originally separate. At the coming of the Messiah God will uproot the Tree of Knowledge and cast it into gehinnom to be burnt, and only then will its true meaning be revealed.

Tree of Life (Hebrew 'etz ha-chaim') Tree in the centre of the Garden of Eden. Adam and Eve were expelled from Eden, after having eaten the fruit of the TREE OF KNOWLEDGE, to prevent them eating the fruit of the Tree of Life and living forever. A Cherub holding a fiery sword guards the way back to Eden to stop man gaining access to the Tree of Life (Gen. 3). The miraculous rod of Moses was cut from this tree, and the torah which God gave to man is called 'a tree of life', for its teachings are the earthly equivalent

Sephardi rabbi reading from the **torah**.

of this plant of Paradise. The fruit of the Tree of Life itself is reserved for the righteous in the World to Come (olam haba), and its branches provide shade for all the inhabitants of the Garden of Eden. So huge is this tree that it would take five hundred years to pass from one side of its trunk to the other. The waters of Paradise, which irrigate the whole world, flow from under the Tree of Life. *See also* ENOCH; NESHAMAH YETERAH.

trees *see* TU BI-SHEVAT

Tribes, The Twelve The twelve sons of Jacob (also known as ISRAEL), Reuben, Simeon, Levi, Judah, Issachar, Zebulun, Dan, Nephtali, Gad, Asher, Joseph and Bejamin, became the eponymous ancestors of the twelve tribes of the Children of Israel. The head of each tribe was called a Nasi. The tribe of LEVI had no portion in the Promised Land since its members, who were in charge of the sacrificial ritual (*see* LEVITES) and religious teaching, were scattered among the other tribes. It is therefore not counted as one of the twelve tribes. Instead, the two sons of Joseph, Ephraim and Manasseh, were regarded as the founders of tribes in their own right. The ten tribes of the Northern Kingdom, who were taken away into captivity by the Assyrians, are known as the TEN LOST TRIBES. The tribe of Judah was regarded as the tribe of kings and counts among its descendants both King David and the Messiah. *See also* AV, FIFTEENTH OF; MATRIARCHS.

tu be-av *see* AV, FIFTEENTH OF

tu bi-shevat (Hebrew for 'Fifteenth of Shevat') The New Year for Trees falls on the fifteenth of Shevat and is celebrated as a minor festival. By this date the main part of the rainy season has passed, and fruit trees are just beginning to bud. Tithes cannot be taken from the fruit of one year for the fruit of another, and the Fifteenth of Shevat represents the beginning of a new tithing year. It is customary to eat fruit on tu bi-shevat, particularly those fruits which grow in the Holy Land. There is a Kabbalistic ritual, held during the night before tu bi-shevat, of studying relevant selections from the Bible and the *Zohar* between the eating of different fruits and of singing songs of praise associated with God's gift of fruit. For the mystics fruit represents the inner divine light in the world, surrounded by the peel or husk which symbolizes evil masking the divine. In some communities individuals offer special prayers on this day, requesting God to grant them a beautiful etrog fruit for the festival of sukkot. In modern Israel children plant young saplings on tu bi-shevat.

tumtum *see* ANDROGYNE

tzaddik (Hebrew for 'righteous man') The righteous man, personified by JOSEPH, is the foundation of the world; he lives by his faith, and in each generation there are at least thirty-six men (*see* LAMED VAVNIK) whose merits support the world. The Creation was undertaken for the tzaddik's sake; he acts as a partner with God and can even annul divine decrees. The angel responsible for conception brings the unformed seminal drop before God and asks what type of person

it will be. Will it be strong or weak, wise or foolish, rich or poor? The angel does not ask whether it will be a tzaddik or a wicked man, because a person has free will to make that choice himself. Even when dead, the tzaddik is still called alive; his soul is taken under the Throne of Glory, and he sits in olam haba with a crown on his head, basking in the radiance of the shekhinah. In the Kabbalah the tzaddik represents the last but one of the sefirot. He is the male generative organ, the channel through which the divine flow comes down to earth. All hidden things are known to him, since he has purified his body.

In the CHASIDIC MOVEMENT a master, or Rebbe, was known as a tzaddik and was thought to have an element of the soul of Moses. As such he was beyond the criticism of his followers. A community leader, who communicated profound mysteries through stories and parables rather than through abstruse analysis of Talmudic texts, he acted as a link between the ordinary Jew and God. His teachings could only be truly understood by those who had attained a similar level, although he was not always a great scholar, but merely a holy person. It was believed that his spiritual powers (*see* RUACH HA-KODESH) were so great that he even instructed God on how to deal with the world of men. His followers sought his spiritual guidance and his blessing for their physical welfare. He could help barren couples and practised exorcism of those possessed by demons. Some Chasidic leaders, such as ISRAEL OF RUZHIN, lived in great splendour on the gifts of their followers. In each age there is one tzaddik who is an incarnation of the soul of the Messiah, and if the generation is worthy, he will usher in the Messianic age (*see* LUBAVITCH). *See also* DEVEKUT; GABBAI; YAHRZEIT.

tzaraat *see* LEPROSY

tzedakah *see* CHARITY

tzimtzum (Hebrew for 'contraction') The self-withdrawal of the Godhead to enable a finite world to come into being through a process of emanation. Since God is infinite, without tzimtzum there would be no vacant 'area' into which the space–time structure of a separate creation could be produced. For the Lurianic Kabbalah (*see* LURIA, ISAAC) the initial tzimtzum, and the further acts of tzimtzum which take place at every stage of creation, generate the restricting sefirot of the left side and ultimately the forces of the SITRA ACHRA. Although a necessary part of creation, the divine self-contraction gives rise to a world in need of rectification (tikkun) because of the clash between the restricting forces and the overflowing divine love. This clash is expressed in the image of the breaking of the vessels which were intended to hold parts of the divine light. The whole doctrine of tzimtzum was understood literally by some Kabbalists, implying the absence of a transcendent God from the created world and the negation of pantheism. They argued that a perfect God could not be found within lowly life-forms. One 18c. Kabbalist, Jacob Emden, claimed that the doctrine of tzimtzum was a rational necessity, explaining how an infinite God could bring something finite into being. Those who understood tzimtzum metaphorically interpreted it as God hiding Himself within the creation so that humans could have a sense of their own separation from God. If God were not hidden, nothing else could be perceived. In fact, however, the world only seems to exist independently, but the otherness of God is an illusion since there cannot be anything empty of the divine infinity. The world therefore exists within God (see PANENTHEISM) and clothes the divine nature which is hidden from everyone but the mystic.

tzitzit (Hebrew for 'fringes') The four threads, doubled over through each corner hole of the TALLIT, which are knotted together five times, leaving a fringe of eight threads. The wearing of tzitzit accords with the biblical prescription, found in the third paragraph of the SHEMA, to have fringes on the corners of one's garments so as to remember God's commandments (Num. 15:38–9). The wearing of tzitzit is considered to be equal to all the other commandments together. It saves man from sin, makes him worthy to receive the divine presence (shekhinah) and protects him from the evil eye and demons. The threads bind man to God, and the fringed garment ensures that one has a clean spiritual garment to clothe the soul after death. Today the threads are white, though originally one thread was dyed blue-purple with the TEKHELET, and when the morning shema is read, they are held in the hand and kissed at the mention of the word 'tzitzit'. Some traditional Jews wear the tzitzit of the tallit katan vest outside their garments, so as to be able to see them at all times. See also SHAATNEZ.

tzom see FAST DAYS

tzom gedaliah see GEDALIAH, FAST OF

unetane tokef see AMNON OF MAYENCE

Uriah the Hittite see BATHSHEBA

Uriel Archangel and leader of the angelic armies. Uriel is an angel of light as his name 'light of God' indicates. He manifested himself as a lion in the fires of the altar in the Temple to consume the sacrifices, appeared as a snake who wanted to swallow Moses when he neglected the circumcision of his son (Exod. 4), dried the Red Sea so that the Israelites could cross (Exod. 14) and appeared to Samson's parents to announce that they would have a son who would save Israel from the Philistines (Judg. 13). Together with Gabriel, Michael and Raphael he is one of the angels who surround the THRONE OF GLORY. His position is in front of God and of man. Uriel's name was written on amulets intended to help people study torah because he represents the light of God's teaching. Uriel is sometimes identified with Raziel.

Urim and Thummim Oracle worn by the High Priest (Num. 27:21). The High Priest's breastplate had twelve stones (see SHAMIR) on which the names of God and of the Twelve Tribes were engraved. Answers were conveyed to the questions of the king or of the

The Twelve **Tribes**, from a fresco in the Dura Europos synagogue (3c. CE).

Funeral of the **Tzaddik** by Samuel Hirszenberg showing a crowd of Chasidim on the way to the burial of their leader.

17c. figure of a High Priest with a jewelled **Urim and Thummim** breastplate, holding a censer.

head of the Sanhedrin by letters of these names being lit up. The Urim and Thummim ceased to be used when the First Temple was destroyed.

Ushpizin (Aramaic for 'guests') The biblical characters ABRAHAM, ISAAC, JACOB, JOSEPH, MOSES, AARON and DAVID, known as the Seven Faithful Shepherds, who come as guests to the SUKKAH on the festival of sukkot. Each evening one of these characters is the main guest, and he is invited in Aramaic to the sukkah and asked to bring the other ushpizin with him. It is recommended that a poor person also be invited each evening, otherwise the holy guests from the spiritual world will not stay, since the poor person is meant to eat their portion. In some communities the name of the ushpizin is hung on the wall of the sukkah for the duration of his day. According to the Kabbalists the guests represent the seven lower sefirot. The last guest, David, the symbol of the king–Messiah, represents both the shekhinah and the coming kingdom of God in the world.

vayikra see CHUMASH

Vilna Gaon see ELIJAH THE VILNA GAON

vine (Hebrew 'gefen') The vine, grapes and WINE made out of them all play a special role in Jewish life and ritual. The fruit-laden vine appears as a symbol of fertility, and unmarried girls seeking husbands used to parade themselves in the vineyards before the eligible bachelors of the locality on two occasions of the year. Noah was the first to plant a vine, and he became drunk after making wine with disastrous consequences (Gen. 9:20). There is even a view that the Tree of Knowledge, of which Adam and Eve ate the forbidden fruit, was a vine.

Vital, Chaim (1542–1620) Palestinian Kabbalist and main disciple of Isaac LURIA. Vital began to study Jewish mysticism when he read that the delay in the coming of the Messiah and the continuation of the long exile of the Jewish people were due to neglect of the study of Kabbalah. God obtains the greatest joy from people engaging in such study, and it alone can hasten the Messianic age. Vital spent two years with Luria in Safed, and the latter once took him in a boat on the Sea of Galilee. At a certain point Luria drew up a cup of water from the lake and gave it to Vital to drink, telling him that it was from MIRIAM'S WELL and would enable him to absorb Kabbalistic teachings quickly. Henceforth, Luria insisted that only Vital should write down his teachings. Although Vital did not want to allow these writings to be published, secret copies were made when he was ill, after his brother had been bribed. Vital regarded all the pre-Lurianic Kabbalistic works, since the time of the Zohar, as based on human understanding or as wordy restatements of a few simple truths. Luria's ideas, by contrast, were divinely inspired. He also regarded other versions of Luria's teachings, recorded by his fellow pupils, as worthless. Vital practised alchemy

and exorcism and seems to have believed that he himself was a character of Messianic significance. He also wrote a book of his dreams. When he died, his writings were buried with him. They were, however, later removed from the grave by Kabbalists, after they had received a message from heaven in a dream telling them that this was permissible. See also DIBBUK.

Wahl, Saul see COURT JEWS; SHTADLAN

Wailing Wall (Hebrew 'kotel ha-maaravi') The western section of the outer wall of the Temple Mount, the only remaining structure of Herod's addition to the Second Temple, which was destroyed in 70 CE. The Wailing Wall has retained the holiness of the Temple in Jewish consciousness, even though it was not actually part of the Temple complex. It has become a site of pilgrimage, and Jews kiss the stones when they come to visit the wall. The midrash states that the shekhinah never departs from the Wailing Wall, basing itself on the verse in the Song of Songs (2:9): 'Behold there He stands behind our wall.' One medieval Kabbalist reported how he saw the shekhinah in the guise of a woman weeping at the wall. It is this belief in the Divine Presence at the wall which is behind the custom of inserting pieces of paper with written requests to God in the cracks of the wall. The wall consists of a lower layer of Herodian blocks, on which there are stones from Roman times, and the whole top section belongs to the Arabic period from the 7c. onwards. It is called the Wailing Wall among non-Jews because Jews used to mourn at the wall for the destruction of the Temple. Their 'wailing' gave the wall its name. Jews themselves refer to it as the Western Wall. See also SHARABI, SHALOM.

Wandering Jew Stories of the Wandering Jew are based on early medieval legends about a Jew called Ahasuerus who disbelieved in Jesus and mocked him. He was told by Jesus that he would be cursed never to die but would wander till the day Jesus returned, only resting long enough to eat his meals. The story has affinities with that of the biblical CAIN who wandered as punishment for his sin, and in the Christian mind it symbolized the condition of the Jewish People who, because of their sin in rejecting Jesus, wander forever, knowing no rest and witnessing to the truth of Christianity. It also provided an anti-Semitic rationale for expelling Jews from Christian lands. People claimed to have met Ahasuerus at different times in different countries; as late as 1868 a Mormon met him in America in Salt Lake City. His appearance was thought to be the harbinger of some natural catastrophe.

Warsaw Ghetto Uprising see GHETTO; HOLOCAUST

water drawing festivities (Hebrew 'simchat bet ha-shoevah', meaning 'rejoicing of the house of water drawing') During Temple times there was a popular celebration when water for the altar was drawn from the Pool of Siloam and brought to the Temple. The festivities began on the second night of SUKKOT, a festival associated with the onset of the rainy season. The Levites chanted Psalms, blew trumpets and played the flute. Prominent rabbis would dance ecstatically all night long, juggling torches of fire and 'drawing up the Holy Spirit' (*see* RUACH HA-KODESH). The main activity took place in the Court of the Women in the Temple, where a temporary gallery was built to separate the sexes and thus avoid any immodest behaviour. Large golden candelabra were lit which illuminated all the courtyards of Jerusalem. It was said that 'he who has never seen the water drawing festivities has never seen true joy.' In modern times the simchat bet ha-shoevah is still celebrated with dancing and singing.

wine (Hebrew 'yayin') Wine is used in the ritual celebration of shabbat (*see* HAVDALAH) and festivals (*see* KIDDUSH), at a circumcision and a MARRIAGE. It is the most important of drinks, warranting a special benediction: 'who creates the fruit of the VINE'. Although there are warnings against DRUNKENNESS in Jewish literature, a minimum measure of wine was prescribed for various rituals and FOUR CUPS have to be drunk at the SEDER (*see also* ELIJAH, CUP OF). Sweet red wine was preferred for ritual use, but it is specifically mentioned that white wine may be used during the pesach meal, so that Jews should not be suspected of drinking Christian blood (*see* BLOOD LIBEL). There were moves to give up wine after the destruction of the Temple as a gesture of mourning, but these were opposed by the Rabbis. Restrictions were placed on Gentile wine, from which libations were once poured out as offerings to idols. Even when idolatry ceased, the prohibition on wine made or handled by a non-Jew remained, to prevent conviviality which might lead to intermarriage. The medicinal properties of old wine are praised in the *Talmud*, and at the great banquet in the age of the Messiah, wine which has been preserved from the beginning of the world will be drunk. *See also* ALCOHOL.

Wisdom Literature *see* ECCLESIASTES; PROVERBS, BOOK OF

witchcraft *see* ABLUTION; CAPITAL PUNISHMENT; DIBBUK; ENDOR, WITCH OF; MAGIC; SIMEON BEN SHET-ACH

woman (Hebrew 'ishah') An Orthodox woman is restricted in her public leadership roles; she cannot serve as a RABBI, a chazzan or as a synagogue lay leader (*see* MECHITZAH), although women light the Sabbath LAMP. She also cannot act as a judge (dayyan) or witness in a bet din and does not inherit her father's property if she has brothers. There are, however, records of female prophets (*see* PROPHECY) and of a number of charismatic women leaders, particularly in the Chasidic Movement. In Reform communities women have greater equality with men in public religious life. In the past women only received a minimum traditional education, since it was believed that teaching a woman torah was equivalent to teaching her to be deceitful, and one Talmudic rabbi maintained that it was better to burn the words of torah than hand them over to a woman. Men may

Photograph of the **Wailing Wall** in 1899 (Gertrude Bell).

Lithograph of the **Wandering Jew** crossing a cemetery, by Gustave Doré.

practise polygamy (*see* CONCUBINE), while women are restricted to MONOGAMY, and according to biblical law, the initiative for DIVORCE rests with the man. Women do not have to perform all the commandments incumbent on men as they are excused positive commandments dependent on time. Despite the fact that men recite a benediction each morning thanking God for not having made them a woman, there is a recognition that a man who does not have a wife is bereft of joy and blessing. The redemption of the Israelites from Egypt is said to have taken place through the merit of the womenfolk. In the Kabbalah there is a recurrent association between women and the demonic. This goes back to the biblical story of Eve, who led Adam astray in Eden, and to legends about LILITH, Adam's first wife, who represents the evil powers of the sitra achra. At the same time the mystical tradition emphasizes the importance of the SHEKHINAH which is the female aspect of the divine. *See also* ADULTERY; BAT MITZVAH; MATRIARCHS; MITZVAH; NIDDAH; PROVERBS, BOOK OF.

yad (Hebrew for 'hand') Pointer in the shape of a hand with an outstretched index finger used during the public reading of the SEFER TORAH. A pointer is needed to follow the text since it is forbidden to touch the scroll with the bare hand. When not in use, the yad is hung by a chain over the torah mantle (*see* GELILAH). It is recorded in ancient times that, when synagogues or Bible schools were attacked, the sharp-pointed yad was used as a weapon of defence. The five fingers of the hand are a prophylactic against evil, and the image of a hand is often put up on a wall of the home by Sephardim and Oriental Jews to ward off evil spirits.

Yad Vashem Centre, Jerusalem *see* RIGHTEOUS GENTILES

yahrzeit (Yiddish for 'anniversary') The anniversary of the DEATH of a near relative, particularly of a parent, is commemorated each year. The yahrzeit is kept on the Hebrew date of death, which may differ from the solar date by several weeks. A special memorial candle which burns for twenty-four hours is lit, based on the idea that 'the soul of man is the lamp of God' (Prov. 20:27), and the KADDISH is recited. Some have the custom of fasting on their parent's yahrzeit, or at least of not eating meat or drinking wine, and of studying those sections of the *Mishnah* which begin with the letters of the name of the deceased. There is a custom among Sephardim of reading the *Zohar* on the night of the yahrzeit. Among followers of the Chasidic Movement the yahrzeit of a parent, or of a great rabbi (tzaddik), is usually a joyous occasion with a repast of alcohol and cakes after the morning service as a 'lechaim', or toast 'to life' in memory of the deceased. This is accompanied by the wish that the soul of the deceased should ascend further into a higher heavenly abode, since it is believed that on each yahrzeit the soul is judged anew (*see* TIKKUN). On the yahrzeit of

a great rabbi, some of the sadder prayers in the service are omitted since death for the righteous is thought of as a spiritual wedding between the soul and God. It is also customary to visit someone's grave on their yahrzeit, and to sit and study torah or recite Psalms beside the graves of the righteous. MEMORIAL PRAYERS are said on the shabbat before the yahrzeit.

yaikelte *see* GENTILE

yarmulke *see* HEAD-COVERING

yayin *see* WINE

yehudi *see* JEW; JUDAH

yekke *see* HEAD-COVERING

yekum porkan *see* EXILARCH

yerushalaim *see* JERUSALEM

Yerushalmi *see* TALMUD

yeshivah (Hebrew for 'sitting'; pl. 'yeshivot') Talmudic college for unmarried male students from their teenage years to their early twenties. Married students usually graduate from a yeshivah to a kolel. Yeshivot originated with the academies of Palestine and Babylonia in the early centuries of the Christian era, and most contemporary ones are modelled on the Lithuanian yeshivot of the 19c. and early 20c. Study is undertaken by two students (chavruta) analysing a talmudic text together with a daily lecture (shiur) by a yeshivah head (rosh yeshivah). The curriculum is devoted almost entirely to the halakhic sections of a small number of Talmudic tractates, with no direct study of the Bible or even of the aggadah. Learning is undertaken for its own sake as a religious duty, so most students leave without any formal qualifications at the end of their period of study. A small number of bachurim, as the students are called, obtain semikhah. This concentration on the most difficult Talmudic texts has led to a highly obtruse method of study known as PILPUL. Various attempts were made by yeshivah heads to avoid such artificial dialectics, but their efforts to broaden the curriculum proved unsuccessful. The early Chasidic Movement opposed yeshivah study because it led to intellectual arrogance, but in the course of time Chasidic yeshivot were opened, some of which copied the very institutions they had criticized. The MUSAR MOVEMENT also tried to reform the yeshivah curriculum, concentrating on the ethical, rather than purely intellectual, development of students. Musar yeshivot aroused strong opposition because too little time was devoted to *Talmud* texts. Even more controversial were various attempts in modern times to introduce secular studies into the yeshivah in the face of resistance by traditionalists. *See also* BET HA-MIDRASH; CHAIM OF VOLOZHIN.

yetzer tov, yetzer ha-ra *see* INCLINATION, GOOD AND EVIL

yetziat mitzraim *see* EXODUS

Yetzirah, Sefer (Hebrew for '*Book of Formation*')
Early mystical work of the MAASEH BERESHIT tradition
existing in two major recensions. The date of composition of the *Sefer Yetzirah* is assumed to be the 3c. CE,
but many mystics believed it was written by the
biblical Patriarch, Abraham. The six chapters of the
work tell of the formation of the cosmos by God
through the ten SEFIROT and the twenty-two letters
of the Hebrew ALPHABET, which were engraved on
the primordial ether. These letters are classified into
different groups, and their structure is reflected in the
three dimensions of space, time and the human soul.
The organs of the body themselves are under the
astrological influence of the planets. Since man is a
MICROCOSM, he has within him the same divine
creative powers as permeate the cosmos and can use
the techniques of combining letters found in the *Sefer
Yetzirah* to unlock these powers. There are many
reports of the use of *Sefer Yetzirah* for theurgic
purposes. Thus we are told that the Tabernacle was
formed by means of such letter combinations and that
they were used to produce artificial animals which
were eaten by their rabbinic creators and also artificial
men (*see* GOLEM) who, though mobile, had the draw-
back that they could not speak. *See also* BAHIR, SEFER
HA-.

yeyashar kochekha *see* GREETINGS

yibbum *see* LEVIRATE MARRIAGE

yichud *see* MARRIAGE

yichus (Yiddish for 'relationship') A term referring
to the honour conferred on an individual from their
family relationship with a famous or outstanding
person. To have yichus is to be related to prominent
living individuals or, more commonly, to be descended
from illustrious ancestors who were famous rabbis or
community leaders. One can also acquire yichus for
oneself from scholarship or wealth. In the latter case
a reputation for the giving of charity is particularly
important in gaining yichus. A better seat in the
SYNAGOGUE was reserved in former times for a yachsan, someone with an impressive yichus. In arranged
marriages (*see* SHADKHAN), the family of the bride or
groom would seek a yachsan as a future spouse, and
rich Jews in particular would try to use their wealth
to marry into a family with inherited yichus. A person
without yichus may be regarded as prost, meaning
'plain', 'ordinary' or 'vulgar'. In the Age of the
Messiah, only those families with yichus, who can
trace their genealogy back without blemish and do
not have a mamzer among their antecedents, will
receive the divine presence (shekhinah). *See also* ZEK-
HUT AVOT.

yid *see* JEW

Yiddish Judaeo-German language spoken by ASHKEN-
AZIM of Eastern European origin, the name being an
abbreviation of Yiddish–Daitsch, 'Jewish–German'.
Yiddish began when Jews moved east into Slavic
countries in the Middle Ages after their expulsion
from German-speaking lands. It is written in Hebrew
characters and contains about 20 per cent of Hebrew
and Aramaic words, some of which were presumably

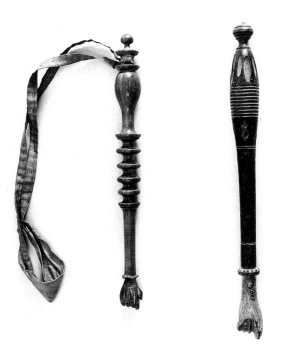

Wooden torah pointers in the shape of a hand
(**yad**).

Seal of the Ashkenazi Magen Avot **Yeshivah** in
Hebron, with a picture of the Cave of Machpelah.

part of the original German dialect used by Jews before their eastward migration. It also has about 10 per cent of Slavonic words, acquired in its formative period in Poland and Russia, and these words, like the Semitic ones, are integrated into the German syntax by being given Teutonic endings. Yiddish was essentially a spoken tongue, while Hebrew and Aramaic served as literary languages. In the course of time, however, a Yiddish literature grew up with works like the SHMUEL BUKH and the Bible translation and commentary, *Tze-ena Ure-ena*, published at the end of the 16c. Women came to know the biblical stories through this work and would cry over its pages as they identified their own sufferings with those of biblical characters. Other popular compositions appeared in Yiddish, such as story-books, ethical literature, Talmudic and midrashic legends and private prayers (*see* LEVI ISAAC OF BER-DICHEV). These were the forerunnners of the great revival of Yiddish literature in the 19c. and early 20c. which produced a new genre of stories (*see* NEBICH), plays, poetry and songs. There was considerable opposition to spoken Yiddish once the walls of the European ghetto began to crumble, since it was regarded as a jargon which Jews had to jettison as a precondition of their entry into Christian society. ZIONISM, too, was interested in the revival of Hebrew and saw Yiddish as the backward-looking language of the SHTETL, where it was traditionally known as MAMA LOSCHEN. Yiddish is still used today by Ultra-Orthodox Jews and by members of the BUND. In recent years there has been a romantic revival of interest in Yiddish among young people, and it is offered on a number of university courses.

yiddishkeyt *see* SHTETL

yigdal (Hebrew for 'may He be magnified') Popular hymn, dating from the 14c., which expresses the thirteen ARTICLES OF FAITH of Maimonides in poetical form. Yigdal is sung on shabbat and festivals to different tunes. The hymn ends with the hope for the coming of the Messiah and the Resurrection of the Dead. Since Kabbalists objected to Maimonides' rationalistic analysis of Judaism, they did not include yigdal in their liturgy, despite its obviously devotional tone. Attempts to have it recited every day in the prayers were unsuccessful although a number of rabbis defended it against criticism.

yizkor (Hebrew for 'remember') Special MEMORIAL PRAYERS for deceased relatives recited on festivals and YOM KIPPUR. The prayers derive their name from the opening words: 'Remember, O God, the soul of my father (or mother, brother, sister, etc.) . . . may his soul be bound up in the bond of life . . . with the righteous in the Garden of Eden.' It is customary for those whose parents are still alive to leave the synagogue before yizkor. This is because staying in synagogue during the prayer is considered a bad omen for living parents, as if one were willing their death. The presence of people not actually praying may also disturb the tearful prayers of the other worshippers. In some communities a slow-burning candle, which lasts for twenty-four hours, is lit the evening before yizkor is said, and money is pledged to charity in memory of the deceased.

yok *see* GENTILE

yom *see* DAY AND NIGHT

yom ha-din *see* DAY OF JUDGMENT

yom kippur (Hebrew for 'Day of Atonement') Fast of the tenth of Tishri and the most sacred day of the Jewish year, which ends the TEN DAYS OF PENITENCE. In ancient times it was the only occasion when the HIGH PRIEST entered the HOLY OF HOLIES, and a scapegoat bearing the sins of Israel was sent off to AZAZEL in the wilderness (Lev. 16:10). The Kabbalists saw this goat as a bribe to Satan to silence his accusations in the heavenly court. Yom kippur is preceded by penitential rituals such as the KAPPAROT ceremony, purification in a MIKVEH and a rite of symbolic flogging. Just before sunset, festival candles and a memorial light are kindled. Yom kippur is a twenty-five hour fast, beginning before sunset and ending with the appearance of the stars the next night. On the preceding day, one is encouraged to eat more than usual, and this is thought of as adding to the fast. During yom kippur Jews are forbidden to wear leather shoes, to engage in sexual relations or to wash. They must cease from all profane work on this Sabbath of Sabbaths (Lev. 23:32). The liturgy begins with KOL NIDREI, and most of the day is spent in prayer, reciting YIZKOR for deceased relatives, confessing sins (*see* ASHAMNU), requesting divine FORGIVENESS, listening to torah readings, to the Book of JONAH and to sermons. It is customary to wear white (*see* KITEL), as a symbol of purity, since on yom kippur Jews are like ANGELS. People greet each other with the wish that they may be sealed in the heavenly book for a good year ahead (*see* GREETINGS). The day ends with the NEILAH service and the blowing of the shofar (*see* JUBILEE). The tenth of Tishri was the date on which Moses brought down the second set of Tablets of the Decalogue, marking forgiveness for the sin of the Golden Calf. In Talmudic times it was customary for the young girls of Jerusalem to go out and dance in the vineyards on yom kippur and during Av (*see* AV, FIFTEENTH OF), encouraging eligible bachelors to choose a marriage partner. *See also* HAVDALAH.

yom tov *see* FESTIVALS

yonah *see* DOVE

yovel *see* JUBILEE

zakan, zaken *see* AGE

zaken mamre *see* MAJORITY OPINION

zayit *see* OLIVE

Zealots *see* JOCHANAN BEN ZAKKAI; JOSEPHUS FLAVIUS; MASADA

zekhut avot (Hebrew for 'merit of the fathers') The merit inherited from the good deeds of one's ancestors, particularly applied to the merit of the PATRIARCHS, which God takes into consideration in his dealings with the People of Israel. Abraham's merits, for example, were so great that 'the world was only created for his sake'. His response to God's demands in the akedah was instrumental in allowing Israel to cross the Red Sea, and his hospitality merited the mercy shown to the Jews by God down the ages. There are references back to the merits of biblical figures in the liturgy when Jews pray for divine help, though people are warned not to rely solely on these merits. Views are also found that these merits are operative only in the Holy Land, that they have ceased, or that they only work for the righteous. Each Jewish community is supported by the merits of its own past members, and the inherited merit of an individual is reflected in his yichus. In Talmudic times rabbis were sometimes appointed to positions because they were descended from saintly ancestors, and their zekhut avot could thus help them withstand the strains of office.

zemirot (Hebrew for 'songs') Table songs sung at family meals on shabbat and to a lesser extent on festivals. The custom of singing at the table is mentioned in a 6c. midrashic text where we are told how the licentious table talk of Gentiles leads God to contemplate destroying the world. The torah comes and pleads with Him to save the world because of the People of Israel who praise Him and bless His name with their songs. Zemirot supply the need for having words of torah at the table. Many of them contain references to the joy and delight of the Sabbath, to the yearnings for the great Sabbath in the age of the Messiah and to Jewish teachings about God and Israel. The Kabbalists wrote their own zemirot, full of the symbolic imagery of the mystical tradition, for the three Sabbath meals. There are references to the Holy Apple Orchard (the female divine principle) on Friday night, to the Lesser Face (the male divine principle) on Saturday lunchtime and to the Holy Ancient One (the union of male and female within God) at the seudah shlishit on Saturday afternoon. Since the mystics saw the Sabbath as a royal bride, they regarded the zemirot as wedding songs and continued to sing them at the melavveh malkah meal on Saturday night after shabbat had ended to accompany the Sabbath queen on her way.

Zion Term meaning a landmark or a sign, which was used of Mount Zion, one of the hills of Jerusalem. Before King David captured Jerusalem, a Jebusite tower stood on Mount Zion, making it a landmark visible from afar. In the course of time Zion came to refer not only to the hill but to the Temple, to Jerusalem and, indeed, to the whole of the Holy Land. Zion came to be identified with the religious centre of Israelite religion, as in the verse: 'For out of Zion shall go forth torah and the word of the Lord from Jerusalem' (Isa. 2:3). It is believed that Zion is the very centre of the world, the place where the shekhinah dwells and from where the world is sustained by the power of God. The prophet Jeremiah once met a woman mourning for her husband who had forsaken

German Jewish soldiers at prayer during **yom kippur**, 1870.

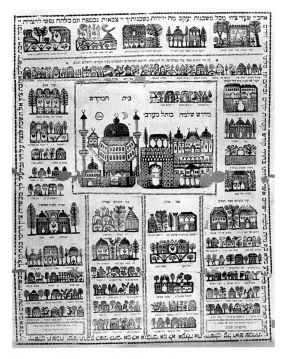

15c. map of **Zion** and the Holy Land.

her and for her seven sons who had died. He told her how mother Zion also weeps for her family who have gone, and the woman answered him: 'I am your mother Zion.' Jeremiah then consoled her with the message that God Himself would rebuild her. There is a whole literature of songs of Zion, mourning the destruction of the Temple, and yearning for the return to the Holy Land and the rebuilding of Jerusalem. The best known of these is Psalm 137 which describes the Judaean exiles weeping in memory of Zion. When asked to sing the songs of Zion in a strange land, they were unable to do so and replied: 'If I forget thee O Jerusalem let my right hand forget her power.' It is said that they even cut off their thumbs so they would be unable to play their harps in exile. The medieval poets, like JUDAH HALEVI, composed hymns of Zion, some of which were incorporated in the liturgy for fast days. At the coming of the Messiah Zion will be illuminated by God's glory, and from there the divine gifts of salvation, strength, blessing and the dew of life will go forth. The modern movement for the re-establishment of a Jewish state in the historic Holy Land adopted the name ZIONISM. *See also* MIZRACH

Zionism Jewish national movement to establish an independent Jewish homeland. Although the belief in the return of the Jews to ZION has always been part of Jewish Messianism (*see* EXILE), the term 'Zionism' was only coined in 1890. Interest in secular nationalism was inspired by 19c. nationalist stirrings in Europe. It was in sharp contrast to the attitudes of many emancipated Jews, who regarded themselves as citizens of their European host nations. The resurgence of anti-Semitism proved to Jewish nationalists that enlightened modernity had failed to integrate Jews into Christian society. At the same time traditional Jews in Poland and Russia formed their own Zionist groups, influenced by the writings of 19c. rabbis who argued that Jews must take the process of redemption into their own hands and not simply wait for the Messiah to gather in the exiles. The Russian pogroms of the 1880s strengthened Zionist feelings and increased Jewish militancy. It was Theodor HERZL, however, who turned Zionism into a political movement, arguing in a number of publications that Jewish survival in the face of anti-Semitism was only possible if Jews lived in their own homeland. Herzl convened the first Zionist Congress in Basle in 1897 in order to promote the establishment of a home for the Jews in Palestine. The BALFOUR DECLARATION of 1917, in which the British Government expressed itself in favour of a Jewish homeland in Palestine, gave the Zionist movement an important boost. Zionist aspirations were only fulfilled, however, when the realization of the extent of Jewish suffering during the Nazi Holocaust generated international sympathy for the plight of the Jewish people. Herzl wrote in his diary after the first Zionist Congress that in Basle he had founded the Jewish state, and perhaps in five years but certainly in fifty years everyone would realize it. The State of Israel was established forty-nine years

later. *See also* HATIKVAH; INGATHERING OF THE EXILES; KOOK, ABRAHAM ISAAC; MIZRACH; NETUREI KARTA.

Ziz Legendary great BIRD about which there are a number of bizarre folktales. The Ziz is as big as the Leviathan. With its ankles on earth, its head reaches into heaven, as far as the Throne of Glory, where it sings songs to God. The bird acts as a windbreaker on earth, yet when it unfurls its wings, it blots out the light of the sun. At the end of summer it frightens birds of prey with its cry so that they do not consume other birds. Travellers once came upon the Ziz standing in a lake, and they assumed that the water was shallow because it only covered the bird's feet. They wanted to bathe but were dissuaded from doing so when they heard that an axe which had been dropped into the water had taken seven years to reach the bottom. Once the egg of a Ziz fell to earth and crushed a forest of three hundred trees. The liquid from the broken egg also flooded sixty cities. At the Messianic banquet the flesh of the Ziz will be served to the righteous.

Zohar (Hebrew for '*Splendour*') Main work of the KABBALAH written as an Aramaic midrash on the Bible. The *Zohar* is ascribed to the followers of SIMEON BAR YOCHAI (2c.) who recorded the mystical teachings he learnt from Elijah during the years he spent hiding in a cave. The text was only published in the 13c. by MOSES DE LEON, who claimed he had an ancient manuscript in his possession, which had been sent to Spain from the Holy Land by Nachmanides. When attempts were made to obtain this manuscript after De Leon's death, his wife admitted that it did not exist and claimed her husband had ascribed his own writings to Simeon Bar Yochai in order to sell them to those interested in ancient mystical texts. Modern scholars accept that De Leon wrote the main part of the *Zohar* himself since it shows the influence of Spanish culture. The *Zohar* describes the esoteric reality that lies behind everyday experience. The world emanates from the Godhead, en sof, by means of the SEFIROT which pulsate with divine life. A by-product of this process of EMANATION is the evil power (*see* SITRA ACHRA) which is led by Samael and his host of demons. Man's task is to help unify the male aspect of the divine with the female aspect (*see* SHEKHINAH), since the latter is continually under attack from the sitra achra. Every word of the torah and every MITZVAH symbolizes some aspect of the sefirot, since the real meaning of the torah lies in its mystical secrets. Fulfilling the commandments has a positive effect on the upper realm, while sin strengthens the sitra achra, since man is a MICROCOSM and the human soul is rooted in the divine. The redemption of the world will come about when each individual, through a process of the TRANSMIGRATION OF SOULS, completes his task of unification. The *Zohar*, paradoxically, had considerable influence both on revitalizing the halakhah and also on the development of anti-halakhic heretical movements. *See also* NESHAMAH YETERAH.

Further Reading
Sources of the Illustrations

Further Reading

Most of the sources for Jewish lore and legend are found in the oral traditions of Jewish communities or in texts as yet untranslated from the original Hebrew, Aramaic, Yiddish or Ladino. Some guidance is offered here to the English-speaking reader about works which deal with both non-rational and rational elements of Judaism and texts containing folkloristic elements available in translation.

Although Jews and Christians share a scriptural belief in the books of the Hebrew Bible, the translated versions of these books differ between the two faiths. The Christian Old Testament usually reflects the belief that Christological elements are foreshadowed in pre-Christian writings. A case in point is the supposed reference in Isaiah to a virgin who 'shall conceive and bear a son' (Isa. 7:14) which was understood by Christians as an allusion to the Virgin Birth, while the Jewish translation about 'a young woman conceiving' is closer to the original Hebrew. The Jewish Publication Society of America has brought out its own version of The Holy Scriptures, based on the accepted masoretic text, which is meant to reflect a Jewish understanding of Scripture. Since, however, traditional Jewish exegesis has often veered away from a too literal understanding of the text, even the JPS version is not acceptable to some Orthodox Jews. The many midrashic stories about biblical characters are ably captured in Louis Ginzberg's classic The Legends of the Jews (Philadelphia, The Jewish Publication Society of America, 1909–38, 6 volumes plus an index volume), the footnotes to which are invaluable in referring the reader to the different versions in which these stories appear.

There is a fine translation of the whole of the Babylonian *Talmud*, the most important work of Rabbinic Judaism, in the Soncino Edition, edited by I. Epstein (London, Soncino Press, 1935, 17 volumes), with helpful footnotes. An index volume enables the reader to locate the aggadic and halakhic subject matter scattered throughout the Talmudic text. There are also many one-volume books about the *Talmud*, its outlook and terminology. A. Cohen's *Everyman's Talmud* (London, Dent, 1932) contains a full survey of the material, though its presentation is a little dry. Adin Steinsaltz, *The Essential Talmud*, translated by C.Galai (London, 1976) is an intelligent modern survey. *A Rabbinic Anthology* (New York, Schocken Books, 1974, first published in 1938), edited by C.G. Montefiore and H. Loewe, is a classic, though it suffers from the embarrassment felt by both its editors towards the more bizarre Rabbinic material. Louis Newman and Samuel Spitz, *The Talmudic Anthology* (New York, Behrman House, 1945) deals with Talmudic biography.

There are many monographs on individual items of Jewish folklore. An important study of major aspects of the whole area is Joshua Trachtenberg, *Jewish Magic and Superstition* (New York, Behrman House, 1939), while his *The Devil and the Jews* (New Haven and London, Yale University Press, 1943) deals with the folklore of Christian anti-Semitism. H.J. Zimmels, *Magicians, Theologians and Doctors* (London, Goldston & Son, 1952) treats of the folk medicine of the pre-modern period, while T.H. Gaster, *The Holy and the Profane* (New York, William Morrow, 1980) analyses the history of folk customs and beliefs. *A Treasury of Jewish Folklore*, edited by Nathan Ausubel (London, Vallentine, Mitchell, 1972), brings together an impressive collection of stories, humour and songs.

Works on Jewish history tend to ignore the legendary material which characterizes the way history is conceived in Jewish consciousness. One-volume surveys like *The Road from Babylon: The Story of Sephardi and Oriental Jews* (London, Weidenfeld & Nicolson, 1985) by Chaim Raphael and *A Short History of the Jewish People* (London, East and West Library, 1969) by Cecil Roth provide useful background information. While Israel Abrahams, *Jewish Life in the Middle Ages* (New York, Atheneum, 1969) and Mark Zborowski and Elizabeth Herzog, *Life Is With People: The Culture of the Shtetl* (New York, Schocken Books, 1962) convey the actual flavour of pre-modern Jewish life.

The main law codes and responsa are mostly not available in English translation. There is, however, a one-volume digest of Jewish law and ritual, *Code of Jewish Law*, a translation of *Kitzur Shulchan Arukh* by H.E. Goldin (New York, Hebrew Publishing Company, 1927) a shortened version of the great *Shulchan Arukh* code. The responsa literature is surveyed in an interesting way in two books by Solomon Freehof, *The Responsa Literature* (Philadelphia, JPS, 1959) and *A Treasury of Responsa* (Philadelphia, JPS, 1963). A collection of the articles about liturgy from the *Encylopedia Judaica* is to be found in *Jewish Liturgy*, edited by Raphael Posner, Uri Kaploun and Shalom Cohen (Jerusalem, Keter Publishing House, 1975). A more analytic approach is found in A.Z. Idelsohn, *Jewish Liturgy and its Development* (New York, Schocken Books, 1967), which

shows how the daily and festival prayerbooks grew out of the informal prayers of early times.

Although some of the works of Jewish mysticism are untranslatable, there is a competent translation of *The Zohar* by Harry Sperling and Maurice Simon (London, Soncino Press, 1934, 5 volumes). The works of Gershom Scholem have opened up the whole subject of the Kabbalah to public awareness, and his *Major Trends in Jewish Mysticism* (New York, Schocken Books, 1946) is both a scholarly and readable introduction to the subject. A short anthology of Jewish mysticism is to be found in Alan Unterman, *The Wisdom of the Jewish Mystics* (London, Sheldon Press, 1976). The standard surveys of Jewish philosophy are Julius Guttmann, *Philosophies of Judaism*, translated from the German by D.W. Silverman (New York, Holt, Rinehart, Winston, 1964), which discusses the history of Jewish philosophical thought from biblical times to the early 20c., and Isaac Husik, *A History of Mediaeval Jewish Philosophy* (New York, Meridian Books, 1958). Alan Unterman, *Jews: Their Religious Beliefs and Practices* (London, Routledge & Kegan Paul, 1981) outlines the main areas of Jewish ritual, while Hayyim Schauss, *Guide to Jewish Holy Days* (New York, Schocken Books, 1962) explains how the sacred calendar was experienced in the environment of the shtetl and suggests explanations of the folk customs associated with the festivals. Itzhak Ben-Zvi, *The Exiled and the Redeemed* (Philadelphia, JPS, 1957), Schifra Strizower, *Exotic Jewish Communities* (London, Thomas Yoseloff, 1962) and Dan Ross, *Acts of Faith: A Journey to the Fringes of Jewish Identity* (New York, Schocken Books, 1984), depict the variety of Jewish and quasi-Jewish communities.

Sources of the Illustrations

a = above, b = below, c = centre

Aachen, Suermondt-Ludwig-Museum (Photo Ann Münchow) 203b. Amsterdam, Rijksmuseum 87a; Stedelijk Museum 23b; Universiteitsbibliotheek 39b. Author's collection 15a, 47a, 51b, 73b, 93a, 183b, 201a. Baghdad Museum 59b. Basel, Historisches Museum 59a. Bern, Burgerbibliothek 111a. British/Israel Public Affairs Centre (Photo Shuki Kook) 169a. C.A.F., Warsaw 29b. Cambridge, University Library 57a. Cambridge, Mass., Fogg Art Museum 89b (Bequest Dr Denman W. Ross). Canterbury Cathedral (Photo A. Lammer) 181a. Cincinnati, Hebrew Union College 35b; American Jewish Archives 131b. Cologne, Stadtmuseum 167c. Coventry Cathedral (Photo Henk Snoek) 135a. Damascus, National Museum 11b, 167b, 171b, 203a. Escorial, Library of Royal Chapel of St Lawrence (Photo Mas) 63b. Frankfurt, Städelsches Kunstinstitut 171a, 173b. Glasgow Museums and Art Galleries, Burrell Collection 103a. The Hague, Mauritshuis 127b. Hamburg, Staats- und Universitätsbibliothek 55a. Hammath-Tiberias, Israel 71a, 183a (Photo Zed Radovan), 199a. Hodonin Museum, Moravia 105a. Israel Tourist Office 175a. Istanbul, Archaeological Museum 85a (Photo J. Powell). Jerusalem, American School of Oriental Research 61a; Central Zionist Archives 93b, 141a, 157b; Israel Museum 25b, 35a, 47b, 49b, 73a, 133b, 143b, 163a, 179b (Feuchtwanger Collection, donated by Baruch and Ruth Rappaport), 207a, 207b, 209b; Jewish National and University Library 57b, 161b, 195b; Rockefeller Archaeological Museum 73c, 121c; Wolfson Museum 155c; Yad Vashem Museum 95a. Johannesburg Art Gallery 79a. Kabul Museum (Photo J. Powell) 125b. Kirchheim Synagogue, Germany, destroyed 1945 (Photo Gundermann) 185a. Kvuzat Hefzibah, Bet Alpha synagogue, Israel 15b, 25a, 45a (Photo Unesco). Richard Lannoy 95b, 101b, 147b, 149b, 155a, 177b. Leipzig University Library 37a, 147a. Leningrad, Saltykov Schendrin Public Library 99a, 129b. London, Bevis Marks synagogue 69b; British Library frontispiece, 11a, 13b, 33a, 43b, 51a, 53c, 59c, 61b, 67b, 77b, 83a, 89a, 105b, 111b, 113b, 123a, 127a, 137b, 175b, 177a, 179a, 195a; British Museum 21b, 27b, 99b, 119b, 155b, 173a; Imperial War Museum 55b; Jewish Museum 21a, 27a, 157a, 175c, 191b, 209a; National Gallery 163b; Board of General Purposes, United Grand Lodge of England 137a. Madrid, Palacio de Liria (Alba Bible) 97b, 193b. Marseilles, Musée Borély 121b. Merseyside County Art Galleries (Lady Lever Art Gallery, Port Sunlight) 31a. Metz, Cathedral 65b. Milan, Biblioteca Ambrosiana 115a. Moscow, Tretyakov Gallery 181b. Mulbarton, Norfolk, Church of St Mary Magdalene (Photo A. Lammer) 75a. Munich, Bayerisches Staatsbibliothek 21c, 107a (Photo Marburg). Newcastle upon Tyne University, Gertrude Bell collection 205a. New York, Jewish Museum 153b (Collection Dr Harry G. Friedman), 187b, 203c; Jewish Theological Seminary of America 93c, 117b; Metropolitan Museum of Art 83b (Fletcher Fund), 145a (Bequest of Mrs H.O. Havemayer, 1929, The H.O. Havemayer Collection); Public Library 63a. Oxford, Bodleian Library 53b, 71b, 101a, 161a. Paris, Alliance Israélite Universelle 139b;

Bibliothèque Nationale 19b, 99c (Photo Giraudon), 103b, 105c, 135b, 205b (Photo Giraudon); Musée du Louvre (Photo Bulloz) 35c; Musée Cognacq Jay 33b; Musée de l'Homme 49a, 129c. Philadelphia, University Museum, University of Pennsylvania 75b. Phototake, New York (Photo Yoav Levy) 41c. Prague, Jewish Museum 143a, 191a; Altneu Synagogue (Photo Karl Neubert) 187a. Private collections 13a, 19a, 23a, 31b, 37c, 81a, 91, 109a, 117a, 129a, 139a, 141b, 159a, 197c. Rome, S. Pietro in Vincoli (Photos Istituto Centrale per il Catalogo e la Documentazione) 119a, 131a. Ronald Sheridan 39a. Tiberias, Church of the Multiplication 79c. United Israel Appeal 17b. Vatican Library and Museums 17c, 167a, 197a (Photo German Archaeological Institute, Rome); Sistine Chapel 77a, 151a (Photo Anderson), 169b. Venice, Basilica di San Marco 79b, 149a (Photo Osvaldo Böhm). Vienna, Albertina 43a; Kunsthistorisches Museum 67c; Österreichische Nationalbibliothek 67a. Washington D.C., National Gallery, Samuel H. Kress Collection 165b. Winchester Cathedral Library 125a. Zabludow Synagogue, Poland 193a.

T.A. Bursink, reconstruction from *Der Tempel von Jerusalem*, Vol. I: *Der Tempel Salomos* 197b. Thomas Coenen, *Ydele Verwachtinge der Joden getoont in der Persoon van Sabethai Zevi* (Amsterdam, 1669) 145b. Gustave Doré, illustrations from *The Holy Bible* (1866) 107b, 153a. An English Person of Quality, *The Counterfeit Messiah* 179a. J. Frellon, *Icones historiarum Veteris Testamenti* (Lyons, 1547 edn) 169c. Haggadah with Marathi translation (Poona, 1874) 37b. Judah Halevi, *Kuzari* (Venice, 1547) 109b. E.M. Lilien, illustration from *Lieder des Ghetto* (Berlin, 1902) 85b; E.M. Lilien, illustration to unpublished poem by Gorki 159b. J. Leuden, *Philologus Hebres Mixtus* (1663) 97a. Mantua Haggadah (1568) 17a. *Sefer Raziel* (Amsterdam, 1701) 41a. Ben Shahn, illustration from *A Partridge in a Pear Tree* (New York, 1949) 65a. Geoffrey Whitney, *A Choice of Emblemes* (Leyden, 1586) 81b.